THE WORLD THE CIVIL WAR MADE

The STEVEN AND JANICE BROSE
LECTURES *in the* CIVIL WAR ERA
William A. Blair, *editor*

THE WORLD THE CIVIL WAR MADE

Edited by
Gregory P. Downs *and* Kate Masur

The University of North Carolina Press CHAPEL HILL

Designed and set in Merope Text by Rebecca Evans
Manufactured in the United States of America

The paper in this book meets the guidelines for permanence
and durability of the Committee on Production Guidelines for
Book Longevity of the Council on Library Resources.

The University of North Carolina Press has been a member
of the Green Press Initiative since 2003.

Cover illustration: © Thinkstock.com/Harm Kruyshaar.

Library of Congress Cataloging-in-Publication Data
The world the Civil War made / edited by Gregory P. Downs and
Kate Masur. — First edition.
pages cm. — (The Steven and Janice Brose lectures in the Civil War era)
Includes bibliographical references and index.
ISBN 978-1-4696-2418-1 (paperback : alkaline paper)
ISBN 978-1-4696-2419-8 (e-book)
1. United States — History — Civil War, 1861–1865 — Influence. 2. Ethnic
groups — Civil rights. 3. Minorities — Civil rights. 4. Human rights.
5. National characteristics, American. 6. Social values — United States —
History. I. Downs, Gregory P., editor of compilation. II. Masur, Kate,
editor of compilation.
E468.9.W754 2015
973.8 — dc23
2014044783

For BILL BLAIR

Contents

Figures and Map

Acknowledgments

Every book is a collaborative effort, but this volume more than most proves that many hands make light work. From the beginning, the book has been a pleasure. Tony Kaye initiated the process when he approached us about putting together a conference on new directions in Reconstruction for the George and Ann Richards Civil War Era Center at Pennsylvania State University. Throughout the process, Tony urged us to think broadly and to take risks.

As the idea for a conference developed, David Perry at the University of North Carolina Press helped us think about the book that would emerge. Although he retired midway through this project, his wisdom has guided us throughout. When David stepped away, Mark Simpson-Vos enthusiastically took his place and proved an invaluable source of advice and assistance. At UNC Press, Lucas Church, Susan Garrett, Jay Mazzocchi, and many others provided important assistance.

The book shifted from an idea to a living and stubbornly breathing thing at a June 2013 conference at Penn State, sponsored by the Richards Center and by Steven H. and Janice Brose, whose generous support also underwrote this volume. At that conference, the participants in this volume, as well as Tony Kaye, Errol Henderson, and many engaged graduate students helped us expand our questions and sharpen our analysis. None of this would have taken place without the amazing logistical work of Barby A. Singer and Matthew R. Isham. At the conference and ever since, the contributors to this book inspired us with their generous commitment to collaboration and the exchange of ideas.

For each of us separately, our families and friends made the book possible in all kinds of ways by helping navigate the obstacle course of parenting, by distracting us from our work, and by reminding us of the hopes for the future we hold in our minds as we contemplate the past. Greg particularly thanks Diane, Sophia, Gabby, his father Monty, his colleagues Cliff Rosenberg, James Oakes, and Judith Stein, and his friends Anthony Guinyard and Michael Washburn. Kate is especially grateful to Peter, Isaac, and Milo Slevin, and to Dylan Penningroth, colleague and comrade extraordinaire.

Finally, none of this would have happened without William A. Blair, the person to whom we dedicate this book. We are the happy beneficiaries of Bill's unwavering commitment to promoting new scholarship and bringing people together. Although Bill did not know either of us at the project's commencement, he from the beginning expressed faith in our judgment, encouraged us to think broadly, supported the project emotionally and financially, provided wise guidance about managing conferences and editing volumes, shared drinks and observations, and sustained our hope that historiographical interventions of the type on display in these pages do matter. He did it all with his characteristic modesty and good humor. His warmth, support, and expertise made us feel like the luckiest historians in the world, and we thank him for it.

THE WORLD THE CIVIL WAR MADE

INTRODUCTION

Echoes of War: Rethinking Post–Civil War
Governance and Politics

Gregory P. Downs *and* Kate Masur

As the final Confederate armies surrendered in May 1865, the nation's interior secretary saw the Civil War's consequences in far-off New Mexico, where the "law abolishing slavery" was "disregarded" and the "practice of selling Indian children still continues." When President Andrew Johnson extended national authority over the rebel states in June, he issued an executive order directing federal officials in New Mexico to end the "barbarous and inhuman practice" of selling captives. The seemingly southern problems of slavery, emancipation, and the defense of federal authority spread far beyond regional boundaries into New Mexico and other places. Throughout the United States, and in some ways around the world, it was clear that a civil war begun in South Carolina and primarily fought east of the Mississippi River had in fact changed politics, policy, and personal life across a much broader canvass. If New Mexican peonage was not, of course, the war's cause, the struggle to destroy it was, in fact, one of the war's consequences. The postwar era tested the reach and authority of the national government over its own territory, and it also brought forward a multitude of challenges to emerging visions of freedom and citizenship. Just as an observer in the South could trace the war's impact in black children singing "John Brown's Body" within sight of John Calhoun's grave, or in the sixty-five white men who dragged the freedman Abram Colby and his daughter from their Georgia house, or in freedpeople like Bella Newton who took white men to court to assert newfound rights, so too could people much farther away see the changes the war had brought. In Wisconsin, "stray bands" of Ho-Chunk Indians, separated from their self-governing tribe and living among white settlers, insisted that they too shared in the newfound constitutional rights the Civil War made. On the floor of the Senate, Democrats and Republicans took those claims seriously, debating whether the logics of war and emancipation had transformed the status not just of freedpeople but of all people who lived under U.S. sovereignty.

Few captured the kaleidoscopic impact of the war better than Ely Parker, a Seneca man who was a wartime general and later became the first Native American to serve as an Indian affairs commissioner. His ambitions had drawn him to the center of the canonical Civil War. As Lt. General Ulysses Grant's aide, he wrote the final copy of the surrender agreement at Appomattox Court House in April 1865. In short order, however, Parker was spinning with the war's consequences across the national landscape. In 1866 at Fort Smith, Arkansas, Parker helped negotiate a treaty with pro-Confederate tribes requiring them to emancipate their slaves and accept increased federal jurisdiction over their affairs. The next year, as he tried to settle the conflict in the Great Plains, he connected South and West, freedman, rebel, Indian, and settler, and envisioned expanded military regulation of the nation's uneasy peripheries. The war's consequences spun farther afield. Across the Atlantic Ocean, Karl Marx saw the "first fruits of the war" in an urban movement for an eight-hour day. The American Civil War, with its attack on the right of white southerners to hold people of African descent as property, had breathed new life into Marx's vision of social revolution. In the United States, as attention turned from the end of slavery to the problem of enduring racial inequality, the bright line between North and South faded. Within a few years, black petitioners from Albany and Brooklyn would join the antislavery icon Charles Sumner and the black congressman Richard Harvey Cain in pressing for an expansive vision of civil rights that included equal access to restaurants, hotels, and theaters.

In this volume we consider some of the ways the Civil War echoed beyond 1865 in a dynamic, crucial postwar period whose contours have often proven difficult to capture.[1] The essays collected here explore several different regions of the United States and the circulation of ideas throughout the nation and the world. Our goal is to do more than just tell new stories. In juxtaposing ostensibly distinct regional stories and approaches to history, we hope to suggest new framing questions and modes of analysis. Rather than presuming that Reconstruction is the best framework for understanding the postwar period—and thus envisioning a Reconstruction of the West or the Plains or the world—in this volume we ask whether thinking across regions might in fact might help us understand not just the regions themselves but the entire nation and its place in nineteenth-century history.[2]

Crucial to this expansive reimagining of the war's consequences are new ways of understanding the size and particular strengths of what we call the Stockade State. Historians have long trained their attention on the extensive and intricate changes in federal policy that characterized the postwar moment. Yet much remains to be learned about practices of governance. The essays in this volume do not assume that the federal government was capable of enforcing the liberal principles to which it had committed or of bringing people and institutions to heel when it wanted. Rather, they ask precisely how the changes that rippled out from the Civil War did—and did not—echo in people's lives and communities. They portray a federal government located in outposts, often beset and besieged, able to enforce its policies in concentrated areas but hard pressed to extend its sovereignty throughout the land. Instead of a nation defined by shared assumptions about democratic processes and peaceful governance, these essays portray a place convulsed by violence and a government stymied by common people's stubborn assertions of power and prerogative. They invite us to envision the enduringly illiberal and chaotic qualities of life in the postwar United States not as imperfections in a consolidating liberal nation, but as central to the American experience. In this context they revisit the enduring question: How did the Civil War, often considered the pivot of American history, change the nation?

THE PERIOD FORMERLY KNOWN AS RECONSTRUCTION

For historians of the U.S. South, the framework for answering that question has long been clear. Reconstruction was both a period and a process, a tumultuous fight over the future of the eleven states that had left the United States in 1861, declared themselves a separate nation, and waged a four-year war for independence. In the fight that became known as Reconstruction, congressional Republicans tried to modify President Abraham Lincoln's early experiments in wartime restoration and then rejected President Johnson's program, refusing to accept the representatives those eleven states sent to Washington in the winter of 1865–66. What followed was an outpouring of Republican-led policymaking that increased the federal government's power vis-à-vis the states and had the potential to change how common people understood themselves in relation to the nation. Historians have long recognized that Washington, D.C., was just one of many centers of action during Reconstruction. Indeed, since W. E. B. Du Bois's canonical *Black Reconstruction* (1935), and especially since the 1960s, most studies of Reconstruction have emphasized ground-level struggles over political power and the organization of labor.[3] As political pleas brought the South to Washington, and as laws and directives pushed outward from the capital into the countryside, white and black southerners struggled to define the contours of freedom in a postwar world. As conventionally understood, then, Reconstruction refers to the dynamic period of political debate and social upheaval in the South that followed the Civil War.

In our own era, the idea of Reconstruction retains its power and its allure. The term is now used more boldly and broadly than ever before, surfacing in studies of other regions and in other disciplines. Linking transformations in the South with those in the North and West, scholars have recently posited a Reconstruction of the North or—in Elliott West's justly influential analysis—a "Greater Reconstruction" of the nation, defined as the project of incorporating western territories that the United States obtained in the war with Mexico. Others have gone even further, suggesting the "reconstruction" of white southern womanhood, race, critical social theory, religion, southern law, southern debtors, American liberalism, Mark Twain, American popular politics, and many other topics. The appeal is understandable. Scholars' multifaceted use of "reconstruction" implicitly recognizes the convergence of a particular problem—the struggle over how the rebel states would rejoin the nation—with the broader and more general phenomena the term implies: crisis, rebuilding, and historical change itself.

For precisely these reasons, however, we have become persuaded that Reconstruction is not the most useful framework for making sense of the many histories of the postwar United States. When historians stretch the concept of Reconstruction to cover the conquest of western land, changing racial dynamics in the North, or the rise of industrial capitalism, the term becomes metaphorical rather than descriptive, emptied of its core meaning. It alludes to everything and nothing. At the same time, such broad uses diminish the specificity of the conventional Reconstruction story, making it more difficult for historians of the South or of federal policy to convey its stakes or significance.

Moreover, when historians frame their analysis around Reconstruction, they tend to foreground certain phenomena while eclipsing others. The concept of Reconstruction carries with it assumptions about the nature of federal power, the relation of region to center, and the stakes of history writing that may inhibit our ability to understand the nineteenth-century United States. Works begun within the framework of Reconstruction tend to move steadily toward a familiar story line of extension and retreat, possibility and disappointment. That narrative reminds us of the importance of the era, both for contemporaries and for our own understandings of the nation in general and the legacies of slavery in particular. Yet that story line may also preclude us from considering postwar history from different angles, from conceiving of this crucial period as something other than three artificially separated textbook topics: Reconstruction, the Gilded Age, and the West.

Because we want to think our way out of some of the frameworks—ideological, regional, and otherwise—that have defined the historical literature, we decided to sidestep Reconstruction as a structure and a keyword for this volume. We called the project "The World the War Made" to emphasize our desire to move away from the assumption that the era can be encapsulated as some version of Reconstruction. We urged the essays' authors to think around that conventional term and to examine the period, in its various complexities, as a postwar moment. Our hope, then, is to consider anew the impact on the nation of a war that cost more than 700,000 lives and 4 billion dollars and freed 4 million slaves from bondage. Perhaps our proposed nomenclature will also help shed presumptions of American exceptionalism that remain embedded in the Reconstruction framework, however much scholars have tried to think broadly and comparatively about the war's end.

Our volume's title is also, however, a nod to the opening chapter of the greatest single work on Reconstruction, Eric Foner's *Reconstruction: America's Unfinished Revolution.*[4] A quarter century after its publication, Foner's *Reconstruction* remains both the standard study of the field and one of the finest works of American history ever written. Although subsequent scholars have produced groundbreaking books on black political organizing, southern labor relations, freedpeople's nationalist visions, the remaking of gender relationships, and many other topics, Foner's synthesis continues to set the standard for interpretations of the era. Indeed, historians of the postwar United States almost inevitably draw on Foner's scholarship, particularly on his ambitious vision of the transformation of Republican ideology and his wide-ranging insights about African American politics. In this volume, rather than attempt to extend Foner's analysis over the entire nation, we instead ask whether a national and international analysis might be based on different framing questions. We step back and ask how, in fact, the Civil War changed the nation. What exactly did the newly invigorated federal government do? Was citizenship the defining way people interacted with that state, or should we look for other ways to characterize people's relationship with the government? Was the postwar moment the origin of a modern, consolidated nation, or did the United States remain fundamentally inchoate, its regions anarchic and chaotic, its modes of governance fundamentally illiberal?

We hope this volume spurs conversation about issues and concerns that cross conventional historical and historiographical boundaries in the period that spans roughly 1865 to the dawn of the twentieth century. By thinking broadly of a postwar era and by asking where it is located and where it ends, we hope to discover new connections between western, southern, and northeastern story lines. We may find new stories altogether, in new settings and told by new characters speaking new words. We may place the United States alongside other postwar nations instead of treating its postconflict moment as a historically unique response to a historically unique civil war. We follow the Americans of the time, who looked to past and contemporary postwar periods in Europe, Asia, and North Africa to understand the challenges the United States faced.

A STOCKADE STATE

This volume particularly emphasizes the shape, size, and power of the U.S. government. The essays collected here reveal the U.S. government as less a "Yankee Leviathan" than a Stockade State, a collection of outposts—both military and civilian—powerful within narrow geographical boundaries but limited in their reach, sometimes capable of enforcing their will, sometimes overpowered, and almost always beset by both competing power centers and individuals who sought to live beyond the reach of most authority. The authors' sensitivity to the government's enduring vulnerability represents a break from prevailing scholarship on Reconstruction, which has often assumed that the state could ultimately have asserted its will over society. Early pro-southern scholarship viewed federal power in the South as overwhelming and malignant. As the historical literature changed, however, the presumption of federal power did not. Writing after the Second World War, many liberal historians assumed that the post–Civil War federal government could have done what it wished and looked for the political, legal, financial, and constitutional factors that limited it.[5]

By contrast, the essays in this collection see the government less in terms of its constitutional prerogatives than in its concrete forms.[6] They depict a state threatened not only by constitutional limitations and political conflict but also by its constituent members, a government less self-restrained than besieged by forces it could not control. The federal government thus appears not as the ultimate arbiter of authority—a vision that may have seemed natural in the context of both Cold War foreign policy and civil rights–era jurisprudence—but as one among many forces scrambling for influence and authority. By seeing the government this way, these essays aim to open new ways of thinking about the postwar world. The battle between state and society, they show, was one the Civil War transformed but did not finally determine.

There can be no doubt that the war brought about a moment of significant rethinking of American governance, the proper role of centralized power, the meaning of citizenship, and the status of individuals within the nation. Such ferment is clear not just in the postwar constitutional amendments and the federal legislation that accompanied them but also in the creation of entirely new agencies, some fleeting—like the Freedmen's Bureau and the Department of Education—and others lasting, including the Justice Department. Even as the War Department sent Civil War volunteers home and Congress cut the military budget, the army attained a newly powerful role in many places. Military officers organized and oversaw the first biracial elections in the South, and in some areas detachments of soldiers remained well into the 1870s. Meanwhile, the army continued its campaigns to contain Native Americans, opening the trans-Mississippi West to railroad construction and white settlement. In both the South and the West, army interventions sparked intense debates about government's proper size, cost, and role. Many Americans condemned governance by force rather than consent, but federal officials were often frustrated by the army's incapacity, its limited size, and its dispersal across vast lands.

Policymakers and social reformers, inspired by liberal visions of freedom and citizenship, attempted newly sweeping efforts to assimilate people they considered racially and culturally different. Drawing on ideas implicit in Republican ideology from the party's founding, policymakers envisioned a nation composed of free and independent individuals capable of entering into contracts, owning land, and raising families. Their liberal worldview generally suggested that people who did not at present appear to live up to those ideals could learn them if properly taught. That belief gave rise to a range of policies—some more coercive, some more voluntaristic—such as primary and secondary schools for freedpeople and Native Americans; worldwide missionary work; and a new Indian policy that rejected treaty making and relied, instead, on incorporation. In the South and the West alike, the Republican fantasy was a nation of free people under federal power, insurgent groups subdued, and racial and cultural outliers brought into the fold through what might today be called "soft power."[7]

Western historians, for good reason, often bristle at the suggestion that the Civil War was the fulcrum of national development and rightly point out continuities in white settler expansion and Indian resistance. Yet the wartime growth of the national government transformed the West as well. In Indian Territory, as Barbara Krauthamer demonstrates, the federal government's actions to end slavery went hand in hand with efforts to expand national sovereignty over Native lands. After the war, spiraling conflicts between white settlers and Plains Indians, spurred by an increased flow of emigrants west during and after the war, led the federal government to stop making treaties with Native American tribes. No longer would Native American groups be treated as "domestic dependent nations," as Chief Justice John Marshal had called them in 1831. As C. Joseph Genetin-Pilawa shows, the change in policy marked a significant (if ambiguous) step toward a vision of Indians as members of the national body politic. As Stacey L. Smith demonstrates, the federal government's new stance against slavery also extended outward into the far West, where it came into conflict with long-standing practices of peonage in New Mexico and, ironically, provided a powerful new framework for the anti-Chinese movement.

Yet the aspiration to govern was not the same as actually governing. Post–Civil War political leaders faced real obstacles to creating the nation they envisioned, including lack of will, lack of capacity, and outright resistance. As historians have amply shown, the Republican Party that dominated Congress and the presidency for years after the war was internally divided over taxation, the relative powers of the states and the federal government, and the potential for transcending racial and cultural divisions in efforts to create a unified American nation.[8] Congressional Republicans argued over appropriate policies toward both the rebel states and Indians even as they sustained unparalleled party unity when confronted with tests to their authority from the White House or the Supreme Court. Yet the most intense attack on the Republicans' newly expansive visions of government came not from within the party but from outside. Democrats, never relegated to the sidelines, proved adept at reading the changing political situation. By raising fears of a standing army, a tyrannical central state, high tax rates, and racial equality, Democrats quickly regained popularity among white northern voters, even as they retained the loyalty of old southern Democrats and acquired the support of old southern Whigs. From the beginning, then, the Republican goal of constructing a powerful central state was avidly contested.

Then there was lack of capacity. Even in situations where the contours of federal policy seem clear, the government often proved unable to follow through. When the Justice Department sent agents to the South to enforce the Civil Rights Acts of 1870 and 1871, for example, those men faced white communities unwilling to cooperate with investigations, witnesses who refused to testify, and juries that would not convict under any circumstances. In Washington, there was no money to put more soldiers or civilian officials on the ground. The federal judges and commissioners crucial to any effort to enforce federally protected rights were often isolated in cities and inaccessible to the rural population. Most freedpeople therefore had no access to the only officers who could help them. Committed officeholders regularly faced obstacles they simply could not overcome. As Smith shows in this volume, federal rulings about the illegality of peonage in New Mexico fell short not because of ideological contradiction or political betrayal, but because the United States was simply not powerful or present enough to assert itself over a vast, distant, and newly conquered territory, no matter what Congress wrote or judges ruled. On the Great Plains, the U.S. Army enjoyed victories but often found it lacked the personnel or capacity to hold them. For years, besieged outposts faced hostile Native groups and disdainful white settlers, and detachments of soldiers chased rebellious bands across enormous territories at great cost. In Indian Territory, as Krauthamer's essay demonstrates, the government struggled to enforce black freedom against Indians reluctant to surrender sovereignty. So, too, as Stephen Kantrowitz shows, did Ho-Chunks and other "stray bands" of Native Americans find it possible to defy federal laws and to remain in place even after they were ostensibly removed. Across the nation, the government did not, in fact, have the organizational structures or staff necessary to execute its policies.[9]

What defined the era, then, was not just the federal government's new reach but the ways people on the ground—southern freedpeople and rebels, western settlers and Indians—managed to deflect or even overthrow its efforts. White southerners' resistance is perhaps best known, and it is most evident here in Kidada E. Williams's powerful analysis of African Americans' descriptions of their feelings and behavior in the wake of terrorist attacks. But it was only one of many examples. Despite the Civil War's seemingly transformative effects, the inhabitants of the United States continued practices long familiar to them, heedless of new policies emanating from Washington and of the federal officials who occasionally appeared in their midst. The widespread refusal of many people to accommodate themselves to government policies in turn stretched the government and diminished its sovereignty. In this light, rebels' ability to stave off federal encroachment in the former Confederacy no longer seems surprising. Instead, they were simply the most powerful, organized, and politically incorporated of the many groups seeking to restrain federal intervention in their locales. The United States still seemed—from the center—distinctly ungoverned, perhaps ungovernable.

By envisioning a dynamic and powerful state whose capacities were nonetheless extremely limited, we begin to catch glimpses of the crucial role of cultural continuity in shaping the postwar era. The Stockade State could place limits on cultural expression—but only within its sight. The state ended, as Luke E. Harlow shows, at the church house doors. Behind them, white southern religious leaders and their congregations produced unifying narratives of righteousness and triumph that strengthened, rather than collapsed, in the face of political change. For K. Stephen Prince, northerners' self-satisfied view of the natural superiority of their way of life led them to expect that defeated white southerners would embrace northern ideals. To many northerners' surprise, however, white southerners did not live among ruins, but instead began to rebuild their surroundings and their societies. Agents of the Stockade State remained, often hunkered down in geographical and political outposts like forts and courthouses, claiming intense authority over narrow bands of space but nearly powerless in the countryside. Unable to regulate or even to see what lay beyond its walls, this federal government aimed to perform its power without risking defeat, as white settlers, ex-Confederates, corporations, Indians, and freedpeople acted not in deference but in defiance.

AN ILLIBERAL LAND?

Recognizing the limits of Washington's power does not mean dismissing the federal government as irrelevant. As the essays in this volume show, the struggle between national aspiration and local resistance is crucial precisely because it helps us think in new ways about the forms of liberal thought that emerged from this period and the extent to which they filtered into American life. Questions about the future of chattel slavery had been at the heart of the Civil War, and as the war ended, slavery's antithesis—freedom—became the subject of significant struggle. Historians have picked up on this, analyzing as struggles over the "meanings of freedom" such phenomena as freedpeople's postwar organizing, debates about labor and wages in the South, the creation of national citizenship through the Fourteenth Amendment, and top-down efforts to assimilate former slaves and Native Americans. Historians have also shown how questions of freedom roiled an industrializing northern society in which an increasingly self-conscious elite insisted that freedom meant little more than the ability to sign one's name to an employment contract and where growing multitudes would spend their lives in drudgery. It is clear that nineteenth-century Americans used the language of freedom to many different ends—to liberate but also to limit and coerce.[10]

Yet leaning on "freedom" as an analytical category, even in such nuanced ways, carries limitations of its own. The concept of freedom aligns easily with liberal values of individual autonomy, contract, and choices unconstrained by institutions. Orienting historical analysis around questions of freedom thus tends to marginalize certain crucial aspects of post–Civil War history, especially the violence and enduring local power relations that made it impossible for the federal government to enforce its own policies or persuade people to accept the principles behind them. Persistently illiberal conditions, rather than odd anomalies to a liberal order, may well constitute the center of a postwar history defined in Smith's essay and in Steven Hahn's afterword less around freedom than around coercion. Or perhaps, as Williams suggests, an emancipation defined not by claims to rights but by brutal violence whose effect was to traumatize and dispossess. We concede that no liberal state is capable of creating a perfectly rationalized system of governance; it would be misleading to judge any era against that ideal. Yet given the persistence and ubiquity of violence, lawlessness, and coercive labor practices, we think it important to ask: Were illiberal forms of power in fact the norm, not the exception, in the post-Civil War era?[11]

To ask such a question is not to suggest that the rise of a national vision of freedom and basic rights made no difference. To the contrary, some aspects of the Republican program were integrated remarkably quickly into the nation's political culture. As Amy Dru Stanley shows, the abolition of slavery opened the door to a wide-ranging debate about fundamental human rights in which African Americans and their white allies made the bold claim—enshrined in the 1875 Civil Rights Act—that all people were entitled not only to pursue a livelihood or to take a case to court but also to spend their money how and where they chose and to enjoy the pleasures of the theater and other public amusements. Yet Republican ideals and legislation could also be brought to bear against the further spread of racial equality and inclusiveness. As Smith shows, for example, Democrats who had earlier opposed the Thirteenth Amendment soon found its categorical rejection of slavery useful in their struggle against Chinese immigration.

At the same time, Republican efforts to construct a racially neutral liberalism, while successful in discrediting some forms of racial discrimination, did not—and were not intended to—stymie other kinds of inequality. The liberal assimilationist policies the government developed for Indians became crucial instruments for dispossessing tribes of their land and power. Political leaders and civic reformers developed new arguments for discrimination and marginalization, including formally color-blind— but in fact racially directed—laws disfranchising southern freedpeople. New and ostensibly scientific ideas about racial difference came into circulation, and Americans mobilized them against not only longtime denizens of the nation but multitudes of new immigrants. The rise of liberal rhetoric, then, did not signal widespread recognition of the dignity and autonomy of every individual.

The ascent of liberal individualism and freedom of contract has sometimes seemed the sine qua non of the postwar period, but the new vision of a frustrated state suggests a less exalted, more pragmatic understanding of rights.[12] Drawing on her influential work on how visions of a corporate "peace" shaped local legal practices in the early national period, Laura F. Edwards captures how local forms of justice survived national efforts to reconfigure rights.[13] As her essay shows, Republicans' attempts to institute a regime of individual rights pushed up against existing forms of communal order that retained their power and utility after the war. In this context, people claimed rights based more on pragmatic assessments of what they thought would work than on a deep, principled commitment. Kantrowitz's Ho-Chunk exemplify this complex relationship between state and subject. Beset by laws that aimed to remove them to the Dakotas and then to Nebraska, they asserted that they had become sedentary farmers and claimed individual land titles. Yet they cared about fulfilling the government's vision of civilization only insofar as it helped them avoid forced relocation. Given the unusual nature of the stray bands, it is tempting to see theirs as a purely exceptional response, but in fact, people across the nation at once grasped for and leaned away from individual rights. Whether they were self-consciously antiliberal or lived in ignorance of liberalism or simply did not believe a liberal order had arrived, their actions help us map out the endurance of competing visions of power in the postwar era.

Meanwhile, the federal government simply could not create a rationalized, legalistic order on the ground. Many of the present essays, like other recent work on the era, place violence at the center of the postwar world. They suggest that rather than a nation of rights undermined by inevitable flashes of violence, the postwar United States was perhaps a nation ruled by violence interrupted by flashes of rights. Night riders attacked former slaves, sparing neither women nor children; whites rioted against Chinese mine workers in Wyoming; New Mexican Hispanos tried to prevent federal officials from freeing their peons; white settlers attacked the Nez Percé in Oregon; and black settlers displaced Native Americans in Indian Territory. Rather than exceptional individual incidents, such moments provide a window into the everyday violence that shaped many communities. New access to the federal state could not stave off, or perhaps even slow, the violence that permeated the South and the West during this period, as local governments proved unable or unwilling to step in. As Williams shows, there was in fact no peace. In her chilling portrayal of postemancipation trauma, violence structured everyone's life even in the moments when it was not occurring, its psychic wounds and economic consequences extending long after the physical injuries healed.

Understanding the growth of both federal power and individual rights in the twentieth century, it is hard not to look backward to find their traces in the post–Civil War era. Some narratives conceive the world the Civil War made as an incomplete, emerging variant of a mostly benevolent contemporary liberalism. Others use the period's limitations and ascriptions to expose the violence and hierarchies inherent in liberalism itself. We agree that liberalism may be, in different ways and in different moments, benevolent, coercive, hierarchical, or equalizing. Yet we are after something different: What happens if we think of the postwar world less as a precursor to what is to come, and more as a jumble of surprisingly open-ended and often illiberal practices? By attempting to stand in the moment itself, instead of looking back with the knowledge of what happened later, we ask whether citizenship, individual rights, and federal authority actually defined the era, and we consider the extent to which Americans continued to experience a world shaped by intimate, personalized power and violence deep into the postwar years.

WAS THE POSTWAR WORLD A NEW WORLD AFTER ALL?

How did the Civil War change the nation? The answer to this question remains surprisingly elusive. However much scholars might reject the historical account offered by D. W. Griffith's famous film, the idea of the Civil War as the birth of the nation echoes through much scholarship on the postwar years. And there is good reason to see the roots of the twentieth-century United States planted deep within the postwar order. The defeat of the slaveholders' rebellion, the concomitant rise of a new national elite, and the volatile period of economic growth that followed the war have captured the attention of historians looking for the origins of what some have called "the American century." Likewise, the political mobilization of freedpeople after emancipation, the unfulfilled promises of a biracial working-class movement, and synergy between grassroots mobilization and legislative change in Washington have suggested connections with the twentieth-century civil rights movement and produced powerful narratives of tragedy, irony, and deferral. In both historical and popular discussion, then, the postwar period has frequently served important political purposes. As Edwards argues, the postwar moment has often taken on an outsized role in national consciousness, used as evidence of what the country could be, or what it must not be, or what it could have been, or what prevents it from becoming something better than it is.

Yet looking backward for the origins of the twentieth-century state risks blinding us to the historical distinctiveness of the post–Civil War United States. It may be tempting to imagine that the twentieth-century national state, an intensely legalistic and powerful hegemon atop a thoroughly capitalist society, had its birth in the triumph of the liberal, bourgeois nationalist Republican Party of the 1860s. As the essays in this volume suggest, however, the nation that emerged after the Civil War was not a Cold War state with training wheels. Rather than using the period as a kind of oracular mirror, the essays offer something more akin to a window into a distant world. They take the transformative nature of the Civil War era as a question, not an assumption. Instead of the moment the United States became modern, the postwar years appear in these essays a period of both massive change and intense continuity.

The possibility of continuity across the Civil War is not new. Economic historians, in particular, have long debated how transformative the Civil War was and whether it spurred the growth of industrial capitalism. From the perspective of southern and African American history, some historians have suggested that war and emancipation did not meaningfully change the larger trajectory of class relations or racial oppression, while others have shown how postwar black politics had roots in antebellum slave communities.[14] In this volume, Harlow finds continuity in the rich field of religious culture. Behind church doors, white Protestants defended their vison of distinct and enduring southern Christian values. Northerners, like those portrayed in Prince's essay, may have hoped to find the South ready to be made anew, but many southern ministers believed northern Christians heretics for doubting slavery's righteousness. Slavery itself had vanished, but race remained a bridge of continuity as white southerners—but also northerners—asserted the enduring power of a white man's democracy. Crystal N. Feimster shows that African American women took advantage of new opportunities offered by the war and the Republican ascendancy to draw attention to their experiences of sexual violation by white men and to insist that they were entitled to dignity and bodily integrity. Yet the broad chronological scope of her essay reveals that their actions were part of much longer quest for sexual justice that dated to before the war and would continue long after it.

As most historians know well, parsing the rhetoric and reality of continuity versus change can be difficult. Sometimes people's claims to be doing what they have always done are reliable; other times they lend cover to new practices. Conversely, declarations of a new policy or approach may in fact be window dressing for more of the same. Amanda Claybaugh's essay shows how literary representations of Washington, D.C., evolved as writers grappled with a federal government whose size and scope had changed dramatically. In the 1870s and 1880s, writers' overtly critical stance against Republican policies shifted easily into seemingly nonpolitical or antipolitical writing that accepted and naturalized a sense of disdain for those who lived and worked in the national capital. Within a few years, an enduring and politicized skepticism of centralized government had been refitted and rearticulated for a new moment.

If continuity emerges as one theme of this volume, meaningful and even revolutionary change is another. Looking both southward and across the ocean to Europe, Andrew Zimmerman makes the transformative nature of the Civil War startlingly clear as he captures its power for European radicals. Rather than regarding it as a bourgeois revolution, much less a moment of continuity, Karl Marx saw the Civil War as a new way to understand what revolution was. Disconcertingly for American historians, Marx interpreted the Civil War not as the American version of the revolutions of 1848 but as an essentially new form, one that superseded failed European models and provided new hope for the world's workers. And Stanley argues that the Congress that passed the 1875 Civil Rights Act, whose members included former slaves and free African Americans, "revolutionized" human rights when it enshrined in federal law a right to enjoy public amusements. If such steps toward democracy and the recognition of human dignity were tenuous and subject to reversal (and they certainly were), they would have been inconceivable before the Civil War.

On the question of continuity and change, as on the precise nature of the postwar state or the exact balance between liberalism and illiberalism, this collection cannot offer final answers. Instead we aim to open up new questions, fresh ways of asking about the people, institutions, and ideas that shaped a crucial era. These questions will, we hope, point to as-yet-unrealized possibilities for transnational, comparative, and global history. While historians of emancipation have long looked to the Caribbean, South America, and Africa for comparisons, an emphasis on the travails of governing opens possibilities for envisioning the postwar period alongside other imperial expansions and state consolidations. It is easy to imagine comparative histories of postwar periods that place the transformation of the United States in constructive dialogue with contemporary experiences in India, Algeria, Hungary, Poland, Mexico, and many other sites of midcentury struggle.

It is a daunting and therefore exciting time to write the history of the post–Civil War United States. In trying to record the ways the war echoed through the postwar years, the essays in this volume range widely across the national landscape and through various modes of historical research and writing. The authors have not only described the path and pitch of the echoes but have also asked about their origins and implications. These essays reveal new possibilities for imagining government, claims-making, and narrative. They show that vital questions remain about this era, but they by no means capture the full range of answers. We hope to see historians venture well beyond any boundaries implied in this volume, asking increasingly global questions, looking westward across the Pacific and southward to the Americas. We also hope they will go further than these essays in incorporating and shaping the scholarship on the history of the nineteenth-century military and the development of capitalism. In all these areas, and in others whose sounds are yet too faint to be heard or too strange to be recognized, the Civil War resonated across the nation and beyond it.

NOTES

1. The postwar period of Reconstruction has produced some of the finest histories and historiographical essays of any period in U.S. history. The standard overview of Reconstruction historiography remains Eric Foner, "Reconstruction Revisited," *Reviews in American History* 10 (December 1982): 82–100. For other historiographical overviews, see , "Introduction," and Eric Foner, "Afterword," in *After Slavery: Race, Labor, and Citizenship in the Reconstruction South*, ed. Bruce E. Baker and Brian Kelly (Gainesville: University Press of Florida, 2013), 1–15, 221–30; Aaron Sheehan-Dean, "The Long Civil War: The Historiography of the Consequences of the Civil War," *Virginia Magazine of History and Biography* 119 (2011): 106–53; Brian Kelly, "Emancipations and Reversals: Labor, Race, and the Boundaries of American Freedom in the Age of Capital," *International Labor and Working-Class History* 75 (Spring 2009): 169–83;

Bruce E. Baker, *What Reconstruction Meant: Historical Memory in the American South* (Charlottesville: University of Virginia Press, 2007); Thomas J. Brown, *Reconstructions: New Perspectives on the Postbellum United States* (New York: Oxford University Press, 2006); Alex Lichtenstein, "Was the Emancipated Slave a Proletarian?" *Reviews in American History* 26 (March 1998): 124–45; Michael Les Benedict, "Preserving the Constitution: The Conservative Basis of Radical Reconstruction," *Journal of American History* 61 (June 1974): 65–90; Kenneth Stampp, "The Tragic Legend of Reconstruction," in *The Era of Reconstruction* (New York: Vintage, 1967), 3–23; Howard K. Beale, "On Rewriting Reconstruction History," *American Historical Review* 45 (July 1959): 807–27; John Hope Franklin, "Whither Reconstruction Historiography," *Journal of Negro Education* (Fall 1948): 446–61; A. A. Taylor, "Historians of the Reconstruction," *Journal of Negro History* 23 (January 1938): 16–34; and W. E. B. Du Bois, "Reconstruction and Its Benefits," *American Historical Review* 15 (July 1910): 781–99.

2. Recent scholars have done crucial work in tying together southern and western history during the Civil War era, especially Elliott West, *The Last Indian War: The Nez Perce Story* (New York: Oxford University Press, 2009); Elliott West, "Reconstructing Race," *Western Historical Quarterly* 34 (Spring 2003): 6–26; Heather Cox Richardson, *West from Appomattox: The Reconstruction of America after the Civil War* (New Haven: Yale University Press, 2008); Adam Arenson, *The Great Heart of the Republic: St. Louis and the Cultural Civil War* (Cambridge: Harvard University Press, 2011); C. Joseph Genetin-Pilawa, *Crooked Paths to Allotment: The Fight over Federal Indian Policy after the Civil War* (Chapel Hill: University of North Carolina Press, 2012); Stacey L. Smith, *Freedom's Frontier: California and the Struggle over Unfree Labor, Emancipation, and Reconstruction* (Chapel Hill: University of North Carolina Press, 2013); Barbara Krauthamer, *Black Slaves, Indian Masters: Slavery, Emancipation, and Citizenship in the Native American South* (Chapel Hill: University of North Carolina Press, 2013); Steven Hahn, "Slave Emancipation, Indian Peoples, and the Projects of a New American Nation State," *Journal of the Civil War Era* 3 (September 2013): 307–30; and Adam Arenson and Andrew R. Graybill, eds., *Civil War Wests: Testing the Limits of the United States* (Berkeley: University of California Press, 2015).

3. W. E. B. Du Bois, *Black Reconstruction: An Essay toward a History of the Part Which Black Folk Played in the Attempt to Reconstruction Democracy in America, 1860–1880* (New York: Harcourt Brace, 1935).

4. Eric Foner, *Reconstruction: America's Unfinished Revolution, 1863–1877* (New York: Harper and Row, 1988).

5. The literature is vast, and we cite just a few examples here. Leon Litwack and C. Vann Woodward emphasized northern racism, while Kenneth Stampp, Eric Foner, and Heather Cox Richardson pointed to ideological brakes. Even historians who emphasized the limits of government capacity, including Richard Bensel and Sven Beckert, made that incapacity evidence of ideology, rather than a factor in and of itself. Leon F. Litwack, *Been in the Storm So Long: The Aftermath of Slavery* (New York: Alfred. A. Knopf, 1979); C. Vann Woodward, particularly in "Equality: The Deferred Commitment," in *The Burden of Southern History*, rev. 3rd ed. (Baton Rouge: Louisiana State University Press, 2008); Kenneth M. Stampp, *The Era of Reconstruc-*

tion, 1865–1877 (New York: Alfred A. Knopf, 1965); Eric Foner, *Reconstruction*; Heather Cox Richardson, *The Death of Reconstruction: Race, Labor, and Politics in the Post–Civil War North, 1865–1901* (Cambridge: Harvard University Press, 2004); Richard Franklin Bensel, *Yankee Leviathan: The Origins of Central State Authority in America, 1859–1877* (New York: Cambridge University Press, 1991); and Sven Beckert, *The Monied Metropolis: New York City and the Consolidation of the American Bourgeoisie, 1850–1896* (New York: Cambridge University Press, 2003).

6. The works in this collection share with recent scholarship in American Political Development (APD) an interest in the size and shape of the nineteenth-century state. While William Novak, Brian Balogh, and others have turned from the weakness of the nineteenth-century state to its surprising strengths, especially at the local level in Novak's analysis, we return to the central question of the weaknesses and paradoxes of the federal government. A crucial early work is Stephen Skowronek, *Building a New American State: The Expansion of National Administrative Capacities, 1877–1920* (New York: Cambridge University Press, 1982). Recent work on the actual administrative capacities of the nineteenth-century federal government that is either part of the APD school or influenced by it includes Theda Skocpol, *Protecting Soldiers and Mothers: The Political Origins of Social Policy in the United States* (Cambridge: Harvard University Press, 1992); Richard R. John, *Spreading the News: The American Postal System from Franklin to Morse* (Cambridge: Harvard University Press, 1995); William J. Novak, *The People's Welfare: Law and Regulation in Nineteenth-Century America* (Chapel Hill: University of North Carolina Press, 1996); Sarah Barringer Gordon, *The Mormon Question: Polygamy and Constitutional Conflict in Nineteenth-Century America* (Chapel Hill: University of North Carolina Press, 2002); Mark R. Wilson, *The Business of Civil War: Military Mobilization and the State, 1861–1865* (Baltimore: Johns Hopkins University Press, 2006); Brian Balogh, *A Government Out of Sight: The Mystery of National Authority in Nineteenth-Century America* (New York: Cambridge University Press, 2009); Stephen J. Rockwell, *Indian Affairs and the Administrative State in the Nineteenth Century* (New York: Cambridge University Press, 2010); and Cathleen D. Cahill, *Federal Fathers and Mothers: A Social History of the United States Indian Service, 1869–1933* (Chapel Hill; University of North Carolina Press, 2011).

7. Some of these points are powerfully explicated in Cahill, *Federal Fathers and Mothers*, 15–59. How reformers and officials directed assimilationist attitudes toward freedpeople is described in scholarship on the Freedmen's Bureau and on freedmen's education. Recent work has given special emphasis to the domestic and gendered aspirations of those efforts. See, for example, Mary Farmer-Kaiser, *Freedwomen and the Freedmen's Bureau: Race, Gender, and Public Policy in the Age of Emancipation* (New York: Fordham University Press, 2010); Kate Masur, *An Example for All the Land: Emancipation and the Struggle over Equality in Washington* (Chapel Hill: University of North Carolina Press, 2010), 51–86; and Catherine Jones, *Intimate Reconstructions: Children in Postemancipation Virginia* (Charlottesville: University of Virginia Press, 2015). Apart from Cahill, the literatures on the South and West remain largely unconnected.

8. See, especially, Michael Les Benedict, *A Compromise of Principle: Congressional Republicans and Reconstruction, 1863–1869* (New York: W. W. Norton, 1974).

9. John Hope Franklin and LaWanda and John Cox a half century ago emphasized deep, inherent limits in federal enforcement: John Hope Franklin, *Reconstruction after the Civil War* (Chicago: University of Chicago Press, 1961) and LaWanda C. Fenlason Cox and John H. Cox, *Politics, Principle, and Prejudice, 1865-1866: The Dilemma of Reconstruction America* (New York: Free Press of Glencoe, 1963). Robert Kaczorowski explored the limits of federal enforcement of postwar legislation in "To Begin the Nation Anew: Congress, Citizenship, and Civil Rights after the Civil War," *American Historical Review* 92 (February 1987): 45-68; and Kaczorowski, *The Politics of Judicial Interpretation: The Federal Courts, Department of Justice, and Civil Rights, 1866-1876* (Dobbs Ferry, N.Y.: Oceana Publications, 1985). Newer works that capture the government's difficulties in responding to southern violence and the resulting toll on freedpeople include Lou Falkner Williams, *The Great South Carolina Ku Klux Klan Trials, 1871-1872* (Athens: University of Georgia Press, 1996); LeeAnna Keith, *The Colfax Massacre: The Untold Story of Black Power, White Terror, and the Death of Reconstruction* (New York: Oxford University Press, 2008); Hannah Rosen, *Terror in the Heart of Freedom: Citizenship, Sexual Violence, and the Meaning of Race in the Postemancipation South* (Chapel Hill: University of North Carolina Press, 2009); and Kidada E. Williams, *They Left Great Marks on Me: African American Testimonies of Racial Violence from Emancipation to World War One* (New York: New York University Press, 2012).

10. The literature is voluminous but perhaps best defined by the work of historians such as David Brion Davis, Barbara J. Fields, Eric Foner, and Thomas C. Holt. See, for example, David Brion Davis, particularly in *The Problem of Slavery in the Age of Revolution, 1770-1823* (Ithaca: Cornell University Press, 1975); Barbara J. Fields, *Slavery and Freedom on the Middle Ground: Maryland during the Nineteenth Century* (New Haven: Yale University Press, 1985); Eric Foner, *Nothing But Freedom: Emancipation and Its Legacy* (Baton Rouge: Louisiana State University Press, 1982); Foner, *Reconstruction*; Thomas C. Holt, *The Problem of Freedom: Race, Labor, and Politics in Jamaica and Britain, 1832-1938* (Baltimore: Johns Hopkins University Press, 1992). See also the work of the Freedmen and Southern Society Project, including Ira Berlin, Barbara J. Fields, Steven F. Miller, Joseph P. Reidy, and Leslie S. Rowland, *Slaves No More: Three Essays on Emancipation and the Civil War* (New York: Cambridge University Press, 1992); and two important postwar volumes of documents and interpretive essays: Steven Hahn, Stephen F. Miller, Susan E. O'Donovan, John C. Rodrigue, and Leslie Rowland, eds., *Land and Labor, 1865*, ser. 3, vol. 1 of *Freedom: A Documentary History of Emancipation, 1861-1867*(Chapel Hill: University of North Carolina Press, 2008); and René Hayden, Anthony E. Kaye, Kate Masur, Steven F. Miller, Susan E. O'Donovan, Leslie S. Rowland, and Stephen A. West, eds., *Land and Labor, 1866-67*, ser. 3, vol. 2 of *Freedom: A Documentary History of Emancipation, 1861-1867* (Chapel Hill: University of North Carolina Press, 2013).

11. That question is also pursued, from different perspectives, in Steven Hahn, *A Nation under Our Feet: Black Political Struggles in the Rural South, from Slavery to the Great Migration* (Cambridge: Harvard University Press, 2003); Gregory P. Downs, *Declarations of Dependence: The Long Reconstruction of Popular Politics in the South, 1861-1908* (Chapel Hill: University of North Carolina Press, 2011); Carole Emberton, *Beyond*

Redemption: Race, Violence, and the American South after the Civil War (Chicago: University of Chicago Press, 2013).

12. The consensus that the postbellum United States was fundamentally liberal appears not just in work celebrating that liberalism, including Louis Hartz's *The Liberal Tradition in American: An Interpretation of American Political Thought since the Revolution* (New York: Harcourt Brace, 1955), but also in critical scholarship of the past decades that finds in the postwar United States proof of liberalism's enduring inequalities. See, notably, Amy Dru Stanley, *From Bondage to Contract: Wage Labor, Marriage, and the Market in the Age of Slave Emancipation* (New York: Oxford University Press, 1998); and Frederick Cooper, Thomas Holt, and Rebecca J. Scott, *Beyond Slavery: Explorations of Race, Labor, and Citizenship in Postemancipation Societies* (Chapel Hill: University of North Carolina Press, 2000).

13. Laura F. Edwards, *The People and Their Peace: Legal Culture and the Transformation of Inequality in the Post-Revolutionary South* (Chapel Hill: University of North Carolina Press, 2009).

14. Reconstruction historians who emphasized continuities between slavery and emancipation were once labeled postrevisionist. Some recent scholars of wartime emancipation have emphasized tragedy and continuity, rejecting the more hopeful sensibility of an earlier generation. See, for example, Susan Eva O'Donovan, *Becoming Free in the Cotton South* (Cambridge; Harvard University Press, 2007); and Jim Downs, *Sick from Freedom: African-American Illness and Suffering during the Civil War and Reconstruction* (New York: Oxford University Press, 2012). For an earlier variation, see Litwack, *Been in the Storm So Long*. Historians interested in the broad sweep of southern history also debated the extent to which emancipation led to a restructuring of the southern economy, the rise of a new elite, or significantly different opportunities for the poor. For a good overview of that literature through the 1990s, see Harold D. Woodman, "The Political Economy of the New South: Retrospect and Prospects," *Journal of Southern History* 67 (November 2001): 789–810.

1 RECONSTRUCTION AND THE HISTORY OF GOVERNANCE

Laura F. Edwards

When historians write about Reconstruction, their attention is usually engaged elsewhere. For better or worse, studies of the period also serve as a way to evaluate the nation's core values: What does the United States stand for? Who are we, as Americans? How do we define our ideals? How do we realize them? Of course, the present always becomes entangled in the past in the discipline of history. Even so, we ask far more of Reconstruction than of other historical moments. The historians of the Dunning School — named for their intellectual mentor, William A. Dunning, a professor at Columbia University — established the precedent, characterizing Reconstruction as a repudiation of national ideals that required a violent "redemption," a term that they took uncritically from southern Democrats who used it to describe the overthrow of democratically elected governments in the region. Recently, the literature has taken a more optimistic tone, with scholars approaching Reconstruction in terms of its possibilities. Optimism, however, also explains the notes of despair that punctuate current scholarship, with analyses highlighting the nation's failure to achieve the very principles that the Dunning School saw as problematic: instead of going too far, the nation did not go — and still has not gone — far enough. Although the conclusions are different than they were in the early twentieth century, the conceptual frame that ties Reconstruction to questions of national development is not. It is as if Reconstruction is the crystal ball in which historians can divine the nation's true character.

The problem with this historiographical frame is that it confuses the history of governance within the United States with the history of the state. I use the term "governance" to refer to the wide range of institutions and practices that exercised legal authority and on which nineteenth-century Americans relied to resolve their conflicts and maintain order. Governance obviously included the state — that is, state governments and the federal government, the institutions that comprise the state and that share governing authority within it, according to the U.S. Constitution. But governance was not limited to the state, particularly in the early nineteenth century. Local government, which included local courts where a great deal of daily business was done, shared authority with governing institutions at the state and federal levels. Governing authority, moreover, also resided in institutions that were relatively private, such as households, churches, and communities. To complicate matters, the line between the categories of private and public forms of governance often blurred.

Historians' tendency to conflate governance with the state is understandable, since the Civil War and Reconstruction rank among the most dramatic events in the history of state formation. It is widely assumed that change in this period concentrated more legal authority at the federal level, creating a government with a truly national reach for the first time in American history and initiating a process that turned the United States into a nation-state. Secession challenged the traditional balance of power between the federal government and the state governments. The exigencies of war then forced the United States and even the Confederacy to locate more power at the federal level. Although many wartime measures proved temporary, the policies of Reconstruction—particularly the three new constitutional amendments—permanently enhanced the power of the federal government in the reconstituted United States. It was a bloody ordeal that extended into the twentieth century. The histories produced by the Dunning School, which emerged from that highly charged context, were so focused on those conflicts over state formation that they subsumed the history of governance within that narrative. The conflation still persists in the historiography, although its presence can be difficult to detect. At first glance, such a perspective might appear entirely at odds with current literature, which no longer confines itself to the business of the nation's statehouses or its political leaders. Nonetheless, much of the literature, particularly that focused on demands for and protection of individual rights, tends to construe questions of law and governance rather narrowly, as matters that lie only (or mainly) in the purview of state and federal jurisdictions.

The federal government and state governments did not have a monopoly on governance in the early nineteenth century, but they did control matters relating to the protection of individual rights, with states handling a much wider variety of such cases than the federal government. Rights were necessary to access and mobilize the power of these jurisdictions, and their denial left people without the means to defend their interests within them. Even so, the operation of rights within these legal jurisdictions did not match the outsized ideals of liberty, freedom, and equality so often attached to them in the popular discourse of the time and in the later historiography. In the Civil War era, Americans routinely used the term "rights" in regards to a wide range of claims on government at all levels. But more often than not, their use of the term referred to their sense of what law and government ought to support—what was right, in their minds—and not a specific right recognized in state or federal law, where rights were few and legal officials tended to define them in narrow, formalized ways that limited their usefulness in the resolution of fluid social conflicts. That was one reason why individual rights played a smaller role in local jurisdictions, which settled disputes and defined justice in different ways, using principles that subordinated individuals to the social order, that resolved discrete wrongs without providing precedent for other cases, and that elevated the maintenance of concrete social relations over the protection of legal abstractions. In these venues the protection of what was right took precedence over the protection of individual rights, which were not the only means of accessing the legal system or the mechanisms of governance. Together, these various jurisdictions constituted a governing system that captured and contained the contradictory impulses of American life: they maintained existing inequalities, while also adjudicating conflicts generated by those inequalities.

As this essay argues, the focus on the state and federal levels has artificially elevated those jurisdictions' focus on rights over other legal practices, extending that framework to explain questions about law and governance that were actually much more complicated. Following popular rhetoric of the Civil War era, historians tend to fall back on the term "rights" to describe all claims on law and government, without stopping to ask whether such claims had any relationship to the actual array of individual rights available in state or federal law. In so doing, we miss the fact that popular conceptions of law, even when expressed in terms of rights, relied on legal principles and governing practices, operative at the local level, which emphasized deeply contextual forms of social justice and active government involvement in the people's daily lives. During and after the Civil War, Americans who had been subordinated at all levels of government picked up legal principles available at the local level and put them to use there and in other jurisdictions. In this sense, this essay builds on one of the most important insights of recent literature: the active participation of ordinary Americans, particularly African Americans, in the conflicts of the Civil War era. But, as this essay argues, the implications were far more profound than the current historiography suggests. Reconstruction-era policy changes drew local, state, and federal jurisdictions into a closer relationship, allowing legal principles operative at the local level to migrate and acquire new meanings at the state and federal levels. In those jurisdictions, local conceptions of law and governance brought questions about what was right into conversation with a legal framework that protected the rights of individuals. The results significantly extended the reach and meaning of individual rights at both the state and federal levels, elevated expectations of federal involvement in the daily business of governance, and introduced new conceptions of social order into the national arena. In this way, Americans built localism into the nation-state, where the principles of local law combined with other legal currents to fuel expansive expectations about what the nation could be and do.

THE FOCUS ON STATE and federal authority reaches back to the turn of the twentieth century and the scholarship associated with the Dunning School. The school's intellectual mentor, William A. Dunning, produced two national studies, *Essays on the Civil War and Reconstruction and Related Topics* and *Reconstruction, Political, and Economic, 1865-1877*, which generated a small fleet of state studies, one for each state of the former Confederacy. Each of those studies followed a similar script, featuring depictions of the misguided policies of congressional Republicans, the resulting inversion of the social order, and the ultimate redemption of the South with the reunion of white southerners and northerners in a shared commitment to white supremacy.[1] Racism permeates the work to the point that it can now be hard to see anything else.[2] Yet for Dunning School historians, the overriding issue was the use—and, for most, the abuse—of federal power. The results not only destroyed the South but also jeopardized the nation's future by undermining the traditional balance of power between states and the federal government. Fortunately, at least as most Dunning School historians saw it, southern redeemers and their northern allies pulled the nation back from the precipice by over-throwing the policies of Reconstruction and returning legal authority to the states, where it belonged.

Although Progressive-era historians placed the emphasis on economic, rather than ideological or political differences between the sections, they still told the history of governance in terms of government at the state and federal levels. Perhaps the most famous rendering of this argument is Charles A. and Mary Beard's *The History of American Civilization*. Reconstruction plays a pivotal role in the narrative as the "second American Revolution," the moment when northern Republicans' economic interests emerged triumphant. Reflecting the goals of the Progressive movement, which hoped to harness federal as well as state authority to resolve the nation's problems, Progressives took a more positive view of the federal government's potential. Yet like historians of the Dunning School, they also tended to take a critical view of the period, blending a healthy respect for what federal authority could accomplish with a deep skepticism of the resulting policies, particularly when it came to racial and economic equality.[3]

By the mid-twentieth century, the New Deal, World War II, and the emerging civil rights movement cast an even more favorable light on federal authority and, ultimately, on Reconstruction policies at both the state and federal levels.[4] Reflecting that viewpoint, a new body of literature emphasized the accomplishments of the era, faulting state and, particularly, federal officials for failing to accomplish their goals. Many revisionists combined optimism with deep disappointment and a note of doubt: optimism in the idealism of America; disappointment that those ideals went unrealized; and sometimes doubt about the success of social change imposed from above, through the federal government.[5]

More recent scholarship contains similar elements of doubt and optimism about the potential of state and federal authority. Much of the work that deals with federal enforcement, for instance, still tends toward pessimism. After the passage of the major legislation and constitutional amendments, a combination of political maneuvering and judicial foot-dragging turned back the clock nearly to where it had been before the war. Not only did white southerners regain control of their state governments, but they were also allowed—even encouraged—to ignore new federal laws and to resurrect a racial system that closely resembled slavery.[6] Other historians who focus on state and federal law and politics wring optimism from this otherwise tragic narrative by taking the long view and emphasizing the enduring legacy of Reconstruction. For them, it was not just the idealism of the moment but also the institutional changes, particularly the Reconstruction amendments, that created a "second American revolution," although one of a very different order than that of the Beards, because it provided the institutional basis for fulfilling the promises of the first: not just racial equality, but also a rights revolution that extended to all Americans and folded them into one nation. Progress came slowly, culminating in the mid-twentieth century with the civil rights movement. Still, those changes never would have been realized at all had it not been for the policies of the Reconstruction era. At times, the scholarship reads like an inverted version of the Dunning School, with a similar take on the collapse of federal power, but a very different interpretation of the implications.[7] In these various assessments, it is often law and government at the state and federal levels that hold the potential to make the promises of the period a reality.

Scholarship since the civil rights movement also has shifted the analytical perspective away from the federal level to explore efforts on the ground to reconstruct southern society and, in a broader sense, the nation. Influenced by W. E. B. Du Bois's *Black Reconstruction: An Essay Toward a History of the Part Which Black Folk Played in an Attempt to Reconstruct Democracy in America, 1860–1880*, the work blends social history with political history, considering the implications of government policy in people's lives, as well as the role of ordinary people in the creation and implementation of policy.[8] In such studies African Americans assume central roles in the major events of the time rather than appearing as inert subjects to whom federal lawmakers gave freedom and rights. Enslaved African Americans' abandonment of the plantations, for instance, created facts on the ground that made the Emancipation Proclamation and the Thirteenth Amendment possible. Similarly, African Americans' claims to full civil and political rights during and immediately after the Civil War set the stage for the passage of the Fourteenth and Fifteenth Amendments. Not all of this scholarship is concerned with African Americans' interactions with local, state, or federal government.[9] But, as this work shows, African Americans made every effort to claim control over their lives, efforts that often entailed claims to civil and political rights that already existed within the legal system and also efforts to expand rights in ways that implied significant changes to social and economic relationships in the nation as a whole.[10]

Yet even as this scholarship has moved further away from the nation's capital, it still continues to define law and governance through the issues that lay within state and federal jurisdictions, particularly the protection of individual rights. Much of recent scholarship is based in the assumption that the actions and ideas of ordinary Americans, particularly African Americans, should be considered central to the conflicts over Reconstruction policies. Yet such work tends to funnel all claims on government into the framework of rights: when African Americans made claims of any kind, the historiography tends to treat them as claims to rights. One result is to extend rights beyond their actual reach in the first half of the nineteenth century. Recent histories, for instance, often assume that African Americans were claiming "rights" that already existed for white people, thus missing the fact that no such rights existed for anyone. Another unintended result is the creation of a conceptual divide between "law" and "society," which locates legal authority in those bodies of law that protect rights—the statutes, case law, and the policies of the state and federal governments. Even scholarship that emphasizes African Americans' efforts to redefine rights falls into this set of assumptions, by positing a dynamic in which those jurisdictions made aspirations into law, often by recognizing them as rights. Although the analytical focus has moved away from state and federal government, they still play a significant role as the entities that enforced law at local level.[11]

Yet neither the federal government nor even state governments controlled law and governance within the United States in the nineteenth century. To be sure, their presence increased after the Civil War. Before the war, however, Americans who lived in states usually encountered federal authority through the postal service or the rituals of electioneering, if they did at all.[12] The federal government figured more prominently in the territories, which lacked the institutional apparatus of state government. But existing states had jurisdiction over the actual work of governance—protecting individual rights, keeping the peace, and looking after the public health and welfare. Even so, the role of state governments was also limited, at least by current standards, because they delegated so much authority to local areas. State law reigned supreme in matters involving property, and local courts followed those rules. But local jurisdictions—courts and local government—had authority over a wide range of matters involving the public interest, from crime to the regulation of businesses and social practices. These venues routinely elevated the collective good of the social order over the rights of individuals. What was right took precedence over individual rights. Of course, southerners had very different ideas about what was right. But experience with the practices of this legal tradition meant that a wide range of southerners—even enslaved people—shared expectations about what law and government should do: government should—at all levels and in all forms—play an active role in people's lives, mediating their interpersonal conflicts and mobilizing the law to maintain the public good.[13]

One of the most problematic results of historians' orientation toward state and federal law is the overemphasis on individual rights in the history of governance. To be sure, questions about individual rights were central to both the Civil War and Reconstruction. The rhetoric of rights was everywhere at the war's outbreak, and the Reconstruction amendments then extended the federal government's jurisdiction over individual rights and made rights more available to more Americans. But rights formed just one element in the legal principles that guided governance in the nineteenth-century United States.

First is the matter of jurisdiction, which is crucial to understanding governance in the nineteenth-century United States. Before the Civil War, conflicts involving individuals' rights lay with the states. The federal government did deal with the rights of those individuals who were not within a state's jurisdiction: in the territories, in relation to Indian nations, in the District of Columbia, and in federal cases. That situation resulted in an uneven experience with federal power, one reflected in this volume's essays. Native Americans, in particular, felt the full weight of federal authority. So did American citizens in the District of Columbia and the territories, although the federal government often protected the interests of western settlers—and their rights—at the expense of Indians.[14] But people who lived within the jurisdiction of existing states—whether citizens or not—encountered federal legal authority only in the context of federal cases, of which there were few, particularly in the first few decades of the nineteenth century.[15] Indeed, it is no coincidence that states' jurisdiction over matters involving individual rights constituted a central point of tension in the conflicts leading up to the Civil War, particularly in the 1850s, when the federal government increasingly involved itself in matters relating to the status of African Americans.

State and local authority mattered far more in most people's lives than did that of the federal government. States' authority even extended to the meaning of citizenship. Before passage of the Fourteenth Amendment, there was no definitive statement about who qualified for U.S. citizenship or what that status meant. The 1790 Naturalization Act did limit citizenship to those who were free and white. But that act and subsequent legislation addressed the situation of new immigrants who sought application for naturalization. Their provisions did not extend to those who resided in the United States at its inception and never applied for citizenship. To the extent that there was a link between U.S. citizenship and rights at all, it was at the state level, where there was a concept of state citizenship, which did establish claims to rights, as defined within states. To complicate matters, the two notions—state citizenship and U.S. citizenship—emerged in an ad hoc way, through statutes and case law, with no clear distinction between the two. States did not usually question the citizenship status of those who lived in their boundaries, although there was considerable discussion about the rights and citizenship status of free blacks in the decades immediately preceding the Civil War.[16] Those debates culminated in the U.S. Supreme Court's decision in *Dred Scott*, which denied all people of African descent U.S. citizenship. But *Dred Scott* was controversial precisely because it upset the status quo and encroached on the jurisdiction of states. In fact, the controversy surrounding *Dred Scott* made its implications ambiguous.[17]

States had purview over individual rights, but those were neither as capacious nor as powerful as the political rhetoric of the time suggests. Nineteenth-century political leaders, regardless of party affiliation, invoked rights in expansive terms, often in connection to liberty, freedom, and equality, with the implication that they could accomplish those ends. To be sure, rights were necessary for individuals to function independently in American society. Without them, it was impossible to claim legal ownership of property, enter into contracts, or defend one's interests in state or federal courts. But, in the legal system, rights did not do the kind of work that the political rhetoric implied. They resolved competing claims among individuals by identifying winners and losers, a situation that undercut the connection between rights and equality posited in political rhetoric. State courts, moreover, were committed to the preservation of rights as such, not to the concerns of the individuals who brought their problems for adjudication. This legal framework actually conflicted with other practices that were widely accepted and even sanctioned in other legal jurisdictions, such as the control of property by people without property rights. The application of rights also produced outcomes of questionable justice: a conviction overturned because of an improperly framed indictment; the seizure of property because of a faulty bill of sale; or a worker denied months of wages because of statutes that specified strict adherence to labor contracts. Decisions did not necessarily conform to popular conceptions of liberty or freedom either, let alone equality. More often, state law preserved existing inequalities, because lawmakers concerned themselves with the rights that governed property ownership and economic exchange, a body of law that tended to protect the interests of those who owned property at the expense of those who did not.[18]

The fact that states also had broad powers to regulate in the name of the public health and welfare also limited people's rights. State constitutions did have bills of rights, but the rights they enumerated were not absolute. In fact, state and local governments exercised wide latitude in limiting or suspending the rights of individuals in the name of the public good. That legal logic sanctioned not just slavery, but also the range of restrictions placed on free blacks, all women, and many white men without property as well. A right was a right only as long as the state decided not to take it away.[19]

To complicate matters, states delegated significant regulatory power to counties and municipalities, where the legal framework of rights was not the only or even the primary one. Local jurisdictions exercised authority over a broad, ambiguous area of public law, which included all crimes as well as a range of ill-defined offenses that disrupted "the peace" of the social order. That situation dates to the American Revolution, when lawmakers turned their colonies into states and decentralized the most important functions of state government. These changes dramatically altered the existing structures of imperial rule by placing a good deal of government business in local courts. The most visible of these venues were the circuit courts, which met on a regular schedule in county seats or court towns, which held jury trials, and which dealt with a great deal of government business. But circuit courts were only the most conspicuous part of a system dominated by even more localized legal proceedings, including magistrates' hearings and trials, inquests, and other ad hoc legal forums. Magistrates not only screened cases and tried minor offenses, but also kept tabs on a range of matters involving markets and morals. In most legal matters, the interested parties collected evidence, gathered witnesses, and represented themselves. Justice was meted out on a case-by-case basis. Each jurisdiction produced inconsistent rulings, aimed at resolving particular matters, rather than producing a uniform, comprehensive body of law. Many saw that situation as natural and just: it made no sense to impose arbitrary rules developed elsewhere without paying attention to the particular attributes of local communities.[20]

Local jurisdictions tended to the peace of their communities. The peace was a well-established, highly gendered concept in Anglo-American law that expressed the ideal order of the metaphorical public body, subordinating everyone (in varying ways) within a hierarchical system. It was inclusive, but only in the sense that it enclosed everyone in its patriarchal embrace, raising its collective interests over those of any given individual. Keeping the peace meant keeping everyone—from the lowest to the highest—in their appropriate places, as defined by rigid inequalities of the early nineteenth century. While this localized system neither protected the interests nor recognized the rights of free women or enslaved people, it still incorporated them into its basic workings, even in the South, because they were part of the social order that the legal process was charged with maintaining. The system regulated their behavior. It relied on information they supplied about community disorder. In fact it *depended* on that information, because free women and enslaved people knew so much about their households and neighborhoods.[21]

Local governing practices were as much about an activist approach to governance as they were about concerns in a specific geographic area. Grand juries in local areas, for instance, issued pronouncements on piracy or the French Revolution only to turn around and demand passage of federal or state laws to address national, regional, local, and even personal issues. Just as the peace blurred the boundaries between international, national, state, and local concerns, it also delved deeply in domestic matters that many historians consider "private" and therefore outside of the law's scope. Neighbors routinely involved legal officials in their quarrels. Masters filed charges against hired servants and slaves whom they could not control; white and free black wives filed charges against husbands; and free children informed on their parents. Free families brought their feuds to court for resolution, with wives, husbands, parents, children, siblings, aunts, uncles, and cousins all lining up to air their dirty laundry. In all these instances, men and women marched off to magistrates, certain that they could mobilize the local legal system to resolve their personal problems and to bring their own vision of order to their communities. Disorder was disorder—when it happened, people expected that their government should listen to them and right the wrongs.[22]

Righting wrongs did not involve the maintenance of individual rights or the production of precedents that others could claim. Local courts did follow state laws regarding rights in procedural respects, particularly in determining who could prosecute cases in their own names. Decisions about the merits of the claims, however, relied on common law in its traditional sense as a flexible collection of principles rooted in local custom, but that also included an array of texts and principles, in addition to statutes and state appellate law, as potential sources for authoritative legal principles. This eclectic legal framework allowed for the handling of situations that might not have had legal standing in other areas of the system. Magistrates recognized that wives and slaves controlled property, even though they could not own it in other areas of law. The point was to keep the property where it belonged, not to uphold property rights. Magistrates prosecuted husbands, fathers, and even masters for violence against their wives, children, and slaves, because the authority granted heads of household was not absolute, but contingent on the maintenance of the social order. The idea was to keep flagrant abuses of power in check so that households did not fall apart, not to attend to the individual rights of either household heads or dependents. The effects of legal decisions thus remained with the particular people involved, because the system was so personalized. One person's experience did not transfer to another person of similar status (defined by such characteristics as gender, race, or class) or predict any other case's outcome. This area of law existed in the lived context of people's lives and existing social relationships—what the historiography tends to identity as elements of social history, distinct from the law.[23]

BEFORE THE CIVIL WAR, local government in the South had protected the peace of a social order based in slavery and committed to white supremacy. Enslaved African Americans could observe, endure, and try to work around the edges, as local officials defined what was right in ways that often worked to their detriment. That situation changed during the Civil War, giving African Americans reason to think that they could assume more active roles in defining the emerging social order, even when their claims to individual rights were still tenuous. They began building a new relationship to the governing system immediately, as existing scholarship has shown. During and immediately after the Civil War, when state and local courts were either nonexistent or hostile, African Americans sought out venues at the federal level, such as military courts or, later, the courts of the Freedmen's Bureau. As the nature of their claims suggest, African Americans expected the federal government to address the same kinds of issues that would have fallen to local courts and that had been handled within the framework of maintaining the peace: interpersonal conflicts, often involving violence and including domestic issues, as well as matters involving broader questions of social justice, such as the treatment of refugees, payment of wages, and reunification of families. The various courts under federal jurisdiction, which lacked an established body of law to handle this diverse array of claims, struggled to keep up. But African Americans persisted, in a manner that legal historians refer to as forum shopping—that is, seeking out a responsive and, hopefully, supportive legal forum. When southern states reconstituted their governments under Congressional Reconstruction and federal venues closed down, African Americans moved back to local and state courts. As they saw it, it was the responsibility of government—at all levels—to protect the peace of the social order, one in which they could now participate actively in ways they had not been able to before.[24]

Consider the case brought by Bella Newton, an African American woman who lived in North Carolina. The incident began in the spring of 1869 when Newton's children, William and Susan, took a shortcut across a white neighbor's land on the way home from school. The neighbor, Alexander Noblin, ordered the children off. From there, the situation deteriorated rapidly. Noblin tried to assault Susan. William threw a rock at Noblin's head, frustrating his attempt. Then, as the children made their escape, Noblin tried to assert his authority one final time. In William's words, he "shook his penis at us." After learning of the incident, Bella Newton first responded in keeping with the local legal process, which extended to informal settlements. She publicized her complaint in the neighborhood and then made an informal bargain with Noblin, agreeing to drop the matter in exchange for one dollar and ten pounds of bacon. Noblin delivered on his end of the deal, but Newton had a change of heart and filed charges with the justice of the peace, turning the incident into a legal matter involving her rights to prosecute a case on behalf of her children. Much to his chagrin, Noblin learned that his actions carried different consequences now than they would have done before the enactment of the Reconstruction amendments: Noblin was indicted for assault at the spring term of the Superior Court.[25]

If she had been enslaved, Bella Newton could not have prosecuted this case. She could in 1869, because of federal policy changes. In particular, the Fourteenth Amendment and related legislation (enacted both before and afterward) gave the federal government supervisory authority over states' handling of rights. Some congressional Republicans argued for a more direct role for the federal government in the form of national standards that would allow *federal* jurisdiction over the rights of all citizens, regardless of where they lived. That position, however, collided with a commitment to maintain states' traditional authority in this area. As a result, the Fourteenth Amendment placed restrictions on states, prohibiting them from making or enforcing "any law which shall abridge the privileges or immunities of citizens of the United States" or depriving any person "of life, liberty, or property, without due process of law." Then it gave the federal government the power to enforce their provisions. But the Fourteenth Amendment itself did not give the federal government the power to define or grant rights in state jurisdictions—although the federal Bill of Rights, of course, still applied to federal cases. Later Civil Rights Acts extended federal authority in ways that brought it into state law more actively, by giving federal officials enhanced discretion over the ways that states interpreted and applied rights by strengthening its enforcement powers. But, given political opposition and the limited resources of federal enforcement agencies, that authority was never fully utilized.[26]

Even so, the Reconstruction amendments and related legislation at the federal level fundamentally altered the American people's relationship to both the federal government and their state governments. These policies not only brought the federal government more directly into the lives of ordinary Americans, but also made individual rights more important and more available than they had been before. At one level, the effects were direct and obvious. Federal policy mandated the extension of individual rights to people, namely African Americans, who could not claim them before. The acquisition of rights, in turn, gave African Americans access to state and federal government, the arenas in which rights were particularly important. The implications of federal policies, however, did not end with African Americans. They extended federal protection to the rights of *all* American citizens—and, potentially, all persons—opening up the possibility that anyone could summon federal authority to challenge states' handling of his or her rights, however they might define those rights. These changes positioned the federal government as an arbiter between individuals and their states, while also elevating the importance of rights as the primary means by which Americans could access federal power.

That context shaped Bella Newton's case. She could file charges because of her civil rights, enshrined in the state's new constitution and protected by the federal government, which ensured access to the legal system at the local and state levels. But the case was not just an assertion of rights, which allowed her access to the local court and the ability to pursue charges in her own name. It was also an assertion of what Newton thought was right. The legal charges that she had to use emphasized the point: she brought charges of assault, which was an offense against the peace of her community, not a violation of her own rights. Such charges offered no monetary awards. People in Newton's situation usually pursued them because they wanted the court to condemn behavior at odds with their view of the social order—in this case, one in which white men like Alexander Noblin could no longer treat African Americans in the way he treated her children, simply because he was white and they were black.

Before the Civil War, claims like those of Bella Newton would have remained in local courts. If the case was appealed to the state level, it would have been done on a procedural point of state law—such as the wording of the indictment—that applied to similar kinds of cases, not on the merits of Newton's claims about the social order. If she and others had petitioned for the legislature's or the governor's intercession, those state leaders would have considered the circumstances of the conflict, but would have rendered a pardon or some other kind of solution as an exception to the laws, which would otherwise remain in force. Reconstruction-era policies gave claims like Newton's entirely new legal possibilities, by allowing them—and legal principles that governed them—to migrate out of local jurisdictions and into state and federal jurisdictions. In those arenas, they had the potential to be something more than a community conflict among particular individuals. Given the governing framework in place there, legal principles that once had nothing to do with rights could acquire the kind of legal power attached to rights—that is, the power of a universal, enforceable claim. They could even acquire the status of rights.

Education provides a particularly compelling example of a claim about what was right becoming something more like an individual right. Access to education was one of the earliest, most common demands from African

American organizations in both the North and the South. In northern states, many of which had well-established public school systems, African Americans advocated desegregation as the best way to provide equal access. The problem of access took a different form in southern states, most of which did not have public schools at all. There, African Americans called for the creation of public education systems, funded through state government, which would serve all the states' residents, white and black. While African Americans argued that education was a public good, they also characterized it in terms akin to other civil rights, something that all individuals could claim and that government could enforce. That characterization stuck, both in popular conceptions of education and the law. The Reconstruction-era constitutions of many southern states gave education all the trappings of a right: a universal claim that was available to everyone within the state and that the state was bound to protect. North Carolina's 1868 constitution even named education as a right. "The people," it declared, "have a right to the privilege of education, and it is the duty of the state to guard and maintain that right."[27]

Conceptions of social justice also found their way into state and federal jurisdictions through claims to existing civil and political rights—particularly the right to access the legal system and the right to vote. Bella Newton's case never moved beyond her local jurisdiction. But thousands of other similar cases involving white violence against African Americans did. While those cases that reached federal courts involved voting rights or other civil rights violations, they were nonetheless similar to Bella Newton's in the sense that they all involved the pervasive level of intimidation employed by white southerners against black southerners to maintain white supremacy. Such tactics were used widely and indiscriminately: not just to keep African Americans from voting or from the courts, but also to keep them from claiming wages, enjoying public space, advancing economically, or even going to school, as was the case with Newton's children. As the cases show, African Americans' claims to the vote and to basic civil rights were inseparable from a larger social vision in which they could live their lives free from the damaging effects of structural racism.[28]

In local courts, African Americans' claims were personalized, when they were recognized at all, because of the legal framework operative there. That jurisdiction still treated such cases as an issue in which a particular person harmed another particular person. Once that particular wrong was righted, social order was restored. In the context of state and federal jurisdictions, such disorderly acts became attached to rights and, in the process, acquired visibility that they would not otherwise have had. They became evidence of the widespread violation of rights that all Americans—or, at least, all American men—should be able to claim and that the federal government should be obligated to protect.

A similar dynamic also brought new kinds of claims into the definition of civil rights, expanding them to cover access to public venues and services, such as streetcars, railroads, restaurants, hotels, and even government jobs. Businesses providing transport and accommodation were not wholly private in state and local law, even though they were privately owned: because they provided services that the public needed and could not do without, they had always been subject to more government regulation than other forms of private property. Such regulation fell under the authority of states and localities to maintain the public welfare—the peace. The fact that these areas were subject to state and local regulation, however, never guaranteed equal access. To the contrary, access to public property—sidewalks, streets, buildings, parks, and even jobs—had always been restricted. The result was a patchwork of local ordinances and longstanding customary practices, upheld in local law, which constrained where African Americans could go and how they could act.[29]

During and after the Civil War, African Americans framed their claims in terms of rights that the state should extend to them and that the federal government should protect. Who, they asked, had a right to access public space and public accommodations if not the public? Was it not the government's duty to ensure and protect access? Those popular conceptions then made their way into legal arenas in these matters, much as they did with education. The Civil Rights Act of 1875 explicitly included access to public space as a right. "All persons within the jurisdiction of the United States," it stated, "shall be entitled to the full and equal enjoyment of the accommodations, advantages, facilities, and privileges of inns, public conveyances on land or water, theaters, and other places of public amusement." As Amy Dru Stanley argues in this volume, this act even included pleasure within the framework of rights. The U.S. Supreme Court ultimately declared the act unconstitutional, but cases involving access to public space continued to cast the issues in terms of civil rights, a characterization ultimately accepted and institutionalized. Issues that had been part of the nebulous category of social rights (privileges established in context and thus varying from one community to another, which were not protected by state or federal law) became civil rights (which implied universal, enforceable standards).[30]

Americans not only drew federal jurisdictions into governing practices that had belonged to localities, but they also brought their expectations about government activism to their interactions with the federal government. They asked it to do a lot. It was not just African Americans in the South who did. Other groups, particularly women reformers and labor activists, increasingly looked to the federal government to do what local government was supposed to have done before the Civil War: to create a just society, to do what was right. In the decades following Reconstruction, federal officials retreated from that vision. The federal courts undercut the U.S. government's power to enforce states' compliance with the Fourteenth and Fifteenth Amendments, and the nation's political leaders also backed away from legislative efforts to achieve sweeping social change. Critics characterized activism, whether through the courts or legislation, as the efforts of particular groups to obtain special consideration, destroy the rights of individuals, and endanger the very concept of equality.

Even though these expansive views of federal power proved unsuccessful at the time, they became firmly embedded in the legal order of the emerging nation—a legal order in which individual rights became linked to conceptions of justice associated with legal principles formerly operative only in local jurisdictions. That link carries its own problems. Individual rights, even in their most expansive form, had definite limits when it came to matters of social justice. Nor was the preservation of an individual's rights always synonymous with the public good. Still, the policy changes of the Reconstruction era allowed the aspirations of diverse groups of Americans to move into the realm of federal law and, once there, to acquire the status of universal legal principles. While those aspirations expressed the unique values of particular groups of Americans, they were also deeply rooted in existing governing practices—practices outside the realm of state and federal government. The results remade the relationship between Americans and the nation-state, raising expectations about the federal government's role in maintaining a just social order. Those expectations could only result in conflict, since no consensus existed among the American people about what constituted a just society. Yet those aspirational visions of rights and social justice guided the nation's development and, ultimately, our own expectations about what the nation should be.

I owe an enormous debt to Kate Masur and Greg Downs, who went above and beyond the call of duty as editors. They not only improved the presentation of the ideas in this essay but also shaped the analysis in important ways. I learned a tremendous amount from them. I also wish to thank the volume's other contributors. The opportunity to share ideas with them at a conference, hosted by the Civil War Era Center at Penn State University, was an inspiring and enriching experience. Many thanks, in particular, to Bill Blair, for his support of the conference and the volume.

1. William Archibald Dunning, *Essays on the Civil War and Reconstruction and Related Topics* (New York: Macmillan, 1898); *Reconstruction, Political, and Economic, 1865-1877* (New York: Harper and Brothers, 1907). For Dunning's protégés, see William Watson Davis, *The Civil War and Reconstruction in Florida* (New York: Columbia University Press, 1913); John Rose Ficklen, *History of Reconstruction in Louisiana (through 1868)* (Baltimore: Johns Hopkins Press, 1910); H. J. Eckenrode, *The Political History of Virginia during Reconstruction* (Baltimore: Johns Hopkins Press, 1904); Walter L. Fleming, *Civil War and Reconstruction in Alabama* (New York : Columbia University Press, 1905); James Wilford Garner, *Reconstruction in Mississippi* (New York: Macmillan, 1901); J. G. de Roulhac Hamilton, *Reconstruction in North Carolina* (New York: Columbia University Press, 1914); Charles W. Ramsdell, *Reconstruction in Texas* (New York: Columbia University, 1910); John S. Reynolds, *Reconstruction in South Carolina, 1865-1877* (Columbia, S.C.: State Co., 1905); Clara Mildred Thompson, *Reconstruction in Georgia: Economic, Social, and Political, 1865-1872* (New York, Columbia University Press, 1915). Not all histories in this period were equally dismissive of federal authority. See, in particular, John W. Burgess, *Reconstruction and the Constitution, 1866-1876* (New York: Scribner's, 1902).

2. For an interesting recent exchange about the contributions of the Dunning School, focused not on racism but on the political feasibility of black suffrage as a matter of policy, see Adam Fairclough, "Was the Grant of Black Suffrage a Political Error? Reconsidering the Views of John W. Burgess, William A. Dunning, and Eric Foner on Congressional Reconstruction," *Journal of the Historical Society* 12 (June 2012): 155–88. A response by Michael A. Ross and Leslie Rowland, "Adam Fairclough, John Burgess, and the Nettlesome Legacy of the 'Dunning School,'" *Journal of the Historical Society* 12 (September 2012): 249–70, takes issue with Fairclough's contention that current historiography has completely dismissed Dunning School scholars, as well as his argument regarding the inadvisability of black suffrage.

3. Charles A. Beard and Mary R. Beard. *The Rise of American Civilization*, 2 vols. (New York: Macmillan, 1927). For another significant revision of federal authority, although not with the economic frame of the Beards, see James G. Randall, *Constitutional Problems under Lincoln* (New York: D. Appleton, 1926). Andrew W. Zimmerman revisits the idea of the Civil War as an economic revolution in a fascinating essay in this volume, "From the Second American Revolution to the First International and Back Again: Marx, Marxists, and the American Civil War."

4. Interestingly, the Progressives' and the revisionists' more positive evaluations of federal authority were also evident in work on the Confederacy, which turned the

Dunning School's logic on its head by recasting the Confederate States of America as models of centralization, not states' rights—something that they did not characterize as entirely negative. See E. Merton Coulter, *The Confederate States of America, 1861–1865* (Baton Rouge: Louisiana State University Press, 1950); Charles W. Ramsdell, "The Confederate Government and the Railroads," *American Historical Review* 22 (July 1917): 794–810; Ramsdell, "The Control of Manufacturing by the Confederate Government," *Mississippi Valley Historical Review* 8 (December 1921): 231–49; Emory M. Thomas, *The Confederate State of Richmond: A Biography of the Capital* (Austin: University of Texas Press, 1971); Thomas, *The Confederacy as a Revolutionary Experience* (Englewood Cliffs, N.J.: Prentice Hall, 1970); Thomas, *The Confederate Nation, 1861–1865* (New York: Harper and Row, 1979); Paul P. Van Riper and Harry N. Scheiber, "The Confederate Civil Service," *Journal of Southern History* 25 (November 1959): 448–70.

5. Historians use the term "revisionist" to apply to a range of work, and there is a lively debate about which works actually fall within that category. I am basing my analysis in the following work, although the points could be extended to other histories as well: Michael Les Benedict, *A Compromise of Principle: Congressional Republicans and Reconstruction, 1863–1869* (New York: W. W. Norton, 1974); Herman Belz, *Reconstructing the Union: Theory and Policy during the Civil War* (Ithaca: Cornell University Press, 1969); LaWanda Cox, *Lincoln and Black Freedom: A Study in Presidential Leadership* (Columbia: University of South Carolina Press, 1981); Harold M. Hyman, *A More Perfect Union: The Impact of the Civil War and Reconstruction on the Constitution* (New York: Knopf, 1973); Kenneth M. Stampp, *The Era of Reconstruction, 1865–1877* (New York: Alfred. A. Knopf, 1965); Allen W. Trelease, *White Terror: The Ku Klux Klan Conspiracy and Southern Reconstruction* (New York: Harper and Row, 1971); Hans L. Trefousse, *The Radical Republicans: Lincoln's Vanguard for Racial Justice* (New York: Alfred A. Knopf, 1969).

6. See, for instance, Robert Goldman, *A Free Ballot and a Fair Count: The Department of Justice and the Enforcement of the Voting Rights Act in the South, 1877–1893* (New York: Fordham University Press, 2001); Robert J. Kaczorowski, *The Politics of Judicial Interpretation: The Federal Courts, Department of Justice, and Civil Rights, 1866–1876* (New York: Oceana Publications, 1985); Lou Falkner Williams, *The Great South Carolina Ku Klux Klan Trials, 1871–1872* (Athens: University of Georgia Press, 2004). Pamela Brandwein's recent reconsideration of the legal interpretation of the Reconstruction amendments moves in a different direction, blaming political will, not the federal courts, but she still finds fault with federal enforcement. See *The Supreme Court, State Action, and Civil Rights: Rethinking the Judicial Settlement of Reconstruction* (New York: Cambridge University Press, 2011).

7. Perhaps the best-known example is Eric Foner, *Reconstruction: America's Unfinished Revolution* (New York: Harper and Row, 1988).

8. W. E. B. Du Bois, *Black Reconstruction: An Essay toward a History of the Part Which Black Folk Played in the Attempt to Reconstruct Democracy in America, 1860–1880* (New York: Russell and Russell, 1935).

9. Leon F. Litwack's magisterial, *Been in the Storm So Long: The Aftermath of Slavery* (New York: Alfred A. Knopf, 1979), is one of the best examples.

10. The work associated with the Freedmen and Southern Society Project provides the framework for much of the literature. See, for instance, Ira Berlin, Joseph P. Reidy, and Leslie S. Rowland, eds., *The Black Military Experience*, ser. 2 of *Freedom: A Documentary History of Emancipation, 1861–1867* (New York: Cambridge University Press, 1982); Ira Berlin, Barbara J. Fields, Thavolia Glymph, Joseph P. Reidy, and Leslie S. Rowland, eds., *The Destruction of Slavery*, ser. 1, vol. 1 of *Freedom: A Documentary History of Emancipation, 1861–1867* (New York: Cambridge University Press, 1985); and Ira Berlin, Stephen F. Miller, and Leslie S. Rowland, "Afro-American Families in the Transition from Slavery to Freedom," *Radical History Review* 42 (Fall 1988): 89–121. Also see Gregory P. Downs, *Declarations of Dependence: The Long Reconstruction of Popular Politics in the South, 1861–1908* (Chapel Hill: University of North Carolina Press, 2011); Laura F. Edwards, *Gendered Strife and Confusion: The Political Culture of Reconstruction* (Urbana: University of Illinois Press, 1997); Barbara J. Fields, *Slavery and Freedom on the Middle Ground: Maryland during the Nineteenth Century* (New Haven: Yale University Press, 1985); Thavolia Glymph, *Out of the House of Bondage: The Transformation of the Plantation Household* (New York: Cambridge University Press, 2008); Steven Hahn, *A Nation under Our Feet: Black Political Struggles in the Rural South from Slavery to the Great Migration* (Cambridge: Harvard University Press, 2003); Kate Masur, *An Example for All the Land: Emancipation and the Struggle Over Equality in Washington, D.C.* (Chapel Hill: University of North Carolina Press, 2010); Susan E. O'Donovan, *Becoming Free in the Cotton South* (Cambridge: Harvard University Press, 2007); Joseph P. Reidy, *From Slavery to Agrarian Capitalism in the Cotton Plantation South: Central Georgia, 1800–1880* (Chapel Hill: University of North Carolina Press, 1992); John C. Rodrigue, *Reconstruction in the Cane Fields: From Slavery to Free Labor in Louisiana's Sugar Parishes, 1862–1880* (Baton Rouge: Louisiana State University Press, 2001); Julie Saville, *The Work of Reconstruction: From Slave to Wage Laborer in South Carolina, 1860–1870* (New York: Cambridge University Press, 1994); Leslie A. Schwalm, *A Hard Fight for We: Women's Transition from Slavery to Freedom in South Carolina* (Urbana: University of Illinois Press, 1997).

11. I would include my own work in this critique: Edwards, *Gendered Strife and Confusion: The Political Culture of Reconstruction* (Urbana: University of Illinois Press, 1997).

12. Richard R. John, *Spreading the News: The American Postal Service from Franklin to Morse* (Cambridge: Harvard University Press, 1995). Political historians have established the popularity of elections in the first half of the nineteenth century.

13. Laura F. Edwards, *The People and Their Peace: Legal Culture and the Transformation of Inequality in the Post-revolutionary South* (Chapel Hill: University of North Carolina Press, 2009). The discussion of local government draws extensively on the analysis in this book. For other accounts of the operation of law on the local level in this period, see Kirt von Daacke, *Freedom Has a Face: Race, Identity, and Community in Jefferson's Virginia* (Charlottesville: University of Virginia Press, 2012), as well forthcoming books by Martha S. Jones, Kelly Kennington, Felicity Turner, and Kimberly Welch.

14. Recent historiography, particularly work in western history and Indian history, reflects the disparity between the experiences of those who lived inside and outside

the jurisdiction of states. Historians in these two fields tend to portray the federal government as not only more powerful, but also more involved in the legal status of individuals than the traditional historiography on Reconstruction. That disparity reflects facts on the ground, namely, the federal government's jurisdiction over Indians and American settlers in the territories. As a result, those people experienced the federal government differently than those who lived in established states to the east. Geography made all the difference. The essays in this volume provide good examples. For analyses that join the regions together, see Steven Hahn, "Slave Emancipation, Indian Peoples, and the Projects of a New American Nation-State" *Journal of the Civil War Era* 3 (September 2013): 307-30; Heather Cox Richardson, *West from Appomattox: The Reconstruction of American after the Civil War* (New Haven: Yale University Press, 2007); Elliott West, *The Last Indian War: The Nez Perce Story* (New York: Oxford University Press, 2009).

15. Some Americans were more likely to be involved in federal courts than others. As the work of Martha S. Jones shows, free blacks actively defended their rights in local, state, and federal jurisdictions precisely because their legal status—and their ability to live within the United States—was so tenuous. See, for instance, Jones, "*Hughes v. Jackson*: Race and Rights beyond *Dred Scott*," *North Carolina Law Review* 91 (June 2013): 1757-83. Also see Stephen D. Kantrowitz, *More than Freedom: Fighting for Black Citizenship in a White Republic, 1829-1889* (New York: Penguin, 2012).

16. "An Act to establish an uniform Rule of Naturalization," U.S. *Statutes at Large* 1, 1790, 103. The definitive analysis of federal citizenship is still James H. Kettner, *The Development of American Citizenship, 1608-1870* (Chapel Hill: University of North Carolina Press, 1978).

17. *Dred Scott v. Sandford* 60 U.S. 393 (1857). In the 1830s and 1840s, northern courts adopted the position that slave law from southern states could not reach into their states. See Leonard W. Levy, *The Law of the Commonwealth and Chief Justice Shaw* (Cambridge: Harvard University Press, 1957); Paul Finkelman, *An Imperfect Union: Slavery, Federalism, and Comity* (Chapel Hill: University of North Carolina Press, 1981). That was why both the Fugitive Slave Act, U.S. *Statutes at Large* 9, 1850, 462, and the decision in *Dred Scott* proved so controversial. Literature on African Americans' attempts to sue for freedom suggests how legally ambiguous the distinction between slavery and freedom was for African Americans in the decades between the Revolution and the Civil War. Martha S. Jones, "Time, Space, and Jurisdiction in Atlantic World Slavery: The Volunbrun Household in Gradual Emancipation New York," *Law and History Review* 29 (November 2011): 1031-60; Edlie L. Wong, *Neither Fugitive nor Free: Atlantic Slavery, Freedom Suits, and the Legal Culture of Travel* (New York: New York University Press, 2009). Questions about freedom were tied to questions about racial identity, which were not easy to resolve either. See Ariela J. Gross, *What Blood Won't Tell: A History of Race on Trial in America* (Cambridge: Harvard University Press, 2008).

18. For a particularly compelling account of the limits of rights, see Christopher L. Tomlins, *Law, Labor, and Ideology in the Early American Republic* (New York: Cambridge University Press, 1993)

19. The best statement on states' regulatory power is William J. Novak, *The People's Welfare: Law and Regulation in Nineteenth-Century America* (Chapel Hill: University of North Carolina Press, 1996).

20. Edwards, *The People and Their Peace*. For the importance of political expectations not based on individualized conceptions of rights, also see Downs, *Declarations of Dependence*.

21. Edwards, *The People and Their Peace*.

22. Ibid.

23. Ibid.

24. Laura F. Edwards, "Status without Rights: African Americans and the Tangled History of Law and Governance in the Nineteenth-Century U.S. South," *American Historical Review* 112 (April 2007): 365–93. Gregory P. Downs's book, *After Appomattox: Military Occupation and the Ends of War* (Cambridge: Harvard University Press, 2015), also emphasizes the pervasiveness and importance of federal legal venues, which often took over for local courts in the years follow Confederate surrender. In addition to the scholarship cited in note 10, see the essays by Kidada E. Williams and Crystal N. Feimster in this volume for particularly striking examples of African Americans' use of the legal system during the Civil War and Reconstruction. For scholarship that emphasizes African Americans' involvement in the legal system throughout the nineteenth century, see Ariela J. Gross, *Double Character: Slavery and Mastery in the Antebellum Southern Courtroom* (Princeton: Princeton University Press, 2000); Dylan C. Penningroth, *The Claims of Kinfolk: African American Property and Community in the Nineteenth-Century South* (Chapel Hill: University of North Carolina Press, 2003).

25. *State v. Alexander Noblin*, 1869, Granville County Criminal Action Papers, North Carolina Department of Archives and History. When I first wrote about this case in "Sexual Violence, Gender, Reconstruction, and the Extension of Patriarchy in Granville County, North Carolina," *North Carolina Historical Review* 68 (July 1991): 237–60, I framed complaints such as this as assertions of rights.

26. This paragraph is based in the discussion in chapter four of my book, *A Legal History of the Civil War and Reconstruction: A Nation of Rights* (New York: Cambridge University Press, 2015).

27. North Carolina's constitution quoted in Emily Zackin, *Looking for Rights in All the Wrong Places: Why State Constitutions Contain America's Positive Rights* (Princeton: Princeton University Press, 2014), 68n4; see 67–105 for a discussion of states' recognition of education as a right. Zackin argues that states recognized an array of positive rights in the late nineteenth century, often at the behest of citizens who actively sought out government protection. For African Americans' efforts to make education accessible, see Heather Williams, *Self-Taught: African American Education in Slavery and Freedom* (Chapel Hill: University of North Carolina Press, 2005). Hugh Davis, *"We Will Be Satisfied with Nothing Less": The African American Struggle for Equal Rights in the North during Reconstruction* (Ithaca: Cornell University Press, 2011); Davison M. Douglas, *Jim Crow Moves North: The Battle over Northern School Segregation, 1865–1954* (New York: Cambridge University Press, 2005).

28. The extent of violence is strikingly evident in Downs, *After Appomattox*. Examples of violence pervade the literature, and some of the most horrific examples were documented in federal hearings. See, for instance, *Select Committee on the Memphis Riots*, 39th Cong., 1st sess., House Rept. 101; *Condition of the Affairs in Georgia*, 40th Cong., 3d sess., House Misc. Doc. 52; *Testimony Taken by the Joint Committee to Enquire into the Condition of Affairs in the Late Insurrectionary States*, 42nd Cong., 2d sess., House Rept. 22 (Ku Klux Klan Hearings); *Condition of Affairs in the South* (Louisiana), 43rd Cong., 2d sess., House Rpt. 261; *Affairs in Alabama*, 43rd Cong., 2d sess., House Rept. 262; *Vicksburg Troubles*, 43rd Cong., 2d sess., House Rept. 265; *Mississippi in 1875*, 44th Cong., 1st sess., Sen. Rept. 527; *Recent Election in South Carolina*, 44th Cong., 2d sess., House Misc. Doc. 31; *Mississippi*, 44th Cong., 2d sess., Sen. Misc. Doc. 45; *South Carolina in 1876*, 44th Cong., 2d sess., Sen. Misc. Doc. 48. The literature on voting rights cases suggests how violence made its way into federal courts through these kinds of cases. See, in particular, the work cited in note 6 above. Also see Hannah D. Rosen, *Terror in the Heart of Freedom: Citizenship, Sexual Violence, and the Meaning of Race in the Postemancipation South* (Chapel Hill: University of North Carolina Press, 2009).

29. For a fascinating discussion of the regulation of public carriers and people's access to them, see Barbara Young Welke, *Recasting American Liberty: Gender, Race, Law, and the Railroad Revolution, 1865–1920* (New York: Cambridge University Press, 2001).

30. Civil Rights Act, *U.S. Statutes at Large* 18, 1875, 335. For a particularly compelling account of such efforts, see Masur, *An Example for All the Land*. See Amy Dru Stanley's essay in this collection for the point about pleasure and rights.

2 EMANCIPATING PEONS, EXCLUDING COOLIES

Reconstructing Coercion in the American West

Stacey L. Smith

In 1873, the U.S. Supreme Court heard the case of a group of white New Orleans butchers who were challenging a Louisiana state corporate charter. The charter gave large slaughterhouse operators a monopoly over butchering and meatpacking in the city. The plaintiffs claimed that in shutting out small operators the state charter restricted their right to pursue their chosen trade, thus denying them the equal protection of the laws guaranteed by the Fourteenth Amendment. In the famous *Slaughterhouse* decision, the court ruled against the butchers and declared that Congress had primarily intended the Fourteenth Amendment to confer citizenship rights on African Americans. Even then, the amendment only guaranteed a narrow range of federal citizenship rights, such as the ability to travel abroad or to run for federal office.[1] Many historians have interpreted the *Slaughterhouse* decision as a critical rollback in the story of expanding postwar freedom.[2] Foreshadowing the Republican Party's retreat from Reconstruction, the Democratic Party's resurgence in the South, and the rise of Jim Crow, *Slaughterhouse* (in the customary view) helped demolish Congress's initial, more expansive vision of African American freedom.

The focus on the court's conservative reading of the Fourteenth Amendment in *Slaughterhouse* has, however, obscured the justices' more expansive interpretation of the Thirteenth Amendment. In their suit, the New Orleans butchers also alleged that the corporate monopoly over animal slaughtering violated the Thirteenth Amendment's ban on slavery and involuntary servitude. The Thirteenth Amendment "comprise[d] much more than the abolition or prohibition of African slavery"; it banned all vestiges of feudalism, serfdom, and seigniorialism. Louisiana's slaughterhouse charter so severely restricted small operators' participation in the market that they were "compelled to refrain from the use of their own land and exercise of their own industry and the improvement of their own property." They therefore suffered a kind of state-imposed involuntary servitude.[3] While the court rejected the butchers' arguments, the majority opinion did confirm that the Thirteenth Amendment's ban on involuntary servitude extended far beyond the prohibition on African American slavery. "While negro slavery was alone in the mind of the Congress which proposed the thirteenth article, it forbids any other kind of slavery, now or hereafter," the justices agreed; "if Mexican peonage or the Chinese coolie labor system shall develop slavery of the Mexican or Chinese race within our territory, this amendment may safely be trusted to make it void." The victims of slavery need not "be of African descent" to receive the protection of the Thirteenth Amendment, and federal officials were constitutionally bound to wipe out a range of coercive labor relationships that resembled African American slavery in practice, if not in name.[4]

The Supreme Court's interpretation of the Thirteenth Amendment in *Slaughterhouse* suggests a new way of conceptualizing the postemancipation era. The central struggles of the postwar era were not just to define the limits of individual freedom but also to map out the boundaries of coercion and to determine how the federal state would intervene to restrain employers, corporations, or states from exercising certain types of coercive power over individuals. In deciding whether the state of Louisiana had deprived New Orleans butchers of their Thirteenth Amendment rights, the justices had first to determine what kinds of coercive behavior were legally acceptable and unacceptable under the amendment. The court ultimately ruled that African slavery and its analogues, "peonage" and "coolieism," belonged firmly in the category of illegitimate and illegal coercion. Meanwhile, other types of compulsion—restraining an individual from pursuing a particular occupation or using his or her productive property to its fullest capacity—constituted acceptable, legitimate coercion (if it was, in fact, coercion at all). At the moment that the postwar federal state played a critical role in transforming millions of enslaved people into rights-bearing individuals with the capacity to exercise a host of new liberties, it also became the arbiter of coercive power relations, determining who could compel whom to do what under which circumstances.[5]

Once we understand that the abolition of slavery raised a host of questions about the boundaries of coercion, how do we go about writing a history of the postwar era? In this essay, I propose the American West as a launching point for exploring postwar visions of the limits and proper exercise of coercive power in the realm of labor relations.[6] As the justices in the *Slaughterhouse Cases* emphasized in their invocation of two western labor systems — Mexican "peonage" and Chinese "coolieism" — the problem of defining the legitimate bounds of labor coercion extended beyond the South and the institution of African American slavery. In the nineteenth century, the American West was a multiracial borderland where labor systems from North America, South America, and Asia overlapped and collided. The region developed distinctive forms of compulsory labor that were not self-evidently free or slave, voluntary or involuntary, and involved people — the "Mexican or Chinese race" — who were neither black nor white.

These amorphous western labor systems persisted well into the postwar era and created a crisis for the Republican Party and the postwar federal state. Republican bureaucrats, jurists, and politicians argued over whether the coercive elements of peonage and Chinese contract labor fell under the Thirteenth Amendment's broad ban on slavery and involuntary servitude. Congressional Republicans finally agreed that the Hispano practice of peonage in New Mexico Territory crossed the line into unacceptable coercion and passed the 1867 Anti-Peonage Act to abolish it. Republicans, however, soon confronted the vexing reality that the postwar federal state in the Southwest lacked the capacity to impose their vision of proper labor relations on the territory. A "Stockade State" of isolated military and bureaucratic outposts, with limited geographic reach, the federal government in New Mexico could not muster enough force to liberate peons from the grasp of resistant Hispano masters. The persistence of peonage in New Mexico thus reveals the incompleteness of the postwar consolidation of federal power and the incapacity of the state to quell rebellious local peoples and divergent labor practices.

In contrast, the struggle over Chinese labor in the West illustrated how the federal state could act in strikingly illiberal ways in instances when it did have the capacity to outlaw certain types of labor coercion. In California, Democrats who had once resisted the Thirteenth Amendment appealed to the amendment's ban on coercive labor relationships to justify the exclusion of Chinese "coolie" immigrants who purportedly arrived under low-paying, long-term contracts. California Republicans, battered by Democrats at the polls, eventually embraced the anti-coolie argument. They contended that the contractual, voluntary, and compensated labor relationships that brought Chinese to the United States involved too much coercion to be tolerated under the Thirteenth Amendment. Instead of seeking to emancipate alleged coolies and bring them into the fold of free laborers, Republicans insisted that Chinese were too servile and dependent to be integrated into a postwar liberal economic order as autonomous, self-owning workers. They then spearheaded a federal campaign for a racially restrictive immigration law excluding all Chinese laborers from the United States. In the West's anti-coolie campaigns we can see the extent to which liberalism failed to permeate postwar law and politics in the wake of slave emancipation.

Struggles over the status of peonage and coolieism, federal power, and liberal visions of free labor did not remain compartmentalized in the West. They boomeranged back across the Rockies to transform national political and legal discourses about the acceptability of coercive labor relations that emerged in the postwar North and South. Federal antipeonage legislation, initially aimed at New Mexico Territory, eventually provoked a contest over the legitimacy of similar southern labor systems aimed at binding African Americans. The result was a much more effective federal initiative that used the 1867 Anti-Peonage Act to suppress southern debt bondage at the turn of the twentieth century. The battle over Chinese labor contracts in California also reverberated back in the industrialized Northeast. There, labor leaders emphasized the capitalist abuse of foreign contract laborers to unmask the distinctly coercive and illiberal nature of the wage bargain. The persistence of coercive labor relations in the West, then, both forged and forced a national postwar conflict over employers' rights to compel labor, the limits of laborers' rights to be free from compulsion, and the power of the state to eradicate certain types of labor coercion. Once we follow the echoes of western labor conflicts into the North and the South, we find that changing visions of coercion were just as central to the unfolding of the postwar era as changing visions of freedom.

ELIMINATING PEONAGE, WEST AND SOUTH

In January 1863, New Mexico's territorial legislators wrote a memorial protesting Congress's recent abolition of slavery in all federal territories.[7] They complained that abolition created special hardships in their territory, where there were "six hundred Indian captives who are now held in servitude." These captives, likely Navajos who had been seized in warfare and incorporated into New Mexican households as domestic servants, would have to be "turned loose by our courts." Released from the benevolent care of New Mexican householders, the emancipated captives would "be placed in a far worse condition than they are now." The legislature requested Congress to allocate money for the welfare of emancipated Indians and to "give a reasonable compensation to the owners of these captives." The Senate received and printed the memorial, but never gave it a serious hearing.[8]

The friction between New Mexican legislators and Congress over the abolition of slavery in the territories foreshadowed a postwar conflict over the enforcement of the Thirteenth Amendment in the Southwest. After a campaign of continental conquest in the 1840s, the United States had acquired New Mexico and inherited a Spanish-Mexican colonial labor regime founded on the forced incorporation of adopted Indian captives and debt-bound mestizo peons into non-Indian households. In the decade before the Civil War, New Mexicans attempted to shore up traditions of borderlands servitude by codifying them in territorial law. After the ratification of the Thirteenth Amendment in 1865, federal officials (mostly Republicans) assailed New Mexican captivity and peonage as illegal and immoral forms of labor coercion that violated the federal prohibition of slavery and involuntary servitude.

Federal officials found, however, that the complex character of these systems—which freely mixed captivity with allegedly benevolent relations of fictive kinship and adoption, and with voluntary, contractual debt peonage—made drawing the line between legally acceptable and unacceptable coercion a vexing task. Aimed at ending African American slavery in the South, the Thirteenth Amendment was silent about the range of coercive labor relations that might be encompassed by its ban on involuntary servitude. The amendment said nothing regarding the coercive labor relationships within families and did nothing to limit the power of male heads of household to extract labor from their dependents. Nor did the Thirteenth Amendment provide guidance about types of voluntary servitude, such as debt peonage, in which debtors ostensibly agreed to serve their creditors until they had repaid their loans. Federal officers struggled to determine whether elite Hispanos (Spanish-speaking New Mexicans) could legitimately command the labor of Indian captives whom they had adopted as fictive kin or of Indian and mestizo peons who had agreed to work off their debts. For their part, Hispanos and Anglo newcomers who profited from captive and debt-bound labor resisted and eventually defeated federal efforts to overhaul the territory's labor arrangements. The thinness of the federal government's power on the ground, its incapacity to impose the Republican Congress's vision of unacceptable coercion onto the territory, revealed the postwar consolidation of federal power as incomplete and imperfect.

The Spanish-Mexican labor system that federal officers confronted in the 1860s was rooted in complex relations of captivity, slavery, debt peonage, household dependence, and kinship ties born of centuries of borderlands raiding and trading. Since the beginning of the Spanish conquest of New Mexico in the sixteenth century, Hispanos and their Pueblo Indian allies had engaged in intermittent wars with equestrian Apaches, Navajos, and Comanches. Hispanos took hundreds of Indians captive in these wars, and they also purchased hundreds more from the Great Plains and the Great Basin during annual trade fairs.

Hispanos justified taking, holding, and buying these captives by arguing that they "redeemed" them from savagery and heathenism. Under Catholic relations of *compadrazgo*, or godparenthood, Hispanos stood as fictive kin to captives at their baptisms and then adopted them into their households. Captives remained in New Mexican homes as lifelong adopted servants, where they were to receive instruction in "civilization" and the Catholic faith. Such practices of Indian captivity frequently bled into debt peonage. Coercive sexual relationships between Hispanos and Indian captives created a class of lower-caste and impoverished mixed-bloods or mestizos. These men and women often became debt-bound servants, *peones*, of elite Hispanos who advanced them cash or goods. By the eve of the U.S. conquest, then, Hispanos had created a tangle of compulsory labor relationships aimed at extracting work, deference, and obedience from Indians and mestizos.[9]

The U.S. acquisition of the Mexican north in 1848 and New Mexico's territorial organization in 1850 left elite Hispanos and their wealthy Anglo allies scrambling to preserve customary relations of servitude under U.S. law. In 1851, Hispano legislators passed a territorial Master and Servant Act. Rooted in the master and servant laws of the Anglo-American common law tradition, the territorial measure enforced contracts in which servants voluntarily bound themselves to labor for their employers. Masters could seize runaways, and servants who failed to "respect their masters as their superior guardians" faced legal prosecution. The law also allowed masters to advance wages and goods to their servants and then extract their labor until they repaid their debts.[10] While the law did not mention captive Indians, it did provide masters with a pretext for holding Native people in debt peonage. Hispanos who bought and "redeemed" Indian captives might claim their services by forcing them to work off their purchase prices.[11]

The U.S. war on the Navajo peoples of the Southwest, a conflict that coincided with the Civil War, stimulated the New Mexico captive trade and fortified Indian servitude in the territory. In the early 1860s, the U.S. Army joined forces with local militias to suppress and remove Navajo bands that lived on New Mexico's western frontier. During these wars, New Mexicans seized a few thousand Navajo women and children, many of whom they baptized and held as domestic servants.[12] Together with countless debt-bound mestizo peons, this growing number of adopted Indian captives—who numbered upwards of three thousand people in a total territorial population of about eighty-seven thousand—became an important source of domestic labor. This explains why New Mexicans contested the abolition of slavery and involuntary servitude in the territories.

Indeed, as reports of Navajo captivity trickled east, Republicans in the federal government challenged New Mexicans' assertion that Indian servitude was a benign form of domestic dependence. They framed it instead as a foreign and barbarous brand of coercion that the United States was now legally bound to eradicate from its national domain. Little more than a month after Abraham Lincoln's assassination, the secretary of the interior, the Republican James Harlan, alerted Andrew Johnson "that the law abolishing slavery in New Mexico is disregarded . . . the practice of selling Indian children still continues."[13] Johnson responded in June 1865 with an executive order commanding federal officers to suppress Indian servitude. Harlan transmitted the order to federal Indian agents and military officers in New Mexico and urged them to "cheerfully co-operate in putting an end to this barbarous and inhuman practice." He emphasized that "such violations of the personal liberty of the Indians, and the extraction from them of unrequited labor, should not be tolerated in a country professing to be free."[14] Similarly, Julius Graves, a Radical Republican and federal Indian agent, fumed that Hispanos clung "tenaciously to their old customs" of capturing and adopting Indians as servants. Congress needed to erase "this remaining blot upon the otherwise fair scroll of freedom." He recommended the creation of a special "freedmen's bureau" for New

Mexico that would protect Indians and the "poor classes" from Hispano exploitation.[15]

By summer 1865, Republicans in Washington, D.C., had concluded that the New Mexican practices of captivity, adoption, and debt peonage constituted illegal, illegitimate, and immoral exercises of labor coercion. New Mexican labor relations violated the soon-to-be ratified Thirteenth Amendment and needed to be destroyed in the United States' territorial possessions. These Republicans soon found, however, that the ambiguous nature of New Mexican labor relations stymied their efforts to redefine them as illegal forms of coercion. Elite Hispano and Anglo residents, vigilant against the imposition of American legal codes that undermined the territory's long-standing labor practices, contested accusations of rampant slavery in the territories. They insisted that captivity and peonage were benevolent and voluntary relationships embedded in kinship relations, and that they violated no federal laws or executive decrees. For instance, Felipe Delgado, New Mexico's Hispano superintendent of Indian affairs, protested Johnson's executive order. Accounts of Indian slavery were "greatly exaggerated," he declared. New Mexicans had trafficked in Indian captives for generations, "but the object in purchasing them has not been to reduce them to slavery." Instead, "Christian piety on the part of the whites to obtain them in order to instruct and educate them in civilization" motivated these transactions. Delgado also insisted that the glue of fictive kinship and paternal benevolence, rather than coercion, bound Indian servants into New Mexican homes. Hispanos stood as "guardians" to Indian servants, their "adopted children." Domestic servitude was a "favorable, humane, and satisfactory" institution for Indians, and Delgado only grudgingly agreed to comply with the executive order.[16] This kind of argument was so convincing that even William Arny, the territory's abolitionist Republican governor, questioned tearing Indians from the homes where they had "voluntarily chosen to remain" and were "clothed, fed and taught to lead a civilized life."[17]

Opponents of emancipation in New Mexico not only claimed that kinship distinguished Indian captivity from chattel slavery; they also denied that debt peonage involved illegitimate or illegal coercion. In August 1865, a Hispano named Don Pedro García complained that a peon had fled his service before paying back a debt he owed. He requested that federal officers stationed at nearby Fort Selden help him capture the man. A captain at the fort refused to comply, arguing that returning a fugitive debtor to the service of his master was "certainly contrary to the established rules and regulations of the government under which we live." A week later, however, the captain's superior officer (who controlled several peons himself) ordered him to assist in returning the servant. "Peonage is voluntary and not involuntary servitude," the commander reasoned. Masters could legitimately hold and extract labor from servants who voluntarily took out debts and consented to work until they paid back what they owed. It mattered not "whether peonage is a good or bad kind of servitude"; the peon had agreed to the arrangement and therefore could be legally compelled into rendering up his services. The officer ordered military personnel to return all runaway peons to their masters.[18]

By 1866, Republicans had decided to test the validity of the idea that Indian captivity and debt peonage were legally acceptable forms of coercion. The ratification of the Thirteenth Amendment in late 1865, followed by the passage of the Civil Rights Act of 1866 a few months later, gave them new legal ammunition against both practices. The Thirteenth Amendment's broad prohibition on slavery and involuntary servitude could be interpreted to prohibit New Mexicans from extracting labor from captives or peons. The Civil Rights Act of 1866, aimed at enforcing the Thirteenth Amendment by conferring basic freedoms on African Americans, was more ambiguous. The act declared that all people born in the United States were citizens and that all citizens, regardless of "race, religion, or previous condition of servitude," enjoyed federal protection of their basic civil rights. Section 4 of the law ordered the U.S. district courts and (crucially) the territorial supreme courts to appoint commissioners to investigate civil rights violations. Commissioners were to receive a fee of ten dollars for every case they pursued. The act's ambiguity came in its very first line that declared that "Indians not taxed" were excluded from citizenship and, presumably, did not enjoy the civil rights protections afforded to citizens. On the other hand, the second section protected "any inhabitant of any State or Territory" from infringements on his or her civil rights, and therefore might be interpreted to encompass Indians and mestizos.[19]

Despite such uncertainties, several federal officials in New Mexico were determined to extend these new laws to the territory. In 1867, the territorial supreme court, under the leadership of the former U.S. general John P. Slough, criminalized peonage and struck down the 1851 Master and Servant Law. According to Slough, peonage constituted "a service which is fled from" and required "compulsory statutes and enactments to recover the fugitive and enforce service." Under its veneer of voluntarism and consent, peonage was actually "involuntary servitude" and was "clearly abolished by the act of Congress [the Civil Rights Act of 1866] and the [Thirteenth] Amendment of the Constitution."[20] The territory's Republican attorney general, Stephen Elkins, then urged the court to enforce section 4 of the Civil Rights Act of 1866 by employing commissioners to investigate whether Hispanos were using coercion to hold captives or peons. They were to scour the territory, hear evidence, liberate any person who was being forcefully detained, and bring charges against masters. They could claim the $10 fee for every case they took up. The commissioners, however, made little headway. Ridiculed in territorial newspapers and stonewalled by elite Hispano and Anglo landholders who refused to testify against their neighbors, they successfully prosecuted only twenty-six cases.[21] The highest court in the territory might have proclaimed that peonage fell into the realm of coercive behavior prohibited by new federal statutes, but the federal government lacked the legal and military capacity to enforce this decree against resistant locals.

The ineffectiveness of antipeonage prosecution under the Civil Rights Act of 1866, which signaled the broader inability of the federal state to impose a particular vision of acceptable coercion onto remote territories, finally drove Congress to formulate the first federal statute aimed at clarifying the scope of the Thirteenth Amendment. In January 1867, the leading Radical senator Charles Sumner took to the Senate floor and proclaimed that he was "astonished" to learn that peonage, "a system of slavery which a Proclamation of the President has down to this day been unable to root out," remained widespread in New Mexico. He requested that the Senate Judiciary Committee investigate these charges and recommend action.[22]

Less than a month after Sumner's appeal, Senator Henry Wilson, a Radical Republican from Massachusetts, proposed an "Act to Abolish and Forever Prohibit the System of Peonage in the Territory of New Mexico and Other Parts of the United States." The Anti-Peonage Act, as it came to be known, set forth an expansive vision of the Thirteenth Amendment's limits on the coercive power of employers. Wilson's bill declared unlawful "the holding of any person to service or labor under the system known as peonage." Crucially, Wilson attempted to stifle objections that holding a worker to labor in exchange for the repayment of a debt was a legitimate exercise of coercion because he or she had voluntarily consented to the arrangement. His bill prohibited "voluntary and involuntary service" whereby any person was held to labor "in liquidation of any debt or obligation, or otherwise." Creditors could only compel debtors to repay them by filing a civil suit against them, not by directly extracting their labor. As one Republican put it, "the creditor shall be left to all his legal means of collecting his debt, but he shall not hold the peon in slavery." The act, in effect, extended the constitutional meaning of slavery and involuntary servitude to encompass all labor relations by which one private party directly compelled another private party to labor, even when such a relationship was ostensibly contractual and voluntary. Like other federal civil rights statutes from the era, it also established that the courts would be the primary recourse for individuals whose rights had been abrogated.[23]

Republicans' efforts to mark the boundaries of legitimate labor coercion in the American West instantly provoked debates about postwar labor coercion in the American South. Wilson's proposal to move voluntary debt servitude into the realm of illegitimate coercion faced immediate challenge from at least one politician who represented a former slave state. The Democratic senator Garrett Davis of Kentucky, who had strongly opposed federal intervention to abolish African American slavery, also resisted federal interference with peonage. Davis demanded that Wilson define the term "peonage" and explain how voluntary debt servitude differed from the basic legal principle that debtors were responsible for repaying their creditors. Davis homed in on the thorny issue of voluntary servitude, arguing that Congress had no need, and, in fact, no power to interfere with consensual agreements between workers and employers. Surely, debtors who worked to pay back loans that they had voluntarily taken out were not equivalent to slaves. If paying back creditors constituted a form of slavery, he joked, "then I have been for a good many years of my life in about the same state of slavery . . . I have owed considerable debts and I have worked mighty hard to pay them." He concluded that "this feature of a man's working to pay the debts that he owes to his creditors, in a modified form at least, ought to exist," and that the Senate should not pass any hasty legislation.[24]

Although Republicans were united against peonage, and they had the votes to pass the legislation easily, they felt compelled to explain why debt servitude constituted an illegal form of coercion that the federal government was bound to eradicate. Wilson contended that peonage was almost never voluntary. He explained that it was "a modified form of servitude, which we have inherited from Mexico . . . in some cases it is voluntary, but in most cases forcible," and he asserted that most peons were Indians "captured and forcibly held in servitude." The Republican senator Henry S. Lane of Indiana interjected that peonage was technically voluntary, but that it amounted to involuntary servitude in practice. Most debtors ended up working in their creditors' homes as domestic servants with the cost of room and board added to their debt. Drowning in debt that they could never repay, peons could never leave the service of their masters and thus suffered "servitude for life." Finally, Wilson pointed out that debt peonage was especially insidious because it knew no racial boundaries. "White men" — by whom he meant mixed-race mestizos — were often peonage's victims. Rhetorically erasing mestizos' Indian heritage and moving them into the racial category of "white," Wilson argued that "slavery of this kind for white men" was equivalent to "negro slavery" and should be eliminated alongside it.[25] In the Republican formulation, then, consent and voluntarism were just smoke screens that hid coercive labor relations as compulsory and permanent as black slavery. Republicans were united in this conclusion. The Senate passed the act, and two weeks later the House followed suit with no discussion or debate. Andrew Johnson approved it on March 2, 1867.[26]

Making peonage legally incompatible with the Thirteenth Amendment initially promised to deliver the final death blow to the institution. Armed with the Anti-Peonage Act, New Mexico Republicans vigorously investigated charges of peonage, prosecuted masters, and emancipated peons. In 1868, the territorial supreme court appointed another commissioner, the Radical Republican William W. Griffin, to investigate violations of the Civil Rights Act of 1866 and the Anti-Peonage Act. Griffin interrogated hundreds of Hispanos "charged with holding Indian slaves and peons, contrary to law." He bound over more than three hundred defendants for a hearing before a grand jury at the U.S. District Court in Santa Fe. Griffin went on to release 289 Indian captives and peons and claimed $2,890 ($10 per person) in compensatory fees under the Civil Rights Act of 1866.[27]

In the end, though, contested visions of coercion, spirited resistance from Hispanos, and the limits of state power on the ground frustrated efforts to punish practitioners of peonage. The U.S. grand jury that reviewed Griffin's cases was made up primarily of Hispanos. These jurors admitted that the "malpractice" of Indian servitude persisted in New Mexico and that Indians were held "as labourers and . . . kept in gross ignorance." Still, they felt that the Hispano defendants' extraction of labor was justifiable, legitimate, and humane, violating no federal law. Reverting to arguments about the benevolent, voluntary, and kinship-based nature of New Mexican labor relations, they concluded that none of the servants in question had "been forcibly detained or ill treated." There was also no evidence that the defendants had "intentionally or maliciously violated the law" by keeping Indian servants or peons in their homes. The defendants had not exercised undue coercion over their adopted captives or peons, nor had they clearly violated any federal law against involuntary servitude in retaining their services. The grand jury dismissed all charges and the defendants went free.[28]

The inability of the federal state to enforce the Anti-Peonage Act became even clearer when the U.S. Treasury refused to pay Griffin the fees he claimed under the Civil Rights Act of 1866. A Treasury agent argued that Congress had intended the act to apply to African Americans and explicitly excluded "Indians not taxed" from its provisions. Since all of Griffin's cases involved Indians or mestizos, he could not receive reimbursement. After four years of petitioning and the intervention of Charles Sumner, Griffin finally got his money.[29] Still, the ambiguity of the Civil Rights Act's protections for people other than African Americans, and the Treasury's narrow interpretation of the act, stalled the campaign to end peonage for good. New Mexico's Republican attorney general lamented that without the power to compensate special commissioners, "the enforcement of the law is paralysed" and "large numbers of Indians are enslaved and persons are held as peons."[30] Republican enthusiasm waned after these repeated setbacks and federal antipeonage prosecutions ceased. In 1877, federal agents continued to report widespread captivity and peonage in rural areas. Peons could be found in New Mexican households into the twentieth century.[31]

While the federal government lacked the power to liberate captives or peons in 1860s New Mexico, the antipeonage debate over unacceptable modes of labor coercion resonated in the turn-of-the-century South. Despite Republican declarations to the contrary, the end of African American slavery did not signal the onset of free and uncoerced labor. The Civil Rights Act of 1866 and the Fourteenth Amendment did undermine coercive tactics—such as vagrancy laws and forcible apprenticeship—that white employers had adopted to bind former slaves in the immediate aftermath of the Civil War. At the same time, Freedmen's Bureau agents, U.S. military officers, and a number of Republicans generally approved white planters' use of annual contracts to bind freedpeople to a specific employer and locale. Annual contracts balanced freedom for former slaves—who could choose their own employers and contract the basic terms of their labor—with the perceived need for labor discipline and market stability.[32] By the last decades of the nineteenth century, this southern style of labor contracting had transitioned into a system of sharecropping that resembled New Mexican peonage. Impoverished black and white southerners signed annual contracts with large landholders who allowed them to cultivate a section of land in return for a share of their annual crop. Most sharecroppers had to take out advances in supplies and cash from landholders at high interest rates and were unable to pay back these debts at the end of the agricultural year. Landholders then used extralegal violence and threats of legal action to bind and hold debtors.[33] By the turn of the twentieth century, peonage became an important mode of labor extraction in the Deep South as mine owners, lumberyard owners, and turpentine producers also began to use debt to bind African American laborers.

The 1860s legal contest over New Mexican peonage both anticipated and directly influenced turn-of-the-century struggles about the legitimacy of southern debt bondage as a method of labor coercion. The Anti-Peonage Act of 1867 found new life in the early twentieth century when attorneys in the U.S. Department of Justice began using it to prosecute white employers who exploited debt-bound black workers. Southern politicians and attorneys offered a spirited resistance to these prosecutions, arguing that the 1867 Congress had lacked the constitutional authority to pass the Anti-Peonage Act in the first place. The Thirteenth Amendment banned only slavery and involuntary servitude; it did not encompass "voluntary service" for debt, they asserted.[34] The U.S. Supreme Court knocked down these arguments in *Clyatt v. the United States*. The court resolved the decades-old question of whether voluntary servitude for debt should be considered a form of unacceptable coercion that violated the Thirteenth Amendment. The justices found that the original intent of the laborer on entering the debt arrangement was irrelevant. Even if the debt relationship began as voluntary and contractual on the part of the laborer, the result was "compulsory service, involuntary servitude," that he or she could not easily escape. Finally, the court asserted that the Thirteenth Amendment was "an absolute declaration that slavery or involuntary servitude shall not exist in any part of the United States" and that it empowered Congress to eradicate "all forms and incidents of slavery and involuntary servitude." Peonage violated the concept of "universal freedom" established by the Thirteenth Amendment and should be extinguished by federal legislation.[35]

Far from being contained in the American West, postwar struggles over peonage radiated outward beyond the region's boundaries. By the first years of the twentieth century, federal prosecutors mobilized the 1867 Anti-Peonage Act to criminalize and partially suppress debt servitude in several southern states. Together these campaigns against peonage, stretching across half a century and thousands of miles, were critical to demarcating the limits of labor coercion in the wake of emancipation. They established that voluntary servitude, no matter how free the laborer appeared to be when making the bargain, was, in fact, always rooted in involuntary, coercive labor relations that violated the Thirteenth Amendment. Moreover, they placed debt service outside the realm of legal tactics that creditors could use to extract labor from workers. Creditors would have to rely on a different kind of legal compulsion—a civil action in the courts—to recoup their money from indebted laborers.

At the same time, efforts to strike down peonage failed to clarify the status of other forms of voluntary and contractual servitude. Chinese contract labor, whereby Chinese workers (allegedly) signed on to long-term agreements in which they pledged to work faithfully in exchange for passage to the United States and a set wage, generated conflict over employers' coercive use of labor contracts. The struggle over Chinese contract labor raised, in turn, new questions about the power of the federal state to police the nation's borders against immigrants who brought intolerable methods of labor coercion to American shores.

"COOLIEISM," COERCION, AND CONTRACT LABOR

As Republicans agonized over the persistence of peonage in New Mexico, the Anti-Coolie Association of the Pacific Coast protested that "a new system of slavery" had appeared in California. The Anti-Coolie Association, a broad coalition of American- and Irish-born workers, proclaimed in an 1869 address that at least one hundred thousand Chinese "coolies" worked "in a state of peonage or slavery" across the state. Chinese merchants bound thousands of their poorer compatriots under long-term contracts at near starvation wages and imported them into the United States. They then hired them out to American corporations eager to replace "free white labor" with the cheap labor of a "semi-barbarous set of slaves." Even more galling, importers and employers carried on this traffic under the "plausible title of 'Chinese immigration.'" Cloaked under the mantle of free immigration, contracted coolie labor evaded the Thirteenth Amendment and reinstated quasi-slavery in the United States.[36] The association proposed to cut off the "coolie trade" by prohibiting the future entry of Chinese into the United States.

In the postwar era, California's campaign for Chinese exclusion revolved around constructing Chinese labor systems as dangerous and undesirable forms of coercion at odds with the Thirteenth Amendment. Justifying Chinese exclusion on Thirteenth Amendment grounds became both a political and legal necessity because Congress's postwar civil rights legislation made it nearly impossible to enforce immigration laws that targeted Chinese on the basis of race or national origin alone. Anti-Chinese politicians in California, first Democrats and later Republicans, realized that a successful campaign for Chinese exclusion rested on casting Chinese labor relationships—which were both voluntary and contractual—as outside the pale of legally acceptable coercion. While the antipeonage campaigns in New Mexico had highlighted the incapacity of the federal state to impose Republicans' views of acceptable coercion, the push to exclude alleged Chinese coolies proved a remarkably effective exercise of state power that transformed national immigration policy.

The debate over Chinese labor and immigration also exposed the limits of liberalism in the postwar nation. Driven by a liberal vision of free labor that emphasized workers' individual autonomy, freedom from coercion, and upward mobility, Republicans proclaimed that Chinese immigrants had to be excluded because they were too servile and dependent to be integrated into the postemancipation labor market as free workers. Republicans' attempts to create a liberal postwar labor order thus ensured the persistence of illiberal racialized immigration policies. Moreover, as the exclusion debate reached eastward into the industrializing North, labor leaders seized on the coolie question to highlight the coercion and unfreedom inherent in the postwar capitalist order and the wage system. Instead of blaming contracted Chinese, labor leaders condemned contract labor as just another capitalist tool that, like the wage bargain, reduced all workers to starvation, servitude, and dependence. The anti-coolie critique thus became a powerful way of laying bare the distinctly illiberal aspects of postwar capitalism.

California's postwar attack on coolie labor had deep historical roots. Starting in the 1830s, coolies became central figures in conversations about labor and race in the postemancipation Atlantic World. The word "coolie," which may be of Urdu-Hindustani, Tamil, or Chinese origin, initially meant "hireling" or "common laborer" and originally designated South Asian and East Asian workers who labored abroad in the eighteenth and nineteenth centuries. The term took on new meaning with the abolition of slavery in the British Caribbean. English authorities hoped that Asian laborers, especially Chinese, would supplement plantation workforces and ease the transition to a free labor economy. In this context, "coolies" denoted contracted or indentured Asians whom British officials recruited to take up the occupations of former slaves.[37] Eventually the kidnapping and abuse that Asian workers suffered raised doubts about the freeness of the "coolie trade" or "coolieism." By 1862, Republicans in the U.S. Congress passed legislation that forbade American ships from trafficking in "coolies."[38]

As the historian Moon-Ho Jung has convincingly demonstrated, however, no coherent, uniform system of long-term coolie contract labor existed by which all or most Asians arrived in the Americas, and "coolie" was never a real, formal legal category designating a particular kind of worker. Instead the coolie was a complex and unstable racial construct, what Jung calls "a conglomeration of racial imaginings that emerged worldwide in the era of slave emancipation, a product of the imaginers rather than the imagined." Variously envisioned as free or enslaved, white or colored, potential citizens or perpetual aliens, coolies came "to embody the hopes, fears, and contradictions" surrounding slave emancipation and the rise of industrial wage labor. Prior to the Civil War, some American abolitionists had identified coolies as a "conduit to freedom," a group of free wageworkers who, by toiling hard and cheap, could help ease the transition from slavery to free labor in the Americas. In contrast, southern proslavery ideologues depicted coolieism as a brutal and degrading method of enslaving free workers, one that demonstrated the folly and hypocrisy of wage labor and abolitionism.[39] The development of the "coolie" as an ambiguous, mutable class and racial construct was well underway before the post–Civil War campaign to ban Chinese immigration.

The unstable meaning of the term "coolie" was especially evident in California. Starting in the 1850s, white Californians asserted that Chinese immigrants were "coolies," by which they meant men who had been imported by Chinese or American employers under fixed, long-term contracts for a set wage (as was the practice in some parts of the Caribbean and Latin America). In reality, the vast majority of Chinese came to California under a more flexible type of temporary debt servitude called the credit-ticket system. Transportation to California was expensive, so would-be migrants often contracted to borrow their passage money from Chinese brokers and merchant houses. The merchants hoped to profit from migrants' California labors by charging them heavy interest on their loans. Once employed, migrants sent regular remittances back to their creditors in China. They were free from any obligation to labor as soon as they paid their debts. As a group of Chinese merchants explained to California's governor in 1852, the state's Chinese were not "'coolies,' if by that word you mean bound men or contract slaves." Instead, the average Chinese man paid his way to the state by taking out loans from merchants, "which they bestow on him safely, because he is industrious and honestly repays them." Chinese workers' only obligation was to pay their debts, which proved that "the Chinamen in this country are not 'serfs' or slaves of any description, but are working for themselves."[40]

Despite Chinese protests, the accusation that all California Chinese were coolies, laboring under fixed-term low-wage contracts, became a staple of anti-Chinese politics by the late 1860s. A postwar economic depression in California, which coincided with increased immigration from China and the movement of Chinese laborers into railroad and factory work, spurred protest against alleged coolie labor competition among working-class whites. Dozens of anti-coolie leagues sprouted up across California. Their members demanded the exclusion of Chinese immigrants and the prohibition of long-term systems of contract labor.[41]

The Democratic Party of California, in shambles during the war, seized on the anti-coolie movement. Postwar Democrats embraced the cause of white labor, promised an end to coolie importation, and fought federal measures that might elevate Chinese immigrants to citizenship alongside African Americans. In 1867, Democrats ran on a platform that promised "no Negro or Chinese suffrage" and vowed to end the "introduction of Mongolian [Chinese] laborers."[42] This strategy brought resounding success. California became one of the first non-slave states to be "redeemed" as Democrats won the governorship, gained a majority in the assembly, and came two seats shy of taking the state senate. Newly elected Democrats used their influence to obstruct congressional civil rights measures.

The state legislature refused to act on the Fourteenth Amendment and then rejected the Fifteenth Amendment outright.[43]

The ultimate ratification of the Fourteenth and Fifteenth Amendments ensured that federal civil rights legislation extended its grasp westward to California. Democrats who wanted to restrict Chinese immigration had to contend with Congress's removal of race-based limitations on civil rights. The Fourteenth Amendment's decree that the states could not deny any person (citizen or non-citizen) due process or the equal protection of the laws could lead to the overturn of anti-Chinese statutes in the federal courts. Moreover, the Civil Rights Act of 1870 explicitly extended equal protection to non-citizen aliens. It also prohibited states from singling out some immigrant groups for special charges or taxes.[44] Finally, the Burlingame Treaty of 1868, the United States' first major treaty with China, reflected the spirit of federal civil rights legislation. Recognizing "the inherent and inalienable right of man to change his home and allegiance," it allowed unrestricted voluntary emigration from China. But the Burlingame Treaty did contain one significant loophole that anti-Chinese forces could (and would) exploit. Reflecting the Republican aversion to slavery, it condemned "any other than an entirely voluntary emigration" and prohibited the importation of Chinese people "without their free and voluntary consent."[45]

Faced with a slate of federal laws and treaties that appeared to preclude immigration restriction on the basis of race, color, or national origin, California Democrats found their remedy in the Thirteenth Amendment's ban on labor coercion. Once notorious for their proslavery politics during the antebellum era and their opposition to emancipation during the Civil War, California Democrats now linked their anti-Chinese campaign to the cause of eradicating coercive labor relationships. They asserted that California Chinese arrived under long-term coolie labor contracts. On the surface, these labor relations looked contractual and voluntary, but the labor contract merely masked a series of intolerable coercions. Employers of Chinese freely bought and sold workers' contracts, thus transferring workers' persons from one master to another. "The Chinese are now sold and passed from master to master, just as slaves were in the South not long ago," one Democrat asserted.[46] Moreover, while Chinese may have consented to their contracts, these contracts could hardly be characterized as free. Coolie contracts bound workers for such long terms (years at a time) for such incredibly low yearly or monthly wages (hardly enough to support human life) that a coolie's employer resembled a slaveholder. The only thing that distinguished the employer of Chinese coolies from the owner of black slaves was that the former could continue to extract labor and obedience from his workers under the false veneer of freedom, consent, and a token bestowal of wages. The latter had been stripped of this power by the Thirteenth Amendment.[47]

In one of the oddest turns of postwar politics, California Democrats not just actively embraced the Thirteenth Amendment but touted themselves as the champions of antislavery. They set out to write anti-Chinese laws that skirted the issue of race by casting Chinese labor relationships as outside of, and antithetical to, the free labor regime established by the Thirteenth Amendment and the Burlingame Treaty's ban on involuntary immigration. Their efforts culminated in California's 1870 "Act to Prevent the Importation of Chinese Criminals and to Prevent the Establishment of Coolie Slavery." This new statute blasted the arrival of "criminals and malefactors . . . constantly imported from Chinese seaports" as coolies. It declared coolie importation "a species of slavery" that was "degrading to the laborer" and "at war with the spirit of the age." The bill then stipulated that every "Chinaman and Mongolian" would have to provide California's commissioner of immigration with satisfactory evidence that he was a voluntary immigrant of good character. Immigrants who failed to meet these requirements would suffer detention and deportation.[48]

Democrats proclaimed this form of immigration restriction fully consonant with federal civil rights law; they merely sought to prevent the spread of dangerous forms of coercion and not to exclude the Chinese based on their race or nationality. The purpose of the statute "was not to prevent Chinese immigration," a Democrat explained, but merely "to prevent the influx of Chinese criminals, or of Chinese brought to this country against their will."[49] One Republican tried to debunk Democrats' claims that "slavery exists among these people in this country" and asserted that these accusations were motivated by racial prejudice and only a "pretense for a necessity for [the bill's] enactment."[50] In the end, though, Democrats' attack on labor coercion was compelling enough to win many Republicans over to their side. When the bill came before the assembly, "several Republicans voted with the ayes."[51] The law went into force in March 1870.

California Republicans' mild approval for Democrats' 1870 anti-coolie bill signaled a shift in the state party's approach to the problem of coolieism and coercion. During the 1860s, California Republicans were both interested in recruiting Chinese laborers for economic development projects and suspicious of race-based legal discrimination. They refuted anti-coolie arguments, protesting that "there [was] no system of slavery or coolieism amongst the Chinese of this State."[52] As late as 1869, the Republican state platform declared Chinese immigration restriction "contrary to the spirit of the age." The state and national postwar resurgence of the Democratic Party, however, left once-dominant Republicans clambering to court the anti-Chinese vote. By 1871, the state's Republicans advocated federal anti-Chinese legislation to "discourage their further immigration to our shores."[53] The transformation of the California Republican Party portended changes in the national organization. Confronting the economic depression of the early 1870s, rising worker protest, and brutal competition with Democrats, Republicans nationwide began to abandon their commitment to civil rights and equal protection. They became more willing to embrace the anti-Chinese cause to attract votes.[54]

California Republicans were at the forefront of the national party's turn toward Chinese exclusion. Like Democrats before them, they realized that singling out Chinese on the basis of race alone made for a losing strategy. Congressional civil rights legislation and the national Republican Party's aversion to racially discriminatory statutes made outright racial exclusion unlikely. California Republicans sought, instead, to cast exclusion as the only way to preserve the Republican legacy of emancipation and to ensure the triumph of a liberal vision of postwar labor relations. Banning Chinese would eliminate contract labor, an intolerable form of coercion by which Chinese merchants used contracts to buy, sell, and bind their compatriots.

Exclusion would also rid the nation of Chinese contract workers who were so poor, servile, and dependent that they willingly consented to these coercive contracts. These men, California Republicans argued, were incapable of exercising postwar freedoms and becoming independent, self-owning workers and citizens. Restricting Chinese immigration, then, was wholly consonant with Republican principles of free labor and antislavery.

The California Republican Horace Page led the charge in reformulating Chinese exclusion as a measure to eradicate an illegitimate form of coercion at odds with liberal visions of free labor. Between 1872 and 1882, Page introduced around a dozen anti-Chinese bills and resolutions into the U.S. House of Representatives. In his 1874 defense of a bill to abolish "coolie labor," Page began by denying that racism lay behind the legislation. He had no "prejudice against any people on account of race or color," and he had always been willing "to accord to every people, of whatever nationality or color, the equal protection of the laws." Yet the Chinese constituted an exception, he argued. They propagated coolieism, a species of labor that, while technically contractual and ostensibly free, lay beyond the limits of acceptable coercion in the postwar nation. Chinese came to California "as slaves to the companies which pay their passage." They were obligated to repay "the companies in such labor as they [the companies] may find for them to do before they can engage in business for themselves."[55] This short-term debt service, though voluntarily undertaken by Chinese immigrants, constituted "serfdom" equivalent to slavery because it "place[d] them entirely within the control of the company whose bidding they must do until the passage money is paid." Chinese contract labor was a form of coercion akin to slavery, and the coolie's servility and dependence made him the antithesis of the self-owning, independent worker of Republicans' liberal free labor vision. An anti-coolie bill would both eliminate Chinese contract labor and exclude a group of workers incapable of assimilating into the ranks of free laborers.

Page's triumph came in early 1875 when he proposed a supplement to the federal immigration code that purported to enforce existing treaty stipulations by ensuring that all immigration from China was "free and voluntary." The Page Law, as the supplement came to be called, charged U.S. consuls in China with examining prospective immigrants to determine whether they emigrated voluntarily and whether they were being held to labor under a contract for a term of service. The law especially targeted the importation of male "cooly" laborers and Chinese women who arrived as prostitutes bound under contracts "for lewd or immoral purposes." Anyone found guilty of importing such people "without their free and voluntary consent, for the purpose of holding them to a term of service" would face fines and jail time. Moreover, the law declared null and void all "contracts and agreements for a term of service" under which Chinese people arrived in the United States. In this, the Page Law established that contractual arrangements by which Chinese financed journeys to the United States were inherently unfree and involuntary and would not be acknowledged, enforced, or tolerated under federal law.[56] In the end, the Page Law passed Congress "with virtually no opposition." Page gloated that even though Democrats had long claimed the mantle of the anti-Chinese cause, "it was left to a Republican Congress to secure some proper legislation on this subject."[57]

After 1875, the so-called Chinese Question became a thoroughly national issue. The debate over the coercions of contract labor echoed back in the industrialized Northeast, where working-class northerners took up the banner of anti-coolieism. While historians have frequently blamed white working-class racism against the Chinese as the driving force behind the national movement for exclusion, workers outside of the West often opposed racial restrictions on immigration. Northern labor leaders condemned capitalists' importation of Chinese workers under long-term contracts, not the presence of Chinese themselves. Contract labor, they argued, allowed capitalists to camouflage bald-faced labor coercion under the veneer of contractualism and voluntarism. Importing Chinese to work under slavery-like conditions, capitalists would eventually drive down wages and reduce all workers to abject poverty and dependence.

Northern workers thus saw anti-coolieism as a way of exposing the labor coercion that underpinned the wage bargain and the postwar capitalist economy. Opposition to contract labor had been a centerpiece of northern labor activism since the middle of the Civil War. In 1864, Congress passed a statute allowing for the recruitment and importation of European workers under long-term contracts. Northern labor leaders, including William Sylvis of the newly formed National Labor Union, protested that European contract laborers, who were sometimes employed as strikebreakers, undercut the bargaining power and wages of American labor. They argued, however, that the real danger to American workers lay in capitalists' power to compel cheap labor from these impoverished immigrants. Much like the wage bargain, the contracts that capitalists used to bind foreign workers appeared free and voluntary, but they concealed a variety of coercions. The men who entered into them were so poor that they had little choice but to sign over their freedom to capitalists or starve. Labor importers subjected these contract workers to all manner of abuse and fraud on their voyages. Worst of all, capitalists used these allegedly free laborers to drive down the wages of all labor. In Sylvis's estimation, contract workers were the blameless "dupes of the wiley agents." He extended a welcoming hand "to our fellows from all parts of the globe." The real enemies of the American workingman were the importers and employers of contract laborers who sought to "reduce us and those who come here to starvation." In the wake of this protest and rising administration costs, Congress quietly repealed the 1864 contract labor law in 1868.[58]

California's anti-coolie agitation and the campaign for Chinese exclusion kept the contract labor debate alive in the northern labor movement after 1868. But even at the height of exclusion fervor, as the historian Andrew Gyory shows, northeastern and midwestern labor activists framed the Chinese problem as an outgrowth of capitalists' corrupt use of contracts, rather than as an immigration or racial question. Chinese might consent to toil under contracts for pitifully low wages, the leaders of Boston's Eight-Hour League observed. But, ultimately, these unbalanced contracts were the work of scheming capitalists who sought to depress wages and force both Chinese and white American labor to endure "coolie" conditions.[59] The corrupt coolie system was the handmaiden to the corrupt wage system. It would eventually drive free wage laborers into perpetual servitude to capital.

For many in the northern labor press, then, the real solution to labor's woes was not the elimination of the Chinese, but the eradication of false forms of free labor — not just contract labor, but the wage bargain itself — which capitalists used to force workers into the impossible choice of working for a pittance under dependent and servile conditions, or starving to death. As one New York socialist newspaper put it starkly, "the coolie is a slave, the wage laborer is a slave, and the capitalist in both cases is a slave-holder." The duty of the American workingman was not to attack the Chinese, but to "organize and agitate for the abolition of the coolie system, and when that is achieved, agitate for the abolition of the capitalist."[60]

Northern labor leaders' opposition to anti-Chinese laws, and their insistence that the labor coercion embedded in the capitalist system and the wage bargain posed the real threat to postwar freedom, ran against the prevailing political current. By 1880, the agitation for outright exclusion ran so high that the United States negotiated a revised treaty with China. The new treaty permitted the United States to restrict or suspend the entrance of Chinese laborers when it felt that these immigrants threatened the nation's "interests" or "good order."[61] Revision laid the groundwork for a broad Chinese exclusion law two years later. In 1882, John F. Miller, a Republican senator from California, proposed a bill suspending the entrance of all Chinese laborers for the following twenty years. Miller and other advocates of Chinese exclusion claimed that this severe restriction on all Chinese workers was the only way to root out a dangerous and illegal form of labor coercion. Anything short of general exclusion, Miller warned, would encourage the coolie trade and allow "all the speculators in human labor, all the importers of human muscle, all the traffickers in human flesh, to ply their infamous trade without impediment under the protection of the American flag."[62]

California Republicans' plea for the wholesale exclusion of Chinese laborers as the only way to eliminate the coercive coolie system did not go unopposed. The exclusion bill provoked weeks of debate in the Senate and the House. East Coast Republicans, mostly aging Radicals, dismissed the clamor against the Chinese as outmoded, illiberal race prejudice. If exclusionists sincerely hoped to eliminate Chinese contract labor, then they would have framed the exclusion law more narrowly. Senator George Frisbie Hoar, a Radical Republican, admitted that contract labor was noxious and that "no person whose labor is not his own property" should be imported into the United States. But the exclusion bill made no distinctions among laborers. It targeted "not importation, but immigration . . . not importation, but the free coming" of Chinese.[63] The harsh twenty-year embargo on all Chinese laborers had but one end in mind: the total exclusion of all Chinese, regardless of whether they were free or coerced.

In its final form, "An Act to Execute Certain Treaty Stipulations Relating to the Chinese" prohibited the landing of "both skilled and unskilled laborers and Chinese employed in mining." To quiet some critics who worried that a twenty-year suspension was too harsh, the bill's proponents agreed to a ten-year exclusion period instead. After these modifications, nearly half the Republicans in Congress joined with Democrats to pass the bill. The Republican president Chester A. Arthur signed it into law in May 1882.[64] The Chinese Exclusion Act, as the law came to be known, shut out vast numbers of Chinese. A swell of 39,579 Chinese arrivals in 1882 dwindled to just 10 by 1887.[65] Immigration eventually rebounded as Chinese people found loopholes in the law, but exclusion became a permanent fixture of U.S. immigration policy. Congress renewed the Exclusion Act twice, extending it until 1904. Then, when China refused to renegotiate its treaty, Congress voted to extend exclusion indefinitely. Chinese exclusion remained in force until World War II.[66]

Both the successful campaign to exclude Chinese workers and the unsuccessful effort to end New Mexican peonage suggest new ways of understanding the world the Civil War made. When we pull apart regionally determined narratives of the postwar era and focus on the American West, the plotline changes. By adding the West to the story, we see that the postwar era revolved around not only expanding and contracting visions of individual freedom, but also changing visions of coercion. The West's ambiguous labor systems, neither self-evidently free or slave, voluntary or involuntary, survived beyond the Civil War. Their persistence generated a regional, and then a national, conversation over what kinds of coercive labor relations were legally and morally (un)acceptable in the aftermath of emancipation. Congressional Republicans' varied success in mobilizing the federal government to eliminate certain brands of unacceptable coercion also helps us map out the contours of state power after the Civil War. Chinese exclusion illustrated the strength of federal power to enforce far-reaching immigration legislation. At the same time, the failure of antipeonage prosecution in New Mexico showed that, in many locales, the federal government remained a Stockade State incapable of imposing congressional will on geographically far-flung and resistant groups of local people.

If the story of western labor systems shows the consolidation of postwar federal power to be incomplete, it also illuminates the uneven and imperfect triumph of postwar liberalism. Republicans' dedication to antislavery and free labor could result in distinctly illiberal immigration policies that severely constrained the liberties of Chinese immigrants. And despite their celebration of laborers' independence and freedom, anti-Chinese Republicans rarely acknowledged northern workers' observation that labor contracts, and the entire wage system itself, perpetuated capital's coercive power and destroyed the liberties of all laborers. Ultimately, then, a West-South-North analysis of the postwar era yields new insights into the relationship between coercion and freedom, the contours and limits of federal power, and the illiberal world that persisted after the Civil War remade the nation.

NOTES

1. *Slaughterhouse Cases*, 83 U.S. (16 Wall.) 36 (1873).
2. See, for instance, Eric Foner, *Reconstruction: America's Unfinished Revolution, 1863–1877* (New York: Harper and Row, 1988), 529–31.
3. *Slaughterhouse Cases*, 83 U.S. (16 Wall.) 49–51 (1873).
4. Ibid., 72.
5. On coercion and its relationship to contractualism in nineteenth-century America, consult Amy Dru Stanley, *From Bondage to Contract: Wage Labor, Marriage, and the Market in the Age of Slave Emancipation* (New York: Cambridge University Press, 1998); Robert J. Steinfeld, *The Invention of Free Labor: The Employment Relation in English and American Law and Culture, 1350–1870* (Chapel Hill: University of North Carolina

Press, 1991); and Christopher Tomlins, *Freedom Bound: Law, Labor, and Civic Identity in Colonizing English America, 1580–1865* (New York: Cambridge University Press, 2010).

6. In this essay, I build on a growing body of scholarship that seeks to integrate the West into the national story of the Civil War, emancipation, and Reconstruction, including Elliott West, *The Last Indian War: The Nez Perce Story* (New York: Oxford University Press, 2009); Heather Cox Richardson, *West from Appomattox: The Reconstruction of America after the Civil War* (New Haven: Yale University Press, 2007); Joshua Paddison, *American Heathens: Religion, Race, and Reconstruction in California* (Berkeley: University of California Press, 2012); D. Michael Bottoms, *An Aristocracy of Color: Race and Reconstruction in California and the West, 1850–1890* (Norman: University of Oklahoma Press, 2013); and Stacey L. Smith, *Freedom's Frontier: California and the Struggle over Unfree Labor, Emancipation, and Reconstruction* (Chapel Hill: University of North Carolina Press, 2013).

7. "An Act to Secure Freedom to All Persons within the Territories of the United States," *U.S. Statutes at Large* 12, 1863, 432.

8. U.S. Senate, *Miscellaneous Documents of the Senate of the United States, for the Third Session of the Thirty-seventh Congress* (Washington, D.C.: Government Printing Office, 1863), Mis. Doc. No. 34; *Congressional. Globe*, 37th Cong., 3rd sess., 1863, 1275.

9. On the captive trade and peonage in New Mexico, see James F. Brooks, *Captives and Cousins: Slavery, Kinship, and Community in the Southwest Borderlands* (Chapel Hill: University of North Carolina Press, 2002), esp. 31–36, 124–38, 327–60; Ned Blackhawk, *Violence over the Land: Indians and Empires in the Early American West* (Cambridge: Harvard University Press, 2006), 24–27, 106–12; and Ramón A. Gutiérrez, *When Jesus Came the Corn Mothers Went Away: Marriage, Sexuality, and Power in New Mexico, 1500–1846* (Stanford: Stanford University Press, 1991), 150–56, 180–90.

10. "Master and Servant Law," July 30, 1851, art. 35, ch. 76, in *Revised Statutes and Laws of the Territory of New Mexico* (St. Louis: E. P. Studley, 1865), 542–50.

11. Brooks, *Captives and Cousins*, 347–48.

12. Ibid., 331–36.

13. John Harlan, quoted in Estéven Rael-Gálvez, "Identifying Captivity and Capturing Identity: Narratives of American Indian Slavery, Colorado and New Mexico, 1776–1934" (Ph.D. diss., University of Michigan, 2002), 221–22.

14. *Report of the Secretary of the Interior, 1865* (Washington, D.C.: Government Printing Office, 1865), 348–49.

15. Ibid., 133–34.

16. Ibid., 349–50.

17. *Second Annual Message of Acting Governor Arny to the Legislative Assembly of New Mexico, December 1866* (Santa Fe: Manderfield and Tucker, 1866), 28.

18. *Report of the Commissioner on Indian Affairs*, 39th Cong., 2nd sess., 1867, Sen. Exec. Doc. 1, 137.

19. Civil Rights Act of 1866, *U.S. Statutes at Large* 14, 1866, 27–30; Robert F. Castro, "Liberty Like Thunder: Law, History, and the Emancipatory Politics of Reconstruction America" (Ph.D. diss., University of Michigan, 2003), 91–94; Rael-Gálvez, "Identifying Captivity," 283.

20. Rael-Gálvez, "Identifying Captivity," 284–86.

21. Ibid.; Lawrence B. Murphy, "Reconstruction in New Mexico," *New Mexico Historical Review* 43 (April 1968): 102–4, 113n26; Castro, "Liberty Like Thunder," 124–26.

22. *Cong. Globe*, 39th Cong., 2nd sess. (1867), 239–40.

23. Ibid., 764, 1571–72; "An Act to Abolish and Forever Prohibit the System of Peonage in the Territory of New Mexico and Other Parts of the United States" [Anti-Peonage Act], *U.S. Statutes at Large* 14, 1867, 546.

24. *Cong. Globe*, 39th Cong., 2nd sess. (1867), 1571.

25. Ibid., 1571–72.

26. Ibid., 1572, 1770, 2004.

27. Brooks, *Captives and Cousins*, 351–53, 385–403; Rael-Gálvez, "Identifying Captivity," 290–93; Murphy, "Reconstruction in New Mexico," 106–8.

28. Rael-Gálvez, "Identifying Captivity," 295–96; Castro, "Liberty Like Thunder," 134.

29. Murphy, "Reconstruction in New Mexico," 108–9; Castro, "Liberty Like Thunder," 139–46.

30. Stephen Elkins, quoted in Rael-Gálvez, "Identifying Captivity," 298.

31. Ibid., chap. 7; Castro, "Liberty Like Thunder," 101–2.

32. Foner, *Reconstruction*, 153–70.

33. Ibid., 173–74; Pete Daniel, *The Shadow of Slavery: Peonage in the South, 1901–1969* (Urbana: University of Illinois Press, 1972), 19–26; Daniel A. Novak, *The Wheel of Servitude: Black Forced Labor after Slavery* (Lexington: University Press of Kentucky, 1978), 36–43.

34. Daniel, *The Shadow of Slavery*, 11–18; *Cong. Record*, 58th Cong., 2nd sess. (1904), 3898–900; *Clyatt v. United States*, 197 U.S. 207 (1905).

35. *Clyatt v. United States*, 197 U.S. 215–18 (1905).

36. *Alta California* (San Francisco), June 24, 1869.

37. Moon-Ho Jung, *Coolies and Cane: Race, Labor, and Sugar in the Age of Emancipation* (Baltimore: Johns Hopkins University Press, 2006), 13–14; Najia Aarim-Heriot, *Chinese Immigrants, African Americans, and Racial Anxiety in the United States* (Urbana: University of Illinois Press, 2003), 30–31; Andrew Gyory, *Closing the Gate: Race, Politics, and the Chinese Exclusion Act* (Chapel Hill: University of North Carolina Press, 1998), 32–33.

38. Jung, *Coolies and Cane*, 36–38.

39. Ibid., 4–5, 9, 13–33.

40. *An Analysis of the Chinese Question* (San Francisco: San Francisco Herald, 1852), 6–7, 13.

41. On the anti-Chinese movement in California, see Alexander Saxton, *The Indispensable Enemy: Labor and the Anti-Chinese Movement in California* (Berkeley: University of California Press, 1971); Charles McClain, *In Search of Equality: The Chinese Struggle against Discrimination in Nineteenth-Century America* (Berkeley: University of California Press, 1994); Gyory, *Closing the Gate*; and Aarim-Heriot, *Chinese Immigrants*.

42. Winfield J. Davis, *History of Political Conventions in California, 1849–1892* (Sacramento: California State Library, 1893), 241–42; Saxton, *The Indispensable Enemy*, 80–91, 264–65.

43. Bottoms, *An Aristocracy of Color*, 86–94.

44. McClain, *In Search of Equality*, 31–42; Aarim-Heriot, *Chinese Immigrants*, 84–92, 140–43.

45. The Burlingame Treaty (July 28, 1868), Art. 5–6, *U.S. Statutes at Large* 16, 1868, 740; McClain, *In Search of Equality*, 30–31; Aarim-Heriot, *Chinese Immigrants*, 109–12; John Schrecker, "'For the Equality of Men — For the Equality of Nations': Anson Burlingame and China's First Embassy to the United States, 1868," *Journal of American-East Asian Relations* 17 (Spring 2010): 9–34.

46. *San Francisco Bulletin*, March 13, 1867.

47. For California Democrats' critique of contract labor, see Smith, *Freedom's Frontier*, 192–98, 207–17.

48. "An Act to Prevent the Importation of Chinese Criminals and to Prevent the Establishment of Coolie Slavery," Act of Mar. 18, 1870, ch. 231, *California Statutes*, 332–33.

49. *Sacramento Union*, March 11, 1870.

50. Ibid., March 1, 1870; *San Francisco Bulletin*, March 1, 1870.

51. *Sacramento Union*, March 1, 1870.

52. Patrick Healy and Ng Poon Chew, *A Statement for Non-Exclusion* (San Francisco: n.p., 1905), 19.

53. Davis, *History of Political Conventions*, 293, 308.

54. Aarim-Heriot, *Chinese Immigrants*, 172–74, 181–82; Gyory, *Closing the Gate*, 72–75.

55. *Cong. Record*, 43rd Cong., 1st sess. (1874), 4534–35, 4537.

56. "An Act Supplementary to the Acts in Relation to Immigration" [The Page Law], *U.S. Statutes at Large* 18, 1875, 477.

57. Aarim-Heriot, *Chinese Immigrants*, 177; *Sacramento Union*, July 26, 1875.

58. Gyory, *Closing the Gate*, 19–25.

59. Ibid., 87–89.

60. Ibid., 88–89.

61. "Treaty of Immigration between the United States and China" (Nov. 17, 1880), *U.S. Statutes at Large* 22, 1883, 826–27; Gyory, *Closing the Gate*, 212–16; Aarim-Heriot, *Chinese Immigrants*, 204–5.

62. *Cong. Record*, 47th Cong., 1st sess. (1882), 1482.

63. Ibid., 1517.

64. "An Act to Execute Certain Treaty Stipulations Relating to the Chinese," *U.S. Statutes at Large* 22, 1882, 58–61; Aarim-Heriot, *Chinese Immigrants*, 210–14; Gyory, *Closing the Gate*, 238–39.

65. Erika Lee, *At America's Gates: Chinese Immigration during the Exclusion Era, 1882–1943* (Chapel Hill: University of North Carolina Press, 2002), 43–44.

66. Ibid., 44–46; Aarim-Heriot, *Chinese Immigrants*, 221–28.

*The Meanings of "Civilization" and the Limits of
Native American Citizenship*

Stephen Kantrowitz

In the spring of 1873, "Dandy's Band," a group of several hundred Ho-Chunk Indians residing in Wisconsin, informed the federal Office of Indian Affairs that they wished to sever their tribal ties, "purchase real estate," and "adopt the habits and customs of civilized life." Their stated goal was to become citizens of the United States, securing "the constitutional and inalienable rights of men."[1] In adopting this language, the petitioners seemed to be aligning themselves with official Indian policy as articulated in President Ulysses S. Grant's 1869 inaugural address, which called for Native Americans' "civilization and ultimate citizenship." More broadly, the Ho-Chunks' language harmonized with the Republican "free-labor" vision of rights-bearing individuals living in well-ordered households and undertaking steady, market-oriented economic activity. Dandy's Band, in other words, appeared to be asking to participate in the national order represented by such Republican policies as the Homestead Act and the Fourteenth Amendment.

Yet none of this talk of real estate and rights was as straightforward as it seemed. The Fourteenth Amendment, which made citizens of all persons "born or naturalized in the United States, and subject to its jurisdiction," had not been intended to embrace Native Americans generally, but to overturn the *Dred Scott* decision and help freedpeople protect themselves from domination by their former owners. The amendment's architects understood the potential pitfalls of their universalizing language where Indians were concerned; they had incorporated the language of "jurisdiction" specifically to define tribal members as something other than citizens, while at the same time asserting authority over individual, detribalized Indians. But the members of Dandy's Band were not easily assigned to either of those categories. They had resisted four decades of attempts to remove them from Wisconsin, and they still refused to join the tribe, now resident in Nebraska, to which officials thought they belonged. Some owned land, but their way of life more generally consisted of seasonal migrations around Wisconsin and a variety of activities that included farming, but also hunting, berrying, and various forms of market engagement. They did not much resemble Republicans' vision of detribalized Indians adopting what decades of lawmaking and public discussion called the "habits and customs of civilization." The Indian Office dubbed the Wisconsin Ho-Chunk a "stray band," and their constitutional status remained uncertain. As Wisconsin Republican Timothy Howe put it in a debate on the floor of the U.S. Senate, they were "not quite constitutionalized."[2]

With their petition, therefore, Dandy's Band probed unanswered questions at the core of Republican Indian policy: what exactly was the "civilization" to which both they and the president referred, and how much of it was necessary to render Native Americans fit for national citizenship? Although the laws and amendments establishing national citizenship spoke only of nativity and allegiance, the framers of that language understood citizenship to require a good deal more. They wanted Native Americans—like freedpeople, non-Protestant immigrants, "beggars," and "tramps"—to demonstrate their fitness by embracing a matrix of values and behaviors: the principles of private property and contract; habits of fixed settlement, market orientation, and patriarchal household organization; and particular modes of dress, speech, and worship. "Civilization" was not a formal requirement of citizenship according to the Fourteenth Amendment, nor did it have a clear, agreed-upon definition. It nevertheless played a significant role when legislators and agents of the government assessed who was fit to vote or to be naturalized, and whom the state would need to deal with more coercively.[3]

Ideological and practical confusion over the relationship between citizenship's formal and unlegislated requirements produced an unexpected opening for the Ho-Chunk during a renewed effort to remove them from Wisconsin in 1873-74. As national and local officials struggled to define the rights of Indians, Dandy's Band and other Ho-Chunk people took advantage of these uncertainties and disputes. They expediently adopted a key form of "civilization"—individual landholding—without embracing the ideological and economic orientation toward free labor that such land ownership was supposed to represent. Uttering the keywords of liberal citizenship without fully embracing their content, the Wisconsin Ho-Chunk baffled their adversaries. They ended up with land, citizenship, and the right to remain in the state, partly insulated from the colonial policies of inspection and detribalization that would soon wrack Indian life throughout the West.

The Ho-Chunks' experience suggests that two key aspects of late nineteenth-century history—the struggle over the limits and meaning of citizenship, and the policy of coercive "civilization" of native populations—informed one another in important ways that were and still are poorly understood. Grant's imagined path through "civilization" to citizenship hints at the problem. The president spoke as though one followed from the other, but while citizenship was a matter of black-letter law, what constituted "civilization" remained amorphous and undefined. This could prove useful to officials, since it allowed them the flexibility to determine individual worthiness. But the ambiguity could also be used for other purposes. Many residents of North America, among them many Native Americans, considered citizenship less a goal to be achieved than a tool to think with or use. So as Republicans pursued their project of creating a unified national citizenship, some of the people they imagined as citizens took up that project, and that name, for purposes of their own.

IN THE DECADES before the Civil War, U.S. settlers and policymakers in the territories west of the Great Lakes had routinely used "civilization" as a flexible standard for differentiating Indians who belonged to the body politic from those who did not. In that region, American policies of conquest and Indian removal were shaped and sometimes limited by long histories of trade and cohabitation between natives and settlers.[4] Although treaties steadily extinguished Indian title and opened ever more land to U.S. settlement and development, not every Indian—or even every tribe—fell on the wrong side of the line between "savagery" and "civilization." In particular, Indians who owned and tilled land and who adopted various other proper "habits and customs" could sometimes cease, in Euro-American eyes, to be Indians at all. Leaving the timeless, unproductive, doomed world of aboriginal life, they stepped into the dynamic present of liberal freedom.[5] Put another way, they entered history. This understanding of what constituted Indian progress shaped federal and state policy in the region. Wisconsin's 1848 constitution enfranchised "Civilized persons of Indian descent not members of any tribe," and similar formulations echoed through the antebellum constitutions of Michigan and Minnesota.[6] In 1840, Wisconsin's territorial governor, James Doty, sought to clarify the meaning of civilization by explaining the fitness of one local group for citizenship: "Their advances in civilization have gradually influenced them to abandon the hunter life. This . . . led them to adopt fixed places of abode, acquire individual property, cultivate the earth, and assume most of those habits and customs, amongst themselves, which go to distinguish the savage and nomadic life from that of educated and civilized man."[7] These were more than words. In 1843 the Stockbridge-Munsee Indians, the group Doty described, successfully petitioned Congress to dissolve them as a tribe, allot land to individual households, and make them all citizens of the United States.[8]

The federal government's policy toward the Stockbridge-Munsee might appear to form part of a coherent policy of Americanization through land ownership, but these policies were also closely tied to the interests of farmers, miners, and others who sought improved access to tribal lands. Many pre–Civil War allotments to Indians were made with the right of alienation, which frequently had the effect of making allotted lands available for purchase by non-Indians. In the Kansas Territory and in Michigan, antebellum allotment quickly abetted outright dispossession, aided by unequal tax policies and official tolerance of white squatting. In Michigan, twenty years after the first allotments began, less than a tenth of the lands allotted to Native Americans remained in their possession.[9] Indeed, the point of allotment often seemed to be to break up Indian control of land as much or more than to encourage individual Indians to embrace land ownership.

Both traders and traditionalists therefore sometimes resisted allotment and citizenship. Traders feared that allotment and tribal dissolution would bring an end to federal annuity payments — the regular disbursements of cash that constituted part of Indians' compensation for lands ceded to the federal government. These annuities injected large sums into the Midwestern economy — the $100,000 per annum received by the Ho-Chunk during the antebellum decades was unusually large, but federal money followed most treaties.[10] On the cash-poor frontier, this "Indian money" constituted a valuable, renewable resource. No wonder that in 1849 the first session of the Minnesota territorial assembly asked the federal government to remove Ojibwe populations *into* the new territory, since that would cause their annuity payments to circulate through St. Paul.[11] Allotment, whether it brought citizenship, dispossession, or both, would end these streams of revenue.

Tribal members who prized their collective life and sought to protect its economic base also understood allotment and citizenship as dangerously powerful solvents. In 1846, just a few years after the Stockbridge-Munsee became U.S. citizens by act of Congress, dissident forces within the tribe managed to have the federal citizenship law repealed. This removed Stockbridge-Munsee people from the jurisdiction of U.S. courts, effectively nullifying three years of real estate transactions that had left substantial former tribal lands in the hands of settlers. The ensuing chaos over land titles prompted delegates to Wisconsin's 1848 constitutional convention to write the Stockbridge-Munsee back into the legal system, enfranchising all Indians declared citizens by Congress at any time. The point, the historian James Oberly explains, was to ensure that these Indians could sue, be sued, and be held responsible for contracts they undertook—that is, that land they had surrendered remained in settlers' hands.[12]

At the time the Stockbridge-Munsee officially embraced landholding and civilization, gaining the right to reside permanently in Wisconsin, the Ho-Chunk people were, in the eyes of the state, either exiles or renegades. A series of treaties in the 1820s and 1830s had whittled away at their lands in northern Illinois and southern Wisconsin. A final treaty in 1837, fraudulently made with people not authorized to speak for the tribe, exchanged their remaining acres of the Wisconsin Territory for a substantial tribal fund and lands in eastern Iowa and southeastern Minnesota. Within a decade, the federal government removed the Ho-Chunk again, this time to the northern part of the Minnesota Territory. Dissatisfied with those lands, in 1855 the Ho-Chunk traded them for a reservation in the southern part of the territory. White settlers flooded into Minnesota throughout the decade, and in 1859 the Ho-Chunk were induced to give up approximately 50 percent of their new land in exchange for an increased annuity and other goods. During this tumultuous period, as many as half the members of the tribe either evaded removal entirely or quickly returned to their former homelands. Some migrated back to Wisconsin from Iowa in the 1840s; hundreds remained in Iowa or returned to Wisconsin in the 1850s. By treaty, the Ho-Chunk belonged on collectively owned lands west of

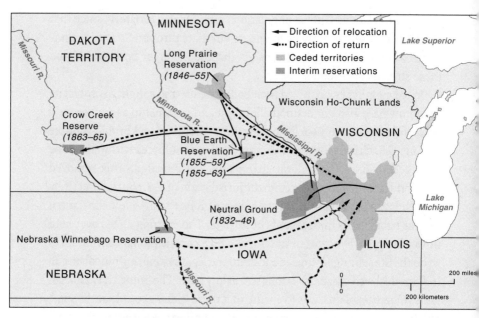

Map 3.1 Ho-Chunk Removals and Returns, 1832–1874

the Mississippi River, but as many as one thousand never left the state at all, fleeing the federal troops sent to corral them and taking refuge in the woods and swamps they knew so well, but to which they held no title.[13]

The Civil War again upended the Ho-Chunks' world. The election of the Republican Abraham Lincoln in 1860 did more than provoke secession; it also brought to power a party committed to a federally subsidized program of nonslaveholding white expansion into the West, a program inaugurated in 1862 with the passage of the Homestead Act, the Morrill Land-Grant College Act, and the Pacific Railroad Act. But while the wartime Republican government found time for these measures, it also failed to meet its treaty obligations to Western tribes, including the Dakota, the Ho-Chunks' Minnesota neighbors. Near starvation, many Dakota rose up in rebellion in the summer and fall of 1862, making war on white settlers. After U.S. forces regained control, the Ho-Chunk—who had not taken part in the uprising—were banished to Crow Creek, a barren camp in the Dakota Territory. A few hundred Ho-Chunk managed to remain in Minnesota despite the removal, while most of the rest quickly abandoned Crow Creek for a variety of destinations. In 1865 the government allowed the Ho-Chunk to trade their land in the Dakota Territory for a hundred thousand acres of eastern Nebraska. As with every previous removal, many Ho-Chunk continued to live where they wished, not where the government demanded.

Once they defeated the Confederacy, the governing Republicans turned their attention to consolidating national authority in and extending free-labor civilization to every corner of North America. Above all, Republicans longed to see the revolution of slave emancipation followed by the transformation of nearly 4 million Southern freedpeople into model free-labor actors. Northern emissaries strove to make former slaves understand what freedom should mean in their domestic and economic lives: "civilization and Christianity," "order, industry, economy, and self-reliance." Many Northerners measured the success of Reconstruction by the degree to which freedpeople approached the ideal of market-oriented workers and householders.[14]

Republicans also began to systematically apply those same metrics to Native Americans, which proved an even more complicated task. As rival claimants to North American land, Indian tribes represented a direct challenge to the idea of free soil—cheap land claimed by the government, marked off into sections, cleared of its indigenous inhabitants, commodified and made alienable—upon which the future of free-labor expansion depended. Republicans and other observers believed that indigenous people must either give way before American settlement or face extinction and that those who accepted confinement to reservations must learn the habits of fixed settlement and steady labor. Postwar Republicans therefore began assembling earlier, scattershot efforts at "civilizing" Indians into a systematic program of detribalization, cultural transformation, and political incorporation—a program they presented as indigenous peoples' only alternative to extinction. The "civilization" and ultimate "citizenship" that Grant had hopefully imagined in 1869 became his administration's "Peace Policy" and defined federal Indian policy in the 1870s and for generations to come.[15]

Despite the language of real estate and rights in their 1873 petition, neither Dandy's Band nor the man from whom they took their name had shown much evidence of embracing Grant's vision. Dandy, a Ho-Chunk leader also known as Roaring Thunder, had spent decades parlaying with and dissembling before white authorities. Until his death in 1869 he consistently asserted the illegitimacy of the 1837 treaty, which formally extinguished Ho-Chunk claims to land in Wisconsin. At times Wisconsin jour-

Figure 3.1 Dandy, ca. 1867 (Wisconsin Historical Society, WHS-61426)

nalists and officials even represented him as a military threat to U.S. order, accusing him of plotting with various Indian or Confederate allies. But his actual desires were perhaps best communicated in his entreaties that his people be allowed to remain where they were, living as they preferred. "He expressed a decided determination to remain in this country," an Indian agent reported in 1863; he "said that his God first showed him the light here, and that he should not go away and live by some other light." If that meant adjusting to life at the margins of white settlement, so be it. "The Indians like to live with the white man," Dandy was reported as saying in a parlay with Governor Salomon that same year. "All [Indians] want is to kill game, pick berries, and fish."[16] Dandy also understood enough of what settlers purported to value to poke at their pretensions of righteousness and consistency. He once persuaded Wisconsin's governor to agree that the Ho-Chunk should do just what the Bible dictated, then asked the governor to show him exactly where in the holy book it said that they should remove to Iowa. This marginal, skeptical engagement with settler society was hardly what the Indian Office or President Grant had in mind.[17]

Before the Civil War ended, the federal Indian Office created a special agency for what it dubbed "stray bands" of Ho-Chunks and Potawatomies in Wisconsin, and during the late 1860s these agents confirmed what Dandy had described—a life of seasonal migration, farming at some seasons but at others living off deer, fish, muskrats, berries, maple sugar, and other fruits of the land. The Ho-Chunk were also part-time capitalists, raising ponies and picking berries for sale and performing agricultural wage work for whites during peak seasons. Perhaps, agents thought, they might at some point be settled on a Wisconsin reservation and there take up "the habits and customs of civilization," but at present the Ho-Chunk showed little interest in that.[18]

The stray bands vexed those seeking a clear distinction between Indians and citizens. James Doolittle, a U.S. senator from Wisconsin and the chairman of the Committee on Indian Affairs, fretted that many Indians, born within the present bounds of the United States, lived under circumstances that made them transparently "subject to its jurisdiction," rather than to that of a tribe or treaty. "In my own state," he explained, "there are the Chippewas, the remnants of the Winnebagoes, and the Pottawatomies."[19] The U.S. Senate Committee on the Judiciary had ruled in 1870 that the Fourteenth Amendment had not made citizens of Indians who belonged to recognized tribes. But in a desultory final paragraph, the committee's report acknowledged that "when the members of a tribe are scattered, they are merged in the mass of our people, and become equally subject to the jurisdiction of the United States." These "fragmentary, straggling bands" had "lost all just pretentions to the tribal character" and ought to be incorporated into and governed by the United States.[20] Dandy's Band, this suggested, had indeed been made American citizens by the Fourteenth Amendment. But this surprising twist in Indian policy raised questions that it failed to answer. The most important of these were how to determine when a group had straggled sufficiently to lose its tribal character, and whether it was reasonable that, simply by disobeying treaty stipulations and remaining in formally ceded territory, such people could transform themselves into citizens of the United States. At what point, that is, did such a group cease to be non-compliant or "hostile" Indians and become "merged in the mass of our people"? At what point were they "constitutionalized"?

By provoking such questions, the Ho-Chunk and other stray bands exposed a conceptual confusion at the heart of Republican ideology: the ill-defined relationship between citizenship and "civilization." President Grant's progressive inaugural vision—that civilization would prepare the ground for citizenship—reflected old and widespread ideas about how Indians could avoid extinction and become part of settler society. But his language of civilization and ultimate citizenship clarified that Indian U.S. citizenship was not a simple matter of birth and allegiance; it was something that must be earned. Citizenship, it turned out, entailed numerous cultural and economic prerequisites, many of them of involving assent to the liberal regime of property and contract. Only those who acknowledged the sanctity of private property and who foreswore collective demands— only those, that is, who showed that they understood what "civilized" life entailed—could confidently claim the rights of citizens.[21] But if the criteria for earning citizenship remained poorly defined, how would anyone know when they had been met? How much civilization was enough? During the 1870s, the reformers of Indian policy set out to answer this question.

Grant's Peace Policy sought to detribalize Native Americans and replace their communal life and collective land ownership with patriarchal agricultural households. That project was carried out by Christian missionaries, who replaced the famously corrupt patronage appointees who had previously run Indian agencies. These new agents were concerned with much more than their charges' spiritual lives. "It was an article of faith" among postbellum reformers, writes Francis Paul Prucha, "that civilization was impossible without the incentive to work that came only from individual ownership of a piece of property."[22] Only that form of civilization would transform Native Americans generally into worthy and virtuous citizens of the United States. Congress resisted elements of Grant's policies, but by 1871 its members assented to his inaugural vision, reaching what Cathleen Cahill describes as "a consensus . . . that tribes should be dissolved and Indians incorporated into the citizenry."[23] And nothing was more important to that process than the individual possession and cultivation of land.

As Indian agents assessed their charges' progress, the Ho-Chunk people who had accepted removal to Nebraska, the Winnebago Nation, offered some grounds for optimism. In 1873, the Office of Indian Affairs described them as being "on the high road to civilization," having taken up land in severalty, built cottages, acquired farming implements and furniture, adopted "civilized costume," and demonstrating a willingness to market their crops, their labor, or both.[24] But a declaration of victory was premature. Tellingly, the Winnebago agent recommended moving the reservation's elections from March to June, since in springtime so many were absent from the reservation, "either at work or hunting and trapping." The Nebraska tribe, he explained, was only "half-civilized."[25]

The Wisconsin Ho-Chunk seemed to stand at a far greater remove from "civilization," but observers could not agree just how far. In 1869 the agent to the stray bands noted many Ho-Chunk people cultivating corn and potatoes, with some owning a few acres, others renting. "I see no reason why they cannot become as good and useful citizens as the Brothertown Indians of this State," he told his superiors, comparing them to a group whose course had paralleled that of the Stockbridge-Munsee.[26] The Ho-Chunk leader Winnishiek was said to have presented the governor with a more mixed, if still heartening, ambition: "I want to stay in Wisconsin and pick huckleberries. Got land here. Want to stay here trade & Keep store. . . . We want to stay in Wisconsin woods."[27] Some officials agreed that this was a reasonable desire. But by the standards of many Wisconsin settlers, the Ho-Chunk were a nuisance.[28] They survived by "pillage and plunder," U.S. senator Timothy Howe hyperbolically suggested in 1873.[29] They begged and lived outside the regime of steady toil, violating the tenets of free-labor society as surely as the tramps and dishonest beggars who haunted the imaginations of urban reformers back east.[30] More generally, they were unfit neighbors for a civilized people: "To all intents and purposes they are as much heathen as the tribes of the interior of Africa," declared an agent in 1866.[31]

By 1870 substantial parts of Wisconsin's settler society were calling for the Ho-Chunks' removal to the Winnebago reservation. Unlike some Native populations west of the Mississippi, Wisconsin's Ho-Chunk possessed neither the military means nor the numbers to challenge white conquest for any period of time. So the question was not whether the United States should "feed or fight" the Ho-Chunk, but whether or not it would choose to use its military to force them onto a distant reservation.[32] In 1870 and again in 1872, Congress appropriated funds to remove the Ho-Chunk; in 1873, as the U.S. Army undertook military operations against hostile Indians in California and elsewhere, it also began preparations for a much more modest operation in the Wisconsin woods—what officials hoped would amount to the final removal of the Ho-Chunk.

For their part, the Wisconsin Ho-Chunk could not help but note that, even as it geared up for removal, the federal government was simultaneously pursuing a policy of "civilization and citizenship" through land ownership—and moreover, pursuing that policy very close by. In the early postwar years, some Sauk and Fox had taken up residence in Iowa, where they purchased land from white settlers. In 1867 Congress authorized them to settle there permanently, allowing them to continue to receive their share of the tribal funds guaranteed by the removal treaty even though they had not honored its terms.[33] Several hundred Ho-Chunk lived near or among these returnees and were certainly in communication with their brethren in Wisconsin. Even more encouraging was the experience of the Minnesota Ho-Chunk. Their 1859 treaty with the federal government allowed individual members of the tribe to purchase land, and many Ho-Chunk had begun the process when the mass of the tribe was removed from the Blue Earth reservation to Crow Creek in 1863. Indeed, several hundred Ho-Chunk, many of them aspiring landowners, had remained in Minnesota with the acquiescence and support of local whites. By 1870, Minnesota's U.S. congressmen began moving to insert appropriations for the Ho-Chunk who remained in the state. The money was earmarked first to reimburse them for the expenses of the removal to Crow Creek (which had, shockingly, been charged against the tribe's trust fund), then to allow individual Minnesota Ho-Chunk to have the use of their share of the tribal funds to purchase lands as previously authorized, and to "withdraw from the tribe and become citizens of the United States."[34]

The General Land Office, which oversaw the sale of public lands, offered a more stringent version of this policy of land acquisition and citizenship to Indians generally. In early 1870, it ruled that those who chose to dissolve their tribal relations formally could enter homesteads under the Homestead Act of 1862, on the same basis as white settlers.[35] The department helpfully provided model forms for the dissolution of tribal identity (figure 3.2).[36]

These forms became the basis for new bureaucratic instruments, including "citizenship certificates" devised for particular local circumstances. In Washington Territory, for example, the Indian agent Robert Milroy "began encouraging Indians to take out the necessary papers for swearing allegiance to their tribes and to apply for homestead claims," and

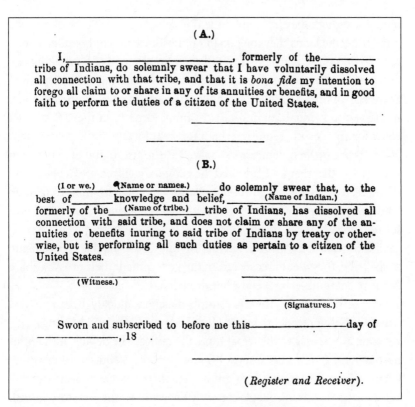

(**A.**)

I,_____, formerly of the_____
tribe of Indians, do solemnly swear that I have voluntarily dissolved
all connection with that tribe, and that it is *bona fide* my intention to
forego all claim to or share in any of its annuities or benefits, and in good
faith to perform the duties of a citizen of the United States.

_____

(**B.**)

(I or we.)   ᐊName or names.)   do solemnly swear that, to the
best of_____knowledge and belief,_____(Name of Indian.)
formerly of the__(Name of tribe.)__tribe of Indians, has dissolved all
connection with said tribe, and does not claim or share any of the annuities or benefits inuring to said tribe of Indians by treaty or otherwise, but is performing all such duties as pertain to a citizen of the
United States.

_____   _____
    (Witness.)
                                 _____
                                         (Signatures.)

Sworn and subscribed to before me this_____day of
_____, 18 .

_____

(*Register and Receiver*).

Figure 3.2 Land Office form for the naturalization of Native Americans, 1870
(Henry N. Copp, *Public Land Laws Passed by Congress From March 4, 1869, to March 3,
1875, with Important Decisions of the Secretary of the Interior, and Commissioner of the
General Land Office . . .* [Washington, D.C.: Henry N. Copp, 1875], 284)

he "began conferring citizenship certificates—of Milroy's own design—
on the Indians under his charge who severed their tribal relations and took
out homestead entries."[37] Crucially, these policies required Indians who
wished to become citizens under the terms of the Fourteenth Amendment
to surrender both their cultural self-definition and their rights to tribal
treaty funds.

With the help of their state's congressmen, the Minnesota Ho-Chunk
soon gained both this and another option through the Indian Appropriations Act of July 15, 1870. Section 9 of the act provided for individual Minnesota Ho-Chunk heads of household to take up land in severalty or to
regularize landholdings they already had. They would be permitted to
remain in Minnesota, where they would continue to receive annuity pay-

ments as though they had joined the Winnebago tribe in Nebraska; at the same time, the lands they took up in Minnesota would not be alienable — they could not turn around and sell them to others. People making use of this provision entered a gray zone between wardship and citizenship. Section 10 of the act, by contrast, pulled the door to citizenship fully open. It allowed individual Minnesota Ho-Chunk to petition the U.S. district court for citizenship, requiring them to swear loyalty to the government and to prove by their demeanor — as well as the attestation of two citizen witnesses — that they had "adopted the habits of civilized life." They would then receive "certificates of naturalization" and be permitted to take up lands in fee simple, with the right of alienation. Formally making themselves "subject to the jurisdiction" of the United States, they would be citizens in the fullest legal sense. Finally, on fully dissolving their relationship to the tribe, they would receive from the government their pro rata share of the tribal fund — about eight hundred dollars.[38]

People throughout the Ho-Chunk diaspora quickly began to test whether these precedents might allow them to claim land holdings, citizenship, and access to the tribal fund all at once. The details of the Minnesota story quickly became well known on the Nebraska reservation, where agents fretted that it might induce their charges to head north.[39] Wisconsin's Ho-Chunk people certainly knew the Minnesota story as well: the 1873 petition of Dandy's Band, in which they asked to become citizens, specifically inquired as to whether the Act of July 15, 1870 provided a way for the Wisconsin Ho-Chunks to acquire land and a right to remain, and asked that if "any other law provides a way by which they may become citizens, their attorney may be so advised."[40]

The 1873 petition may also have represented Wisconsin Ho-Chunks' knowledge that they had unlikely allies in Washington: anti-Reconstruction Democrats eager to expose Republican hypocrisy. The Wisconsin Ho-Chunks' fiercest advocate in the Senate was Ohio's Allen Thurman, a former War Democrat who became a fierce opponent of many elements of Republican Reconstruction policy, especially the Fourteenth and Fifteenth Amendments. Thurman indicted the Republicans for hypocrisy. While they demanded that white Southerners accept the citizenship and enfranchisement of millions of former slaves, he noted, Wisconsin's Republicans refused to contemplate the same for even a few thousand Native Americans in their own state. Instead, despite the 1870 report asserting the U.S. citizenship of the members of stray bands, Wisconsin's

Republican leadership repeatedly sought federal funds for the Ho-Chunks' expulsion.

The Fourteenth Amendment, Thurman insisted in Senate debates, could not mean different things in different regions. Indians who abandoned their tribal ties became—under the terms of the amendment—citizens of the nation and of the state in which they resided, with all the rights of other citizens. "There are people in Wisconsin who would be very glad to get rid of them," Thurman acknowledged. "They are not comfortable neighbors, and they want to get rid of them." But the citizens of Wisconsin had no such right. Indeed, according to the universal language of the Fourteenth Amendment, the Ho-Chunk—who were subject to the jurisdiction of no recognized tribe—were themselves citizens of Wisconsin. Thurman delightedly pointed out the irony: Wisconsin's ardent congressional supporters of the Fourteenth Amendment "helped very much to make these people citizens . . . and she [Wisconsin, through her elected leaders] denounced everybody who did not like that amendment as being an old fogy who was behind the age, a pro-slavery old fogy. . . . Now, she made these people citizens, and let her keep her citizens." It was too late to remove the Ho-Chunk again; they had already been "constitutionalized."[41]

Wisconsin's Republicans demurred. "Not quite constitutionalized, I think," replied Senator Timothy Howe, who sought to draw a bright line between the citizenship status of the freedpeople and that of Native Americans. The Fourteenth Amendment, Howe asserted, "was carefully drawn for the express purpose of excluding all the Indians from citizenship." Further, the logic of Native sovereignty argued against seeing the stray bands as de jure national citizens. If the simple act of leaving the reservation made Indians into citizens, he explained, "American citizenship is gained or lost simply by crossing the boundary between an Indian reservation and the territory adjoining!"[42] Native Americans remained wards of the federal government, ineligible to acquire real estate or to obtain political privileges; these disabilities made a mockery of any notional citizenship the Fourteenth Amendment might have conveyed. "They have no home in Wisconsin," Howe explained, "not a foot of land there, not even the poor right to vote there." It made no sense to "leave them in Wisconsin, where they have not a right and cannot get a right, to live on pillage and plunder."[43] Stateless, without either individual property or reservations, they possessed neither the rights and responsibilities of citizens nor the clearly subordinate status of wards. That state of affairs could not continue.

Even as he made these arguments denying the citizenship of members of the stray bands, Howe seemed aware of the 1870 Senate report that took the contrary position. He solved this conundrum by keying his argument in the register of humane sentiment. Removing the Ho-Chunk from Wisconsin was the Christian solution to their miserable, marginal state, and the constitutional lacuna should not stand in the way of that impulse. Thurman's "love for humanity far transcends his love for the Constitution," Howe suggested, cunningly digging at Thurman's opposition to the very amendment on which his argument was based. But with his next step the Wisconsin senator's footing failed him: Thurman, he suggested, would ultimately "give way to his humanitarian views and 'let the Constitution slide' for the present."[44]

Howe had stumbled into Thurman's rhetorical thicket. His desire to "let the Constitution slide" confirmed that Republicans' commitment to equal, universal citizenship depended on how well that principle jibed with the achievement of a white man's republic in the West. Thurman was right, it seemed: Howe and likeminded Republicans asserted the broad principle of equality where the freedpeople were concerned, but they denied it with reference to their own nonwhite populations. Thurman lit into Howe's assertion that Wisconsin's Ho-Chunks could not be considered citizens because they lacked the right of suffrage, comparing his pro-Reconstruction colleague to anti-Reconstruction vigilantes. The Wisconsin Ho-Chunk were citizens, the Democrat repeated, under the meaning of the Fourteenth Amendment,

> and if they are not allowed to vote, if they offer to vote, my friend ought to get after the men who refuse them with the enforcement act. I think he supported that act. He ought not to confine it entirely to the Ku Klux and that class of people. If there are Ku Klux in Wisconsin who will not allow these people to vote, I pray my friend to be after them with the enforcement act, and punish them, and vindicate the right of suffrage, which belongs to all the people without distinction of race, color, or previous condition of servitude. [laughter] Vindicate it up in Wisconsin before you ask the southern people to vindicate it.[45]

Thurman's larger point was not the virtues of consistency—he himself was an ardent opponent of the Ku Klux Klan Act and of nonwhite political citizenship. Instead, Thurman underlined Republican inconsistency to suggest that the principles of national citizenship, like the Enforcement Acts, were nothing more than partisan enactments.

Thurman scored rhetorical points in this debate, but in another he secured a far more meaningful victory for the Ho-Chunks' cause. When the Senate debated an appropriation for the removal of the Ho-Chunks from Wisconsin, Thurman loudly insisted that this removal could only take place with the consent of the removed, and that the legislation must therefore explicitly foreswear the use of force. His position gained enough support that Republicans agreed to add the phrase "with their consent" to the legislation authorizing and funding Ho-Chunk removal.[46] In 1873, as preparations for removal proceeded, Republican colleagues reassured Thurman that no compulsion would be used.[47] Commissioner of Indian Affairs E. P. Smith repeated that promise to a delegation of Ho-Chunks in February.

Despite these promises, and as the threat of federal removal from Wisconsin seemed to grow greater during 1873, Ho-Chunks and their representatives tested the possibility that land ownership could protect them. In May, the attorney Henry Lee of Portage, whom Dandy's Band had hired to represent them, told the Indian Office that "they do not wish to be removed [and] are willing to do anything to be allowed to stay would gladly become citizens if there is any way for them to do so." "[S]ome of them now own real estate," he underlined. "Is there any law by which they can become citizens?"[48] He did more than ask questions. He and some other whites encouraged Ho-Chunk people to purchase parcels of land, no matter how small, in an effort to establish themselves as on the path to "civilization," and therefore as the kind of citizen-Indians the removal might leave undisturbed.

State officials from the governor on down sought to douse this flame of hope, insisting that the Ho-Chunk lacked the legal rights of citizens, including the right to purchase land. At a meeting near Sparta, Wisconsin, in June 1873, Governor Washburn told the four hundred Ho-Chunk people assembled that they could not legitimately own land in the state: "I am informed that some of you think you can avoid going by buying land here. In your present condition you are the wards of the government, and cannot hold lands without its consent."[49] Charles A. Hunt, the special commissioner appointed to remove the Ho-Chunks from Wisconsin, even asked the federal Commission of Indian Affairs to have the state's land offices closed to them.[50]

But some Ho-Chunk had already taken up small parcels of land, provoking a debate among white Wisconsinites about the relationship of landholding, "civilization," and citizenship. Even white advocates of removal seemed to think that at least some of these Indian landowners ought to be allowed to remain. A man who had purchased and (especially) improved land had, in the words of a Madison journalist, "performed those acts which secure to him citizenship, just as any Indian who wants to become civilized may do." But he cautioned that this embrace of American patterns of life—the performance of those "acts"—must be earnest and unstinting; it could not be a fig leaf of a few acres, intended to mask a preconquest mode of life. "If they will adopt the manners of white men and become citizens, all right, but if they insist on being Indians let them go to an Indian land. This playing Indian in the settlements is what is objected to."[51] That "playing Indian" provoked the Portage editor Andrew Jackson Turner (father of the historian Frederick Jackson Turner) to a disdainful description of the Ho-Chunks' "strolling, vagabond life" of "a muskrat f[o]r Monday, a turtle for Tuesday, a few berries for Wednesday, begging for Thursday, strapping up their belt for their Friday's meal and going hungry Saturday with the possibilities of a catfish for Sunday."[52]

On the other hand, some whites stood to gain economically from the Ho-Chunks' presence. The Ho-Chunks' aspirations to live "as citizens and not as a tribe" did not quite match the yeoman ideal, but they had in fact come to play important roles as suppliers of berries and other goods, and as wage laborers at peak seasons. One trading partner and staunch political ally, Jacob Spaulding of Black River Falls, noted that the Ho-Chunks with whom he traded desired "swamp lands adapted to the raising of cranberries, huckleberries, and grass," and that some were even now picking hops and working in the pineries.[53] Proponents of removal usually claimed that Native Americans' primary trading relationship was the purchase of liquor, but Spaulding, one of the first English-speaking settlers in northwestern Wisconsin, wrote that Ho-Chunks had sold as much as $30,000 worth of huckleberries during the 1873 season.[54] As the historian Brad Asher writes of a similar economic situation in Washington Territory, "[h]aving obtained Indian lands through warfare, treaties, and statutes of dubious legality, many settlers . . . found that they could not dispense with Indians," either with their labor or the goods they produced.[55]

Both Spaulding and Henry Lee also imagined reaping a windfall if the stray bands were allowed to cash out from the vast tribal fund.[56] Lee worked on a contingency basis to get the Wisconsin Ho-Chunks an arrangement similar to that obtained by their Minnesota cousins. Spaulding may also have thought that Lee's contingency agreement promised him future riches; he allegedly offered to buy Lee out of his arrangement with the Ho-Chunk for the sum of $20,000.[57] Some might feel, as Thurman noted, that the Ho-Chunk were "not comfortable neighbors," but many people stood to gain from an outcome other than removal.

Removal proceeded nonetheless, and officials quickly broke their promise not to use force. In July 1873, shortly after Dandy's Band offered their petition, the commissioner of Indian affairs issued an order for the Ho-Chunks' removal "nolens volens." Soon he and a Wisconsin congressman journeyed to the council grounds outside Sparta to inform the Ho-Chunk of the new order, accompanied by Charles A. Hunt, the official appointed to oversee the removal. Only a minority of those present agreed to leave, and in August Hunt met with a smaller group to issue another ultimatum. Henry Lee pled the Ho-Chunks' case in a succession of letters to federal officials, to no avail.[58] In early December, about fifty soldiers of the Twentieth U.S. Infantry were deployed from Minnesota to a temporary base in Sparta, Wisconsin, to support Hunt's campaign of removal.[59]

Shortly before Christmas, Hunt and the soldiers sprang into action. Parties of between eight and several dozen federals, often accompanied by Hunt himself, sought out Ho-Chunk families and bands in their winter camps, the locations of which were apparently well known to local U.S. residents. They captured nearly two hundred people and sent them west by rail to the Winnebago Reservation.[60] During the next month they captured about seven hundred more. The prisoners, often hurried out of their shelters and corralled into freezing boxcars, suffered terribly. A number died en route or shortly after arriving in Nebraska. And soon, as after every previous removal, significant numbers of Ho-Chunk began to return.

But the uncertain relationships between land ownership and citizenship vexed removal officials at every turn. Some of the people his troops rounded up, Hunt complained, "claim citizenship by virtue of ownership of real estate." Hunt was unsure how to deal with these cases, and he sometimes exempted those Indians who could demonstrate that they owned land. But where were the limits? Did the ownership of very small parcels—as little as three acres—provide grounds for allowing households to remain?

And what about cases in which they had come into these holdings only a short time before, in an effort to evade removal? Hunt was particularly frustrated by the expediency and speed with which some Ho-Chunk had acquired titles to land. Forty-one Indians near Reedsburg claimed membership in families holding two deeds, both made out in June 1873. Lee doubted both the legitimacy of the kinship claims and the intentions behind the acquisition of land. "They claim all connections as their families," he complained, either failing to understand the nature of kinship in a clan society or — more likely— simply assuming that the claimants' intent was to deceive. In any case, "there will not be many to move if we recognize the recent deeds."[61] In the end, Hunt grumpily reported that he had allowed 249 to remain by virtue of owning real estate.[62]

Removal officials sought to plumb the deeper meanings of Indians' title to real estate, evaluating it in the context of the landowner's adherence to the matrix of values and behaviors that constituted "civilization." One of the officers working with Hunt, Captain H. G. Thomas, explained that in many instances the purchase of small tracts of "worthless" land was simply "fraud": "[W]here the owner was a wandering, blanket, Indian, living in a tepe, hunting for a subsistence, . . . the mere fact of a 'deed' conveying a few acres of worthless unimproved land, on which it was evident, that no one could get a living, would not convert him into a 'bona fide' citizen." On the other hand, "when the Indian lived in a house, however humble, in a place at all improved, and raised a crop &c &C &c, that it made no difference whether he owned it or hired it, that he carried the evidence of civilization about him. I have taken none such away, and have released several, giving them sometimes the benefit of the doubt."[63] He claimed to see past the shallow surface of a land title and into the character of the individual holding it, assessing "civilization" by a variety of signs, and using those to determine the person's fate.

Many pro-removal whites rued such fine distinctions, presenting all Indian claims of landholding and citizenship as nothing more than a dodge. "Citizens of Caledonia" demanded the removal of returned Ho-Chunks who "claim to have acquired title to a forty acre tract . . . and further claim that they are citizens." In a meandering argument that showed no awareness of its own circularity, they held that the Ho-Chunks claiming citizenship had "cultivated no land, paid no taxes, do not send their children to our schools, pay no poll taxes, do not offer to vote, and could hardly be permitted to vote if they should offer to, until they give more evidence than they yet have done, that they have abandoned their tribal relations and become citizens."[64] That is, they had not demonstrated their fitness for citizenship, and could not be allowed to do so.

But other whites challenged federal agents' assessments of which Ho-Chunks were civilized neighbors and which were savages. When soldiers loaded eighty-three captives onto railcars at Portage, numerous "citizens of Portage" defied the military, staring down Hunt and his men until they released two families who owned land in the area.[65] On another occasion, Hunt attempted to remove the family of a landowner named Ah-ha-Cho-Ker; they had been found far from the lands he owned, "dressed the same as other of the tribe and liv[ing] the same with no ways to distinguish them from the others."[66] But when Hunt brought these people to Reedsburg for transportation west, several hundred white citizens overpowered the federal detachment and "by force" secured the release of ten members of Ah-Ha-Cho-Ker's family.[67] The white citizens of central Wisconsin claimed the right to determine which of their Indian neighbors should be allowed to remain.

The confusion sown by Ho-Chunk land ownership soon combined with growing official unease about potential clashes between federal troops and white citizens. By the second week of January, Hunt reported nearly nine hundred people removed or in captivity, with about two hundred remaining at large,[68] but the forces of opposition were rallying. Lee and Spaulding protested to the state legislature, which called Hunt to testify.[69] An outraged Allen Thurman presented a petition from the Ho-Chunk on the Senate floor, reminding his colleagues that during the previous year's debate everyone had promised not to use force.[70] The War Department jumped in, concerned that its troops had been employed in violation of the terms of the congressional authorization, and worried about the collision with white citizens at Reedsburg.[71] Military officials had almost certainly received word of one removal officer's alarming query, issued after the Reedsburg incident, as to "how far I am authorized by law and the Dept. Commander to resist such a mob . . . whether I can fire upon them."[72] General William Tecumseh Sherman soon reported to the secretary of war that removal officials would abandon the use of force.[73] By April 1874 Hunt was squarely on the defensive, promising the secretary of the interior that, "I have not knowingly removed any one against his will who had a shadow of title to any real estate."[74]

Having foresworn the use of force, officials became helpless to prevent Ho-Chunk individuals, families, and bands from "daily returning" to

Wisconsin by the spring of 1874.[75] The Ho-Chunk seemed to understand that landholding offered significant protection from any further removal effort. "Nearly every Indian returning purchases small worthless tracts of land for the purpose of evading removal," Hunt fumed.[76] "This is what is being constantly planned," he reported: "[O]ne returning & buying a small worthless piece of land & then getting his family back and if not stopped will get the whole tribe back here."[77] By the fall the Nebraska Winnebago agent glumly reported that as many as two-thirds of the removed Ho-Chunk population had returned to Wisconsin.[78]

The Ho-Chunk confronted what Kate Masur and Gregory Downs call the "Stockade State" in two senses. From the perspective of those who confronted fear, hardship, and death during the winter removal, federal power was real and—at least in the moment—beyond their capacity to resist. The state, if not precisely a stockade, took the form of a boxcar. But as early as the spring of 1874, as it became clear that federal troops and Indian agents neither would nor could prevent their return to Wisconsin, the Ho-Chunk might well have agreed that the federal government's vision and ambitions far outstripped its capacities. It could corral them for a time, but it could not exercise power with the consistency or effectiveness that its policies demanded.

Soon other events forced Congress to clarify its intentions with regard to Indian use of the land office. In 1874, the Department of the Interior reversed its 1870 ruling that detribalized Indians had full rights under existing land laws. This may have been a response to the Ho-Chunks' use of the land office in evading removal. It may also have been in response to the recently announced *Slaughterhouse* decision, in which the U.S. Supreme Court radically truncated the rights of national citizenship; in announcing the change, Secretary Columbus Delano argued that his predecessor's extension of the Homestead Act to Indians exceeded Congress's intent in the Fourteenth Amendment.[79] If Congress wished to make Indians eligible for public lands, it would have to enact a special law for that purpose. A large group of Ho-Chunk retained Henry Lee to lobby Congress for such a law, while Jacob Spaulding took part in a parallel movement to have the Ho-Chunk "declared citizens" of Wisconsin.[80] Frank Moore, one of Wisconsin's leading journalists, thought Spaulding's campaign was "either idiocy or knavery," perhaps nothing more than a merchant seeking the loyalty of his trading partners; the state constitution already made "citizens and electors" of "civilized persons of Indian descent, not members of any tribe." But Moore admitted that "[p]erhaps our law ought to define a little more clearly what constitutes 'civilization,' so that that an Indian can know when he has earned the right to pay taxes and go to the polls and vote."[81]

In the aftermath of the failed removal, and with no clear policy in place to govern Indian use of the land office, congressmen seem to have grabbed at the solution offered by Henry Lee. In February 1875 Lee traveled to Washington, D.C., with the draft text of a bill that would make citizens of the Wisconsin Ho-Chunk while allowing them to retain their pro rata shares of tribal funds. He was rejected by the Indian commissioner, E. P. Smith, but better received by Secretary Delano, who referred him to the chair of the Senate Committee on Indian Affairs.[82] On March 3, 1875, the last day of its session, Congress passed an appropriation act for Indian affairs that included a provision making Native Americans who abandoned tribal ties eligible to take up land under the Homestead Act of 1862. Neither the title they acquired nor the terms were the same as those offered other homesteaders: like section 9 of the act of 1870, this "Indian Homestead Act" conveyed the land without the right of alienation. It also required Indians acquiring such land to abandon tribal relations, while allowing them to retain their right to annuities and tribal funds.[83] No congressional debate took place over these provisions, and the records of the Senate Committee on Indian Affairs contain no discussion of them, but Lee claimed then and later that the "Indian Homestead Act" was his creation.[84] The law seems to have been a hasty insertion, resolving an ambiguity with a minimum amount of fuss. It made no mention of citizenship, or of civilization.

Poverty prevented many Ho-Chunk from taking advantage of the new opening, but local observers in Wisconsin intuited that, as in previous cases, pro rata distribution of the tribal fund would soon follow. Fifty or more Ho-Chunk property owners took up contiguous forty-acre tracts near Black River Falls, where they found both a ready market for their produce and the services of Jacob Spaulding as an intermediary. "There is reason to believe they will make their location permanent," wrote a sympathetic observer, "and become producers as well as consumers, and good citizens as well as good Indians."[85] Other whites were not so sure. "A few seem to be making a sincere effort to take care of themselves by taking land under the homestead act," wrote the Nebraska Winnebago agent. "The larger portion of them, however, are probably the victims of interested parties, who are endeavoring to bring them within the operation of the homestead act, in order to show them what to do with their portion of the tribal funds which it is expected will be distributed to those who separate from the tribe."[86] Whatever the case, in other parts of the state matters proceeded more slowly. In May 1875 a Ho-Chunk assembly (including Dandy's son and many members of the prominent Decora family) hired Henry Lee on a contingency basis to help them enter homesteads and obtain the money due them from the tribal funds—money without which many could not afford to take or hold such lands.[87] It took six years to wrangle those funds from the federal government, but finally in 1881, an "Act for the Relief of the Winnebago Indians in Wisconsin" mandated the creation of a tribal roll and the distribution of tribal funds to those who had entered homesteads under the 1875 act. A Chicago newspaper declared that this "practically makes citizens of them."[88]

This citizenship did not rest on a foundation of "civilization." Wisconsin's Ho-Chunks regained access to their tribal fund and gained the right to take up lands, but many continued to migrate seasonally, pursuing a varied subsistence. During the fall 1879 cranberry harvest, bands of Ho-Chunks worked alongside Norwegians and other pickers. These were the same "strolling bands that they have been for many years," one observer thought, "but they have learned something of the rights of settlers and have preempted certain wild lands, which they affect to occupy, and thus become entitled to the privileges of citizens, and enjoy immunity from government interference."[89] The citizenship they claimed gave the right to remain, immunity from removal, and insulation from the worst features of wardship. But their civilization remained in important ways their own.

In retrospect, it is possible to view the developing policy of the early 1870s, from the 1870 Minnesota naturalization policy through the 1875 homestead provision, as stepping-stones toward the Dawes Act of 1887—possible, but not quite correct. Both the Ho-Chunk acquisition of individual plots and the dissolution of reservations into individual homesteads seem to follow from the same official desire: to see Native Americans detribalized and transformed into citizens through the adoption of U.S. practices of agricultural improvement, household structure, production, and consumption.[90] In C. Joseph Genetin-Pilawa's analysis of the overall trajectory of Indian policy in this era, "allotment and forced assimilation were potentially to serve as the means, with citizenship and all that that status entailed (including the end of tribal sovereignty and tribal relations) as the end." But the road to allotment, he notes, was less a straight line than a crooked path.[91] The Ho-Chunk took one fork of that path, during the brief window of its existence.

When the Ho-Chunk used the words "citizenship" and "civilization," they seem to have attached meanings and hopes to them quite different from those intended by policymakers. They did not seek assimilation into the U.S. order, nor did they imagine they could fully escape it. Neither simply embracing nor simply rebelling against liberal individualism and market-oriented activity, they engaged with those regimes as part—but only part—of the reality shaping their individual and collective lives.[92] By so doing, they achieved citizenship during the brief moment when Grant's Reconstruction-era vision of incorporation seemed imminently achievable, but before the colonial project of "killing the Indian to save the man" had sufficiently developed to wrap them in its smothering embrace.[93]

As the essays in this volume demonstrate, liberalism's challengers were legion during the postwar era. Most notably, freedpeople and their descendants practiced politics in ways that diverged from liberal individualism and U.S. nationalism: they treated the vote as a collective possession and sometimes organized to promote a national future outside the United States.[94] Over the next decades, labor activists, Plains Indians, Populists, and Philippine insurgents all demanded different political and economic arrangements than those envisioned by U.S. policymakers. Unlike the Ho-Chunk, however, these later insurgents confronted and were defeated by a liberal capitalist order of enormous military and administrative capacity. Public and private armies played their parts, as did the consolidation of effective political power in two parties, both of them committed to white supremacy and liberal capitalism. By the turn of the century, the federal government was well on its way to colonial rule over Native life, and courts, governments, and bands of white citizens had emptied national citizenship of much of its emancipatory content.

In that new era, citizenship functioned as a racial entitlement and a disciplinary tool of the state, not as a path to partial autonomy.[95] Nightriding vigilantes and intellectual elites agreed that universalist readings of the Fourteenth Amendment were relics of a misguided era. Supreme Court decisions—from the *Civil Rights Cases* and *Elk v. Wilkins* in the 1880s to *Plessy v. Ferguson* and the *Insular Cases* at the turn of the century—radically delimited citizenship's scope and power, relegating entire geographies and social groups to a "waiting room of history."[96] More than "not quite constitutionalized," the people encompassed by those policies remained simultaneously outside the borders of citizenship and within the bounds of what Stacey L. Smith calls "acceptable coercion." In that zone of economic subjection and political quarantine, the vision of "civilization and ultimate citizenship" became less a pathway to self-determination than a promise of indefinite confinement.

NOTES

Thanks to the colleagues whose generous sharing of work and ideas have helped me find my way in a new field of study—Larry Nesper, Aaron Bird Bear, Janice Rice, Patty Loew, Ari Kelman, Miranda Johnson, Richard Monette, Andrew Fisher, and Damon Akins; the conveners of and participants in "The World the Civil War Made" (Pennsylvania State University, June 2013), particularly Joe Genetin-Pilawa, Kate Masur, and Greg Downs; and the students in "Native Madison after Removal" (University of Wisconsin–Madison, fall 2011).

1. Petition of "Indians of the Winnebago Tribe, and more particularly described as the descendants of what was known in the year 1837, and subsequent, as Dandy's Band," [May] 1873, Letters Received by the Office of Indian Affairs, 1824–1881, Microcopy No. 234, (Washington, 1956), Winnebago Agency [hereinafter cited as OIA-Winnebago], Roll 944. During the nineteenth century and much of the twentieth, the Ho-Chunk were known to English speakers as the Winnebago; the Winnebago Nation of Nebraska, part of the diaspora from the tribe's long-standing homeland in what is now southern Wisconsin and northern Illinois, retains that name.

2. *Congressional Globe*, 42nd Cong., 3d sess., 1873, 374.

3. On liberal visions of property and contract, see Amy Dru Stanley, *From Bondage to Contract: Wage Labor, Marriage, and the Market in the Age of Slave Emancipation* (New York: Cambridge University Press 1998). On postbellum ideas about Indians and civilization, see David Wallace Adams, *Education for Extinction: American Indians and the Boarding School Experience, 1875–1928* (Lawrence: University Press of Kansas, 1995), esp. 12–21.

4. For representative scholarly approaches to these dynamics, see Richard White, *The Middle Ground: Indians, Empires, and Republics in the Great Lakes Region, 1650–1815* (New York: Cambridge University Press, 1991); Susan Sleeper-Smith, *Indian Women and French Men: Rethinking Cultural Encounter in the Western Great Lakes* (Amherst, Mass.: University of Massachusetts Press, 2001); Sophie White, *Wild Frenchmen and Frenchified Indians: Material Culture and Race in Colonial Louisiana* (Philadelphia: University of Pennsylvania Press, 2012).

5. "[I]ndividual ownership of land was one of the main criteria for measuring whether an Indian was 'civilized.'" Deborah Rosen, *American Indians and State Law: Sovereignty, Race, and Citizenship, 1790–1880* (Lincoln: University of Nebraska Press, 2007), 136. See, e.g., the distinction between "nonproducing Indians" and civilization, in Lyman Copeland Draper, ed., *Collections of the State Historical Society of Wisconsin*, 20

vols. (Madison, 1855–1915) [hereafter cited as *WHC*], 28:274, and of land as valueless until cultivated by white settlers, selections from *Wisconsin Democrat, WHC*, vol. 28.

6. Rosen, *American Indians and State Law*, 132–41; *Constitution of the State of Wisconsin, Adopted in Convention, at Madison, on the First Day of February, in the Year of Our Lord 1848* (Madison: Beriah Brown, 1848), Article 3, sec. 1.

7. Quoted in James W. Oberly, *A Nation of Statesmen: The Political Culture of the Stockbridge-Munsee Mohicans, 1815–1972* (Norman: University of Oklahoma Press, 2005), 71.

8. Ibid., 63–72.

9. Paul W. Gates, "Indian Allotments Preceding the Dawes Act," in *The Frontier Challenge: Responses to the Trans-Mississippi West*, ed. John G. Clark (Lawrence: University Press of Kansas, 1971), 141–70.

10. Ibid., 154.

11. Bruce M. White, "The Power of Whiteness: Or, the Life and Times of Joseph Rolette, Jr.," *Minnesota History* 56, no. 4 (Winter 1998–99): 178–97.

12. Oberly, *Nation of Statesmen*, 62–78.

13. The story of the Wisconsin Ho-Chunks' resistance to removal and emergence as a distinct group is best told in Lawrence W. Onsager, "The Removal of the Winnebago Indians from Wisconsin in 1873–74" (M.A. thesis, Loma Linda University, 1985). See also Nancy O. Lurie, "Winnebago," in *Northeast*, vol. 15 of *Handbook of North American Indians*, ed. Bruce G. Trigger (Washington, D.C.: Smithsonian Institution, 1978), 690–707; Bethel Saler, *The Settler's Empire: Colonialism and State Formation in America's Old Northwest* (Philadelphia: University of Pennsylvania Press, 2014); and Tom Jones et al., *People of the Big Voice: Photographs of Ho-Chunk Families by Charles Van Schaick, 1879–1942* (Madison: Wisconsin Historical Society Press, 2011).

14. The essential explication of free-labor ideology is Eric Foner, *Free Soil, Free Labor, Free Men: The Ideology of the Republican Party before the Civil War* (New York: Oxford University Press, 1970). Crucial works exploring the wartime and postbellum elaboration of this ideology with reference to freedpeople and other (non-Indian) groups include Willie Lee Rose, *Rehearsal for Reconstruction: The Port Royal Experiment* (reprint; Athens: University of Georgia Press, 1999); Stanley, *From Bondage to Contract*; and Kate Masur, *An Example for All the Land: Emancipation and the Struggle over Equality in Washington* (Chapel Hill: University of North Carolina Press, 2010), 51–86. William A. White to Edward A. Atkinson, February 21, 1862, quoted in Rose, *Rehearsal*, 41.

15. On the triumph of the policy of allotment later in the century, and the alternative policies promoted along the way, see C. Joseph Genetin-Pilawa, *Crooked Paths to Allotment: The Fight over Federal Indian Policy after the Civil War* (Chapel Hill: University of North Carolina Press, 2012).

16. Quoted in Onsager, "The Removal of the Winnebago Indians," 107, 113.

17. In this respect, the Ho-Chunks' superficial acquiescence masked profound cultural persistence in ways comparable to Luke Harlow's finding, in this volume, that pro-slavery Christianity survived emancipation.

18. Onsager, "The Removal of the Winnebago Indians," 117–19.

19. *Congressional Globe*, 39th Cong., 1st sess., 2892.

20. *Effect of the Fourteenth Amendment upon Indian Tribes*, 41st Cong., 3d sess., 1870, S. Rep. 268, 11. The report appears to have been commissioned in response to claims that the Fourteenth Amendment, lacking the theretofore typical exclusion of "Indians not taxed," had made U.S. citizens of Indians generally. The question of the status of the "straggling bands" amounts to an afterthought. For careful elucidation of the relevant congressional debates, see Earl M. Maltz, "The Fourteenth Amendment and Native American Citizenship," *Constitutional Commentary* 17 (Winter 2000): 555–73.

21. For a closely related set of questions and concerns about freedpeople's fitness for citizenship, see Masur, *An Example for All the Land*, 51–86.

22. Francis Paul Prucha, *The Great Father: The United States Government and the American Indians* (Lincoln: University of Nebraska Press, 1984), 609–86, quote on 660.

23. Cathleen D. Cahill, *Federal Mothers and Fathers: A Social History of the Indian Service, 1869–1933* (Chapel Hill: University of North Carolina Press, 2011), 17–20.

24. *Annual Report of the Commissioner of Indian Affairs to the Secretary of the Interior for the Year 1873* (Washington, D.C.: Government Printing Office, 1874), 184–85. On clothing, see Stephen Kantrowitz, "'Citizen's Clothing': Reconstruction, Ho-Chunk Persistence, and the Politics of Dress," in *Civil War Wests: Testing the Limits of the United States*, ed. Adam Arenson and Andrew Graybill (Berkeley: University of California Press, 2015).

25. *Annual Report of the Commissioner of Indian Affairs to the Secretary of the Interior for the Year 1876* (Washington, D.C.: Government Printing Office, 1876), 94; *Annual Report of the Commissioner of Indian Affairs to the Secretary of the Interior for the Year 1875* (Washington, D.C.: Government Printing Office, 1875), 325.

26. *Annual Report of the Commissioner of Indian Affairs to the Secretary of the Interior for the Year 1870* (Washington, D.C.: Government Printing Office, 1870), 323–24.

27. Quoted in Onsager, "Removal of the Winnebago Indians," 130.

28. Compare this to the concerns in Genetin-Pilawa, *Crooked Paths*, 80–82.

29. *Congressional Globe*, 42nd Cong., 3d sess., 1873, 372.

30. See Stanley, *Bondage to Contract*, esp. 100–137.

31. *Report of the Commissioner of Indian Affairs for the Year 1866* (Washington, D.C.: Government Printing Office, 1866), 59.

32. "Feed or fight" taken from Genetin-Pilawa, *Crooked Paths*, 81. Other groups faced similar challenges during this era: numerous Indian groups around Puget Sound, for example, resisted being confined to reservations, or to the particular reservations designated for them. They were sometimes derided as "roaming" or "renegade" Indians, just as Ho-Chunks were "stray bands." Brad Asher, *Beyond the Reservation: Indians, Settlers, and the Law in Washington Territory, 1853–1889* (Norman: University of Oklahoma Press, 1999), 42–48. See also Andrew Fisher, *Shadow Tribe: The Making of Columbia River Indian Identity* (Seattle: University of Washington Press, 2010).

33. *Annual Report of the Commissioner of Indian Affairs to the Secretary of the Interior for the Year 1874* (Washington, D.C.: Government Printing Office, 1874), 31–32.

34. *Congressional Globe*, 41st Cong., 2d sess., 1870, 4133.

35. Henry N. Copp, *Public Land Laws Passed by Congress from March 4, 1869, to March 3, 1875, with Important Decisions of the Secretary of the Interior, and Commissioner of the General Land Office.* . . . (Washington, D.C.: Henry N. Copp, 1875), 283–85.

36. Ibid., 284.

37. Asher, *Beyond the Reservation*, 76–77.

38. "General Incidental Expenses of the Indian Service," *U.S. Statutes at Large 16*, 1870, 361–62. "Certificates of Naturalization," OIA-Winnebago, Roll 944.

39. *Annual Report of the Commissioner . . . 1874*, 37–38.

40. Petition of "Indians of the Winnebago Tribe, and more particularly described as the descendants of what was known in the year 1837, and subsequent, as Dandy's Band," [May], 1873, OIA-Winnebago, Roll 944.

41. Quotations in the next paragraphs are from *Congressional Globe*, 42nd Cong., 3d sess., 1873, 362–80.

42. *Congressional Globe*, 42nd Cong., 3d sess., 1873, 484.

43. *Congressional Globe*, 42nd Cong., 3d sess., 1873, 372.

44. Ibid.

45. Ibid.

46. *Congressional Globe*, 42nd Cong., 2d sess., 1872, 2200.

47. *Congressional Globe*, 42nd Cong., 3d sess., 1873, 375–77.

48. H. W. Lee to H. R. Blum, May 1, 1873, OIA-Winnebago, Roll 944.

49. "Indian Council," Madison *Wisconsin State Register*, June 21, 1873, 2.

50. Telegram, C. A. Hunt to E. P. Smith, July 8, 1873, OIA-Winnebago, Roll 944.

51. *Wisconsin State Register*, July 5, 1873, vol. 2, col. 4.

52. Quoted in Onsager, "Removal of the Winnebago Indians," 183.

53. Jacob Spaulding to U.S. Grant, Sept. 1, 1873, OIA-Winnebago, Roll 944.

54. Spaulding to Pres. U.S. Grant, Sept. 1, 1873, OIA-Winnebago, Roll 944.

55. Asher, *Beyond the Reservation*, 51.

56. In 1871, the commissioner of Indian affairs, Ely S. Parker, calculated the Ho-Chunk tribal fund to be more than 1.25 million dollars. Letter from Ely S. Parker quoted in *Congressional Globe*, 41st Cong., 3d sess., 1871, 763.

57. *Henry W. Lee*, 56th Cong., 1st sess., 1900, S. Doc. 144, part 2, 7.

58. H. W. Lee to Columbus Delano, June 23, Dec. 5, 1873, OIA-Winnebago, Roll 944.

59. Onsager, "Removal of the Winnebago Indians," 209–10.

60. Telegram, C. A. Hunt to E. P. Smith, Dec. 26, 1873, OIA-Winnebago, Roll 944.

61. Telegram, C. A. Hunt to E. P. Smith, Apr. 4, 1874, OIA-Winnebago, Roll 945.

62. C. A. Hunt to E. P. Smith, June 23, 1874, OIA-Winnebago, Roll 945.

63. H. G. Thomas to Asst. Adjutant General, Dept. of Dakota, Jan. 2, 1874, OIA-Winnebago, Roll 945.

64. Petition of W. W. Owens and others to remove the Winnebago Indians from the State of Wis., n. d., OIA-Winnebago, Roll 945.

65. C. A. Hunt to E. P. Smith, Dec. 29, 1873, OIA-Winnebago, Roll 945.

66. Ibid.

67. W. H. H. Cash to C. A. Hunt, Dec. 27, 1873, OIA-Winnebago, Roll 945.

68. Telegram, C. A. Hunt to E. P. Smith, Jan. 9, 1874, OIA-Winnebago, Roll 945.

69. C. A. Hunt to E. P. Smith, Feb. 12, 1874, OIA-Winnebago, Roll 945.

70. *Congressional Globe*, 43rd Cong., 1st sess., 1874, 743–44.

71. Telegram, P. H. Sheridan to W. T. Sherman, Jan. 3, 1874; C. Delano to W. W. Belknap, Jan. 5, 187[4], OIA-Winnebago, Roll 945.

72. Report of Capt. H. G. Thomas, submitted by Secretary of War Belknap to the Secretary of the Interior, Jan. 16, 1874, OIA-Winnebago, Roll 945.

73. Telegram, W. T. Sherman to Secretary of War, Jan. 22, 1874, OIA-Winnebago, Roll 945; Genetin-Pilawa, *Crooked Paths*, 79.

74. Telegram, C. A. Hunt to E. P. Smith, Apr. 1, 1874, OIA-Winnebago, Roll 945.

75. Telegram, C. A. Hunt to E. P. Smith, May 4, 1874; D. B. Bon to C. A. Hunt, July 6, 1874, OIA-Winnebago, Roll 945.

76. Telegram, Hunt to Smith, May 4, 1874, OIA-Winnebago, Roll 945.

77. C. A. Hunt to E. P. Smith, May 8, 1874, OIA-Winnebago, Roll 945.

78. Taylor Bradley to E. P. Smith, Nov. 5, 1874, OIA-Winnebago, Roll 945.

79. Asher, *Beyond the Reservation*, 78–79.

80. "Stevens Point," *Milwaukee Daily News*, February 17, 1875.

81. "Citizens of Indians," *Wisconsin State Register*, January 9, 1875.

82. "The Winnebago Indians in Wisc.," *Wisconsin State Register*, February 27, 1875.

83. "An act making appropriations for the current and contingent expenses of the Indian Department, and for fulfilling treaty stipulations with various Indian tribes, for the year ending June thirtieth, eighteen hundred and seventy-six, and for other purposes," *U.S. Statutes at Large* 18, 1875, 420. For discussion of the Indian Homestead Act, see Fisher, *Shadow Tribe*, 91–92.

84. The U.S. National Archives has a bound volume of the committee's minutes, but it contains no discussions of these provisions in February and no minutes from February 14 through the end of the session. The center does not possess the corresponding docket volume. Author correspondence with Rodney A. Ross, Center for Legislative Archives, June 14, 2012.

85. "Sensible Indians," *Chicago Inter Ocean*, May 31, 1875, 5; "Indian Civilization," *Wisconsin State Register*, June 5, 1875.

86. *Annual Report of the Commissioner . . . 1875*, 100.

87. *Henry W. Lee*, 2–5.

88. "Winnebago Indians," *Chicago Daily Inter Ocean*, January 8, 1881, 1–2; "An act for the relief of the Winnebago Indians in Wisconsin, and to aid them to obtain subsistence by agricultural pursuits, and to promote their civilization," *U.S. Statutes at Large* 21, 1881, 315; *Henry W. Lee*, 36; *Copp's Land-Owner*, March 15, 1884, 406.

89. "Harvesting Cranberries," *St. Louis Globe-Democrat*, January 12, 1879, 9.

90. Genetin-Pilawa, *Crooked Paths*, 108–11.

91. Ibid., 114.

92. The history represented by the story here—from the 1873 petition of Dandy's Band to the enactment of the Indian Homestead Act two years later—thus occupies something closely akin to what the political scientist Kevin Bruyneel has dubbed the "third space of sovereignty." In his analysis, this is a domain of activity distinct from both colonial rule and native resistance to it, constituted by native people's

exploitation of the "inconsistencies in the application of colonial rule." Bruyneel's understanding of indigenous efforts to exploit the unstable boundaries of American political life "to gain the fullest possible expression of political agency, identity, and autonomy" closely tracks my findings here, with the significant difference that Bruyneel locates the forging of a "third space" between national citizenship and native resistance in the 1920s, a half century later than the struggles outlined in this essay. Bruyneel, *The Third Space of Sovereignty: The Postcolonial Politics of U.S.-Indigenous Relations* (Minneapolis: University of Minnesota Press, 2007), quotes on 10, 6.

Another way to frame this is to suggest that Ho-Chunk activity during this period may not be best understood as (or only as) "resistance." Walter Johnson has argued that interpreting the history of African American slaves in terms of "agency" and "resistance" effectively "overcodes . . . discussions of human subjectivity and political organization" with "a notion of the universality of a liberal notion of selfhood, with its emphasis on independence and choice." He further warns against replacing that liberal "agent" with a monolithic "culture" of resistance. Instead, he urges historians to see subordinated peoples' activity neither as individual acts of resistance nor as an unthinking expression of cultural values, but as "an ongoing argument about what elements of a shared past were relevant to a current situation." Johnson, "On Agency," *Journal of Social History* 37 (Autumn 2003): 113–24, quotes on 114–15, 119. At many moments during the Civil War era, Ho-Chunk people effectively resisted official U.S. desires in ways and for reasons rooted in their material circumstances, desires, and cosmology, not because resistance as such was the Ho-Chunks' primary purpose.

93. For an intriguingly similar story of a group of Nez Percé deliberately "detribalizing" themselves in 1877 to secure homesteads, thereby escaping removal to a reservation, see Asher, *Beyond the Reservation*, 147.

94. Steven Hahn, *A Nation under Our Feet: Black Political Struggles in the Rural South from Slavery to the Great Migration* (Cambridge: Harvard University Press, 2003), esp. 5–10; quite differently, Stephen Kantrowitz, "'Intended for the Better Government of Man': The Political History of African American Freemasonry in the Era of Emancipation," *Journal of American History* 96 (March 2010), 1001–26.

95. See Kevin Bruyneel, "Challenging American Boundaries: Indigenous People and the 'Gift' of U.S. Citizenship," *Studies in American Political Development*, 18 (Spring 2004): 30–43.

96. Dipesh Chakrabarty, *Provincializing Europe: Postcolonial Thought and Historical Difference*, rev. ed. (Princeton: Princeton University Press, 2009), 8.

4 THE BURNT DISTRICT

Making Sense of Ruins in the Postwar South
K. Stephen Prince

When George Barnard arrived in Charleston, South Carolina, in early 1865, his camera was ready. Having traveled with the army of William Tecumseh Sherman, the photographer was no stranger to the effects of war. The ruins of Charleston's once prosperous buildings and residences, however, threw the city's desolation and suffering into bold relief. Charleston had been the playground of the Slave Power, the birthplace of South Carolina's secession ordinance, and the scene of the first shots of the Civil War, lending a profound symbolic meaning to the city's utter devastation. When Barnard published his wartime photographs in a monumental 1866 collection called *Photographic Views of Sherman's Campaign*, he chose the Charleston ruins to close the work. This arrangement offered a convenient narrative of the war, one well suited to the northern parlors in which Barnard's book was likely to sit. The ordering implied causation. Southern secession, Barnard suggested, led inexorably to southern destruction. The ruins of Charleston were the logical endpoint, the last chapter of the Civil War.[1]

But there is another way to understand Barnard's images of ruined Charleston. With a slight alteration of historical perspective, these same images can be recast as the opening vista of a postwar world. Throughout much of 1865, northerners turned to ruins—real and metaphorical—in an attempt to make sense of the postwar South. Depictions and discussion of the war-torn southern landscape saturated northern print and visual culture. Southern ruins appeared in newspaper articles, speeches, sermons, travel narratives, photographs, and illustrations. Though physical ruins were largely confined to the South, representations of ruins did important work in the cultural spaces of the North. In photographic views and

Figure 4.1 George Barnard's photograph of Charleston, South Carolina, 1865
(Library of Congress)

popular discussions of southern devastation, northerners glimpsed the
challenge—and the opportunity—of the postwar era.[2]

Ruins are easier to recognize than to define. For the purposes of this
essay, however, at least a partial definition is necessary. When they used
the word "ruin" (or related words and phrases), postwar northern commentators generally referred to man-made structures that had been damaged to a point where they could no longer perform their appointed task.
The structures, however, remained recognizable; it was clear what the
ruin once was, even if it no longer functioned as designed. Born out of
sudden, catastrophic damage, southern ruins were visually striking, even
picturesque. Perhaps most significant, ruins told a story. They possessed
(or seemed to possess) narrative and pedagogical significance. To call a
structure a ruin—as opposed to, say, a pile of junk—was to immediately

affirm its cultural and symbolic power. "When we frame an object as a ruin," the critic Michael S. Roth argues, "we reclaim that object *from* its fall into decay and oblivion and often *for* some kind of cultural attention and care that, in a sense, elevates its value."[3] When they used the term "ruin" or offered comparisons to sites of ancient ruination, northern commentators tapped into a well-established vocabulary rife with historical, political, and cultural significance. In so doing, they affirmed that the ruins of the South offered important lessons for the postbellum United States.

In this essay, I use popular conversations about southern ruination to map the intellectual and cultural terrain of the early postwar period. My interest is not in the actual rebuilding of southern cities, towns, and plantations, but in the ways that images and discussion of ruination reflected larger notions about the North, the South, and the legacies of the Civil War. I have limited my chronological focus to the thirteen months between the burning of Atlanta in November 1864 and the convening of the Thirty-Ninth U.S. Congress in December 1865. A study of the treatment of southern ruins in the print and visual culture of the North in these months helps capture the complex range of emotions—pride, resolve, conceit, optimism—with which the northern public greeted the dawn of the postwar era. As they gazed on images of southern ruination, northerners pondered the meanings of war, but they also looked to the future. Ruins carried within them the promise of a new and reformed South. The victorious North had, it seemed, been given a blank slate, a chance to re-create the South from the ground up. After four years of bloody war and three hundred thousand Union dead, this was not merely an opportunity, but an obligation. From the desolation of the Confederacy, northerners would build the South of the future.

Engagement with ruin discourse helps us recognize that the immediate postwar moment posed cultural and intellectual problems, not just political ones. Such an approach helps illuminate all that was at stake in the world the Civil War made. Federal Reconstruction policy would realign the South's political structures, rebuild its economic base, and recalibrate its social order, but this was only a start. The South—defined as a place— would be re-created, but so would the South *as an idea*. Out of the ashes of the Civil War, a new South would emerge. Defining the character of that South would prove a central concern of the era. Such conversations occurred in the halls of Congress, in southern state capitols, in military headquarters, and on individual southern plantations. But they also took place in the periodical press, in travel writing, in popular oratory, and in the visual culture of the North. Ruin discourse was an essential component of this imaginative work. When they engaged with the ruins of the former Confederacy, northern commentators were actually struggling with the very meaning and identity of the South in the postwar world.

Though it is impossible to draw a direct correlation between popular ruin discourse and Reconstruction policy, the two are intertwined. Cultural representations created the context in which politics was practiced, in which power was won, lost, and contested. To fully understand the era's political developments, it is necessary to explore the cultural and intellectual world in which they transpired. Though ruination was certainly not the only intellectual framework through which northerners approached the postwar South, popular ruin discourse established a set of expectations regarding the revolutionary transformations to be wrought in the South. Of course, such notions would prove fundamentally unrealistic on a number of levels. Faced with white southern hostility to the postemancipation racial order, the stubborn inflexibility of deeply engrained economic and political structures, and the limits of the federal government's administrative capabilities, most northerners eventually lost faith in the revolution that ruin discourse had promised. Even so, the sheer visibility and dogged persistence of ruin discourse in the early postwar months demand an explanation. A study of the ways that northern commentators responded to the Burnt Districts of the South promises to illuminate the meaning, possibilities, and limitations of the postwar world.

ENCOUNTERING SOUTHERN RUINS

As the Civil War came to a close, southern ruins posed a problem that was intellectual as well as architectural. On the most basic level, the homes and cities of the South would have to be rebuilt—literally reconstructed. Even before the physical work of restoration got under way, however, northern commentators grappled with the nature and significance of southern devastation. Throughout late 1864 and 1865, northern journalists, travel writers, photographers, illustrators, and speakers toured the South and reported on their findings. They visited sites from Richmond to Vicksburg, using all the tools at their disposal to make the state of the South comprehensible to northern audiences. Those who relied on the printed word scoured the English language for the necessary verbiage, offering historical allusions and biblical analogies, even ranking southern locales according to their degree of desolation. Artists and photographers were equally quick to recognize the power of ruination as they plied their trade in towns and cities across the region. Through the agency of these travelers, northern civilians vicariously experienced the destruction war had wrought in the major cities and small towns of the South. They toured the South's devastated plantations and walked the scorched earth that General Sherman had left in his wake. In the process, they began the difficult work of ascribing meaning to southern ruination.

Between November 1864 and April 1865, the collapse of the Confederacy presented northern journalists with newfound access to much of the South. In these months, a quartet of southern cities that would loom large in subsequent discussions of the ruined South—Atlanta, Georgia; Charleston and Columbia, South Carolina; and Richmond, Virginia—opened to northern correspondents in rapid succession. In November of 1864, Sherman's siege of Atlanta culminated in a fire that destroyed much of the city. Almost immediately, northern journalists sought to make sense of the damage. A *Chicago Tribune* correspondent reported that, on Sherman's command, "the torch was to be applied to all public buildings, manufactories, and store-houses," and everything "which would not burn, was to be blown up." Soon, "the Gate City" was "sent reeling to ruin."[4] Shortly thereafter, another correspondent offered a stark description of the devastation that Sherman had wrought. "Atlanta is no more," the correspondent wrote. "The Babylon of the South has fallen, the voice and hum of busy industry has ceased. Its splendid homes and broad streets are deserted. The houses are in ruins, the streets will soon be overgrown with grass." The plight of Atlanta, the article continued, offered a "lesson to rebels of the fruits of their wicked efforts to rend their country in pieces."[5]

Similar processes took place in Charleston, Columbia, and Richmond. As soon as the retreat of Confederate forces made it feasible to do so, northern journalists flocked to report on the damage they found. A *New York Tribune* reporter was amazed at what he saw in Charleston in early March. "No pen, no pencil, no tongue can do justice to the scene," he wrote. "No imagination can conceive of the utter wreck, the universal ruin, the stupendous desolation. Ruin—ruin—ruin—above and below; on the right hand and the left; ruin, ruin, ruin, everywhere and always."[6] The journalist Sidney Andrews opened his travelogue, *The South since the War*, with a remarkable description of Charleston: "A city of ruins, of desolation, of vacant houses, of widowed women, of rotting wharves, of deserted warehouses, of weed-wild gardens, of miles of grass-grown streets, of acres of pitiful and voiceful barrenness."[7] David Conyngham, a correspondent for the *New York Herald*, wrote that Columbia was a "city of ruins" after a mid-February fire. Conyngham found little besides "tall spectre looking chimneys" and "groups of crouching, desponding, weeping, helpless women and children."[8] By the time they arrived in Richmond in early April, correspondents familiar with other sites of ruin had begun to write in a sort of comparative shorthand. One journalist declared Richmond's "Burnt District" to be "the most complete scene of desolation I ever beheld, excepting Charleston."[9] Another insisted that the extent of the damage in Richmond made it "almost a second Charleston, but not so bad as Columbia."[10] A third disagreed, arguing that even Columbia could not match "the ruin apparent here in Richmond."[11] Though they could not agree which city—Richmond, Charleston, or Columbia—was the most desolate, the act of comparison itself is highly significant. As early as April 1865, southern ruination had become a familiar part of the nation's rhetorical and intellectual landscape.

Though Atlanta, Charleston, Columbia, and Richmond attracted more than their fair share of attention, northern correspondents also expanded their geographical scope, reporting on the damage they encountered in smaller cities and in the backcountry. In the early fall of 1865, a traveler found much of the southern heartland in a state of ruination. "Rome, Athens, Savannah, Andersonville, Millen, Macon, Augusta, all stand blasted monuments of the anger of God upon slavery and its fiend-like instruments," he wrote. "In Alabama the spectacle is the same, or worse. From Mobile to Montgomery—including Huntsville, Selma, and other places of equal importance—the work of war is hideously complete."[12] The journalist Whitelaw Reid made three separate tours of the South in 1865 and 1866, collecting his thoughts in a volume titled *After the War*. Reid visited the ruins of Atlanta, Charleston, Columbia, and Richmond, but he also testified to devastation in a number of other locales. In Selma, Alabama, he reported, "a third or more of the city was in ruins."[13] In Knoxville, Tennessee, Reid found "burnt houses and solitary chimneys over one whole quarter of the city."[14] Bolivar, Mississippi, "the former site of a once bustling town," consisted of "a single standing chimney."[15]

Southern ruins were also well represented in northern visual culture. The Civil War was the first widely photographed conflict in U.S. history.

New technology and the ingenuity of war photographers, including George Barnard and his better-known contemporary Alexander Gardner, allowed curious northerners to have seemingly unfettered visual access to the war-ravaged South. Though it is difficult to measure the precise impact of Barnard's depictions of ruination in South Carolina or Gardner's photographs of Richmond's Burnt District, circumstantial evidence suggests that such images circulated widely. Barnard and Gardner each sold affordable prints of individual photographs for home consumption. Both shot many of their Civil War photographs (including most of Gardner's Burnt District images and many of Barnard's photos of Charleston) in stereograph format.[16] Stereograph cameras took two nearly identical pictures at the same time. When seen through a special viewer—by the mid-1860s, a relatively common accessory in upper- and middle-class northern homes—the stereograph created the illusion of three dimensions. It is impossible to tell exactly how many northerners saw fit to purchase stereographs of southern ruins. Even so, thanks to Gardner and Barnard, ruins could quite literally be brought into northern homes.

While stereographs may have circulated widely, it is likely that a greater number of northerners encountered southern ruination through the more democratic means of the illustrated newspaper. The nation's major illustrated weeklies, *Harper's Weekly* and *Frank Leslie's Illustrated Weekly*, both gave pride of place to southern ruins. On the front page of its March 25, 1865 issue, *Leslie's* printed five engravings highlighting devastation in Charleston.[17] In April, the paper ran a pair of large images of Columbia, one depicting a panoramic view of the city before the fire, the other showing the devastation the morning after the conflagration.[18] The paper's June 24 issue featured a large image of the ruins of the Confederate arsenal in Richmond.[19] During the same period, *Harper's Weekly* featured scenes of destruction its illustrators found in Richmond, Columbia, Charleston, and Norfolk, Virginia.[20] The Charleston engraving, which filled a full page of the journal, was based on one of Barnard's more famous photographs. It features a man sitting on a pile of rubble, smoking a pipe. Behind him loom the city's famous ruins. The man's identity has been lost to history, but in his meditation on the ruins of Charleston, he can stand as a proxy for many a curious Yankee.

Ruins, in short, were everywhere. For much of 1865, the desolate South was a constant in northern print and visual culture. In newspapers, travel books, and memoirs, in photographs and illustrations, in thanksgiving sermons and political speeches, northern commentators were endlessly drawn to the imagery of southern ruination. This fascination had roots in any number of understandable impulses—the remnants of wartime jingoism; a voyeuristic interest in destruction and decay; a genuine concern for the plight of the South's homeless and poverty stricken. However, the sheer volume of commentary suggests that something greater was at work. Northern travelers were not just interested in the ruins themselves, but in the metaphorical value of those ruins. Simply put, ruins generated such extensive popular commentary because they proved intellectually useful. Ruins were potent cultural symbols, signifiers that pointed to issues much larger than themselves. In this guise, they proved invaluable in helping northerners conceptualize the character of the defeated South and articulate the challenges and possibilities of the postwar period.

RUIN AS METAPHOR: THREE APPROACHES

Like any other cultural symbol, ruins do not mean the same thing in all times and all places. Postwar ruin discourse was a reflection of its particular moment: the transition from civil war to an uneasy peace. Discussion of postwar southern ruination can be helpfully divided into three broad conceptual categories. Ruins, first of all, were frequently read as a justification of the northern cause. In southern ruination, Yankees found confirmation of their own righteousness, evidence of the superiority of their political structures and labor system, and, frequently, proof of divine favor in the war's outcome. The flip side to these notions, of course, was a conviction of southern guilt. In affirming the idea of a "guilty South," ruins ratified the results of the Civil War and affirmed the northern right—indeed, duty—to preside over the postwar re-creation of the South. Second, physical ruins were frequently assumed to be emblematic of an entire civilization in ruins. Northern commentators claimed that the Civil War had destroyed the political, economic, and social structures of the South just as surely as it had destroyed the region's homes and cities. The South was an empty vessel, a blank slate, a society that had ceased to be. Ruins provided the perfect metaphor for these claims, a vehicle through which to discuss the "end of the South." This framing fed naturally into a third face of postwar ruination: a notion that southern ruins spelled northern opportunity. If the South, as it had been, was no more, it fell to victorious Yankees to rebuild and reinvent the region. Northerners would reconstruct the South, and they would do so largely in the image of the North. Ruins, therefore, pointed to the promise of "the South reborn." Admittedly, these categories—the guilty South, the end of the South, the South reborn—were closely related, even mutually constitutive. When read together, however, they offer a useful guide to the contours of postwar ruin discourse.

The Guilty South

On the night of April 14, 1865, at a dinner in the Charleston Hotel, Judge Advocate General Joseph Holt stood to give a toast. Earlier that day, Holt and a crowd of dignitaries had gathered to witness the ceremonial return of the American flag to Fort Sumter. Though Holt insisted that he had never doubted "the final success of the Government in putting the accursed rebellion under its feet," the raising of the flag offered powerful confirmation of the righteousness of the Union cause. This, of course, was precisely the message that the carefully staged ceremony at Fort Sumter was designed to send. Significantly, however, Holt found a similar moral in a more unlikely place: the ruins of the Confederacy. Just as surely as the flag waving above Sumter, he claimed, "the ruined fortresses and devastated cities of the rebellion" provided evidence of the rectitude of the nation's struggle. The state of the South—"its palaces and homes in ashes, its people exhausted and impoverished"—seemed to Holt fitting comeuppance for slavery, treason, and war.[21] God had shown His favor in the outcome of the war. The raising of the American flag proved as much, but so did the devastated buildings and desolate streets of Charleston. Ruins, in this context, did not bespeak destruction, but justification.

Such sentiments were quite common in the immediate postwar period. In the ruins of the South, Northerners found confirmation of southern guilt and proof of their own virtue. The region's desolation, they argued, had less to do with Yankee shells than with the underlying wickedness of the southern cause. Assertions of southern barbarism had been common currency in the antebellum North.[22] For many commentators, postwar southern ruination retroactively affirmed such visions. Ruins became the best evidence of the failures of the South, physical confirmation of the region's long-term, deep-rooted malfeasance. At the same time, they offered proof of the superiority of northern society and the righteousness of the Union cause. Such a reading of southern ruination sent a powerful message about the postwar order. Inspired by residual wartime patriotism, and, in many cases, a belief in the active agency of God in worldly affairs, northern commentators read into southern ruins a moral and political mandate.

For this reason, commentators often treated southern ruins as a cause for celebration rather than mourning. In his 1865 memoir of Sherman's March, George Ward Nichols described the "terrible gladness" with which he watched the destruction of South Carolina. "Houses are burning, and South Carolina has commenced to pay an installment, long overdue, on her debt to justice and humanity," he wrote. "With the help of God, we will have principal and interest before we leave her borders."[23] South Carolina burned, but only because it deserved to burn. Sherman's ruins were the final settlement for generations of southern iniquity. Another veteran of Sherman's March declared, "with an approving nod," that the "widespread surrounding desolation" of the southern interior represented "the just fruits of treason and rebellion."[24] A poem published in *Harper's Weekly*, simply titled "South Carolina, 1865," made a similar point. The poem opened with an image of a ruined state:

> Behold her now, with restless, flashing eyes,
> Crouching, a thing forlorn, beside the way!
> Behold her ruined altars heaped to-day
> With ashes of her costly sacrifice!

Finding a subtle self-satisfaction—even a touch of glee—in the misfortune of South Carolina, the poet measured the Union's victory by the ruin of the South. The state's devastation was evidence of "righteous retribution, great and just!"[25] There was more than Schadenfreude at work here. Commentators insisted on a direct causal link between southern conduct and the war's terrible consequences. The South was in ruins because it had been unjust, unrighteous, and cruel.

Such arguments were frequently couched in religious terms. The Civil War and its aftermath proved profoundly spiritual experiences for many Americans.[26] The direct involvement of God in the course of the war was widely assumed, and clergy on both sides sought and claimed divine favor throughout the conflict. After the war, northern ministers joined secular commentators in their embrace of the explanatory power of ruins. Southern ruination, they argued, offered confirmation that God favored the Union cause. The plight of the South reminded a Massachusetts clergyman named Robert C. Mills of the curse of Pharaoh, whose "hardened heart" assured his downfall. "As we look on the desolate and vanquished Southern States," Mills declared, "it does now seem as if they had been hardened to pursue the course of self-destruction." It was the South's dangerous and foolish course that had brought about its "own complete ruin."[27] The Presbyterian pastor W. S. Leavitt told his parishioners that the government of God "is just in its retributions." The devastation that gripped the South was fit punishment for slavery, secession, and war. "When a guilty people brings upon itself the desolations of war," Leavitt said, "and for its sins the land is laid waste, — its cities burned and captured, — its inhabitants plunged into poverty and wretchedness," the faithful would find proof of God's awful power, but also His enduring justice.[28] Reverend William W. Patton wrote that Charleston's "blackened ruins testified as mute witnesses to the retributive justice of God." Such desolation, however, caused him neither worry nor concern for the well-being of his fellow man. Instead, Patton saw the hand of a righteous and all-powerful God. Ruins, in fact, prompted him to recall the words of a patriotic (and religious) anthem: "Mine eyes have seen the glory of the coming of the Lord."[29]

By its very nature, a ruin exists simultaneously in the past and the present tense. The ruin itself confronts the viewer in the here and now, but it simultaneously conjures images of its earlier appearance and function. As the historian Megan Kate Nelson puts it, "the rubble simultaneously suggests what is and what was, referencing the absence of the whole (past) in its piles of fragments (present)."[30] Northern commentators made frequent use of this duality, ascribing meaning to southern ruins with explicit reference to the structure's previous usage. Such juxtapositions naturalized the devastation of the Civil War, suggesting that ruination was the necessary and wholly deserved result of a structure's past iniquity. More than this, they made a powerful claim about the character of the South and the future course of the sectional relationship.

A correspondent for the *Christian Recorder*, an African American newspaper based in Philadelphia, found Richmond's Burnt District to be a "ghastly sight." It was not the ruins themselves that troubled him, however, but their connection to the city's violent past. "The ghost of Richmond 1860," he mused, "the ghost of slavery, that hydra-headed monster, the father of all evil," was etched into the ruins.[31] Other commentators betrayed no squeamishness when confronting southern ruins. In fact, many considered ruin to be a positive good, preferable to what had come before. Passing an abandoned plantation, another *Christian Recorder* correspondent found surprising beauty in its "desolation," due to the fact that "the stately dwelling will no more be inhabited by its cruel owners, nor the blood of poor slaves dampen its soil."[32] In Salisbury, North Carolina, at the site of a Confederate military prison destroyed by George Stoneman's cavalry, the travel writer Sidney Andrews spoke with a black man who offered his own take on the transformative power of ruination. "Does ye call dis yer hor'ble?'" the man asked Andrews. "I calls it beautiful since Stoneman polished it up."[33] Because ruins naturally recalled that which had come before, it proved extraordinarily easy to read causation into destruction. Past misdeeds explained present ruination. The ruined South was the guilty South.

Though Yankees found validation in devastation throughout the region, the ruins of Charleston proved especially compelling. Indeed, northern travelers could not help but revel in the desolation they found there. "Charleston is a doomed city," wrote an early correspondent. "The haughty populace that taught the South to rebel, and defied the national government by the first appeal to arms, lie[s] prostrate in the dust. Desolating fires have swept away her finest structures, hostile shells have torn up her streets and battered down her dwellings." The city, he predicted with savage delight, "will decline into ruin, unhonored, unpitied."[34] Admittedly, the ruin in Charleston was extensive, but this only partially explains the volume of commentary it generated. Postwar northerners found the city's desolation to be both richly deserved and deeply poetic. Calling Charleston "the most blasted, blighted, broken-hearted desolation on this continent," the *New York Evangelist* insisted that the devastation was "not one whit more than her stupendous sin has richly deserved."[35] The fate of Charleston, concluded A. O. Abbott, who spent time in the city as a Union prisoner of war, was "but *justice* to this city of sin."[36]

While commentators discussed ruination in Charleston with unparalleled frequency and unmitigated ferocity, their treatment of the city was not out of keeping with larger trends. The difference was one of degree, rather than kind. The arguments that northerners made about Charleston—that the city had brought devastation upon itself, that its ruins offered final proof of southern wickedness and northern righteousness—were precisely the arguments that they made about the South as a whole. Ruins, in Charleston and elsewhere, reaffirmed and naturalized the long-lasting differences between North and South. Northern discussions of the desolate South tended to encourage regional chauvinism and self-satisfaction. Ruin discourse turned the Civil War into a morality tale, confirming the superiority of northern culture and offering a rationale for the spread of that culture into the postwar South. This was clearly an oversimplification of an extraordinarily complex social, economic, and political moment. Such visions, however, were written into the ruins of the South.

The End of the South

With some regularity, northern travelers evoked the ruins of ancient civilizations in an attempt to come to terms with what they found in the South. "Not Pompeii nor Herculaneum, nor Thebes nor the Nile have ruins so complete, so saddening, so plaintively eloquent," a *New York Tribune* correspondent wrote of Charleston. The city was "dead, dead, dead, as silent as the grave of the Pharaohs, as deserted as the bazaars of the merchant princes of Old Tyre."[37] When David Conyngham gazed on the remains of Columbia, he was reminded of "the ruins of Pompeii and Herculaneum."[38] A short ride through Charleston made Henry Ward Beecher, the most influential clergyman of the era, feel "as though I was a pilgrim in some Oriental city—in some city like Tadmor or Palmyra of the desert—rather than in one of the cities of my own native land."[39]

It may be that travelers who conjured ancient ruins were simply searching for a convenient comparison by which to make real the devastation they found in the South. These associations, however, were hardly value neutral. Linking the postwar South to the ruins of Pompeii or Palmyra made a powerful statement about the past and future of the region. Such comparisons reflect a tendency among northern commentators to move from a discussion of actual, physical ruins to a larger discussion of a *society* in ruins. Southern ruin, northern travelers insisted, went deeper than the region's buildings and homes. An entire way of life had been destroyed. The society of Charleston in 1860 had vanished just as surely as had Pompeii's. The South, as it had been, was gone. What remained was a ruin, the shell of what once was. In gazing on southern ruins, Yankees saw more than the remnants of a house, an office, or a plantation. They saw the end of the South.

In the photographs of Barnard and Gardner, physical devastation

Figure 4.2 Alexander Gardner's photograph of Richmond, Virginia, 1865
(Library of Congress)

seemed to herald larger ruptures in southern life. Barnard's images of
Charleston functioned largely through familiarity. The sites of ruin that
he captured in the city—Fort Sumter, St. Philip's Church, Secession
Hall—would have been recognizable to northern viewers, if not by sight
then certainly by name. In demonstrating the decay into which the war
had thrown these emblems of the slave South, Barnard dramatized the
changes wrought by the war. The hotbed of southern radicalism, the home
base of the Slave Power, had fallen. Barnard's images of the burned-out
capitol building in Columbia, South Carolina, carried a similar message.
Gardner's photographs of Richmond's Burnt District functioned a bit differently. In contrast to Charleston, Richmond's most significant structures
largely escaped destruction. The gutted warehouses that populate Gardner's Richmond photographs are noteworthy for their lack of specificity.
Indeed, the photographs could have been taken anywhere. Gardner captures a barren, almost alien landscape. Hulking skeletons of once-proud
buildings loom over ash-lined streets. Empty windows stare blindly onto

massive piles of rubble. A haphazard assortment of chimneys and wall fragments point skyward. One shell of a building is almost indistinguishable from the next, denying the viewer any sense of their shape or function before the fire. Without Gardner's explanatory captions, viewers would have been hard-pressed to identify the locale as Richmond. Robbed of all identifying features, the capital of the Confederacy had been reduced to a generic ruin. Such images bespoke a single hard truth: the South, as it had been, was gone forever.

Northern travel writers employed similar practices in their discussions of southern ruins. Though they commented widely on all the city's sites of ruination, postwar travelers to Charleston were particularly drawn to the burial grounds of John C. Calhoun. "Down in the churchyard of St. Philip's," Sidney Andrews wrote, "is a grave which every stranger is curious to see. It is the grave of the father of the Rebellion, and on the marble slab there is cut the one word, — 'CALHOUN.'" The churchyard, like the city of Charleston, had seen better days: "Children and goats crawl through a convenient hole in the front wall, and play at will among the sunken graves and broken tombstones. There is everywhere a wealth of offal and garbage and beef-bones. A mangy cur was slinking among the stones, and I found a hole three feet deep which he had dug at the foot of one of the graves." Scavengers had even broken off pieces of the great statesman's grave for keepsakes. "Time was when South Carolina guarded this grave as a holy spot," Andrews concluded. "Now it lies in ruin with her chief city."[40] Andrews could not ignore the symbolic value of the scene. Calhoun's burial site lay damaged and desecrated. The grave — once a revered monument to the intellectual champion of slavery and states' rights — lay in ruin. So did the society that Calhoun had loved and defended to his last day. Other travelers found similar meaning in the ruins of Calhoun's burial site. When a group of northern preachers and abolitionists visited Calhoun's grave, one wondered, "Did none of the bones in that sepulchre *rattle* when the voice of William Lloyd Garrison was heard at the grave's mouth?"[41] For the Union general Carl Schurz, the sound of a group of black children singing "John Brown's Body" within earshot of the ruined grave perfectly encapsulated the revolution that had taken place.[42] Calhoun's South was dead and gone, never to return.

In their zeal to record the new dispensation in the South, travelers eagerly sought evidence of slavery's destruction. As often as not, they found it in the ruins of physical structures once associated with the peculiar institution. Henry McNeal Turner, an army chaplain to the United States Colored Troops and a *Christian Recorder* correspondent, offered a vivid description of the fate of one South Carolina plantation. The plantation owner, a "mean old wretch" named Herron, had been notoriously cruel to his three hundred slaves. When Turner's regiment passed the plantation, the black soldiers in blue exacted revenge. "They gutted his mansion of some of the finest furniture in the world. With an axe they shattered his piano, bureaus, side-boards, tore his fine carpet to pieces, and gave what they did not destroy to his slaves," Turner wrote. "And on his speaking rather saucily to one of the boys, he was sent headlong to the floor by a blow across the mouth, his downward tendency being materially accelerated by an application of boot-leather to his 'latter end.'"[43] For Herron, the world had quite literally been turned upside down, but the ruins of his plantation empire simply mirrored the larger fate of the slave South. Another writer described a similar reversal of fortune he had witnessed amid the ruined mansions of Charleston, marveling that while "the grandees" had been forced to flee "penniless and ruined into the interior," their former slaves, "now 'free as I am,' nestle in the ancient homes, and hold their fantastic jubilees in the self-same halls, which once echoed to their oppressor's revels."[44] The physical damage done by northern shells was but a reflection of a deeper sort of ruination. The system of slavery—the lifeblood of the antebellum South—appeared to be the greatest ruin of all.

In a similar vein, northern travelers indulged in extended descriptions of the ruin into which the antebellum South's economic and cultural elite—the much maligned "aristocracy"—had fallen. Like their homes, businesses, and plantations, this elite class was a mere shell of its former self, the trappings of its power and prestige having fallen victim to Yankee shells and soldiers. The travel writer Whitelaw Reid sketched the domestic ruin that had beset the first families of Mobile, Alabama. "Mobile houses showed the straits to which the people had been reduced," Reid wrote. "The pianos all jangled, and the legs of parlor chairs were out of tune quite as badly. Sofas had grown dangerous places for any but the most slow-motioned and sedate. . . . The glories of fine window-curtains had departed. Carpets had in many cases gone for army blankets." Worst of all, Reid joked, Mobile's elite now had to take their champagne "in plain tumblers."[45] David Conyngham offered a more poignant image of an aristocracy in ruin. In the streets of Columbia, Conyngham "saw a lady richly dressed, with three pretty little children clinging to her. She was sitting on a mattress, while round her were strewn some rich paintings." He concluded: "It was a picture of hopeless misery surrounded by the trappings of refined taste and wealth."[46] The war had destroyed a way of life. What remained was a ruin, a pale shadow of what had come before.

The "end of the South" framing also proved particularly useful when travelers considered the human toll of the war.[47] Travel writers and journalists described a southern white population decimated after four years of conflict. "The white population of the Southern States, never as dense as that of the North, has been greatly diminished in consequence of the war," the journalist Thomas Wallace Knox wrote. "In many localities more than half the able-bodied male inhabitants have been swept away, and everywhere the loss of men is severely felt."[48] In South Carolina, Sidney Andrews noted that "one marks now how few young men there are, how generally the young women are dressed in black. The flower of their proud aristocracy is buried on scores of battle-fields."[49] In a May 1865 article fittingly titled "Desolation," the *New York Tribune* offered a stark summation of the human ruins of the South. "Persons who have recently passed through the accessible portions of the Atlantic Slave States report a frightful scarcity of able-bodied males," the paper reported. "A few old men; a few cripples; not many boys able to shoulder a musket, with a sad abundance of widows, and orphans, ill clad, coarsely and scantily fed, woe-begone, shoeless."[50] Beyond burnt buildings and cities, Southern ruination could be measured in broken families, empty chairs, and disfigured countenances. The population of the former Confederacy perfectly matched its landscape. The ravages of war had robbed the region of its youth and its strength, leaving a population that was a mere shadow of its former self.

During his southern travels, Whitelaw Reid encountered human ruins of a different sort. In Key West, Florida, Reid spoke with a black man named Sandie Cornish, and was sufficiently interested in Cornish's tale to reproduce it at some length in his travelogue. Born a slave in Maryland, Cornish had purchased his freedom and settled in Key West in the late antebellum period. When a gang of slave traders attempted to kidnap and reenslave him, Cornish took drastic action. In Key West's main square, Cornish severed his own Achilles tendon, cut off the fingers of his left hand, plunged a knife deep into his hip, and then dared the astonished crowd to try to sell a free man into slavery. By the time Reid encountered him, Cornish had recovered from his injuries and established himself as an independent farmer and "one of the wealthiest and one of the most respected citizens of Key West."[51] Reid noted, moreover, that Cornish frequently told his story and proudly displayed his scars to visitors and guests. In so doing, Cornish made a powerful claim regarding the nature of slavery. He was the physical embodiment of the South's slave past, his own physical ruination perfectly matching the larger devastation wrought by the peculiar institution. Significantly, however, Cornish's story also pointed the way to a brighter future. His body was in ruins, but Sandie Cornish was free. Out of the ruins of slavery, a new South might yet grow.

As they toured the ruins of the postwar South, northern travelers found evidence of radical changes in southern life. The ruins of southern cities and homes seemed to reflect an absolute break with the southern past—the end of the South. It was here that northern commentators located both the challenge and the promise facing the nation. It would be relatively easy to rebuild cities and buildings. But these were simply the outward trappings of southern society. The changes in the region must be—like its ruins—deeper than this. The postwar period would replace the ruins of southern society with something new, something better. It was a matter of construction, not just reconstruction; the process must be transformative, not simply restorative. Convinced that the war had laid bare the ruined foundations of southern civilization, northerners would build anew.

The South Reborn

In his study of U.S. responses to disaster, *The Culture of Calamity*, the historian Kevin Rozario argues that catastrophe has frequently been seen as an opportunity for improvement, advancement, and change. Throughout most of the nation's history, in fact, disaster has been viewed as productive, helpful, even necessary.[52] Though Rozario does not address the Civil War, his claims regarding devastation and opportunity nicely frame a central element of postwar ruin discourse. On their face, ruins appeared to signify only emptiness and desolation, but they also carried a deeper meaning. Ruins symbolized opportunity. Southern desolation presented northerners with a chance to recreate the South, and by extension, the nation. As they emphasized the untold devastation and destruction that the war had caused, northerners recognized that destruction brought with it the possibility of change. Ruins held the promise of a new and reformed South.

For this reason, vistas of southern ruination stimulated a remarkable degree of optimism. Despite the almost endless stream of despair, damage, and devastation they reported, travelers remained surprisingly, even discomfortingly, upbeat. Ruins invited northerners to imagine a new South. The Civil War had wiped away the remnants of a debauched civilization. Now they would build anew. Of course, such thinking did not constitute an actual plan or program. The travelers' forecasts were often thin on specifics, and the actual steps by which the ruined South would be reborn remained stubbornly opaque. Even so, the sense of radical possibility that ruin discourse inspired should be recognized as a significant part of the intellectual apparatus with which the nation entered the postwar moment. Looking out on the ruins of 1865, anything seemed possible.

In a speech in Somerville, Massachusetts, dedicated to "The Condition and Prospects of the South," Reverend Charles Lowe nicely summarized this sense of optimism. During his travels in early 1865, Lowe found "mingled features of prostration and promise" in the South. Lowe recognized the scope of the physical destruction and economic distress in the region, but he saw opportunity in precisely this devastation. "The promise," he explained, "is almost wholly because of the prostration, and the greatest hope for the future is from the completeness with which the old has been overthrown."[53] Lowe's logic here was willfully counterintuitive, but it reflects larger trends in postwar northern thought. In ruins lay possibility. Had the ruins been less complete, had more traces of the old ways survived the war, there would have been cause for concern. Because the devastation was so total, however, Lowe could express confidence in the South's eminent recovery and regeneration.

In his oration at the flag-raising ceremony at Fort Sumter, Henry Ward Beecher likewise promised that southern ruination would prove salutary. Reflecting familiar notions of the guilty South, Beecher argued that the war had destroyed a diseased social order rooted in treason and slavery. "Society here is like a broken loom," he told the crowd, "and the piece which rebellion put in, and was weaving, has been cut, and every thread broken."[54] The re-creation of southern civilization—replacing the fabric of its society with something more just and beautiful—was the work now confronting the nation. Beecher was confident that "there is a good day coming for the South." This bright future, however, was possible only because southern ruin was so all encompassing. "Her institutions before were deadly; she nourished death in her bosom; the greater her secular prosperity, the more sure was her ruin," Beecher claimed. "Now, by an earthquake, the evil is shaken down; and her own historians, in a better day, shall write, that from the day the sword cut off the cancer, she began to find her health."[55] The South's prostration, Beecher insisted, actually gave cause for hope. A new South would spring from the ground prepared by the ruin of the old.

Significantly, these commentators assumed that northerners would drive the South's recovery. Implicit in much discussion of southern ruination was a deeply held conviction that the ruined South could only be reconstructed by northerners and along northern lines. Ruin discourse depicted the South as a landscape almost entirely lacking in people. Gardner's images of Richmond's Burnt District offer a case in point. Most of Gardner's ruin photographs do not contain people. When human figures do appear, they tend to be distant, out of focus, of secondary importance. Gardner's subject is the empty, desolate, vacant landscape of the South. Travel writers and correspondents followed suit. The actual residents of the South were relegated to the background, becoming a part of the ruin, local color used to round out the atmosphere of desolation: Confederate widows in mourning black; a mother huddling with her children in the street; a former slave occupying the crumbling dwelling of his old master. In their discussion of ruins, northern commentators largely ignored the possibility of active southern involvement (or interference) in the rebuilding process. As they insisted that there was no South, northern travelers were actually announcing their intention to reinvent the region in their own image.

Postwar commentators put great faith in the ability of northern immigrants to rebuild and reconstruct the ruined South. When Sidney Andrews arrived in Charleston, he found the city damaged almost beyond recognition. He offered a stark prediction. "If Northern capital and Northern energy do not come here, the ruin, they say, must remain a ruin," Andrews claimed, "and if this time five years finds here a handsome and thriving city; it will be the creation of New England."[56] Carl Schurz offered a similar prediction about the same city. "It will require a long time to restore the former prosperity of this place unless Northern capital and Northern enterprises step in," he wrote in the *Boston Daily Advertiser*. "The Yankee has to invade this country again, a peaceable invader, to clear away the rubbish and to reopen the avenues of wealth." Charleston, he concluded, was poised to become a "Yankee city."[57]

If one started from the premise that the South was empty, it was a small step to imagine northern migrants filling the void. In early 1865, the *New York Times* called for an infusion of northern capital and ingenuity. "It is hardly possible to overestimate the results which will be produced in the rich cotton and rice fields of South Carolina and Georgia, and the river bottoms of Mississippi and Louisiana," the paper wrote, "by the application to them of the skill, energy, enterprise and industry which have made the stony hills of Massachusetts bloom like a garden, and converted the storm-driven plains of the Norwest into the granaries of the world."[58] The *Boston Herald* agreed. "A southward movement of our population has been going on for the last four years, but the emigrants have carried muskets and cannons," the paper noted. "The next southward movement will be of a different character—the emigrants will carry the arts and machinery of peaceful industry, and will go to make homes in the fertile regions restored to the Union and to law, and to invigorate the slip shod society of the South with the spirit of free and educated labor."[59] The conviction that the South was in ruins carried with it a northern obligation to repair its waste places. Northern migrants would rebuild and restore the ruined South.

As northerners looked South in 1865, therefore, they saw destruction and desolation, but they also saw opportunity. In emphasizing southern ruination, Yankee travelers were also looking to the future. Out of ruins would spring a renewed and revivified South. The region became a blank slate, a screen on which northerners could imagine a rejuvenated and perfected union. The South had long been a problem in American life. The postwar period offered an unprecedented opportunity to recreate the region from the ground up. Out of ruins would spring a renewed, revivified, and *northernized* South.[60]

THE RUINS OF HISTORY

Despite its popularity, northern engagement with the ruined South was fleeting. By the end of 1865, northern interest in southern ruins had faded, as had the particular vision of the South that ruin discourse bred. In part, this was simply due to overexposure and waning novelty. At a certain point, southern ruins ceased to be surprising or noteworthy. In addition, the literal reconstruction of southern towns and cities made ruins a less visible part of the landscape. However, troubling changes within the South played a role as well. By the end of 1865, the self-congratulations and naive optimism that underlay much popular discussion of ruins appeared untenable. In the face of near constant white-on-black violence, the passage of harshly discriminatory Black Codes across the South, and the electoral victories of Confederate sympathizers and veterans, the notion of an "empty" or "ruined" South began to seem misguided, problematic, even dangerous. As Luke Harlow's essay in this volume demonstrates, southern white elites had not resigned themselves to ruination and northernization—far from it. In the final analysis, the postwar discussion of southern ruins had more to do with northern predilections and preconceptions than it did with southern reality. Though it had helped northerners think through the sectional relationship in the immediate postwar moment, the idea of a ruined South quickly outlived its usefulness.

Of course, some commentators had never been comfortable with the facile notion that a ruined South awaited only the rejuvenating touch of northern culture. In January of 1865, the abolitionist and African American leader Frederick Douglass predicted that a "rank undergrowth of treason" would remain in the South long after the close of the Civil War. Southern whites would continue "interfering with and thwarting the quiet operation of the Federal Government in those States," Douglass told a Boston audience. "You will see those traitors handing down from sire to son the same malignant spirit which they have manifested and which they are now exhibiting . . . that spirit will still remain; and whoever sees the Federal Government extended over those Southern States will see that government in a strange land and not only in a strange land but in an enemy's land."[61] Such a vision directly contradicted the most basic assumptions built into the discourse of the ruined South. Douglass pointed to an obvious fact, one that popular discussion of southern ruination largely overlooked: the South was *not empty*. While northerners painted the South as a blank slate and vacuum waiting to be filled with northern ideas and idealism, an embittered southern white population had other intentions.

Even those northerners who did embrace the explanatory power of southern ruins had begun to change their tune by late 1865 or early 1866. By the end of their respective southern tours, Sidney Andrews and Whitelaw Reid had each grown noticeably pessimistic. Both travel writers recognized a hardening of attitudes among white southerners, and both began to doubt the malleability of southern institutions. Looking back on his trip, Reid could make out a fleeting moment of possibility. In May and June of 1865, Reid claimed, the white South had been ready to accept whatever conditions the government laid out. "They expected nothing; were prepared for the worst; would have been thankful for anything," he wrote. "They were defeated and helpless—they submitted." By the end of Reid's travels, however, rebellious intransigence had largely replaced ruined submission.[62] Andrews likewise admitted that his early optimism had been misplaced. "Possibly we were wrong to hope that one season could sow the grain of reconstruction and gather its fruitage of good order and fair respect for human rights," he wrote. "At least this season has not done that."[63] In their focus on ruins, northern travelers had fundamentally misinterpreted the state of the South and the determination of its white residents. The postwar period would be more difficult, more dangerous, and more divisive than they could have imagined.

A central theme of this volume is the relationship between change and continuity in the world the Civil War made. Ruins (and postwar ruin discourse) speak directly to this matter, for ruins embody, at a fundamental level, *both* continuity and change. Postwar ruin enthusiasts, however, failed to account for this dual character. Emphasizing transformation and novelty, they overlooked the persistence of prewar behaviors, ideologies, and social structures. Indeed, ruin discourse had little to say about entrenched patterns of race-based political and economic inequality in the South. It also neglected to address the limits of northern popular will or the inadequacies of the U.S. government's "Stockade State." Ruin discourse promised a rebuilding process that was simple, natural, automatic, and largely uncontested. The guilty South had brought ruination on itself; a debauched slaveholding society had been washed away; it now fell to the superior culture of the victorious North to repair, enliven, and reform the ruined region. Such a narrative had an undeniable appeal to a war-weary population, but northerners would have done well to look a bit more closely at the ruins they described. If they had, perhaps they would have been better prepared to grapple with the challenge of rebuilding the postwar South. For a ruin may promise growth and development, but it simultaneously contains the remnants of what has come before. Change, in other words, coexists with continuity. Optimistic—even certain—that a new South would emerge from the ruins of the war, many northern commentators failed to recognize the stubborn tenacity of the past. In our own work on the postwar era, historians would do well to remember this lesson.

NOTES

1. See Alan Trachtenberg, *Reading American Photographs: Images as History, Mathew Brady to Walker Evans* (New York: Hill and Wang, 1989), 93–111.

2. On the cultural and intellectual history of Civil War ruins, see Megan Kate Nelson, *Ruin Nation: Destruction and the American Civil War* (Athens: University of Georgia Press, 2012).

3. Michael S. Roth, et al., *Irresistible Decay: Ruins Reclaimed* (Los Angeles: Getty Research Institute, 1997), 1. See also Michel Makarius, *Ruins* (Paris: Flammarion, 2004); Julia Hell and Andreas Schönle, eds. *Ruins of Modernity* (Durham: Duke University Press, 2010); Christopher Woodward, *In Ruins* (New York: Pantheon, 2001).

4. "Sherman's March," *Chicago Tribune*, November 24, 1864, 3.

5. "The Devastation at Atlanta," *Hartford Daily Courant*, November 26, 1864, 1. See William A. Link, *Atlanta, Cradle of the New South: Race and Remembering in the Civil War's Aftermath* (Chapel Hill: University of North Carolina Press, 2013), 33–60; Anne Sarah Rubin, *Through the Heart of Dixie: Sherman's March and American Memory* (Chapel Hill: University of North Carolina Press, 2014).

6. "Account by Our Special Correspondent," *New York Tribune*, March 2, 1865, 1.

7. Sidney Andrews, *The South since the War* (Boston: Ticknor and Fields, 1866), 1.

8. D. P. Conyngham, "Sherman," *New York Herald*, March 20, 1865, 1.

9. "The Capture of Richmond," *Liberator*, April 14, 1865, 59.

10. "Richmond after Evacuation," *Boston Herald*, April 10, 1865, 4.

11. "The Victory," *New York Times*, April 10, 1865, 1.

12. "Destitution of the South," *Liberator*, September 15, 1865, 1.

13. Whitelaw Reid, *After the War: A Tour of the Southern States* (1865; New York: Harper Torchbooks, 1965), 384.

14. Ibid., 351.

15. Ibid., 292.

16. *Catalogue of Photographic Incidents of the War, from the Gallery of Alexander Gardner* (Washington, D.C.: H. Polkinhorn, 1863), 3.

17. "Charleston—Five Sketches," *Frank Leslie's Illustrated Newspaper*, March 25, 1865, 1.

18. "Columbia—Two Sketches," *Frank Leslie's Illustrated Newspaper*, April 8, 1865, 40.

19. "Ruins of the Confederate Arsenal, Richmond," *Frank Leslie's Illustrated Newspaper*, June 24, 1865, 220.

20. "Ruins on Main Street, Richmond," *Harper's Weekly*, April 22, 1865, 252; "Ruins of the Norfolk Navy-Yard," *Harper's Weekly*, April 8, 1865; "Scenes in Columbia, South Carolina, the Morning after the Fire," *Harper's Weekly*, April 1, 1865, 200–201; "Ruins in the Heart of Charleston," *Harper's Weekly*, July 8, 1865, 428.

21. Joseph Holt, *Remarks of Hon. J. Holt at a Dinner in Charleston, South Carolina on Evening of April 14, 1865* (Washington, D.C.: Gibson Brothers, 1865), 4.

22. See Susan-Mary Grant, *North Over South: Northern Nationalism and American Identity in the Antebellum Era* (Lawrence: University of Kansas Press, 2000).

23. Quoted in A. H. Guernsey, "Sherman's Great March," *Harper's New Monthly Magazine*, October 1865, 579.

24. George Sharland, *Knapsack Notes of Gen. Sherman's Grand Campaign through the Empire State of the South* (Springfield, Ill.: Jackson and Bradford, 1865), 6.

25. "South Carolina, 1865," *Harper's Weekly*, March 18, 1865.

26. Mark A. Noll, *The Civil War as a Theological Crisis* (Chapel Hill: University of North Carolina Press, 2006); George C. Rable, *God's Almost Chosen Peoples: A Religious History of the American Civil War* (Chapel Hill: University of North Carolina Press, 2010); Daniel W. Stowell, *Rebuilding Zion: The Religious Reconstruction of the South, 1863–1877* (New York: Oxford University Press, 1998).

27. Robert C. Mills, *The Southern States Hardened Until Ruined: A Sermon Preached in Salem on Fast Day, April 13, 1865* (Boston: J. M. Hewes, 1865).

28. W. S. Leavitt, *A Sermon, Preached April 9, 1865, the Sunday after the Capture of Richmond* (Hudson: Bryan and Webb, 1865), 9.

29. W[illia]m W. Patton, "In Richmond," *Chicago Tribune*, April 20, 1865, 2.

30. Nelson, *Ruin Nation*, 22.

31. "Letter from Richmond," *Christian Recorder*, October 28, 1865, 169.

32. "Letter from South Carolina," *Christian Recorder*, February 25, 1865. 30.

33. Andrews, *South since the War*, 105.

34. "Evacuation of Charleston," *Hartford Daily Courant*, February 21, 1865, 2.

35. "A Trip to Fort Sumter, and the Doomed City," *New York Evangelist*, April 27, 1865, 1.

36. A. O. Abbott, *Prison life in the South* (New York: Harper, 1865), 109.

37. "Account by Our Special Correspondent," *New York Daily Tribune*, March 2, 1865, 1.

38. David P. Conyngham, *Sherman's March through the South* (New York: Sheldon, 1865), 333.

39. Henry Ward Beecher, "Narrative of His Trip to South Carolina," *Independent*, May 11, 1865, 2.

40. Andrews, *South since the War*, 10.

41. T. L., "A Trip to Fort Sumter and the Doomed City," *New York Evangelist*, April 27, 1865, 1.

42. [Carl Schurz], "Letters from the South," *Boston Daily Advertiser*, July 21, 1865, 2.

43. "Army Correspondence by Chaplain Turner," *Christian Recorder*, April 15, 1865, 57.

44. *Trip of the Steamer Oceanus to Fort Sumter and Charleston, SC* (Brooklyn, N.Y.: "The Union" Steam Printing House, 1865), 40.

45. Reid, *After the War*, 219.

46. Conyngham, *Sherman's March*, 333.

47. On human ruins, see Nelson, *Ruin Nation*, 160–227. See also Drew Gilpin Faust, *This Republic of Suffering: Death and the American Civil War* (New York: Vintage Books, 2009); Mark S. Schantz, *Awaiting the Heavenly Country: The Civil War and America's Culture of Death* (Ithaca: Cornell University Press, 2008).

48. Thomas Wallace Knox, *Camp-Fire and Cotton-Field: Southern Adventure in Time of War* (New York: Blelock, 1865), 493.

49. Andrews, *South since the War*, 2.

50. "Desolation," *New York Tribune*, May 4, 1865, 4.

51. Reid, *After the War*, 183–87, 189–93, quote on 189.

52. Kevin Rozario, *The Culture of Calamity: Disaster and the Making of Modern America* (Chicago: University of Chicago Press, 2007). See also Nick Yablon, *Untimely Ruins: An Archaeology of American Urban Modernity, 1819–1919* (Chicago: University of Chicago Press, 2009).

53. Charles Lowe, *The Condition and Prospects of the South: A Discourse Delivered in Somerville, Mass, June 4, 1865* (Boston: Walker, Fuller, 1865), 7.

54. Henry Ward Beecher, *Oration at the Raising of 'The Old Flag' at Fort Sumter, and Sermon on the Death of Abraham Lincoln, President of the United States* (Manchester, UK: Alexander Ireland, 1865), 18.

55. Ibid., 31.

56. Andrews, *South since the War*, 2.

57. [Carl Schurz], "Letters from the South," 2.

58. "The Resurrection of the South," *New York Times*, January 20, 1865, 4.

59. "A Southward Movement," *Boston Herald*, May 3, 1865, 4.

60. Richard N. Current, *Northernizing the South* (Athens: University of Georgia Press, 1983).

61. John W. Blassingame and John R. McKivingan, eds., *The Frederick Douglass Papers*, ser. 1, vol. 4 (New Haven: Yale University Press, 1997), 64.

62. Reid, *After the War*, 295–97.

63. Andrews, *South since the War*, 384.

5

THE LONG LIFE OF PROSLAVERY RELIGION

Luke E. Harlow

Historians know well the central role proslavery religion played in the antebellum white South. American Protestantism faced an intractable crisis over slavery before the Civil War, and the United States' three largest antebellum religious denominations — Methodists, Baptists, and Presbyterians — suffered schisms into northern and southern branches over the slavery question. The South's white Protestants grounded their argument in a conservative reading of the Bible that demonstrated unequivocally that their Triune God of Grace sanctioned the right of white masters to own black slaves. Breaking from northern Protestants strengthened the voice of the white southerners on slavery, and proslavery theology became the critical ideological building block in the making of southern sectionalism and, ultimately, the Confederacy.[1]

The Confederate political project ended in defeat, but that did not mean the defeat of proslavery theology. White Protestants throughout the once-slaveholding South made that argument long after slavery's demise. As a widely circulated official statement from southern Presbyterians put it boldly in 1871:

> The dogma which denies the lawfulness of [slavery] under any circumstances; which condemns it as always contrary to the Divine will; which asserts its inherent sinfulness, is completely contradicted by the plainest facts and teachings of the Old Testament and New; is a doctrine unknown to the Church until recent times; is a pernicious heresy, embracing a principle not only infidel and fanatical, but subversive of every relation of life, and every civil government on earth.[2]

This was not merely a conservative white supremacist statement, pining for a bygone slaveholding era. Their denomination had come into existence in December 1861 as the Presbyterian Church in the Confederate States of America, founded on a proslavery platform. But here a decade later these southern Presbyterians expressly denied "that it was the duty of the Church to *perpetuate* the institution of slavery." Instead, they rejected the approach of their northern counterparts' theology on the issue. They claimed they defended slavery not for slavery's sake, but because the Christian God had sanctioned it in Holy Scripture. To take issue with that God was to take issue with the right order of things.[3]

Such bold and defiant rhetoric, several years after the end of American slavery, calls us to consider cultural continuities that spanned the era of the American Civil War. It forces us to reevaluate what the Civil War accomplished and, furthermore, what was possible after the fact. To say that the ideas that drove the Confederacy survived the Civil War is to question our collective confidence in the power of formal politics, as well as our faith in the force of military might to reshape cultures.

To raise questions about cultural continuity during the Civil War era does not mean that the conflict was unnecessary or pointless. But it does suggest that for all the war accomplished, it did not wipe clean the cultural slate. In the war's aftermath many northern leaders looked on the South, as Stephen Prince's essay in this volume shows, as a ruined region ready for remaking in the image of the North. But that ambition ran headlong into manifest white southern resistance—often in the form of violent intimidation directed at those who preached an emancipatory gospel, whether northern whites or freedpeople.[4]

Historians generally agree in calling the white southern opposition to the post–Civil War expansion of civil and voting rights to freedpeople a "counterrevolution." Yet much disagreement persists about where the white southern counterrevolution came from—especially its causes, and relatedly, its timing. Attention to religion, however, can clarify much in this debate. With as much as 40 percent of the United States' population affiliated with evangelical Protestantism on the eve of the Civil War, evangelical churches were the most politically significant voluntary organizations everywhere in mid-nineteenth-century America, but their influence was particularly outsized in the South.[5] Furthermore, in a United States that guaranteed the state's noninterference with matters of church, no mechanisms existed to compel proslavery believers to change their minds, no matter how many laws might change. White southern churches, in short, were intentionally protected spaces where the Fourteenth and Fifteenth Amendments would not apply.

Notwithstanding the importance of religious observance and institutions to white southerners, social and political historians have all but ignored the role of religion in the postwar period—save for its role in defining the meaning of freedom among freedpeople.[6] But that oversight, which fails to consider the most ubiquitous source of cultural values in the American South, substantially limits the field's interpretive horizons when it comes to discerning what was possible following emancipation. Some historians have noted the disorganized and fractured nature of white southern politics during the war and early years of Reconstruction, arguing that white opposition to federal policy did not fully coalesce until after 1867's Reconstruction Acts led to black enfranchisement and biracial Republican coalitions that challenged Democratic domination. In this view, dedicated counterrevolutionary opposition flowed from political sources external to the white South, did not appear until well after Confederate surrender, and was expressly tied to African American suffrage. By contrast, others have argued that the backlash against southern black and white Republicans in the wake of emancipation was "nothing new" and "hardly could have been unanticipated," part of a continuous white supremacist program that extended from the antebellum era, fueled by an irrational racism.[7]

The history of the South's white churches challenges these assumptions. It shows that the counterrevolution was not sustained by simple white supremacist paranoia or basic desires for Democratic hegemony triggered by external political forces—profound as both these realities were. The roots of southern whites' postwar resistance extended backward in time, to long before the Civil War itself could have been imagined. Before U.S. victory, before Radical Republicans ever sat down to determine the fate of the conquered South, the region's white churches had long been mobilized against any attempts to meddle with what they saw as timeless Christian truth. The counterrevolution drew from the deep well of white Christian moral reasoning that had constituted a coherent and continuous aspect of the white South's political culture.

This essay establishes the antebellum and Civil War context for religious dispute over the slavery question before focusing closely on white southern Protestants' proslavery arguments after emancipation. It makes its claims based on formal statements from leading clergy from the South's three largest denominations: the Southern Baptist Convention (founded 1845), the Methodist Episcopal Church, South (founded 1845), and the Presbyterian Church in the United States (formerly the Presbyterian Church in the Confederate States of America). Throughout the long Civil War era, the slavery question remained the key source of division between southern and northern believers. Long after emancipation, southern white denominations continued to assert the justness of their independent existence and, more generally, the slaveholding southern way of life. In turn, they refused fellowship with any who disagreed. In the antebellum context, proslavery theology fueled white supremacist politics. When slavery died, the beliefs that had sustained slavery breathed life into the counterrevolutionary white supremacist order.

The proslavery theology itself never concerned the slavery question alone: it was, at root, about how Christians claimed to read Holy Scripture. In the context of the American nineteenth century, evangelical notions of orthodoxy drew from a belief in the supreme authority of the "Bible alone" for shaping matters of faith and practice, which led to a common method of interpreting the text. This reading deemed the Bible an eminently readable book containing Holy Spirit—inspired teachings that any individual Christian could plainly apprehend. Drawn from the legacies of the Scottish Enlightenment and American political philosophy, this democratized, commonsense methodology led to literalistic biblical interpretation. Ubiquitous among evangelicals of the period, the hermeneutic stressed the immediate relevance and applicability of scriptural teaching to practical affairs of everyday nineteenth-century life. This plain reading of the Bible emphasized the text's ostensibly obvious meanings.[8]

For white believers accustomed to the hegemonic place of white Protestant values in the nineteenth-century American South, claims for the theological relevance of the slavery question after emancipation did not indicate a facile unwillingness to admit the ostensible "wrongness" of slavery. No, it cut far deeper than that. This was an argument about how the Christian God called his people to live. For theologically conservative Protestants, the Bible revealed that standard; inspired biblical teachings clearly taught that slavery was a Christian institution. Whether in the Mosaic Code or the Pauline epistles, Holy Scripture depicted a world of divinely sanctioned slaveholding. Given Jesus of Nazareth's silence on the issue in the Gospels—despite condemning many other sins—proslavery believers read a text that described slaveholding as God given. Slavery therefore concerned divine economy as much as political economy. And for believers who saw no distinction between those two spheres, proslavery religion represented a totalizing worldview. It was shorthand for the way things were meant to be. As historians have come to understand, the slavery debates and antislavery activism paved the way—prior to Darwin or biblical higher criticism—for the rise of Protestant liberalism. To challenge slavery was to challenge everything, because it meant questioning God's revelation to humanity. For white Christians in the American South, however, there would be no quick transition to the postemancipation world. There would be no getting over slavery, for there was no way to go beyond the biblical witness without becoming a heretic.[9]

The biblical mandate for slavery was widely understood—if not always unchallenged—among evangelical Protestants in America prior to the Civil War. Southern proslavery divines made much of the biblical warrant for slavery, but many otherwise antislavery ministers in the North—including the Presbyterian Charles Hodge, the Baptist Francis Wayland, and the Congregationalist Moses Stuart—also conceded the biblical imprimatur for slavery. Such concessions did not mean that emancipationist clergy rejected the narrow proslavery biblical argument, but rather that they distinguished between ancient and American slavery. While some antislavery activists, including the constellation of abolitionists associated with Boston's William Lloyd Garrison, argued from a radical perspective that a higher human law demonstrated the Bible's erroneous character given its endorsement of slavery, more moderate antislavery religious voices held to biblical authority yet attempted to show how the slavery in scripture differed greatly from American slavery. They pointed out that the American system ripped apart families in the slave trade and neither recognized such biblical concepts as the Jubilee Year (in Mosaic Law, when all slaves were set free every seven years) nor allowed for marriage between slaves. Most significantly, they insisted that biblical slavery was not based on racial difference, while American slavery clearly was. Thus antebellum American evangelicals grew deeply divided over the slavery question. By 1861, two factions had emerged, more or less divided sectionally, both claiming to read the Bible the same way, both denouncing the other as sinful. On one side were southern proslavery divines who insisted on following the letter of the biblical text and who saw a direct divine sanction of American slavery. On the other side were antislavery clergy who maintained that a deeper understanding of the gospel's broad intent, revealed through the Bible, denounced American slavery because it differed from the slavery of biblical times.[10]

The conclusions each side reached gave shape to different understandings of how Christians ought to engage the world. In many ways, therefore, the Civil War represented the clash of two distinct political theologies—both framed and forged by religious conflict over the slavery question. Throughout the war the North's leading denominations made overtly nationalistic statements that demanded Unionist loyalty from adherents and reflected a robustly providential view of the United States' place in world history. Northern Protestants' conviction of the divinely elevated nature of the American project resonated broadly with a theological understanding of the church's relationship to the state that had persisted north of the Mason-Dixon line since the Puritan era. For many northern Protestants, the Civil War represented the culmination of a millenarian vision, a necessarily violent hurdle to be cleared before inaugurating an age of peace and ultimate divine favor on the American people. Since the slaveholding South had rejected the providentially ordained United States by seceding, Protestant northerners, understanding themselves as participating in a divine covenant with the Christian God, believed they must eradicate rebellious elements of society in what might amount, as one historian memorably put it, to an "American Apocalypse."[11]

Similar ideas persisted in the slaveholding South. When the Confederate States of America ratified its constitution in March 1861, the southern document—in sharp contrast to the nonsectarian and religiously neutral U.S. Constitution—signaled to all readers that the new nation "invok[ed] the favor and guidance of Almighty God." As in the North, the people of the South developed the belief that they were a chosen people who participated in a covenant relationship with God. From a southern religious perspective, the Confederate cause—and war in its name—was a Christian one. White southerners entered the Civil War convinced of having God on their side.[12]

But that move broke with historic southern Protestant political-theological tradition. For at least a century, dating to the colonial era, southern evangelicals had refrained from wielding religion in direct political engagement, believing the church a purely spiritual institution that should not meddle with the purely secular affairs of state. That pervasive southern Protestant doctrine, which achieved its fullest articulation as the "spirituality of the church," was implicitly proslavery. Its adherents asserted that the church's proper role was to aid in the saving of souls and the cultivating of individual piety, not to work for the Christianization of society at large. White southerners could be certain of slavery's morality because of the institution's biblical foundation. As a result, they argued, churches ought not haggle over and meddle with the legality of slavery. It was a righteous institution but, as a legal matter, best left to the state. Shifting definitions of the political rendered a commitment to the spirituality of the church somewhat arbitrary in practice. Yet many white southerners nonetheless sincerely believed that they lived by the doctrine that the church had no business weighing in on purely political matters. They cited the words of Jesus of Nazareth who, on trial before crucifixion, refused to claim earthly power for himself and argued, "My kingdom is not of this world."[13]

Yet with the rise of more aggressive antislavery activism in the 1830s and the rhetorical attacks on southern society that followed, southern Protestants became increasingly vocal about supposedly secular political affairs. They insisted that slavery, the bedrock of antebellum white southern society, was ordained of God—and that theological claim held significant political weight. As the most famous southern minister in the period, the Presbyterian James Henley Thornwell of South Carolina, had argued in 1850, the stakes were high. "It is not the narrow question of Abolitionism or Slavery—not simply whether we shall emancipate our negroes or not; the real question is the relations of man to society, of States to the individual, and of the individual to the States—a question as broad as the interests of the human race." Thornwell had characterized the antebellum slavery debates in dualistic terms, claiming, "in one word, the world is the battle ground, Christianity and Atheism the combatants, and the progress of humanity the stake." A fundamental distinction existed between those who sought slavery's end and those Christians who affirmed the institution. In Thornwell's analysis, "One party seems to regard society . . . as the machinery of man, which, as it has been invented and arranged by his ingenuity and skill, may be taken to pieces, reconstructed, altered or repaired, as experience shall indicate defects or confusion in the original plan." However, this misguided social vision was countered by "the other party," who "beholds in [society] the ordinance of God." According to Thornwell, social problems were thus ultimately inscrutable to human minds. In his argument, "irregularity is the confession of our ignorance, disorder the proof of our blindness, and with which it is as awful temerity to tamper as to sport with the name of God." Humans were not divine, and "the weakness of man can never make that straight which God hath made crooked." Opponents of slavery thus erred gravely—not simply with regard to political order, but with regard to divine order as well.[14]

In short, antislavery northerners were heterodox. Southerners believed they ignored the plain, commonsense, literal teaching of the Bible about slavery. Thus the election of Abraham Lincoln to the U.S. presidency in November 1860 proved decisive in securing southern religious support for the Confederacy. White southerners convinced of the righteousness of slavery came to believe that an abolitionist conspiracy had taken over the American government. In 1861 the evangelical South suddenly laid claim to the same sort of politicized religious identity that had persisted in the Protestant North for more than two centuries.[15]

For those northern Protestants whose political theology went through no transformation in the period, the political and military aspects of the Civil War were often indistinguishable from their religious goals. In their view, the war provided the occasion to remake southern religion as much as it might remake southern society at large. As northern believers saw it, they needed to send missionaries from their antislavery faith to help the South transition from a benighted slaveholding society to one free. Outside the realm of denominational polities, the effort began in earnest when the nonsectarian, evangelical abolitionist American Missionary Association (AMA) established a school for fugitive slaves at Fortress Monroe, Virginia, in September 1861.[16] Within a year, the North's leading Protestant denominations began likeminded efforts. An early overture came from the northern American Baptist Home Mission Society (ABHMS) in June 1862. By their lights, "Divine Providence" was at work in the "recent abolition of slavery in the District of Columbia, and in the setting free of thousands of bondmen by the advancement of our national armies into insurgent States." The Christian God was "about to break the chains of the enslaved millions in our land," and, as a result, the ABHMS anticipated "the entire reorganization of the social and religious state of the South, which must inevitably follow the successful overthrow of the rebellion." That inevitably bore the mark of the "Divine Hand," who would "thus furnish an unobstructed entrance for the Gospel among vast multitudes who have hitherto been shut out from its pure teachings." Northern Baptists moved to respond immediately to these new conditions. They commissioned "missionaries and teachers" for "emancipated slaves" to help usher in the new order.[17] During the next two years, other leading religious denominations in the North, black and white, joined the cause. By the spring of 1865, the Methodist Episcopal Church, the Old and New School Presbyterian Churches, the African Methodist Episcopal Church, and the African Methodist Episcopal Zion Church had all sent missionaries to the South. Along with missionaries from the AMA and the Quaker and Unitarian-supported American Freedmen's Union Commission, their numbers would greatly increase in the aftermath of the war.[18]

Northern missionaries often cooperated directly with the U.S. Army, and they received the blessing of members of the Lincoln administration. With the mass destruction the Civil War brought, as well as the social disruption to local communities, many southern churches wound up abandoned. Or so it appeared to the northern Methodist bishops Matthew Simpson and Edward Ames, who appealed to Secretary of War Edwin M. Stanton for the authority to manage vacated church properties. Stanton agreed, and in late November 1863, he ordered U.S. military officials to allow Methodists to occupy or take control over churches in rebellious states "in which a loyal minister . . . does not now officiate." By the early months of 1864, Stanton had spread that same mandate to the leadership of other northern Protestant denominations. For religious bodies that had split over the slavery question in the antebellum period, the orders represented a chance to reclaim a previously lost connection to old memberships. Moreover, as many northerners asserted late in the war, it allowed the restoration of national, rather than sectional churches.[19]

But Stanton's church orders were short lived. Though northern missionaries came to control several dozen Baptist and Methodist churches in the South, by 1865 the Lincoln administration had rescinded the orders and restored a number of congregations to their former owners. Then Andrew Johnson's administration oversaw the return of all remaining southern churches by the spring of 1866. The aegis of the United States military could not be brought to bear interminably on the shape of American religious life.[20]

More to the point, white southern believers did not see such overtures as signs of goodwill. They saw a meddlesome and blatantly political attempt to use the federal government's power for the ends of Yankee Protestantism. The charge held some truth. In their annual address in 1864, the northern Methodist bishops had collectively stated their "solemn judgment that none should be admitted to [northern Methodist] fellowship who are either slaveholders or are tainted with treason." On the heels of the surrender of various Confederate armies, northern Baptists and Presbyterians made similar pronouncements at their denominational meetings in May 1865. The Presbyterian approach was particularly strident. Noting that some ministers who had sided with the Presbyterian Church in the Confederate States of America during the war might reapply for ordination in the northern Presbyterian Church USA (PCUSA), the northern church required two tests. First, ministers who had in "any way, directly or indirectly" been involved in "aiding or countenancing the rebellion and the war" were required to "confess and forsake" that action as sin. Second, ministers had to disavow the idea that "the system of negro slavery in the South is a Divine institution, and that it is 'the peculiar mission of the Southern Church to conserve the institution of slavery as there maintained.'" Any southern minister who refused to repent of these errors would not be allowed to preach in the PCUSA.[21]

Such proclamations, while couched in language of sectional reconciliation, only served to intensify the schism between northern and southern believers. Having lost a war prosecuted in the name of a Christian God who ordained slavery, southern Protestants hardly entertained sectional rapprochement—particularly on these terms. White southerners viewed the sweep of northern religious activity during the war—from missionary efforts to an ostensibly unredeemed South, to the colonizing of churches devastated by war through government force, to religious reunion on northern terms—as confirmation of their old antebellum feeling that their northern counterparts were a heterodox people, unworthy of Christian fellowship.[22]

It was in this context that white southern Protestants also reasserted their righteousness, which derived from their doctrinal fidelity. By mid-1865, the military work of the Civil War had concluded, but the religious fights that the war represented were by no means resolved. Although the Thirteenth Amendment had been passed by Congress and would soon become law, the freedom of many thousands of enslaved people had not yet been secured. Regardless of what was happening on the ground, however, southern Protestants insisted that slavery remained a divinely approved institution. Legal and military realities had not changed their Christian truth, nor had they changed the nature of the white South's religious identity.[23]

In March 1865, one of the leading lights of postbellum southern Presbyterianism, Louisville's Stuart Robinson, published a treatise titled *Slavery, As Recognized in the Mosaic Civil Law, Recognized . . . and Allowed, in the . . . Christian Church*. In the main, Robinson did not offer a novel argument. But appearing just weeks after Lincoln's second inaugural address, it was remarkable for its insistence on the righteousness of slavery. It furthermore condemned Lincoln's speech for its appropriation of Christian abolitionist arguments—and the quoting of biblical chapter and verse to that end—in the name of the Civil War. Robinson contended that, after reading his treatise on slavery, true believers would give abolitionist ideas a "sober second thought" and understand the "relation of master and slave" as divinely sanctioned.[24]

By the summer of 1865, a chorus of white southerners was making similar arguments about the ongoing salience of the proslavery position, all with official denominational sanction. In June, a group of Methodists comprising laity and clergy and joined by the Methodist Episcopal Church, South (MECS) bishop Hubbard H. Kavanaugh, gathered in Palmyra, Missouri, to denounce the wartime efforts of northern Methodists to take over southern churches with military support. The slavery question loomed large in the so-called Palmyra Manifesto they produced to explain their position. "Those who publish to the world that all the differences between [northern and southern Methodists are] swept away with the institution of slavery are either ignorant of the facts or are trying to mislead the public," they argued. "The question upon which the Church divided was not whether the institution of slavery was right or wrong, per se, but whether it was a legitimate subject for ecclesiastical legislation. The right or wrong of the institution, its existence or non-existence, could not affect this vital question." Their next words were significant: slavery was "now abolished by Federal and State legislation, which event we accept as a political measure with which we have nothing to do as a Church." Read one way, the statement might be taken to mean that these southern Methodists in Missouri accepted the death of American slavery. Perhaps they did. But read in the context of all other white southern Protestant writing on slavery during the period, it seems more likely that they meant that the political resolution to the slavery question had no bearing on the church's teaching on the subject.[25]

Robinson's *Slavery* volume and the southern Methodist Palmyra Manifesto precipitated two major southern denominational statements that appeared in the latter half of 1865, both nationally circulated "pastoral letters." One was issued in August by three leading MECS bishops; the other came in December from the General Assembly of the southern Presbyterian Church. The southern Presbyterians' pastoral letter succinctly summarized the white Christian South's view of the stakes of the old religion-and-slavery dispute for the postslavery order. The "relation" of slavery "is now overthrown," it argued, "suddenly, violently." It was for "history" and the Christian God to decide "whether [slavery's end came] justly or unjustly, in wrath or in mercy, for weal or for woe." But the church remained resolutely committed to two core principles it had long held.[26]

The first was that abolitionism was a grievous error. Because their 1865 language so closely mirrored what might be called the thesis of the antebellum white Christian South, it merits quotation at length:

> While the existence of slavery may, in its civil aspects, be regarded as a settled question, an issue now gone . . . the lawfulness of the relation as a question of social morality, and of Scriptural truth, has lost nothing of its importance. When we solemnly declare to you brethren, that the [abolition] dogma which asserts the inherent sinfulness of this relation, is unscriptural and fanatical; that it is condemned not only by the word of God, but by the voice of the Church in all ages; that it is one of the most pernicious heresies of modern times; that its countenance by any Church is a just cause of separation from it, (1 Tim. 6:1–5.) we have surely said enough to warn you away from this insidious error, as from a fatal shore.[27]

The laws of the state had changed, but God's law was eternal. White southerners' distinctiveness on the slavery question lived on, in spite of the death of slavery. They would preserve the true faith.

Relatedly, and secondarily, these southern Presbyterians argued that they had nothing to apologize for in their slaveholding past. "Whatever . . . we may have to lament before God, either for neglect of duty to our servants, or for actual wrong while the relation lasted, we are not called, now that is has been abolished, to bow the head in humiliation before men." There was no cause "to admit that the memory of our dear kindred is to be covered with shame." Southern slaveholders were no different than biblical patriarchs. As was the case with biblical slavery, they argued, American slavery had served an evangelistic purpose. "Abraham, Isaac, and Jacob" held "bond-servants born in their own houses," but they were "redeemed by the same precious blood," and thus they "sit down together in the kingdom of God." Abolitionists would have to answer to God for their heresy. But whatever the sins committed by slaveholders, the biblical record showed that holding other humans in bondage brought no judgment. White southerners could have been better masters, even better Christians. But that was in spite of slavery, not because of it.[28]

Such arguments closely aligned with the southern Methodists' pastoral letter. In classically paternalistic prose, they called for an ongoing mission to African Americans: "In the change from slaves to freedmen, which has providentially befallen the negroes of the Southern States, our obligations to promote their spiritual welfare have not ceased. We are still debtor to them free, as before to them bond. Under the divine blessing, our church has done a great work for this people." As these southern Methodists saw it, Christianity — given by whites — had made African Americans properly contented in their condition of servitude. Thus, when the Civil War came, rather than moving toward freedom themselves, the enslaved experienced a "safe though sudden passage from a state of bondage to liberty" that was "accompanied by no violence or tumult on their part." White Christianity could be thanked for such a docile populace.[29]

It is worth noting how willfully incorrect these white southern Christians were in interpreting antebellum blacks' religious claims and aspirations. In the antebellum era, the proslavery gospel depended on missions to the enslaved. Though many southern blacks responded to the Christian message, they overwhelmingly rejected white oversight — whether spiritual or physical. When emancipation came, the mass exodus from biracial southern churches confirmed that these organizations were incapable of sustaining black members without slavery's coercion. The southern Methodist bishops preferred to see things differently. They contended that African Americans in the Methodist Episcopal Church, South, numbered 240,000 and that the slave missions had proven a successful venture. In reality, southern African Americans were fleeing the MECS. In 1860, southern Methodists had claimed just fewer than 208,000 African American members; by 1866, fewer than 79,000 remained.[30]

Given southern white believers' long-standing conflict over "orthodoxy" with abolitionists, it is no surprise that these southern Methodist bishops believed abolitionists were the prime movers behind all that they saw as wrong with the recent American past. Southern whites were "often reviled while prosecuting the evangelization of the colored people, by those who claimed to be their better friends," but "Southern Methodists have persevered in it—not without blessed results. We might have done more, but we should be thankful to the grace of God, that we have not done less. Our labor has not been in vain in the Lord." Like that of their southern Presbyterian coreligionists, their commitment to slaveholding showed the depth of their true belief. Southern Methodists had labored in earnest for the faith once delivered to the saints.[31]

They could not say the same about abolition-minded northern Methodists. These antislavery heretics "have incorporated social dogmas and political tests into their church creeds. They have gone on to impose conditions upon discipleship that Christ did not impose." Instead of an otherworldly spiritual kingdom that cultivated "personal piety," the southern bishops argued, northern "pulpits are perverted to agitations and questions" that ensured "political and ecclesiastical discord." Northerners had long been wayward on the slavery question, and it was a litmus test for all doctrine.[32]

Such arguments from leading white southern Protestants in 1865 proved continuous with decades of dispute about the slavery question before the war. Those prewar debates were no distant memory. As the three bishops in the MECS asserted in their 1865 pastoral letter, their own denomination's split of 1844 came because "a large proportion, if not a majority of Northern Methodists [became] incurably radical. . . . They preach another gospel." Even though they lamented that their division affronted biblical calls for Christian unity, they refused to give up their proslavery position. They required the acknowledgment that the antebellum South's defense of slavery was biblically correct. [33]

Much of their language from 1865 would have been right at home in the antebellum period. And it would continue to carry weight in the decade to come. As they put it, "The abolition, for military and political considerations, of the institution of domestic slavery in the United States does not effect the question that was prominent in our separation [from northern Methodists] in 1844. Nor is this the only difference or the principal one between us and them." The political theology of slavery shaped the ecclesiastical terrain of the antebellum United States. It would continue to do so after emancipation.[34]

Even so, northern believers from the Baptist, Methodist, and Presbyterian traditions all hoped that the death of slavery would end the strife between the sections and pave the way for denominational reunion. Starting at the end of the Civil War, northern Methodists implored their white southern counterparts to let go of their past grievances and reunite the denomination that, prior to 1844, had been America's largest religious body. As northern Methodist bishops first claimed in June 1865, the end of the Civil War and of American slavery meant that there was no reason to continue with two sectional churches: "The great cause which led to the separation from us . . . has passed away, and we trust the day is not far distant when there shall be but one organization which shall embrace the whole Methodist family of the United States."[35]

For the next several years, however, southern Methodists remained steadfast in their rejection of such overtures. The process picked up in May 1869, when two bishops from the northern church, Matthew Simpson and Edmund S. Janes, attended a meeting of southern bishops in St. Louis to consider "the propriety, practicability, and methods of reunion." Responding on behalf of their southern church, the MECS bishops Holland N. McTyeire and Robert Paine argued that the northern church misunderstood what was at stake in the slavery question: "Slavery was not, in any proper sense, the cause, but the occasion only of [the 1844] separation, the necessity of which we regretted as much as you. But certain principles were developed in relation to the political aspects of that question . . . which we could not accept." In sum, it was northerners who had erred on slavery, not the white South. In truth, slavery had existed throughout the United States in 1784, the date of the Methodist Episcopal Church's founding. It furthermore existed widespread throughout American Methodism, with untold numbers of slaveholders in the denomination. As Paine and McTyeire explained to their northern guests in 1869, "That which you are pleased to call, no doubt sincerely thinking it so, 'the great cause' of separation, existed in the Church from its organization, and yet for sixty years there was no separation." From the view of these white southerners, northern Methodist theology had changed. It was thus impossible to consider denomination reunion on such grounds.[36]

Southern Methodists' reluctance rested entirely on old disputes over the political theology connected to the slavery question. In 1874, a committee of the General Conference of the MECS flatly summarized the matter at stake in analyzing the 1844 denominational fracture: "The existence of slavery in the southern States furnished an occasion, with its connected questions, fruitful of disturbance; and to this division has been mainly attributed. The position of southern Methodism on that subject was scriptural." Because northern Methodists refused to acknowledge that white southerners in fact held a monopoly on biblical orthodoxy, a breach in American Methodism—as well as in the United States' other evangelical Protestant denominations—became inevitable and irreparable. At that late date white Methodists in the South were direct about their views: "Our opinions have undergone no change." The death of slavery by military force and law had not destroyed these white southerners' faith: "The causes which led to the division in 1844 . . . have not disappeared. Some of them exist in their original form and force, and others have been modified, but not diminished."[37]

Despite the force and clarity of that argument, however, southern Methodists did deem it possible to engage in "fraternal relations." That is, they participated in a process of mutual recognition of each denomination and in an agreement to labor in harmony rather than discord. After mutual exchanges between the general conferences of northern and southern Methodism, a joint commission convened in Cape May, New Jersey, in August 1876. There, they agreed that both the northern and southern churches were "a legitimate Branch of Episcopal Methodism in the United States, having a common origin in the Methodist Episcopal Church organized in 1784." Moreover, the Methodist Episcopal Church, South, was affirmed as "an evangelical Church, reared on Scriptural foundations, and her ministers and members, with those of the Methodist Episcopal Church, have constituted one Methodist family, though in distinct ecclesiastical connections." The meaning of the Cape May declaration was plain for anyone paying attention: white southern Methodism and all that was bound up in that identity—principally the biblical defense of slavery, which they did not apologize for or concede—remained a legitimate form of Christian expression. It was distinct from northern belief, but a true faith all the same.[38]

This veneer of cooperation masked an underlying and deep hostility that had come to mark religious life throughout the postwar South. Southern Baptist Convention (SBC) leaders were far less explicit than the Methodists in their use of historical disputes over slavery to justify ongoing ecclesiastical independence from their northern counterpart, the American Baptist Home Mission Society. That had something to do with particular matters of church polity. More than any other American denomination, Baptists maintained a rigid commitment to the autonomy of local congregations. Unlike Protestant counterparts in the Episcopal,

Methodist, or Presbyterian traditions, Baptists constituted more a constellation of likeminded churches than a formal denomination. They had no authoritative body that exercised congregational oversight. For Baptists, Christian identity was an individual matter expressed through the local congregation. Slavery—in fact, all questions of moral and political import—was a matter to be sorted out in local churches, not aired in the context of denominational debate.[39]

Because of congregational autonomy, Baptists had come together historically for one purpose: to raise funds for missionaries. As white southerners had claimed at the 1845 founding of the Southern Baptist Convention in Augusta, Georgia, "We have constructed for our basis [as the SBC] no new creed; acting in this matter upon a Baptist aversion for all creeds but the Bible." Although they took for granted that the Bible revealed a proslavery God and a proslavery faith, they wrote that the SBC "Constitution knows no difference between slaveholding and non-slaveholders." Like southern Methodists, they claimed that northern Baptists had caused the separation when the ABHMS's General Convention, after more than a decade of pressure from antislavery northern members, ruled in 1844 that no slaveholder could be a missionary. White southerners in turn read that decision as an "[attempt] to eject us."[40]

Southern Baptist interpretation of their split from northern Baptists in 1844 and 1845 guided their postwar conduct. Representatives from the ABHMS brought a "Christian greeting" to the Southern Baptist Convention meeting in Baltimore in 1868, hoping to "'work together,' in relation to a common end" in the "great transition period" that followed the Civil War. Principally, that social change required individuals willing to deal with the "numerous, varied, conflicting, and demoralizing forces" that had been "brought to bear upon the emancipated millions of the Southern States." Predictably, however, their southern coreligionists gave an icy reply to this overture. While a committee recommended "reciprocat[ing] the expressions of Christian kindness and fraternity" to the ABHMS, the SBC claimed its own white mandate for the religious shape of the South—especially its African American population.[41]

The new postemancipation world was not the same as the one prior to the Civil War, but those old ways of seeing racial dependency profoundly influenced how these southern whites conceptualized the world the war made. As Southern Baptists argued, freedpeople were "now without adequate guardianship"—presumably the paternalist kind provided by a

Christian master class. Southern blacks could therefore not resist "the appeals of passion and the terrors of superstition, and the heartlessness of intrigue, and the imminence of vice and crime." Despite emancipation, the white Christian role in the South remained the same. The new racial landscape of the postemancipation order could only be explained with reference to the old proslavery faith. What were once missions to the slaves—affirming a proslavery gospel—became paternalistic missions to freedpeople. Given their generations of mastery, these southern whites believed themselves particularly suited for the task. As Southern Baptists had argued in 1866, "it is our decided conviction, from our knowledge of the character of these people, and of the feelings our citizens, that this work must be done mainly by ourselves." Thus the SBC had little time for northern Baptist overtures. "Two bodies exist; the divisions of history remain," they argued in 1868. "As we ask no concession of principle, we make none." Southern Baptists could "thank God" that northerners shared "a common interest with us in one Lord, one faith, one baptism, one hope, one God and Father of all." But the sectional division would remain unhealed. The legacy of slavery meant that they did not worship in the same church.[42]

More virulent than southern Methodists or Southern Baptists were southern Presbyterians. Like the Methodists, some Presbyterians had expressed interest in the late 1860s in reconciling the sectional denominations. In 1868 the northern PCUSA's General Assembly recognized the existence of the southern Presbyterian Church in the United States (PCUS); then in 1869 the PCUSA wrote to the PCUS's General Assembly in hopes of establishing fraternal relations between the two bodies. But unlike southern Methodists, southern Presbyterians rebuffed these northern overtures in 1870, when their General Assembly, led by three vocal defenders of slavery—Benjamin M. Palmer of New Orleans, Stuart Robinson of Louisville, and Robert L. Dabney of Hampden Sydney, Virginia—overwhelmingly voted against them. Where southern Methodists were willing to entertain fraternal relations with the northern church, southern Presbyterians saw even that move as a sign of doctrinal laxity. The PCUS General Assembly then explained its position in a pastoral letter written by Palmer and sent to the northern Presbyterian denomination. Arguing that during the Civil War the northern church had abrogated its mission to keep the affairs of state separate from the church, the PCUS claimed the reason for the breech had not been resolved.[43]

In a widely circulated compendium that followed, southern Presbyterians documented the history of their denomination since 1861 and clarified the reasons for the separate existence of their church. Among the denomination's "distinctives" in 1870, slavery played a central role. "The essential principle of slavery is submission or subjection to control by the will of another," the document argued. "This is an essential element in every form of civil government, also, and in the family relation itself." In this formulation slavery was "not an institution essential to the social state; and therefore is not of universal obligation." Thus the contrast existed in what southern Presbyterians argued were foundational aspects of their society: "civil government, as opposed to anarchy" and "marriage" rather than "concubinage, polygamy, and general licentiousness."[44]

But if slavery was a second-order institution, it was nonetheless "of divine appointment." Citing a series of biblical passages from both the Old and New Testaments, these white southerners argued that "in certain conditions of society it has been expressly recognized by God, permitted and appointed." The point was not an abstract one. In this view, "the circumstances of [slavery] in this country made it right and best that such should be the relation, in general, of the negro to the white population." Many proslavery ministers had called for a reform of slavery as it existed in America—whether to decry the domestic slave trade that destroyed families, to denounce the prohibition against slave marriage, or to disparage a system that made slave literacy illegal—and saw the failure to do so as a key reason for Confederate defeat in the Civil War. Nevertheless, "the existence of wrong laws and usages connected with [slavery], no more disproves the lawfulness of the relation itself, than such things disprove the lawfulness of marriage or of civil government." Slavery might have needed reform. But slavery was right all the same.[45]

In the antebellum context of pro- and antislavery rivalry, such arguments make sense. Yet historians currently lack much understanding of the significance of proslavery thought after emancipation—despite fine work by a growing number of scholars who have explained the religious world of the postwar South. Commonly, religious histories of the period begin or end with 1861 or 1865, which implicitly suggests that the Civil War fully determined the fate of the slavery question. To be sure, U.S. military victory ended the legal fight over the status of American slavery. But the religious battle had not ended for white believers in the South. To the contrary, for white southern Christians, the primary doctrinal questions at stake in the conflict had not been satisfactorily resolved and would not be well into the twentieth century—and in some cases not at all.[46]

For biblical literalists, especially those in the American South, the Civil War thus constituted an ironic blessing to their faith. They continued to read the Bible through the frame of commonsense literalism, but without its most unsavory aspect from the perspective of emerging liberal democracy: slaveholding. The death of slavery gave biblical literalism a new lease on life, and a way of defending not simply the so-called southern way of life—slaveholding—as it had existed after the war. Shorn of slavery, biblical literalism was not simplistically backward looking. Rather, it remained the hermeneutic that gave shape and meaning to the white South's postwar order.

But the end of slavery also made literal interpretations more palatable throughout all of America moving forward. In this way, the proslavery reading of Holy Scripture metastasized well beyond the South, drawing in solidarity all religious conservatives who hoped to stand against social change. Reconciliation, a concept so familiar to our historical notions of what came after the Civil War as a way of excluding African Americans from the American political project as whites understood it, could only happen religiously on terms dictated by white southerners. As antislavery Christians were becoming protoliberals, the white South paved the way for the national movement that would be called fundamentalism. Often portrayed as a northern and western movement, historians have generally understated or ignored the significance of the Civil War in the making of fundamentalism. But it is impossible to imagine the fundamentalist-modernist controversy of the late nineteenth and early twentieth centuries without reference to slavery and emancipation. At bottom, fundamentalists read the Bible like the proslavery Christians of an earlier generation.[47]

For many decades to come, white southerners used their biblicism— deeply influenced by the debates of the Civil War and Reconstruction eras—to forestall any efforts at denominational reunion. While the Methodists achieved tepid fraternal relations—with language dictated by southern whites—in 1876, a true rejoining of the northern and southern branches of Methodism did not occur until 1939, and only then in a Jim Crow America that preserved segregated church structures. Presbyterians agreed to their own version of fraternal relations in 1882, though it required no concession of southern distinctiveness on the theology of slavery. Their denominational reunion did not come for a century, in

1983—and then only after a significant number of biblicist theological conservatives, in large part white southerners, chose in 1973 to found an alternate polity called the Presbyterian Church in America. For Southern Baptists, who continued to lean on the belief of congregational autonomy, some cooperative work occurred with ABHMS organizations at the local level in the late nineteenth century. But nothing resembling fraternal relations existed, and no denominational reunion ever happened.[48]

As Protestantism proved central to the making of the antebellum Bible Belt, so it was also constitutive for the postwar Solid South. Thus white Protestants cleared an intellectual and religious path for the emergence of the region's post-Reconstruction political order, where the term "redemption" connoted as much politically as it did religiously. It was built on a white conservative Democratic bloc, opposed to civil rights for African Americans and averse to overtures from northern religious and political agents—unless such overtures came on white southern terms. These were all staples of the slavery debates that informed churches before, during, and after the Civil War. In historical perspective, we fail to understand many white southerners if we fail to see that, from their vantage point, to give up on slavery seemed tantamount to giving up on the Christian God; and they were not about to do that.[49]

NOTES

1. The literature on the church splits, as well as on proslavery Christianity and the making of Confederate identity is vast, but for representative examples, see C. C. Goen, *Broken Churches, Broken Nation: Denominational Schisms and the Coming of the American Civil War* (Macon, Ga.: Mercer University Press, 1985); Drew Gilpin Faust, *The Creation of Confederate Nationalism: Ideology and Identity in the Civil War South* (Baton Rogue: Louisiana State University Press, 1988), 22–40; Mitchell Snay, *Gospel of Disunion: Religion and Separatism in the Antebellum South* (1993; Chapel Hill: University of North Carolina Press, 1997); Eugene D. Genovese, *A Consuming Fire: The Fall of the Confederacy in the Mind of the White Christian South* (Athens: University of Georgia Press, 1998); Elizabeth Fox-Genovese and Eugene D. Genovese, *The Mind of the Master Class: History and Faith in the Southern Slaveholders' Worldview* (New York: Cambridge University Press, 2005); and Mark A. Noll, *The Civil War as a Theological Crisis* (Chapel Hill: University of North Carolina Press, 2006).

2. *The Distinctive Principles of the Presbyterian Church in the United States, Commonly Called the Southern Presbyterian Church, as Set Forth in the Formal Declarations, and Illustrated by Extracts from Proceedings of the General Assembly, from 1861–70* (Richmond, Va.: Presbyterian Committee of Publication, [1871]), 131–32.

3. Ibid., 132–33.

4. On white missionaries and African American churches as targets of white terrorist violence, see Edward J. Blum, *Reforging the White Republic: Race, Religion, and American Nationalism, 1865–1898* (Baton Rouge: Louisiana State University Press, 2005), 76–82; and Margaret M. Storey, "The Crucible of Reconstruction: Unionists and the Struggle for Alabama's Postwar Homefront," in *The Great Task Remaining before Us: Reconstruction as America's Continuing Civil War*, ed. Paul A. Cimbala and Randall M. Miller (New York: Fordham University Press, 2010), 84–86.

5. On overall evangelical adherence and political influence, see Richard Carwardine, *Evangelicals and Politics in Antebellum America* (New Haven: Yale University Press, 1993). Churches—especially evangelical Protestant churches—were arguably the most prominent social, cultural, political, and intellectual institutions in the nineteenth-century white South. In 1860, in the states that comprised the future Confederacy plus Kentucky, churches held seating capacity for just under 100 percent of the free population (97.7 percent). South Carolina (149.8 percent), Georgia (128.4 percent), Mississippi (125.7 percent), North Carolina (122.7 percent), and Alabama (104 percent) all had church seating for more than the state's entire free population. In 1870, the numbers are more complicated to interpret. In general, the census's basic accounting was deeply flawed, and in the South especially it showed far fewer African Americans—in places 20 to 30 percent fewer—than lived there at the time. Moreover, the postemancipation boom of autonomous black churches is not shown on the census, nor does it account for the minority of northern "missionary" churches in the South (only broad denominations are given), nor is there a clear accounting for churches destroyed by the Civil War. Given those significant limitations, the 1870 numbers are still revealing. Overall, churches held seating capacity for 94.6 percent of the white population. South Carolina (169.7 percent), Mississippi (126.8 percent), Georgia (125.4 percent), Virginia (107.4 percent), and North Carolina (105.9 percent) all had church space for more whites than lived in the state, though, as in the antebellum period, those numbers were inflated by locales that had large churchgoing populations of African Americans. Numbers taken from the 1860 and 1870 U.S. census, Historical Census Browser, University of Virginia, Geospatial and Statistical Data Center, http://mapserver.lib.virginia.edu/index.html. On the flaws in the 1870 census, see Richard Reid, "The 1870 United States Census and Black Under-enumeration: A Test Case from North Carolina," *Historie Sociale/Social History* 28 (November 1995): 487–99.

These numbers are significantly higher than indicated by the period's church membership records. Membership numbers are suggestive, but they vastly undercount the number of religious adherents in nineteenth-century America. Because of relatively restrictive membership standards, most churches saw many more regular church attendees—perhaps double or triple the number—than actual members. (The nineteenth century was roughly the reverse of the twentieth century on this issue, as membership standards and regular attendance grew more relaxed.) As a result, ascertaining the actual number of Christian adherents in the period is highly imprecise. Most careful historians of American religion tend to rely on the U.S. census tally of church accommodations but currently lack effective ways of determining just how many people considered themselves active faith practitioners in the period. See George C. Rable, *God's Almost Chosen Peoples: A Religious History of the American Civil War* (Chapel Hill: University of North Carolina Press, 2010), 11–12. For an elucidation of this problem as it applies to antebellum Virginia, see Charles F. Irons, *The Origins of Proslavery Christianity: White and Black Evangelicals in Colonial and Antebellum Virginia* (Chapel Hill: University of North Carolina Press, 2008), 3–10.

6. Notable counterexamples include Daniel Stowell, *Rebuilding Zion: The Religious Reconstruction of the South, 1863-1877* (New York: Oxford University Press, 1998); and Blum, *Reforging the White Republic*. For examples of the most significant works on freedpeople's religion, see Katherine L. Dvorak, *An African-American Exodus: The Segregation of the Southern Churches* (New York: Carlson, 1991); William E. Montgomery, *Under Their Own Vine and Fig Tree: The African-American Church in the South* (Baton Rouge: Louisiana State University Press, 1993); and Reginald F. Hildebrand, *The Times Were Strange and Stirring: Methodist Preachers and the Crisis of Emancipation* (Durham: Duke University Press, 1995).

7. For a classic perspective on the continuity of southern white supremacy before, during, and after the war, see John Hope Franklin, *Reconstruction after the Civil War* (Chicago: University of Chicago Press, 1961), 152–73, quotes 152, 154. See also W. E. B. Du Bois, *Black Reconstruction in America, 1860-1880* (1935; New York: Free Press, 1992), 670–710. Works that suggest that the counterrevolution came later do not necessarily agree about the causes for or ends sought by white southerners opposed to Reconstruction. See William Archibald Dunning, *Reconstruction, Political and Economic, 1865-1877* (New York: Harper and Brothers, 1907), 121–23; George Rable, *But There Was No Peace: The Role of Violence in the Politics of Reconstruction* (1984; Athens: University of Georgia Press, 2007); Eric Foner, *Reconstruction: America's Unfinished Revolution, 1863-1877* (New York: Harper and Row, 1988), 412–59; and Adam Fairclough, "Was the Grant of Black Suffrage a Political Error? Reconsidering the Views of John W. Burgess, William A. Dunning, and Eric Foner on Congressional Reconstruction," *Journal of the Historical Society* 12 (June 2012): 155–88. For a survey of this literature that sides with Du Bois and Franklin, see Michael Perman, "Counter Reconstruction: The Role of Violence in Southern Redemption," in *The Facts of Reconstruction: Essays in Honor of John Hope Franklin*, ed. Eric Anderson and Alfred A. Moss Jr. (Baton Rouge: Louisiana State University Press, 1991), 121–40.

8. See Mark A. Noll, *America's God: From Jonathan Edwards to Abraham Lincoln* (New York: Oxford University Press, 2002), 367–401. This and subsequent paragraphs first appeared and are elaborated on in Luke E. Harlow, *Religion, Race, and the Making of Confederate Kentucky, 1830-1880* (New York: Cambridge University Press, 2014), used with permission.

9. On nineteenth-century methods of biblical interpretation and the slavery question, see Noll, *America's God*, 367–401. On antislavery and the origins of Protestant liberalism, see Molly Oshatz, *Slavery and Sin: The Fight against Slavery and the Rise of Liberal Protestantism* (New York: Oxford University Press, 2011).

10. Noll, *The Civil War as a Theological Crisis*, 31–50; and Noll, *America's God*, 386–401. See also J. Albert Harrill, "The Use of the New Testament in the American Slave

Controversy: A Case History in the Hermeneutical Tension between Biblical Criticism and Christian Moral Debate," *Religion and American Culture* 10 (Summer 2000): 149–86; and E. Brooks Holifield, *Theology in America: Christian Thought from the Age of the Puritans to the Civil War* (New Haven: Yale University Press, 2003), 494–504.

11. See Timothy L. Wesley, *The Politics of Faith during the Civil War* (Baton Rouge: Louisiana State University Press, 2013), 78–80; and James H. Moorhead, *American Apocalypse: Yankee Protestants and the Civil War* (New Haven: Yale University Press, 1978).

12. *Provisional and Permanent Constitutions, Together with the Acts and Resolutions of the Three Sessions of the Provisional Congress of the Confederate States* (Richmond, Va.: Tyler, Wise, Allegre, and Smith, 1861), 3. See Snay, *Gospel of Disunion*; and Harry S. Stout, *Upon the Altar of the Nation: A Moral History of the Civil War* (New York: Viking, 2006), 47–52.

13. Much historiographic debate has surrounded the "spirituality of the church" doctrine, its sources, and its legacy. Jack Maddex, "From Theocracy to Spirituality: The Southern Presbyterian Reversal on Church and State," *Journal of Presbyterian History* 54 (Winter 1976): 438–57, has argued that the Presbyterian idea of the church's "spirituality" was a particular postbellum innovation, but other historians tend to disagree in varying ways. Several historians contend that the Civil War–era doctrine drew from historic roots in colonial America. For example, see Preston D. Graham Jr., *A Kingdom Not of This World: Stuart Robinson's Struggle to Distinguish the Sacred from the Secular During the Civil War* (Macon, Ga.: Mercer University Press, 2002), 169–73; James Oscar Farmer Jr., *The Metaphysical Confederacy: James Henley Thornwell and the Synthesis of Southern Values* (Macon, Ga.: Mercer University Press, 1986), 256–60; and John B. Boles, *The Irony of Southern Religion* (New York: Peter Lang, 1994). For the most recent and cogent explanation for the complex series of ecclesiological negotiations that led white southern evangelicals to arrive at the "spirituality of the church" stance in the postrevolutionary era, see Irons, *Origins of Proslavery Christianity*, 55–96. See also Wesley, *Politics of Faith*, 103–4. The biblical quote from Jesus of Nazareth is from John 18:36.

14. James Henley Thornwell, "The Christian Doctrine of Slavery," in *The Collected Writings of James Henley Thornwell*, 4 vols., ed. John B. Adger and John L. Girardeau (1873; Carlisle, Pa.: Banner of Truth, 1974), 4:405–6.

15. On the transformation of a historically apolitical southern religion to politicization on slavery and the sectional crisis, see Boles, *Irony of Southern Religion*, 75–89. Analyzing the emergence of religious Confederate rituals in Richmond, Virginia, Harry Stout and Christopher Grasso compellingly explain the transformation in white southern church-state ideas: "Where the Puritans had taken two generations to invent a rhetoric of nationhood and war around the ritual convention of the fast and the thanksgiving day, the Confederacy would achieve it in a year, and it would grow thereafter until the very last battles were lost." Stout and Grasso, "Civil War, Religion, and Communications: The Case of Richmond," in *Religion and the American Civil War*, ed. Randall M. Miller, Harry S. Stout, and Charles Reagan Wilson (New York: Oxford University Press, 1998), 320.

16. Joe M. Richardson, *Christian Reconstruction: The American Missionary Association and Southern Blacks, 1861–1890* (Athens: University of Georgia Press, 1986), 3–4.

17. *Baptist Home Missions in North America; Including a Full Report of the Proceedings and Addresses of the Jubilee Meeting, and a Historical Sketch of the American Baptist Home Mission Society, Historical Tables, Etc., 1832–1882* (New York: Baptist Home Mission Books, 1883), 397; and Stowell, *Rebuilding Zion*, 27–28. The ABHMS was the body the South's white Baptists vacated when they created the Southern Baptist Convention in 1845.

18. Stowell, *Rebuilding Zion*, 28–29; Blum, *Reforging the White Republic*, 51–52.

19. The quote comes from the first of the orders, issued on November 30, 1863, and authorizing the Methodist Episcopal Church Bishop Edward R. Ames to occupy disloyal Methodist Episcopal Church, South, churches. For the order, see *The War of the Rebellion: A Compilation of the Official Records of the Union and Confederate States*, ser. 1, vol. 34, part 2 (Washington, D.C.: Government Printing Office, 1891), 311. For the details and broader impact of these "religious Reconstruction" orders, see Stowell, *Rebuilding Zion*, 30–31; Rable, *God's Almost Chosen Peoples*, 330–34; and Wesley, *Politics of Faith*, 67–72.

20. While Lincoln saw the orders as important for silencing the treasonous and rebellious speech he believed emanated from churches, he also thought they undermined the separation of church and state. See Richard Carwardine, *Lincoln: A Life of Purpose and Power* (2003; New York: Knopf, 2006), 277–78; Stowell, *Rebuilding Zion*, 30–31; Rable, *God's Almost Chosen Peoples*, 330–34; and Wesley, *Politics of Faith*, 67–72.

21. *Journal of the General Conference of the Methodist Episcopal Church, Held in Philadelphia, Pa., 1864* (New York: Carlton and Porter, 1864), 279; "St. Louis Anniversaries," *Western Recorder*, June 10, 1865; and Joseph M. Wilson, *Presbyterian Historical Almanac and Annual Remembrancer for the Church, for 1866* (Philadelphia: Joseph M. Wilson, 1866), 45.

22. See Stowell, *Rebuilding Zion*, 49–64.

23. Though the Emancipation Proclamation applied to at least 3 million of the South's 4 million slaves, estimated conservatively, only some five hundred thousand enslaved people had achieved freedom by the spring of 1865. See Steven Hahn et al., eds., *Land and Labor, 1865*, ser. 3, vol. 3 of *Freedom: A Documentary History of Emancipation, 1861–1867* (Chapel Hill: University of North Carolina Press, 2008), 1–4; and Ira Berlin et al., eds., *The Wartime Genesis of Free Labor: The Lower South*, ser. 1, vol. 3 of *Freedom* (New York: Cambridge University Press, 1990), 77–80.

24. Stuart Robinson, *Slavery, As Recognized in the Mosaic Civil Law, Recognized also, and Allowed, in the Abrahamic, Mosaic, and Christian Church* (Toronto: Rollo and Adam, 1865), v, 20.

25. "Palmyra Manifesto," in *Sourcebook of American Methodism*, ed. Frederick A. Norwood (Nashville: Abingdon Press, 1982), 330–31. See also Charles T. Thrift, "Rebuilding the Southern Church," in *The History of American Methodism*, vol. 2, ed. Emory Stevens Bucke et al. (New York: Abingdon Press, 1964), 267–69.

26. *The American Annual Cyclopedia and Register of Important Events of the Year 1865*, vol. 5 (New York: Appleton, 1870), 706.

27. Ibid.

28. Ibid.

29. "The South: The Methodist Church; Pastoral Address of the Southern Methodist Bishops," *New York Times*, September 10, 1865.

30. Ibid. Also see Irons, *Origins of Proslavery Christianity*, 169–209; and Hildebrand, *The Times Were Strange and Stirring*, 3–7.

31. "The South: The Methodist Church."

32. Ibid.

33. Ibid.

34. Ibid.

35. *Formal Fraternity. Proceedings of the General Conference of the Methodist Episcopal Church and of the Methodist Episcopal Church, South, in 1872, 1874, and 1876, and of the Joint Commission of the Two Churches on Fraternal Relations, at Cape May, New Jersey, August 16–23, 1876* (New York: Nelson and Phillips, 1876), 9.

36. Ibid., 11.

37. Ibid., 37, 38. On the antebellum Methodist schism over slavery and its implications, see Donald G. Mathews, *Slavery and Methodism: A Chapter in American Morality, 1780–1845* (Princeton: Princeton University Press, 1965); Goen, *Broken Churches, Broken Nation*, 78–90; and Richard Carwardine, "Methodists, Politics, and the Coming of the American Civil War," in *Religion and American Politics: From the Colonial Period to the Present*, ed. Mark A. Noll and Luke E. Harlow, 2nd ed. (New York: Oxford University Press, 2007), 185–93.

38. *Formal Fraternity*, 67. On fraternal relations among Methodists, see also Stowell, *Rebuilding Zion*, 172–75; and Thrift, "Rebuilding the Southern Church," 299–303.

39. On Baptist ecclesiological principles, see Gregory A. Wills, *Democratic Religion: Freedom, Authority, and Church Discipline in the Baptist South, 1785–1900* (New York: Oxford University Press, 1997), 26–36.

40. *Proceedings of the Southern Baptist Convention, Held in Augusta, Georgia, May 8th, 9th, 10th, 11th, and 12th, 1845* (Richmond, Va.: H. K. Ellyson, 1845), 18–19; and Goen, *Broken Churches*, 90–98.

41. *Proceedings of the Thirteenth Meeting of the Southern Baptist Convention, Held in the Seventh Baptist Church, Baltimore, May 7th, 8th, 9th, 11th, and 12th, 1868* (Baltimore: John F. Weishampel Jr., 1868), 17–18, 20–21.

42. Ibid., 20–21; and *Proceedings of the Southern Baptist Convention, Held at Russellville, Kentucky, May 22nd, 23rd, 24th, 25th, and 26th, 1866* (Richmond, Va.: Dispatch Steam Presses, 1866), 85–86.

43. Stowell, *Rebuilding Zion*, 169–70; Ernest Trice Thompson, *1861–1890*, vol. 2 of *Presbyterians in the South* (Richmond, Va.: John Knox Press, 1973), 223–26; and *Distinctive Principles*, 91–107.

44. *Distinctive Principles*, 131.

45. Ibid. See also Genovese, *Consuming Fire*, 3–33.

46. Several excellent books do note, often in passing, the salience of proslavery religion for the postslavery order. See Charles Reagan Wilson, *Baptized in Blood: The Religion of the Lost Cause, 1865–1920* (Athens: University of Georgia Press, 1980); Paul

Harvey, *Redeeming the South: Religious Cultures and Racial Identities among Southern Baptists, 1865-1925* (Chapel Hill: University of North Carolina Press, 1997); Beth Barton Schweiger, *The Gospel Working Up: Progress and the Pulpit in Nineteenth-Century Virginia* (New York: Oxford University Press, 1999); Stowell, *Rebuilding Zion*; and Blum, *Reforging the White Republic*.

47. See David W. Blight, *Race and Reunion: The Civil War in American Memory* (Cambridge: Belknap Press of Harvard University Press, 2001); and Blum, *Reforging the White Republic*. The classic accounts of the origins of fundamentalism and modern evangelicalism do not discuss the Civil War, slavery, or race. See Ernest R. Sandeen, *The Roots of Fundamentalism: British and American Millenarianism, 1800-1930* (Chicago: University of Chicago Press, 1970); and George M. Marsden, *Fundamentalism and American Culture: The Shaping of Twentieth-Century Evangelicalism, 1870-1925* (New York: Oxford University Press, 1980). Though not attuned to the role of the slavery question, more recent work has shown expressly the role of racial division in the shaping of fundamentalism, especially Matthew Avery Sutton, *American Apocalypse: A History of Modern Evangelicalism* (Cambridge: Belknap Press of Harvard University Press, 2014), 109-12.

48. On these church efforts at reunion, or lack thereof, see Stowell, *Rebuilding Zion*, 170-78. For an arresting account of the role of white supremacy in southern denominational resistance to civil rights, see Carolyn Renée Dupont, *Mississippi Praying: Southern White Evangelicals and the Civil Rights Movement, 1945-1975* (New York: New York University Press, 2013).

49. See Daniel W. Stowell, "Why 'Redemption'?: Religion and the End of Reconstruction, 1869-1877," in *Vale of Tears: New Essays on Religion and Reconstruction*, ed. Edward J. Blum and W. Scott Poole (Macon, Ga.: Mercer University Press, 2005), 133-46.

6

*Reckoning with African Americans' Testimonies of
Trauma and Suffering from Night Riding*

Kidada E. Williams

On October 29, 1869, sixty-five white men surrounded the Georgia residence of Abram Colby. He testified at the 1871 congressional hearings on the "affairs in the late insurrectionary states" that night riders had raided his home to punish him for insisting on his and other black men's right to vote and serve in office. The men had kidnapped and whipped Colby with "sticks and straps that had buckles on the end of them," before leaving him alone.[1]

African Americans like Colby were on the front lines of southern white Democrats' wars against Republicans' efforts to create a more inclusive democracy in the postwar South.[2] Republican policymakers faced significant challenges achieving their objective of asserting federal control throughout the nation. White southerners were particularly effective in using violent terror to roll back black people's newly gained civil and political rights. Historians have used the transcripts of the Ku Klux Klan hearings to illuminate the consequences of Republicans' failure to recognize that it would take more resources to vanquish the Confederate spirit and to advance "a new birth of freedom" than it had taken to defeat the Confederate army.[3] In this essay, however, I will show that these records do more than provide documentation of political or physical injury; they also expose how African Americans experienced federal failure and processed the resulting injuries in their inner lives.

When I reread survivors' accounts of terrorism after studying scholarship on how people experience violence, I realized that, in addition to reporting the basic facts of what happened, African Americans created a history of the postwar period that documents how much the violent insurgency against freedom undermined their ability to fashion themselves as free people. Survivors of night riding like Colby told lawmakers the details of experiencing earth-shattering attacks that did not always allow either escape or resistance. In telling their stories, black southerners reported a wide range of wounds. Traumatic suffering is one of the easiest injuries to miss because African Americans did not always use terms associated with psychological harm. Yet these people's descriptions of their feelings during paramilitary strikes are filled with what Judith Herman has identified as markers of trauma—"intense fear, helplessness, loss of control, and [the] threat of annihilation."[4] Survivors also pointed to problems they had with coping months and years after violence.

Common sense would suggest to historians that postwar violence wrought significant damage in African Americans' lives. I want to build on existing works that have unearthed the racial atrocities that followed the Civil War by showing how survivors understood and explained the harm they experienced. In this essay, I use scholarship on trauma and suffering to narrate the history of this violence in a new way by attempting to conduct what Nell Irvin Painter might call a "fully loaded cost accounting" of night riding.[5] I do this by focusing my analysis on victims' representations of the moments of attack and what they faced in the days that followed.[6] I take this approach because survivors' stories suggest that deeper psychological and sociological wounds troubled victims of night riding than historians have thus far understood.

CONTENDING WITH TRAUMATIC SUFFERING
IN THE ARCHIVE OF NIGHT RIDING

Research on African Americans' experiences of the consequences of the Civil War has uncovered and focused on continuities of hardship. In *Black Reconstruction*, W. E. B. Du Bois initiated the process of producing histories of emancipation that balance black southerners' triumphs and disappointments in their efforts to fulfill their goals for freedom.[7] His successors exhumed emancipation's complexities regarding labor, family, and politics.[8] What this scholarship has shown historians is that with abolition, civil and political rights, and a belief that Republican officials would protect them, blacks focused on doing what they could to control their own destinies. As a people who harbored distinctive visions of freedom, they did not wait for Congress to pass legislation or need instructions on how to forge their new lives.[9] Black southerners acted locally, using the resources and insights they found at their disposal. As Laura Edwards's and Amy Dru Stanley's essays in this volume show, African Americans pushed for equal access to public institutions and the franchise, transforming what had been privileges into civil and political rights. Although most blacks struggled, some of them successfully reconstituted their families, purchased land, established thriving business, and served in political office. Conservative whites responded to their accomplishments by waging war against freedom and escalating the scale of violence in deadly paramilitary attacks.[10]

I wanted to recover survivors' representations of the terror they endured during night-riding strikes and the continuing wounds they experienced. To illuminate survivors' experiences of this violence I had to cast a wide theoretical net, become more agile methodologically, and utilize research on traumatic suffering.[11] In search of guidance for interpreting survivors' accounts of their injuries, I turned to scholars in the social sciences who studied people's reactions to similar catastrophes and the multitude of injuries victims endured. These researchers' ability to interact with living survivors allowed them to demonstrate how violence, as Veena Das explains, "attaches itself with its tentacles into everyday life and folds itself into the recesses" of people's existence.[12] Seeing the tentacles of violence changed how I interpreted black survivors' accounts of night riding.

Using social scientists' work to make better sense of how people experience violent conflict and explain traumatic events enabled me to see and understand material that I had overlooked when I first started investigating African Americans' testimonies of racial brutality.[13] Looking at violence differently helped me push beyond obvious physical or political injuries and into damages that are more opaque.[14] It also allowed me to consider the Ku Klux Klan hearings' influence on the testimonies' structure.[15] With a road map to navigate the labyrinth of lights and shadows in the articulations and silences of victims' stories, I managed to see what I believe survivors like Abram Colby tried to communicate about how night riding violence became stitched into the fabric of their lives.

My goal is to better understand what African Americans thought it meant to endure postwar violence and how it affected their ability to achieve their goals for freedom. I want to, as Saidiya Hartman writes, "listen for the unsaid, translate misconstrued words, and refashion disfigured lives," and to "reckon with the precarious lives which are visible only in the moment [of their appearance in the archive]."[16] Therefore I am less interested in the documentation of injury than I am in the ways black victims made sense of the harm these injuries created in their lives. I take the approach I do because although African Americans' testimonies of traumatic injury and suffering appear frequently in the archive, scholars have only made them visible for brief moments in the process of writing about other topics. Bringing these moments from the margins to the center of historical analysis helps scholars understand the lived costs of policymakers' failure to stabilize the peace.

NIGHT RIDING STRIKES

When I reread Colby's testimony to see beyond his straightforward account of what had happened, I noticed that he wanted the committee to know that although the night riders came for him, his family got caught in the violent scrum. According to Colby, when the men seized him, his mother, wife, and daughter tried to protect him. The night riders responded with enough force that the women—appreciating the dangerous consequences continued resistance posed—stood down; Colby's young daughter did not. He testified that when she "begged [the white men] not to carry" him away, one of them responded by drawing his gun on her, a terrifying act that finally subdued her. Colby's daughter lived through the attack, but he believed the emotional wound of experiencing the raid contributed to her death shortly thereafter. She "never got over it until she died," he explained. Colby also remarked that her death was "the part that grieves me the most of all."[17] Colby's testimony about his daughter and his own grief points to children being victimized and to victims carrying with them the horrors of what happened to them long after white terror strikes ended.

Night riding involved gangs of armed white men who rejected the Republican goal of black and white southerners coexisting peacefully under the auspices of the federal government. In waging fragmentary attacks, night riders took advantage of the gaps between centers of federal power—whether in Washington, D.C., or Freedmen's Bureau and army outposts—and the disparate places in the margins where most black southerners lived. These men inflicted considerable damage because policymakers had neither the foresight to see how conservative whites would continue fighting to achieve their goals of limiting black people's freedom nor the resources to assert their complete authority over the South's wide terrain.

Night riders surprised families in their homes during the nighttime hours and denied them the possibility of leaving, as they held their victims hostage in a state of what Judith Herman has called "domestic captivity."[18] Although these men used force and violence, they did not always have to do so to control their captives. Oftentimes, the night riders' mere presence and black people's fear of physical harm or annihilation had the power to reduce, as Herman puts it, "victims' sense of autonomy" and undermine their willingness and ability to resist.[19]

Night riders conducted both indiscriminate raids and targeted hits. White men's desire to stop blacks who threatened their power often triggered specific attacks. Night riders went after Doc Rountree for owning more land than they believed a freedman should acquire and for refusing to let his former master apprentice his children in 1869.[20] Other blacks who refused to stand by while whites burned black churches or schools were visited, as were people who insisted on receiving their share of a crop.

Survivors of night riding gave similar accounts of being trapped in their homes, feeling powerless, anticipating death, and enduring a range of injuries. A raid on the Garrisons provides an illustration of what happened to families. In October 1868, white men surrounded the home of Jerry and Leanna Garrison. The couple and their children were sitting around the fire when the men started shooting. Family members scrambled to hide but the gunfire killed Jerry, struck an adult son, Samuel, in the arm, and hit another son in the hip. Hits such as these often happened without warning, so the home's occupants had little recourse other than trying to dodge the bullets.[21]

In night riding's early stages, some African Americans may have dismissed accounts of white men raiding black people's homes in the middle of the night, kidnapping, assaulting, and killing them. Those who knew of these attacks may have persuaded themselves that they would not become victims, assuring themselves that night riders only hit people who deserved it. Augustus Blair testified that he had seen whites "run all the rest of [his black neighbors] away" but "didn't think anybody would ever interfere with me."[22] For Mack Tinker, it took the killing of Lem Campbell, a man whom everyone said was "a good citizen as there was in the country, colored or white," for him to conclude that "if they killed such a man, they will kill me or any other man," and to leave until things calmed down.[23] For a time, this type of rationalization allowed people to believe they would not become victims, but as the attacks continued, blacks learned that everyone was vulnerable.[24]

Survivors testified that the terror of night riding permeated their communities so much that they came to expect and dread it.[25] Letty Mills reported that armed white men's arrival outside her home did not surprise her, because "there had been so much talk of Ku Klux about [Walton County, Georgia,] that I had been expecting them. We had heard of their going about so much that I said they would come down on us next."[26] Internalized terror was a common response of people living in night-riding zones. Henry Reed described people's fear of raids as turning his community in Marianna, Florida, into as "terrible a place at that time as ever there was in the world."[27]

The news of this violence circulated quickly, making it easier for African Americans to comprehend what could happen to them. Some prayed for the best, but others braced for attack. Caroline Smith testified that her family "sat up . . . the better part of the night" watching for night riders.[28] Joseph Turner and Joshua Hairston informed the committee that they started carrying pistols for protection.[29] Some families even reported sleeping outdoors for days and weeks at a time to avoid being trapped by white men in an enclosed space.

As night riders invaded his community, William Coleman reported witnessing strikes, including one on a man named Nathan Cannon. He also testified that he was afraid to share with his wife details of his investigation into the violence he saw for fear that she would "get so uneasy and tore up in mind," suggesting that she had already expressed to him her fears of attack. The Colemans' concerns about night riders visiting them were justified; a raid, which left William bloodied and bruised, forced the family to flee.[30]

The constant fear of attack engendered feelings of intense anxiety and worry among blacks. Listening to or hearing about other people's accounts of experiencing a raid portended the harm that might befall them. Nocturnal noises took on new meaning, as did routine encounters with whites. Letty Mills explained, "I kept feeling afraid all the time of the Ku Klux. Every noise I would hear in the night, after they had begun to get near, I would fear they were coming in on us."[31] African Americans likely imagined various scenarios of what might happen if night riders came for them. This kind of fear proved mentally distressing and physically taxing, likely triggering problems that affected people's health and their ability to fulfill their social obligations.

Hannah Tutson's testimony about the raid on her family opens another window onto the tragedies that befell victims. When I first read her account, I focused on her report that the deputy sheriff, George McCrea, had sexually assaulted her. Rereading her testimony, I discovered that she wanted witnesses to understand much more about what had happened to her family.

Night riders struck Hannah and Samuel Tutson's home after the couple had refused to surrender their land. The white men's invasion of the family's home sent their terrified children fleeing into the woods. The men snatched the couple's toddler from Hannah's arms and threw the baby across the cabin. They then separated Hannah and Samuel, whipped him, and sexually assaulted her. In one of their last moves, the men destroyed the family's property. Tutson testified that because the men had separated her from her family and she could not find her loved ones after the assault, she spent considerable time experiencing the dread of thinking that the white men had killed her entire family. She staggered through her community's thoroughfare half-dressed, battered, bloodied, and calling out "murder" to anyone she encountered. Tutson testified that her neighbors had turned her away and encouraged her to go find her family, which she did—to discover they had all survived.[32] Although all the Tutsons lived through the strike, fear of subsequent attacks forced them to leave their community.

Having heard as much as they had about night riding, families like the Tutsons would have known what to expect when the white men came for them. They would have had few opportunities to escape unharmed. In describing raids, survivors recounted situations akin to what Cathy Caruth has called victims' "waking into consciousness" about their presence amid situational forces spiraling out of their control.[33] Tilda Walthall reported that disguised white men burst into her family's home so quickly that her husband John barely had enough time to crawl under the house before they discovered his hiding spot and killed him.[34] Caroline Benson testified that men "came charging up like a party of cavalry; they scared me very much."[35] One night, Daniel Lane opened his door slightly, possibly after hearing a noise or because he intended to go outside, when white men "burst right in" and whipped him with hickory sticks.[36] These testimonies point to the chaos of attacks and the sense of peril African Americans faced as they found themselves exposed to white men in every possible way.

Scholars who do not know the range of human responses to terror might assume that most people fought back. Yet resistance was not a given. Research shows that people often experience paralytic fright, mutism, or hysterical blindness during catastrophic events.[37] Shock from life-threatening situations can cause fear to invade all the senses and render people physically immobile. Unexpected threats to life can also cause people to panic or misread the situation and act in ways contrary to survival. Maria Carter testified that a gang "came hollering and knocking at the door, and they scared my husband so bad he could not speak when they first came."[38] In light of research on trauma, we must consider that Carter was not speaking hyperbolically but rather describing a literal moment of mutism. People injured in raids' initial moments might have felt the type of pain that Elaine Scarry describes as making people lose their sense of self and place in the world.[39] The fright and pain survivors described experiencing or witnessing suggest that victims could not always choose how they responded to violent attacks. This is why night riders easily overpowered many of their targets.

An individual's sense of helplessness is often exacerbated and people's vulnerability increased when they are attacked in the presence of their kin. Black families in communities with a history of night riding knew what would happen when the white men came and that there was little they could do to save themselves. In his research on Argentina's Dirty War, Marcelo Suárez-Orozco found that violence meted out to families during raids had the effect of "reorganizing the basic social unit, the family. The family's affective bond was manipulated in skillful games of horror."[40] During these games, night riders played on family members' fear of physical harm. They forced captives to make impossible decisions about resisting or deferring to the white men and protecting a loved one or themselves. Family members likely carried with them the "terror and guilt over selective survival in the face of the often inexplicable death and suffering of others."[41] A victim's failure to honor his or her responsibilities to the unit during strikes could wound families. Jacobo Timerman observed of his imprisonment and time reporting on the Dirty War that "nothing can compare to those family groups who were [terrorized] together, sometimes separately but in view of one another, or in different [areas] while one was aware of the other being tortured. . . . The entire affective world, constructed over the years with utmost difficulty, collapses. . . . Suddenly an entire culture based on familial love, devotion, the capacity for mutual sacrifice collapses. Nothing is possible in such a universe, and that is precisely what the torturers know."[42]

Such theories appear to be borne out in the testimonies of black men, who often said the presence of their loved ones intensified their feelings of terror and powerlessness. Reuben Sheets might have resisted, but he was "scared nearly about to death" the men would shoot him. He also explained that he had to consider that his "wife and children got scared."[43] Alfred Richardson testified that when his wife cried out to neighbors for help, the men shot at her "some twelve or fifteen times." Richardson responded by firing on the men, killing one, which forced them to retreat.[44] Lewis Jackson was armed with his pistol "all loaded six times, and I had a hole to shoot at them" but his wife Sally said, "don't shoot them; they are too many; they'll overpower you and kill you." He listened, which probably saved their lives.[45] Henry Johnson did not fight the men who came for him because his wife "was in the family way. I couldn't do nothing, and I just stood and took it. I couldn't help myself no way."[46] These men made decisions knowing that if they tried to defend their families and did not succeed, or if their family members intervened, the white men might retaliate by killing everyone. None of them used the terms "guilt" or "shame" as they explained where they could not protect their families, but ethnographers' and psychologists' interviews with male survivors of other conflicts suggest that these feelings might have plagued them long after the night riders departed.[47]

Research on youth amid conflict made it easier for me to follow parents' testimonies of what happened to their children and to consider the physical and psychic impact that night-riding attacks may have had on young people.[48] The presence of children, ranging from newborns to young adults, during strikes had subduing effects on parents, according to survivors' stories. Martin Anthony testified that he did not defend himself and his home from night riders, because "my wife was not at home, and there was nobody there but me and my daughter." The men did not touch the fifteen-year-old girl because she "ran under the bed as they came in." Anthony explained that he was terrified that if he tried to defend himself, the men would kill both him and his child. He tried to deescalate the situation by allowing the men to beat and carry him from his home. Anthony did not resist, he explained, "because I was afraid they would shoot me" and attack or kill his daughter if they discovered her. When a congressman interviewing Anthony asked, "Why did you not get away?" Anthony responded, "There was no chance." What remained unspoken was that running away would have meant leaving his daughter to face the men alone, which was something Anthony could not do.[49]

Black youths' capriciousness could lead to their victimization. Parents' testimonies suggest that some kids cried uncontrollably, either out of fear or because they could not understand what was happening around them. Crying children intensified the situation inside homes, because perpetrators wanted to silence them and forced parents to choose between complying with night riders' commands and protecting their children. The parents had reason for concern. Anthony probably knew that if he ran, his daughter might have tried to follow and put herself in harm's way. Wild panic drove Henry Reed's son William to jump out of a window, an act that drew a blast of gunfire. Reed described being paralyzed by fear. "I did not know what to do," he explained. It was only when Reed fled the house in search of William that he discovered his son was injured but alive. During a raid on Sampson Reed's home, white men pistol-whipped his sixteen-year-old son Andy, and he was unable to intervene.[50]

Parents did what they could to shield their children from violence, including refusing to follow white men's demands. The presence of Sir Daniel's two-day-old child informed his refusal to leave his home when night riders ordered him to do so, as well as his threat, after some discussion with his wife, that they would have to come take him at their own risk.[51] The men left the family alone, but the Daniels fled for their future safety. Strikes like these rendered all family members vulnerable, deepening their suffering.

As these cases show, African Americans could not always stop night riders from carrying out their attacks. The white men killed many of the people who tried to defend themselves. Survivors all recounted similar stories—a seemingly normal day altered by an inescapable attack.

TRAUMATIZING WOUNDS

Witnesses at the hearings were people who lived and *lived with* what had happened for the rest of their lives.[52] Studying victims' processing of traumatic experiences as they tried to resume their lives, Caruth argues that researchers cannot locate trauma in the event, "but rather in . . . [what] returns to the haunt the survivor."[53] The stories told by survivors of night riding indicate that their wounds—which social science research suggests included not only physical aches but also intrusive memories of the attacks and anxieties about the future—formed part of what returned to haunt them. These wounds, Caruth writes, represent trauma, which is "more than a pathology, or the simple illness of a wounded psyche: it is always the story of a wound that cries out, that addresses us in the attempt to tells us of a reality or truth that is not otherwise available."[54] The wounds that returned to haunt survivors also included attempts to make sense of what happened to them, to consider how they might have acted differently, and to figure out how to contend with living after violence.

One of the most obvious indications of the psychological wounds African Americans suffered from night riding are survivors' detailed testimonies about the physical injuries they endured. Hannah Tutson explained, "I was just raw. The blood oozed out from my frock all around my waist, clean through . . . I could not bear my clothes fastened on me." Tutson also testified about the wounds her child suffered and her efforts to heal the baby. When the toddler tried to walk, "one of its hips was very bad, and every time you would stand it up it would scream," Tutson explained. The physical pain was likely also a reminder to the child and its parents of what had happened. Hannah reported that she "rubbed and rubbed it," and thought that the baby was finally "outgrowing" the wounds.[55] In the attack on him, Joseph Turner tried to defend himself by putting his arms up. He testified that "they killed my arms dead, and they struck me over the head. . . . It was six weeks before I could grab anything with my hand." Turner provided even more evidence of his ongoing suffering by explaining that "I never laid down the whole night; I could not lay. When I would lay down it felt like my arms would all burst off of me. I walked about all night in the yard or in the house. I could not sit, I was in such misery. They liked to have broken both my arms."[56] Daniel Lane explained, "I could not go about. My wife had to wash me with salt and water, and grease me good; I could not get about for about a week."[57] Scipio Eager was whipped and his brother killed when night riders raided his home in response to the three Eager brothers' insistence on voting. Eager testified, "they took off every rag of clothes I had, and laid me down on the ground, and some stood on my head some on my feet . . . I did not do any work in the three weeks afterward."[58]

Some survivors reported experiencing physical pain months and years after their attacks. Jesse Brown, whose skull was cracked when a night rider kicked him with a brass spur, complained that "it pains me now; every time it goes to rain it bothers me a heap."[59] Henry Hamlin claimed he was "never whipped so much in all the days of my life" and that three years later he still sometimes felt "the pain coming back in my back now; I have never got well from it; it hurt me so bad."[60] Victims' wounds and pains manifested as both physical and mental reminders of night-riding strikes.

Witnesses not only described their discomfort, but they also presented their bodies as evidence of their victimization. Women and men displayed fresh stripes from whippings, scars from bullet wounds and stabbings, and rope burns from being hanged or dragged. The transcript of Jack Johnson's testimony reads, "here is the scar of his lick. [Indicating]. He struck me here, and struck me again, and this finger he broke entirely so that I cannot turn a drill in my hand."[61] Others showed different evidence to prove what happened. George Roper presented one of the pistol balls doctors removed from his breast after having been shot in the back.[62] Because these displays came unprompted, we can conclude that victims likely believed that showing physical evidence might attend to some committee members' questions about the veracity of their testimonies.

In explaining their injuries, witnesses also discussed the medical care they had received. Some people treated physical wounds themselves, with the healing practices of washing lacerations or applying poultices, but others testified that they called on doctors. Victims made their decisions based on a family member's medical knowledge or whether they could find a doctor they trusted to treat them. Some witnesses' testimonies described doctors as empathetic and providing good care, but others did not.[63] A Dr. Estell charged Charles Powell $10 "just to look at" his gunshot wound and tell his wife to wash it, but Drs. Edmonds and Seal took the ball out for $5.[64] Augustus Blair contacted several doctors to care for his son Billy whom night riders had beaten and stabbed. He testified that a Dr. Henry Bedford hounded him for "forty or fifty dollars" even after he had lost everything and Billy had died from his injuries.[65]

Families whose members were incapacitated by violence had to rely on kin and neighbors until the wounded could resume their work and provide for their families. Jack Johnson could no longer use a drill for work. Abram Colby was unable to work as a barber or to haul wood because of the physical injuries he had sustained, including to his left hand, which he declared was "not of much use to me."[66] Major Gardiner testified that after night riders whipped his brother so badly, he "never expected to see him alive." Gardiner's brother lived, but he could not work for a year and had to "let his children stay out to work to get him something to live on."[67] Even if they felt the need to relocate, many victims testified that they could not do so until they had healed to earn enough money to move. Understanding the immediate and possible long-term implications of these injuries helps us understand the different types of suffering that African Americans endured.

Less obvious to researchers are survivors' representations of psychological wounds that came from losing loved ones or suffering from posttraumatic stress. Henry Reed described himself as being "badly disturbed" by the hit on his family.[68] Reuben Sheets reported, "I have never rested since."[69] Although he might have been afraid of being struck again, trying to understand what happened to his family and why might have been the source of Sheets's agitation. Abram Colby added a phrase that elucidated his belief about the totalizing effect of the raid on his life when he explained, "they broke something inside of me." In saying this, Colby seemed to want members of the committee to know that he had suffered more than just physical or financial injury; the repercussions were psychological and emotional as well.[70] Alfred Richardson described his wife, whose cries during the raid on their family drew gunfire, as being "injured [by what happened] a good deal. She was in a delicate state at the time they came to my house, and it has injured her. She will never be of any more account, I think." The transcripts do not indicate whether Mrs. Richardson's delicacy involved pregnancy or a fragile mental state. However, Richardson's statement that the violence had "injured" his wife and that he thought she would "never be of any more account," echoed by other survivors, seems to indicate a belief that neither they nor their families would ever be the same.[71] Richardson did not describe any emotional injuries he or his children endured from the attack, but they certainly would have suffered and probably had to balance managing their own distress with helping Mrs. Richardson cope. In describing emotional injuries, survivors seem to have attempted to make their humanity visible to officials listening.[72]

The social science literature suggests that victims of terrorist violence often end up displaced from their homes and communities, and this was often the case for African Americans in the South. Night riders destroyed African Americans' crops and property, and many survivors fled their homes. "I had to come away," Floridian Joseph Nelson testified.[73] Daniel Lane explained, "Now, if a man is warned of danger and he stays and is caught again, it's his own fault."[74] Warren Jones informed the committee, "[Whites] got so bad I could not stand it; they threatened to take my life."[75] Nelson reported, "they did not tell me I could not say, but they were going to kill me."[76] Continued threats to their lives forced victims to leave the homes and communities in which they had made their lives after slavery.

The primary targets of night riding were the first to decamp. Some, like Augustus Blair, left his family behind, but others fled alongside their kin. Caleb Jenkins bolted with eight children in tow. His family went from living together in a home fitted for material comfort to living separately with no property but the clothes on their backs. Jenkins found employment as a cook and a place for him to sleep, but his employer would not agree to allow his children to reside on the property, so he had to rent a room for them.[77]

In escaping from violence, survivors reported leaving everything behind, pointing to economic dispossession as a consequence of night riding. Warren Jones testified, "I gathered up what I could in my arms, and with my wife and child, I came away."[78] William Coleman and his family quickly deserted their land and the home he built on it. He reported, "I have lost my year's crop, and my land, and everything else. I can't get nothing out of it, nor do anything about it."[79] Daniel Lane explained that he "left it all [his property], corn, cotton, horse, wagon, and everything."[80] According to Abram Colby, "I have a small plantation, and I could make as comfortable a living there as anywhere in the world if they would leave me alone. I cannot live [there]."[81] Augustus Blair cited thirty head of hogs, four bales of cotton worth "$200 at 20 cents a pound," and forty acres of corn still in the ground as the losses he sustained when he left right after the attack. When he returned home, he found everything "destroyed and taken." He estimated his total loss at about $500.[82] After night riders raided Eliza Lyon's home and killed her husband, Abe, she reported the family lost $600 in cash they had been saving to move to Demopolis to buy land and build a new home, hogs, a $75 wagon, and a "great many other little things."[83] Fear of returning to their communities and an inability to find representation to navigate the legal system prevented many families from filing lawsuits to recoup their financial losses, which left them destitute, compounding their victimization.

From accounts of physical and psychological wounds to descriptions of the economic losses they sustained, these survivors' testimonies are rich in direct and indirect representations of the hardships African Americans endured from night riding. Henry Reed testified, "They deprived me of everything I owned in there in the world."[84] It is clear, even from the snippets of information survivors like Reed provided, that victims still struggled to manage the effects of violence months and years after strikes had occurred.

SOCIAL SUFFERING AND NIGHT RIDING'S IMPACT ON FREEDOM

African Americans who testified at the hearings made clear distinctions when they described their lives before and after a strike, underscoring what they understood to be night riding's transformative nature.[85] Witnesses' accounts of "the after" indicate what anthropologists refer to as "social suffering," which include the myriad difficulties people face in the wake of calamities. These problems are not only individual; they are shared across families and communities and influence how people respond to the societies in which they live.[86] Analyzing the survivors' lexicon made it easier to apprehend how raids subverted black southerners' efforts to build new lives after slavery.

Emancipation allowed many African Americans to assert new control over their lives. Postwar research reveals that many people made good use of freedom's economic promises, whether they were in the United States or, as Barbara Krauthamer's essay in this volume shows, in Indian Territory. They not only found viable work by securing contracts or opening their own businesses but balanced work with valuable leisure activities. Some black southerners purchased land and planted crops to feed their families and generate profit. Even with inefficient southern economic institutions and limited economic growth, black people's material income increased significantly after slavery.[87]

African Americans took advantage of freedom's social and political benefits too. They reconstituted families and negotiated gender relations in ways that made sense to them. Black southerners built homes to their liking and, using their power as consumers, furnished them with goods that suited their personal tastes. Once enough of them congregated in a neighborhood, they built community institutions to try to eliminate the disadvantages that had come with slavery.[88] Thanks to the Fifteenth

Amendment black men voted in elections, held elective and appointed offices, and helped create democratic governments and policies. They tried to defend their right to vote as they saw fit and to protect themselves against attacks. Even amid extraordinary political violence, in many places, black men continued to vote and even hold office well into the late nineteenth century.

After throwing their full weight behind making freedom real, black southerners fought to keep what they had built. They did this not only because they had worked so hard but also because they understood the precariousness of their situation after the war. Victims reported violence to U.S. troops and agents of the Freedmen's Bureau, claiming their citizenship rights and demanding protection as Crystal Feimster's essay shows. Some demanded better wages and working conditions, and when those demands failed, they stopped working or found new employment. They also filed lawsuits to recover lost property or stolen wages and defended themselves and their communities against violence. Daily life could be a struggle but witnesses at the hearings seemed to have managed the transition to freedom well until the night riders' attacks began.[89]

Survivors' testimonies about losing cash and property suggest that night riding robbed African Americans of financial resources they had accumulated after slavery. Victims' accounts about murdered loved ones and displacement from their homes and communities hint at significant social disruptions. Deadly campaigns against black politicians and voters resulted not only in the loss of these men but possibly in fear of engaging politically in future elections.[90] Disfranchisement by violence made it even more difficult for blacks to protect their social and economic interests. Night riding had many reverberations in survivors' lives.

Lawmakers conducting the hearings were charged with investigating political violence; they could not restore what victims had lost. Few survivors testified about recovering their property or receiving humanitarian aid. Although victims may have been denied official justice, the investigations into this violence did help drive the Ku Klux Klan underground. African Americans who testified also had the opportunity to proclaim night riding's impact on their interior lives.

These survivors' stories show that experiencing violence disrupted some African Americans' ability to meet the obligations and responsibilities of freedom. Night riders stripped families like the Lanes and the Joneses of the wealth they had accumulated after slavery, depriving them of the opportunity to pass on property and cash to their heirs. Augustus Blair's daughters would not be able to inherit the wealth he had been accruing before the raid. Indeed, his ability to provide for his family as he had done previously remained compromised even at the time of his testimony. Families like the Lyons and the Garrisons, who lost family members in attacks, experienced immense emotional grief. Women widowed by night riding, like Eliza Lyon and Leanna Garrison, lost the labor and income their husbands Abe and Jerry provided, forcing them to work harder or to rely on relatives to bear their economic burdens. The murder of craftsmen and tradesmen meant fathers could not pass on skills to their sons, which would have constrained families' wealth for generations. Jack Johnson and Stewart Samuel survived the raids on their families, but both men's injuries left them unable to provide from their work in carpentry and blacksmithing, forcing their families to live on less than they had before.[91] When the Nelsons and the Tutsons fled their communities, they left behind property and social networks. Once they arrived in new locations they had to rebuild their support systems and find housing and work. Caleb Jenkins's inability to live under the same roof as his children reveals some of the difficulties families faced when starting over. Communities that lost political leaders, elders, and other political actors to violence were vulnerable to subsequent attacks and even more repression. All of this points to long-term and intergenerational factors in the contrails of suffering that flowed out from the attacks.

This is not to say that African Americans could not meet the responsibilities of freedom. Some black southerners' success, even in the face of violent white supremacy, shows that many of them could and did. However, when one considers how night riding violence attached itself to people's lives for the long term, it becomes easier to see the magnitude of the challenges that many African Americans faced in this period. Most former slaves were vulnerable to the harsh realities of postwar life; experiencing a terrorist strike made them even more so.

Survivors did not simply accept their oppression; many of them fought against it. Some rebounded, though others never recovered. For those who rallied, scholars should consider the complex and situational nature of recovery. Although some individuals or families may have managed to heal physical wounds or rebuild some of their wealth, they were probably not as strong as before the attacks. It is also worth contemplating how much more successful some blacks might have been had they not endured such catastrophes so close to slavery's end. For those who did not recover, historians should consider the impact of conditions that did not yet have a name—chronic anxiety and pain, trauma, and complicated grief—on survivors' families and communities.

Attempting to historicize African American suffering from night riding has its risks. As Judith Herman notes, trauma "provokes such controversy that it periodically becomes anathema" because it leads us "into the realms of the unthinkable and founder[s] on questions of belief."[92] For some historians, something as indeterminate as the traumatic suffering caused by night riding remains beyond historical analysis.

Scholars investigating the effects of racial violence have reason to proceed with particular care. The controversies surrounding Stanley Elkins's *Slavery* (1959) and *The Moynihan Report* (1965) illuminate the hazards of pathologizing African Americans.[93] However, too much caution seems to have constrained historians' ability to conduct a comprehensive "cost-accounting" of postwar violence and has prevented us from understanding its devastating truths.

My effort to bring to light some of night riding's underanalyzed truths is consistent with the work of scholars excavating the harsh realities of the war and its aftermath.[94] In her work on the atrocities noncombatants and freedom seekers faced during the war, Thavolia Glymph, in particular, called on scholars to write about the "history of hurt," one that resists triumphant narratives and allows for the comprehensive analysis of people's suffering.[95] The effects of night riding belong in the same category as the histories of individual and collective pain.

Historicizing African Americans' experiences of night riding is difficult, and some of the conclusions drawn from testimonies will remain speculative as scholars cannot themselves interview the survivors. The potential rewards of fostering a deeper appreciation for the difficulties black southerners faced in their initial efforts to make freedom real outweigh those challenges, however. In doing this work, historians do not need to speak for or give voice to victims of violence; they simply need to let the survivors speak for themselves and pay even closer attention to what they did or did not say and how they said it. Bringing night-riding victims' wounds from the shadows of this history into the light helps us convey the horrors black southerners experienced and what they believed they lost when there was no peace.

I want to thank Lisa Ze Winters, Liette Gidlow, Danielle McGuire, William Blair, Laura Edwards, Crystal Feimster, and Anthony Kaye for their invaluable feedback in the development of this essay. I am also deeply appreciative of the precise suggestions Greg Downs, Kate Masur, Jay Mazzocchi, and the anonymous reviewers made to render the essay stronger.

1. Abram Colby, Oct. 27, 1871, in U. S. Congress, *Testimony Taken by the Joint Select Committee to Inquire into the Condition of Affairs in the Late Insurrectionary States: Georgia* (Washington, D.C.: Government Printing Office, 1872), 695–97 (cited hereafter as GAKT for Georgia Klan Testimony).

2. Boyle argues that postwar violence was "not a replay of the Civil War but rather a new conflict, largely conducted at a subterranean fashion by new actors or by splinters from existing groups." See Michael J. Boyle, *Violence after War: Explaining Instability in Post-conflict States* (Baltimore: Johns Hopkins University Press, 2014), 7, and 5–8, for a larger discussion. See also George C. Rable, *But There Was No Peace: The Role of Violence in the Politics of Reconstruction* (Athens: University of Georgia Press, 1984).

3. For the miscalculation of resources, see Boyle, *Violence after War*, 3–5.

4. Judith Lewis Herman, *Trauma and Recovery*, rev. ed. (New York: BasicBooks, 1997), 33.

5. See Nell Irvin Painter, *Soul Murder and Slavery* (Waco, Tex.: Markham Press Fund, Baylor University Press, 1995). See also Saidiya V. Hartman, *Scenes of Subjection: Terror, Slavery, and Self-Making in Nineteenth-Century America* (New York: Oxford University Press, 1997); Michel-Rolph Trouillot, *Silencing the Past: Power and the Production of History* (Boston: Beacon Press, 1995); Wendy Anne Warren, "'The Cause of Her Grief': The Rape of a Slave in Early New England," *Journal of American History* 93, no. 4 (2007): 1031–49; Marisa J. Fuentes, "Power and Historical Figuring: Rachael Pringle Polgreen's Troubled Archive," *Gender and History* 22, no. 3 (2010): 564–84.

6. I use "stories" and "representations" to describe survivors' accounts to illuminate the processes by which historical actors produced these records. It is not clear that witnesses who testified at congressional hearings were able to authenticate the transcriptions of their statements. Additionally, using traumatic suffering to analyze historical accounts of violence means conceding that these testimonies are *representations* of what survivors *remembered* and *believed* happened to them during attacks. It also means acknowledging that survivors' memories could be fragmented or characterized by gaps and inconsistencies. For insight on analyzing testimonies, I turned to Helmut Walser Smith, *The Holocaust and Other Genocides: History, Representation, Ethics* (Nashville: Vanderbilt University Press, 2002); Shoshana Felman and Dori Laub, *Testimony: Crises of Witnessing in Literature, Psychoanalysis, and History* (New York: Routledge, 1991); Andrea Frisch, "The Ethics of Testimony: A Genealogical Perspective," *Discourse* 25, nos. 1–2 (2003): 36–54; Herman, *Trauma and Recovery*, 175–95; Trouillot, *Silencing the Past*.

7. W. E. B. Du Bois, *Black Reconstruction: An Essay toward a History of the Part Which*

Black Folk Played in the Attempt to Reconstruct Democracy in America, 1860–1880 (New York: Harcourt, Brace, 1935); Eric Foner, *Reconstruction: America's Unfinished Revolution, 1863–1877* (New York: Harper and Row, 1988).

8. See Steven Hahn, *A Nation under Our Feet: Black Political Struggles in the Rural South, from Slavery to the Great Migration* (Cambridge: Belknap Press of Harvard University Press, 2003). See the following for scholarship on families: Laura F. Edwards, *Gendered Strife and Confusion: The Political Culture of Reconstruction* (Urbana: University of Illinois Press, 1997); Noralee Frankel, *Freedom's Women: Black Women and Families in Civil War Era Mississippi* (Bloomington: Indiana University Press, 1999); Heather Andrea Williams, *Help Me to Find My People: The African American Search for Family Lost in Slavery* (Chapel Hill: University of North Carolina Press, 2012). For insight on the economic transformations brought on by emancipation, see Amy Dru Stanley, *From Bondage to Contract: Wage Labor, Marriage, and the Market in the Age of Slave Emancipation* (Cambridge: New York: Cambridge University Press, 1998); Tera W. Hunter, *To 'Joy My Freedom: Southern Black Women's Lives and Labors after the Civil War* (Cambridge: Harvard University Press, 1997).

9. Elsa Barkley Brown, "To Catch the Vision of Freedom: Reconstructing Southern Black Women's Political History, 1865–1880," in *African American Women and the Vote, 1837–1960*, ed. Ann D. Gordon, Bettye Collier-Thomas, John H. Bracey, Arlene Avakian, and Joyce Berkman (Amherst: University of Massachusetts Press, 1997).

10. See Allen W. Trelease, *White Terror: The Ku Klux Klan Conspiracy and Southern Reconstruction* (Baton Rouge: Louisiana State University Press, 1995). See also Lou Falkner Williams, *The Great South Carolina Ku Klux Klan Trials, 1871–1872* (Athens: University of Georgia Press, 1996). For an analysis of African Americans in the context of this violence, see Gladys-Marie Fry, *Night Riders in Black Folk History* (Knoxville: University of Tennessee Press, 1975); V. P. Franklin, *Black Self-Determination: A Cultural History of African-American Resistance* (Brooklyn, N.Y.: Lawrence Hill Books, 1992).

11. Several scholars discuss the constraints historical methods place on understanding trauma. See Saidiya V. Hartman, "Venus in Two Acts," *Small Axe* 26, no. 2 (2008): 1–14; Dominic LaCapra, *Writing History, Writing Trauma* (Baltimore: Johns Hopkins University Press, 2000); Cathy Caruth, *Unclaimed Experience: Trauma, Narrative, and History* (Baltimore: Johns Hopkins University Press, 1996).

12. Veena Das, *Life and Words: Violence and the Descent into the Ordinary* (Berkeley: University of California Press, 2007), 1.

13. For insight on how people become socialized to terror, see Linda L. Green, *Fear as a Way of Life: Mayan Widows in Rural Guatemala* (New York: Columbia University Press, 1999); Nancy Scheper-Hughes, *Death without Weeping: The Violence of Everyday Life in Brazil* (Berkeley: University of California Press, 1992); Michael T. Taussig, "Culture of Terror — Space of Death: Roger Casement's Putumayo Report and the Explanation of Torture," in *Violence: A Reader*, ed. Catherine Lowe Besteman (New York: New York University Press, 2002), 211–43. See also Fiona C. Ross, "Speech and Silence: Women's Testimony in the First Five Weeks of Public Hearings of the South African Truth and Reconciliation Commission," in *Remaking a World: Violence, Social Suffering,*

and Recovery, ed. Veena Das, Arthur Kleinman, Margaret Lock, Mamphela Ramphele, and Pamela Reynolds (Berkeley: University of California Press, 2001), 250–80. For deciphering testimony and accounting for the settings in which it is recorded, see Thomas Trezise, "Between History and Psychoanalysis: A Cast Study in the Reception of Holocaust Testimony," *History and Memory* 20, no. 1 (2008): 7–47.

14. For debates on psychohistory and historicizing trauma, see Saul Friedländer, *History and Psychoanalysis: An Inquiry into the Possibilities and Limits of Psychohistory* (New York: Holmes and Meier, 1978); Gerald M. Sider and Gavin A. Smith, *Between History and Histories: The Making of Silences and Commemorations* (Toronto: University of Toronto Press, 1997); Trezise, "Between History and Pscyhoanalysis"; Herman, *Trauma and Recovery*, 34.

15. The committee was charged with investigating election-related violence, which informed the witnesses they called, the scope of their investigation (violence occurring between 1869 and 1871), and the questions they asked. In a work that has cast a brilliant light on the intersections of gender, sexual violence, and political terror after the war, Hannah Rosen has shown that witnesses had to fit their testimonies into a narrow legal framework by answering the questions they were asked, responding to interruptions or questions about their character, who owned them, and whether they could read or write. Hannah Rosen, *Terror in the Heart of Freedom: Citizenship, Sexual Violence, and the Meaning of Race in the Postemancipation South* (Chapel Hill: University of North Carolina Press, 2009). For more on sexual violence, see also Lisa Cardyn, "Sexualized Racism/Gendered Violence: Outraging the Body Politic in the Reconstruction South," *Michigan Law Review* 100, no. 4 (2002): 675–867.

16. Hartman, "Venus in Two Acts," 2–3, 12.

17. Abram Colby, GAKT, 697.

18. Herman, *Trauma and Recovery*, 74–96.

19. For a discussion of captives' interpretations of their captors' power, see ibid., 74–78.

20. Doc Rountree, Nov. 14, 1871, in U. S. Congress, *Joint Select Committee on the Condition of Affairs in the Late Insurrectionary States: Miscellaneous and Florida* (Washington, D.C.: Government Printing Office, 1872), 279–81 (cited hereafter as FLKT for Florida Klan Testimony).

21. Leanna Garrison, Oct. 27, 1871, GAKT, 666–68; Samuel Garrison, Oct. 27, 1871, GAKT, 688.

22. Augustus Blair, Oct. 9, 1871, U. S. Congress, *Joint Select Committee on the Condition of Affairs in the Late Insurrectionary States: Alabama* (Washington, D.C.: Government Printing Office, 1872), 678 (cited hereafter as ALKT for Alabama Klan Testimony).

23. Mack Tinker, Oct. 26, 1871, ALKT, 1361, 1362.

24. Suárez-Orozco discusses internalization as one of three phases of communities' coming to terms with terror. See Marcelo M. Suárez-Orozco, "Speaking of the Unspeakable: Toward a Psychosocial Understanding of Responses to Terror," *Ethos* 18, no. 1 (1990): 367–70.

25. Michael Taussig describes violence as creating a culture of terror. Taussig invoked Walter Benjamin's theory of "terror as usual" to understand how people

internalize terror. See Michael T. Taussig, "Terror as Usual," in *The Nervous System* (New York: Routledge, 1992), 11–54.

26. Letty Mills, Oct. 23, 1871, GAKT, 468.

27. Henry Reed, Nov. 11, 1871, FLKT, 110.

28. Caroline Smith, Oct. 21, 1871, GAKT, 400–401.

29. Joshua Hairston, Nov. 11, 1871, in U.S. Congress, *Testimony Taken by the Joint Select Committee to Inquire into The Condition of Affairs in the Late Insurrectionary States: Mississippi* (Washington, D.C.: Government Printing Office, 1872), 798 (cited hereafter as MSKT for Mississippi Klan Testimony); Joseph Turner, Nov. 11, 1871, MSKT, 770–71, 772.

30. William Coleman, Nov. 6, 1871, MSKT, 486, 485.

31. Letty Mills, GAKT, 468.

32. Hannah Tutson, Nov. 10, 1871, FLKT, 59–64.

33. Caruth, *Unclaimed Experience*, 64.

34. Tilda Walthall, Oct. 21, 1871, GAKT, 407–8.

35. Caroline Benson, Oct. 21, 1871, GAKT, 387

36. Daniel Lane, Oct. 27, 1871, GAKT, 653.

37. John Leach, "Why People 'Freeze' in an Emergency: Temporal and Cognitive Constraints on Survival Responses," *Aviation, Space, and Environmental Medicine* 75, no. 6 (2004): 539–42.

38. Maria Carter, Oct. 21, 1871, GAKT, 411.

39. Elaine Scarry, *The Body in Pain: The Making and Unmaking of the World* (New York: Oxford University Press, 1985), 35.

40. Marcelo M. Suárez-Orozco, "The Treatment of Children in the 'Dirty War': Ideology, State Terrorism, and the Abuse of Children in Argentina" in *Violence in War and Peace: An Anthology*, ed. Nancy Scheper-Hughes and Philippe Bourgois (Malden, Mass.: Blackwell, 2003), 386.

41. Suárez-Orozco, "Speaking of the Unspeakable," 355.

42. Jacobo Timerman, *Prisoner without a Name, Cell without a Number* (New York: Vintage, 1981), 148–49.

43. Reuben Sheets, Oct. 27, 1871, GAKT, 651.

44. Alfred Richardson, July 7, 1871, GAKT, 2–3.

45. Lewis Jackson, Oct. 14, 1871, ALKT, 983.

46. Henry Johnson, Oct. 14, 1871, ALKT, 954.

47. For an enlightening discussion of gendered guilt in cultures of terror, see Frantz Fanon, "Colonial Wars and Mental Disorders," in *The Wretched of the Earth* (New York: Grove, 1963; reprint 2005; translated from French by Richard Philcox).

48. James Quesada, "Suffering Child: An Embodiment of War and Its Aftermath in Post-Sandinista Nicaragua," in *Violence in War and Peace*, 290–96; Suárez-Orozco, "The Treatment of Children in the 'Dirty War,'" 378–88.

49. Martin Anthony, Oct. 27, 1871, GAKT, 692–93.

50. Henry Reed, FLKT, 109; Sampson Reed and Andy Reed, Oct. 27, 1871, GAKT, 644–46.

51. Sir Daniel, Oct. 14, 1871, ALKT, 994.

52. Herman's work underscores the long-term effects of surviving traumatic events. See *Trauma and Recovery*.

53. Caruth, *Unclaimed Experience*, 4

54. Ibid., 4.

55. Samuel Tutson, Nov. 10, 1871, FLKT, 54–59; Hannah Tutson, FLKT, 60–61.

56. Joseph Turner, Nov. 11, 1871, MSKT, 770, 772.

57. Daniel Lane, GAKT, 653.

58. Scipio Eager, Oct. 27, 1871, GAKT, 668.

59. Jesse Brown, Oct. 12, 1871, ALKT, 861.

60. Henry Hamlin, Oct. 12, 1871, ALKT, 858.

61. Jack Johnson, July 20, 1871, in U. S. Congress, *Joint Select Committee on the Condition of Affairs in the Late Insurrectionary States: South Carolina* (Washington, D.C.: Government Printing Office, 1872), 1169 (cited hereafter as SCKT for South Carolina Klan Testimony).

62. George Roper, Oct. 9, 1871, ALKT, 688.

63. See Sharla Fett, *Working Cures: Healing, Health, and Power on Southern Slave Plantations* (Chapel Hill: University of North Carolina Press, 2002); Gretchen Long, *Doctoring Freedom: The Politics of African American Medical Care* (Chapel Hill: University of North Carolina Press, 2012); Todd Savitt, *Race and Medicine in Nineteenth and Early Twentieth Century America* (Kent, Ohio: Kent State University Press, 2006); Harriet A. Washington, *Medical Apartheid: The Dark History of Medical Experimentation on Black Americans from Colonial Times to the Present* (New York: Anchor, 2008).

64. Charles Powell, Nov. 3, 1871, ALKT, 1848.

65. Augustus Blair, ALKT, 676.

66. Abram Colby, GAKT, 697.

67. Major Gardiner, Oct. 12, 1871, ALKT, 863.

68. Henry Reed, FLKT, 112.

69. Reuben Sheets, GAKT, 651.

70. Abram Colby, GAKT, 697.

71. Alfred Richardson, GAKT, 9.

72. Lisa Ze Winters, in July 15, 2014, conversation with the author.

73. Joseph Nelson, Nov. 11, 1871, FLKT, 136.

74. Daniel Lane, GAKT, 654.

75. Warren Jones, Oct. 27, 1871, GAKT, 689.

76. Joseph Nelson, FLKT, 136.

77. Caleb Jenkins, July 12, 1871, SCKT, 696–98.

78. Warren Jones, GAKT, 689.

79. William Coleman, MSKT, 486.

80. Daniel Lane, GAKT, 654.

81. Abram Colby, GAKT, 697.

82. Augustus Blair, ALKT, 676, 678. Victims named white men, including census workers and their employers, who could verify their calculations, which informs my use of these figures here.

83. Eliza Lyon, Oct. 24, 1871, ALKT, 1263, 1264.

84. Henry Reed, FLKT, 109.

85. For a discussion of terror and violence as temporal markers, see Kidada E. Williams, *They Left Great Marks on Me: African American Testimonies of Racial Violence from Emancipation to World War I* (New York: New York University Press, 2012), 7; Sasanka Perera, "Spirit Possessions and Avenging Ghosts: Stories of Supernatual Activity as Narratives of Terror and Mechanisms of Coping and Remembering," in Das et al., *Remaking a World*, 159.

86. Arthur Kleinman, Veena Das, and Margaret M. Lock, eds., *Social Suffering* (Berkeley: University of California Press, 1997), x.

87. Roger L. Ransom and Richard Sutch, *One Kind of Freedom: The Economic Consequences of Emancipation* (New York: Cambridge University Press, 2001); Leon F. Litwack, *Been in the Storm So Long: The Aftermath of Slavery* (New York: Vintage Books, 1980), 292–502.

88. Nancy Bercaw, *Gendered Freedoms: Race, Rights, and the Politics of Household in the Delta, 1861–1875* (Gainesville: University Press of Florida, 2003); Anthony E. Kaye, *Joining Places: Slave Neighborhoods in the Old South* (Chapel Hill: University of North Carolina Press, 2007).

89. For research on the interior worlds of African Americans at emancipation, see for example, Litwack, *Been in the Storm So Long*; Lawrence W. Levine, *Black Culture and Black Consciousness: Afro-American Folk Thought from Slavery to Freedom* (New York: Oxford University Press, 1978); Herbert G. Gutman, *The Black Family in Slavery and Freedom, 1750–1925* (New York: Vintage Books, 1977).

90. Litwack, *Been in the Storm So Long*, 221–91; Hahn, *Nation under Our Feet*; Rable, *But There Was No Peace*.

91. Jack Johnson, ALKT, 1169; Samuel Stewart, Oct. 26, 1871, GAKT, 592–93.

92. Herman, *Trauma and Recovery*, 7, 183.

93. Stanley Elkins, *Slavery: A Problem in American Institutional and Intellectual Life* (Chicago: University of Chicago Press, 1959); U. S. Department of Labor, Office of Policy Planning and Research, *The Negro Family: The Case for National Action* (Washington, D.C.: Government Printing Office, 1965).

94. See Chandra Manning, "Working for Citizenship in Civil War Contraband Camps," *Journal of the Civil War Era* 4, no. 2 (2014): 172–204; Jim Downs, *Sick from Freedom: African-American Illness and Suffering during the Civil War and Reconstruction* (New York: Oxford University Press, 2012).

95. According to Chandra Manning, on May 23, 2011, Glymph delivered a talk addressing histories of hurt titled "Preserving and Interpreting Historic Places Associated with Civil War–Era Freedom Seekers." Manning, "Working for Citizenship," 191, 203–4n86.

C. Joseph Genetin-Pilawa

In September 1861, Ely S. Parker, a Tonawanda Seneca and friend of Ulysses S. Grant, approached Secretary of State William Seward requesting a commission in the United States Army. Seward refused, telling Parker that the war was "an affair between white men." "Go home, cultivate your farm," Seward instructed. "We will settle our own troubles among ourselves, without any Indian aid." This was the third time Parker had attempted to volunteer for service, and the third time he had been rebuffed.[1] Despite these early rejections, Parker went on to serve ably as General Grant's military secretary and aide-de-camp, eventually penning the surrender documents at Appomattox Court House, and standing beside Grant as General Robert E. Lee signed those documents that marked the beginning of the end of the Civil War. Parker's allegiance to Grant eventually propelled him to the office of commissioner of Indian affairs (1869–71). From this vantage point, the end of the Civil War seemingly marks a period of transition, whereby the United States embraces inclusivity and the incorporation of previously marginalized groups, including Native Americans.

Yet Parker's meteoric rise proved short lived. Six years after Appomattox, he again found himself rejected by the government he wished to serve. In December 1871, he reluctantly relinquished his post as commissioner. In a tersely worded resignation letter, Parker complained that the office of commissioner, in his opinion, had been stripped of "all its original importance, duties, and proper responsibilities." His own position as commissioner, he believed, had been reduced to the occupation of "a clerk."[2] Moreover, he had been the target of congressmen, powerful businessmen, and even clergy who believed that Native people were to be subjects of federal policy, not voices in its creation. The Republican/Unionist senator Joseph Fowler from Tennessee, for example, argued before the Senate that it was "ridiculous in itself" that an Indian had been appointed to run the Office of Indian Affairs. Parker, he said, was "a wild man."[3] While Parker might not have acknowledged it directly, the message from powerful white men echoed Seward's earlier rejection—federal Indian policy in the postwar era would proceed "without any Indian aid."

These two moments—Seward's rejection and Parker's ouster as commissioner—might lead us to read the postwar narrative of Indian affairs as similar to the story of Reconstruction in the American South: as the rise and fall of an optimistic moment for disenfranchised people or as an "unfinished revolution." Indeed, many scholars have reached this conclusion. Yet simply wedging Indian affairs into the story of Reconstruction obscures more than it reveals. Instead, it might be more accurate to examine postwar events in Indian Country as a result of the competing legacies of the Civil War itself. On one hand, Parker welcomed the possibility of inclusion, as he and other Native leaders believed that an active federal government could reconfigure racial politics and empower Native people as agents in their own destinies. On the other hand, the postwar ambitions of Americans to fulfill the promises of Manifest Destiny also drove a national ethos of western expansion that threatened the livelihoods and lives of Native people in the West.

The Fourteenth Amendment certainly can be credited with producing much of the early optimism among Native reformers, including Parker, just as it had among African American leaders and their allies in the South.[4] Clearly, Native reformers viewed the establishment of the Freedmen's Bureau, the attempt to incorporate African Americans into the American electorate, and military enforcement of postwar civil rights legislation as signs of better things to come. Yet as any novice historian of the period can attest, the optimism toward and the enforcement of federal policies in the Reconstruction South were ephemeral moments within a larger history of abuse and subjugation. It has been easy to map this broader declension narrative onto the West, but the failure of Native reformers differed quite dramatically from that of their African American counterparts. Unfortunately for many Native communities, continued tribal sovereignty represented an impediment to westward development in the eyes of powerful white politicians and businessmen. The optimism expressed in the Office of Indian Affairs ended not as a result of terror and political intimidation (as Reconstruction had in the South), but instead because policymakers and western settlers ceased to understand tribal sovereignty as a central pillar of federal Indian policy. The period from the end of the Civil War until 1871 marks a dramatic and significant moment in the development of American settler colonialism and yet scholars have only just begun to contextualize this development within the broader contours of the postwar nation.[5]

A fuller understanding of this period—one that also considers the development of settler colonialism in relation to Reconstruction and Indian policy reform—demands that we take seriously several important events and trajectories within the Office of Indian Affairs in the late 1860s. This approach places Ely Parker at the center of the story.[6] Parker's enthusiasm toward inclusion was tempered by his argument for Native American sovereignty and participation in the formation of Indian policy. He argued that the government needed to honor existing treaties, protect Native communities from settler violence, and provide opportunities for Native people to assimilate on their own terms. These issues, which differed dramatically from the events happening in the U.S. South, remind us that the history of the postwar era is more complicated than a simple division between former Union and Confederate states, a racialized politics drawn in black and white, or a partisan fight between Democrats and Republicans (or between factions of Republicans against other Republicans). This essay attempts to provide a nuanced, though brief, story of Native American and U.S. history in the period between 1865 and 1871 that might complicate our understanding of the Reconstruction era and shed light on the difficult decisions that Native people faced in the postwar years. In particular, the following pages focus on two key developments in the Office of Indian Affairs (OIA) in which Parker played a large role: an attempt to transfer the OIA from the Interior to the War Department, and Congress's 1871 initiative to end treaty making. In both instances, Parker's arguments demonstrate that tribal sovereignty in the West was incompatible with the nation's new policy of racial assimilation.

Parker's wartime experience weighed heavily on the work he did in Indian affairs in the late 1860s. In the army, he began at the rank of captain in 1863 and worked as an engineer, but his administrative skills were recognized quickly and he served next as an assistant adjutant general. He joined Grant at the Battle of Vicksburg and became his military secretary and a prominent advisor. As the war ended, Parker stayed on as Grant's aide-de-camp in Washington, D.C., and at the general's request began working as a military advisor on Indian affairs in the mid-1860s.[7] Parker next served as an army representative on the Fort Smith peace council that met with southern Indian nations, some of whom had signed treaties and fought alongside the Confederate Army. His work on the council convinced some policymakers that Native representatives should be involved in the development of Indian affairs policy itself. The Choctaw and Chickasaw diplomats at Fort Smith stated that "the fact that the United States Government have seen fit to include a member of an Indian tribe with its commissioners, has inspired us with confidence . . . we are anxious to have the benefit of his presence and counsel in any deliberations or interviews."[8]

As Parker's role in federal Indian affairs expanded, he began to articulate a vision of policy reform that focused on using the army to protect tribal communities, while providing money, goods, education, and opportunities to Native individuals. In 1867, Parker moved out of his advisory role and served, with General Alfred Sully, as an investigator of the military encounter known as the "Fetterman Fight," a battle during Red Cloud's war that resulted in the deaths of eighty U.S. soldiers near Fort Phil Kearney at the hands of Lakota, Northern Cheyenne, and Arapaho attackers. In meetings with the Lakota, Cheyenne, and others along the Missouri River in Nebraska and the Montana Territory, Parker focused on the treatment of Indigenous allies. "The Great Grandfather will take care of and protect the friendly Indians from their Indian enemies, and from bad whites," Parker told a group of Brule and Oglala leaders at California Crossing in April.[9] Many reformers were becoming hesitant to vest too much hope in the army, as its reputation in the West had suffered. Parker's statements, though, reveal an important bit of nuance. From his perspective, western settlers posed a far greater risk to Native people than did U.S. soldiers. This perspective would continue to shape his reform agenda in important ways.

As he began his work on the Kearney investigation, Parker also submitted a letter to the secretary of war, Edwin Stanton, outlining his thoughts on Indian policy reform. He described it as a program for "the establishment of a permanent and perpetual peace . . . between the United States and the various Indian tribes," and in important ways foreshadowed the Peace Policy, a set of federal programs developed and administered in the West during Reconstruction that included an effort to place the OIA in the War Department.[10] When we compare the ideas expressed in this letter to the final report of the Kearney investigation, Parker clearly emerges as the report's primary author. The final Kearney report has been almost completely overlooked, especially the influence it had on the other major peace commission of that time—often referred to as the Peace Commission of 1867–1868, or simply the 1868 Peace Commission.[11] In fact, because Parker and Sully initially reported that many Native communities on the Great Plains desired an end to war and violence, Congress authorized the second peace commission to meet with and negotiate treaties among them.

The 1868 Peace Commission consumes almost the entirety of the historical literature on Indian policy in the late 1860s for two reasons: first, it was granted treaty-making authority, something that many of the other commissions and expeditions were not; and second, the men who served on the 1868 Peace Commission tended to be powerful and influential in both the civilian and military elements of Indian policymaking. Nonetheless, Parker played a key role in shaping the language that framed these peace commissions and illustrated how an attempt to balance tribal sovereignty and racial inclusion emerged as an important, if at times contradictory, discourse in the Peace Policy/Reconstruction era.[12]

A close reading of Parker's 1867 letter to Stanton provides insight into why he advocated the transfer of the Office of Indian Affairs into the War Department and demonstrates how an investment in tribal sovereignty shaped that advocacy. Parker proposed that the government create a committee made up of both Native and non-Native individuals to oversee the administration of federal policy. He also wanted the government to establish and protect specific land rights for Native communities. He argued that transferring the Office of Indian Affairs (OIA) back to the War Department, where it had been housed prior to 1849, would curb corruption, allow the army to enforce treaty stipulations, and insulate the OIA from the influence of land companies and other business interests that sought continued dispossession. The War Department increasingly engaged in foreign policy after the Civil War, defining and policing relationships between separate sovereigns, while the Department of the Interior, the OIA's current home, helped facilitate the work of mineral extraction, logging, and railroad construction in the West, processes that threatened Native homelands. Finally, Parker articulated the view that the federal government should provide money, goods, services, and new opportunities for Native people, particularly in the form of education, in an effort to counterbalance dispossession and the history of colonization. In outlining his thoughts on Indian policy, Parker essentially argued that the federal government should use the army to protect and defend Native sovereignty by enforcing treaties and policing the boundaries of Indian Country from the incursions of settlers, land speculators, and spurious businessmen.

Historians and others have read backwards through the western violence of the late 1800s and assumed that the effort to move the OIA to the War Department reflected a larger desire among government officials to deploy troops and engage Native communities militarily (or at least threatening to do so) with more frequency. A recent example of this narrative arc exists in Karl Jacoby's *Shadows at Dawn*. The author suggests that tensions surrounding the transfer debate were a holdover from the 1849 decision to house the OIA in the Interior Department. "Many in the military," he writes, "still resented the intrusion of what they regarded to be corrupt civilians into the army's proper sphere."[13] And while there is certainly evidence to suggest such an interpretation, especially if one focuses on the arguments made by General George Crook, as Jacoby does, or by Generals Philip Sheridan, William Tecumseh Sherman, and Nelson Miles, the issue was far more complex and connected to broader questions of bureaucratization, inclusion, expansion, and the responsibilities of the state to those who made up its constituencies in the postwar nation. But viewing the transfer debate as one about increased militarism on the Plains allows little room to understand Parker's position.

In his 1867 letter, Parker advanced several arguments in support of the transfer. First, he asserted that the military was best suited to protect Indian communities from avaricious whites. He characterized civilian agents as "absolutely powerless" in this regard. Parker also pointed to the role of the military in enforcing treaty stipulations. As the "hardy pioneer and adventurous miner" traveled west, he noted, he "found no rights possessed by the Indians that they were bound to respect . . . the faith of treaties solemnly entered into were totally disregarded, and Indian territory wantonly violated." If "any tribe remonstrated against this violation of their natural and treaty rights . . . [they] were inhumanely shot down and . . . treated as mere dogs." He concluded that the "military alone can give the Indians the needed protection."[14] In a related vein, Parker saw the civilian agents working in Indian affairs at this time as especially prone to fraud. He believed that they sought "to avoid all trouble and responsibility, and to make as much money as possible out of their offices." While the military officer's "honor and interest is at stake, and impels him to discharge his duty honestly and faithfully."[15]

Parker viewed the American military as a force that could enable Native communities to act on their own accord, and could shield them from threats posed by settlers and businessmen. He drew this belief both from experiences earlier in life, when he had advocated on behalf of his Tonawanda Seneca community as it fought against a local land company's effort to remove them to Kansas Territory, and from more recent experiences with military bureaucracy before and after the Civil War. From Parker's perspective, local settlers, land speculation, mining, and railroads posed far greater risks for Native peoples than the army, especially if it were properly led and bureaucratically efficient. In addition, as a prominent member of Grant's inner circle, he also supported the army as a reflection of the general goodwill—especially in the Republican North—extended to Grant (and evidenced by his overwhelming electoral victories), as well as of the popularity of the Grand Army of the Republic, and even the establishment of and popular support for federal soldiers' pensions.[16]

Parker's advocacy of the transfer reflected his interest in creating an effective and impartial bureaucracy. It also revealed a larger optimism about using the military to enforce social change in the Reconstruction Era. It was not, though, indicative of any movement in the direction of increased military action against Indian people. Parker acknowledged recent evidence of army misconduct, but he viewed those occurrences from the perspective of a bureaucrat, not a soldier, and clearly distinguished individual actions from institutional practice. For example, in the Fort Phil Kearney investigation, he asserted that Colonel Henry Carrington, the commander at the fort, "had no sort of discipline in his garrison" and took "no unusual precautions" against the potential for violence between the Indians and the soldiers.[17] He saw the deficiencies of individual soldiers and officers as the root cause of institutional failures—not the bureaucratic structures of the military itself. He concluded that the "whole conduct of Indian Affairs shows a great lack of judgment and efficiency on *some one's* part."[18] Parker's own military experience as an "indoor man" may have led him to distinguish between voluntary soldiers or militias and the pared-down, postwar, professional military, which he viewed as much more efficient and trustworthy.

At the end of the Civil War, the War Department housed the most complex and well-developed bureaucratic system of any of the executive agencies; it consumed the lion's share of the federal budget. The necessities of war had helped develop a complex infrastructure that distributed supplies, food, and pay to nearly 2.25 million soldiers during the four-year conflict.[19] The War Department and the U.S. Army also played an important role in implementing Reconstruction programs in the South by feeding black refugees, protecting Freedmen's Bureau offices, and ensuring access of freedmen to the polls."[20] Beginning in 1867, following the Radical Republicans' usurpation of control over the direction of congressional policy, Congress placed the ten "unreconstructed" states under military jurisdiction, an action Parker and Grant both supported.[21]

During a brief window in the history of the American South, the U.S. military sought to protect and facilitate African American inclusion and participation into American politics, and a comparison to Parker's ideas for deploying the army to enforce Indian policy reform is intriguing. He envisioned using the army to protect Native people from local settlers, thereby maintaining tribal sovereignty, allowing Native communities to live in "permanent and perpetual peace" and to assimilate at their own pace, or not at all. On the one hand, it is easy to see how Parker was influenced by the army's role in Reconstruction in the South, part of which involved defending freedpeople from aggressive and intrusive citizens. On the other hand, in the immediate postwar formulation, inclusion, at least from the perspective of federal legislators, was premised on national homogeneity, not on the continued existence of tribal communities as "neither fully foreign nor domestic," or on what the political theorist Kevin Bruyneel has referred to as the "third space of sovereignty."[22] Parker would not necessarily have understood his simultaneous support for tribal sovereignty and transferring the OIA to the War Department as contradictory at the time, but the contradiction has certainly posed a problem for historians looking to conveniently fit Parker into a larger narrative trajectory of Indian affairs that traces a direct route from removal to allotment.

Some scholars have dismissed Parker's ideas as having had little traction, yet he received significant support for the agenda he outlined in his 1867 letter, especially from Radical Republicans. Henry Wilson, for example, a leading Radical Republican politician and Massachusetts senator (1855–73) who would be elected as Grant's vice president in 1872, wrote to him only four days after Parker penned the letter. "I have read your interesting and able report on Indian Affairs," Wilson stated, "and would feel much obliged if you would draw up and send me a bill for presentation to Congress, embodying the ideas and propositions embraced in your report."[23] Because he was sent west on the Fort Phil Kearney investigation,

Parker was unable to fulfill the request, but this expression of support was significant. Christopher Columbus Andrews, a U.S. Army veteran and Radical Republican who had supervised early Reconstruction programs in Texas, also followed Parker's efforts, even after he was sent to Sweden as a foreign minister. He wrote a letter, forwarded through Paris, to "urge upon the Administration the great importance of at once setting in motion" Parker's reforms.[24]

The 1868 Peace Commission weighed in on the transfer debate as well, but it struggled to find a clear consensus given the complexities of this issue. In its initial report to Congress, the commission argued that Indian affairs should not be transferred to the War Department. The commissioners wrote that the new federal policy goals should be "emphatically civil, and not military." Yet they also argued that the Interior Department was not a good home for the Office of Indian Affairs; instead, they proposed a new "independent bureau or department."[25] An independent bureau, the commissioners asserted, would help remove the influence of political patronage from the office. They even went so far as to suggest that on a given date, Congress should dismiss all employees of the Indian Office, review their performances, and rehire only those who had "proved themselves competent and faithful." As an effort to forestall patronage appointments—postwar reformers in Indian affairs were early advocates of civil service reform—they stated explicitly that "professions of party zeal" could not be a factor in reappointment.[26] While all seven of the original commissioners signed the peace commissioners' report, only a simple majority approved the recommendations. In an 1869 letter to Senator E. G. Ross, General William Tecumseh Sherman revealed that the civilian members of the commission had voted in favor of the recommendations, while he and Generals Terry and Harney had not. "We did not favor the conclusion arrived at, but being out-voted," he wrote, "we had to sign the report."[27] Sherman's faction likely supported the transfer because, as would be revealed in their final report, they anticipated active military engagements with Native peoples.

In its final report to Congress, the 1868 Peace Commission recommended housing the Office of Indian Affairs in the War Department and, in so doing, appeared as Parker's ally. Yet it quickly became clear that the commissioners' motivation was to facilitate military conquests, not bureaucratization. As violence re-erupted in the southern Plains in October 1868, the generals, this time with an additional vote from the newly appointed peace commissioner General C. C. Augur, managed to sway the opinions of all the civilian peace commissioners but one: Nathaniel Taylor.[28] It is instructive to consider this final recommendation in relation to Parker's position and to the larger historiography of federal Indian policy. While the peace commissioners appeared to be Parker's allies in advocating the transfer, their motivation differed. A statement from the earlier report, likely Sherman's voice, seems to typify this standpoint: "If the savage resists, civilization, with the ten commandments in one hand and the sword in the other, demands his immediate extermination."[29] Parker explicitly rejected such a stance. On the other hand, in arguing against the transfer, Commissioner Taylor used a logic that Parker not only supported but also espoused constantly in his advocacy for reform. Taylor wrote, "respect their wishes, fulfill our treaty stipulations promptly and faithfully, keep them well fed, and there will be no need of armies among them."[30]

By the time Parker was appointed to head the Indian Office in 1869, it had become clear that the transfer debate was a potential political minefield. The shifting recommendations of the 1868 Peace Commission might have offered some early insight. In his first annual report in 1869, Parker noted a break from the previously complex and confusing relationship between the civilian and military branches. There was, he wrote, "now a perfect understanding between the officers of this department [OIA] and those of the military, with respect to their relative duties and responsibilities in reference to Indian affairs."[31] Parker also circulated a statement of proper protocol for the administration of Indian affairs to the members of the Interior Department and asked that military leaders issue similar orders. The result, Parker reported, was a "harmony of action between the two departments" with "no conflict of opinion having arisen as to the duty, power and responsibility of either."[32]

Religious organizations, such as the Society of Friends, favored keeping the OIA in the Department of Interior. In a memorial to Congress in 1869, the Friends wrote that they appreciated the "evident desire of Congress to remedy the gross evils and abuses of our Indian system" and were sure that the "proposal to place the Indian affairs in the control of the War Department has been dictated by motives of humanity, both to the interest of the Indians and the honor of the nation." Yet they argued that the transfer proposal should be abandoned due to the deleterious effect of alcoholism that often characterized interactions near western army forts, often leading to violent encounters. The "loathsome disease which has destroyed thousands," they argued, could be "traced to licentious intercourse between the soldiers and the Indians."[33] Importantly, too, Quaker reformers were enmeshed in the broader Reconstruction era discourse of racial inclusion. Many had worked in "contraband" camps during the war and remained involved with the Freedmen's Bureau in the late-1860s.[34] Since the Interior Department was the executive agency that administered domestic policy, it likely made sense to them as the proper home for Indian affairs.

The events that ultimately ended the transfer debate reinforced those who foresaw and feared violence in the presence of the military on the western Plains. In January 1870, General Phillip Sheridan, one of most effective defenders of African Americans in the U.S. Army, authorized an attack on Piegan Indians in northern Montana (Department of Dakota). During actions that would come to be known as the Marias Massacre, Major Eugene Baker and the soldiers of the Second Cavalry attacked thirty-seven Piegan lodges—Chief Heavy Runner's settlement—that had been granted "safe conduct" by the Indian Office. They killed 173 Indians (at least 53 of whom were women and children) while taking another 140 prisoner.[35] This event raised important questions about the military's ability to simultaneously punish so-called hostile Indian groups while protecting "friendlies." When the Illinois congressman and chairman of the Committee on Military Affairs, John A. Logan, read the details of the massacre in early 1870, "his blood ran cold in his veins," and he asked the committee to "let the Indian Bureau remain" where it was. The committee agreed.[36] In an effort to further confine President Grant's interference in congressional patronage in the Indian service, the House and Senate also made regular army officers ineligible for civil positions.

The Plains Wars of the 1870s illustrate a clear difference between the narratives of the American South and federal Indian affairs in the postwar era. Immediately following the Civil War, many Americans, based on Union victories late in the conflict, viewed the military as a vehicle for good. In the South, though, where the army struggled to reform the political system against an entrenched and aggressive white population, its eventual withdrawal allowed local racism to corrupt politics. In essence, the army was unable to protect freedmen in their effort to be included as full citizens into the nation. The army's role in the West, however, played out differently, especially in its incursions into the sovereignty of Native communities. There the military did not withdraw. Instead, it actively campaigned and attacked communities as a means of eroding Native sovereignty. It became, as some had feared, a powerful agent of American settler colonialism. Despite the Marias Massacre, Parker's continued optimism drove him to seek bureaucratic efficiency and a clear relationship between the War Department and the OIA in which the military could be useful in protecting tribal sovereignty. Even as Congress limited Grant's power and ended the transfer movement, the president encouraged the interior secretary Jacob Cox "to harmonize the action of the two branches." He argued that this more than anything else would "promote the efficiency and usefulness of the Agents in charge of the Indians."[37]

CONGRESSIONAL REPUBLICANS' opposition to the OIA transfer did not spring from sympathy for Native autonomy. In fact, in the late-1860s, Congress intensified its assault on tribal sovereignty. Formal treaty making with Native nations had characterized U.S.-Indigenous relations from the 1780s forward. The treaty enshrined the concept of tribal sovereignty in the American legal system, and over the years more than 370 treaties had been ratified. In 1870, in a rider attached to the Indian appropriations bill, Congress ended the practice of treaty making. Ely Parker served as commissioner of Indian affairs and, interestingly, he argued both in support of the existing treaties and against the continuation of treaty making. Much like his advocacy for transferring the OIA to the War Department, his opposition to treaty making reveals the difficulties of wedding the discussions of tribal sovereignty to the Reconstruction-era ethos of inclusion. Parker was swept up in the optimism of the postwar moment and was influenced by broader arguments for racial inclusion and a national reconciliation.[38] An obvious question, then, is why he would, as a Native activist and reformer, support the cessation of treaty making when treaties seemingly provided the foundation for tribal communities' efforts to maintain autonomy from the United States?

To begin to answer this question, it is instructive to look at experiences earlier in Parker's life, as well as at events in the immediate postwar moment. As a young man, he witnessed the destructive forces unleashed by powerful land companies and how difficult it was for a Native nation to ensure that the United States would negotiate fairly. The same investment in tribal sovereignty that led Parker to advocate for the transfer of the OIA to the War Department in the late-1860s and early-1870s also motivated his support for the cessation of treaty making in 1871. This is why historians have struggled to fit Parker within analytical binaries. At its heart, his support for tribal autonomy drove him toward policy decisions that seem illogical at face value. Yet Parker's position on this issue is instructive because it also illustrates the larger Reconstruction-era shift in settler colonial thought within which he operated. As the grammar of racial inclusion pervaded the discourse on race politics and reform following the passage of the Fourteenth Amendment, indigeneity came to represent a racial identity and was increasingly separated from the notion of autonomy and sovereignty. Theorists of settler colonialism remind us to be wary of such "shiftiness of language." As Jodi Byrd had argued, "colonization relies upon racialization," but that process often hides the violence of colonialism and conflates all experiences of oppression.[39]

Mapping Parker's efforts onto the narrative of national development during the Reconstruction era helps clarify how and why the optimism he and others expressed proved so fleeting in the face of rapid western expansion. As Parker attempted to introduce economic and educational opportunities for Native people, the importance of state building, western expansion, and the solidification of U.S. sovereignty in the wake of an incredibly traumatic war facilitated a process of spatial and legal confinement for Native communities. Some scholars, such as the political theorist Kevin Bruyneel, have asserted that Parker's willingness to end treaty making demonstrated a certain kind of colonial collaboration, that his support for the cessation of treaty making revealed a "linked articulation of progress, rule, rationality, and the state."[40] In short, Bruyneel and others believe that Parker, despite his Seneca heritage, helped facilitate U.S. colonialism.

Judging by many of Parker's own statements, it would appear that this interpretation is correct. In his first annual report as commissioner, Parker suggested that the treaty system should no longer continue. He denied Chief Justice John Marshall's findings earlier in the century, asserting instead that the "Indian tribes of the United States are not sovereign nations, capable of making treaties."[41] In a letter to William Welsh, the first chairman of the Board of Indian Commissioners, Parker foreshadowed congressional actions by stating, "Congress intends a radical change in the Indian policy by discontinuing the treaty system and hereafter legislating for Indians as for wards of the government which they really are."[42]

There is an alternate interpretation, however. Parker's position on treaty making in 1871 might be understood as an expression of realpolitik. As a leading voice in the Seneca resistance campaign against forced removal in the 1840s and 1850s, Parker had seen firsthand how devastating political discord could be—even within a powerful and populous Indian community. He had watched as numerous western New York tribes jockeyed for position against one another and then, in 1848, as a political revolution swept through the Allegheny and Cattaraugus communities. At that time he asserted that internal political conflict "has made so much trouble" and "caused so much bitter and hard feeling among our leading men."[43] "If ever the Tonawandas were required to be united in their plans and purposes," he advised his own community, "it is now."[44] Drawing on those experiences, Parker may have decided that Native communities lacked the political, economic, and military might to force external agents of colonialism (land speculators and other private interests) to negotiate fairly or to compel the federal government to honor their treaty agreements. The resulting pressures at times caused destructive political disputes that further weakened Native nations. Ending treaty making, Parker believed, would limit one of the United States' most effective tools of colonization.

Although he did not make explicit reference to his antebellum experiences, Parker's own words as commissioner revealed that his prewar work indeed motivated his support for an end to treaty making. In the same annual report in which he asserted that Indian tribes were not sovereign nations, Parker argued that "great injury has been done by the government in deluding this people into the belief of their being independent sovereignties, *while they were at the same time recognized only as its dependents and wards.*" He also suggested that no Indian nation had "an organized government of such inherent strength as would secure a faithful obedience of its [the United States] people in the observance of compacts of this character [treaties]."[45] In other words, he suggested that the federal government exploited power and resource inequities by encouraging Native nations to sign treaties they could neither negotiate advantageously nor force the United States to honor.

Even after he left the OIA, Parker continued to criticize the treaty regime. In a draft of a lecture he was preparing in 1878, Parker wrote, "here I may mention the absurdity of the United States Gov't making treaties with the Indian tribes of the country. . . . They have all been declared the wards of the government, and they all live within its jurisdiction, and yet these dependent people are treated as though they were independent sovereign nations." He continued:

I perhaps ought to be the last person to find fault with such a condition of things. I suppose that I ought to be very proud, I ought to swell out as a turkey cock that with a few hundred ignorant Indians at my back I can consider myself the head of a strong independent sovereignty, and treat with the great United States as if I were Russia or Germany or China or Japan. But I have no such feeling. On the contrary I am humiliated. For I know too well the great wrecks of violated Indian treaties that are strewn in the historical pathway of the U.S. I know too well that a violation of a treaty on the part of the Indians means their forcible expulsion from their homes and their extermination. These things are like the handle to a jug. The advantages and the power of execution are all on one side.[46]

In the end, he appealed to policymakers for a "wise, liberal, and just" approach to Indian affairs, because, though pessimistic, he realized that this was the best hope for Indian people.

Parker advocated for an end to treaty making because be believed that Native nations could never force the United States to negotiate fairly. However, the 1871 rider that ended treaty making also reflected Reconstruction-era politics more broadly; it exposed partisan divisions and disputes concerning congressional procedures.[47] In this way, one of the most significant developments in nineteenth-century Indian affairs — the unilateral decision to end treaty making — is intimately bound up with postwar political issues and arguments only tangentially connected to the OIA itself. For example, most Republicans supported Parker and early Peace Policy reforms, but western party leaders who were focused on expansion, including Thomas Tipton from Nebraska, broke ranks. In a debate over an Indian appropriations bill, Tipton argued, "You say [the Office of Indian Affairs'] policy is a success, and the only way to keep the peace is to feed and feed and feed, and let one portion of this country work and work and work and toil, in order that your agents may go and feed and feed and feed. . . . The system is rotten; the system is false; the system can no longer be maintained or endured."[48]

The debates over treaty making also provided Democrats an opportunity to attack policies and individuals supported by Radical Republicans. Congressman James Beck, a Kentucky Democrat and the former law partner of John C. Breckenridge, commented on the jurisdictional benefits an end to treaty making would provide to the House of Representatives. "I desire to say that the House, in my judgment, has gained almost everything that it had a right to expect," he said. No longer would the House have to figure out ways to fund the treaty annuities ratified by the Senate alone. The bill formalized "a distinct agreement between the two Houses," thereby ending the Senate's exclusive control of Indian policy.[49]

Senator Eugene Casserly, a California Democrat, used the creation of the 1871 rider to complain about Senate procedures. He argued that legislators had created the rider behind closed doors and that the trend was to take important bills from open debate and "decide them by conferences held in some committee-room, with closed doors, without the knowledge of either House, and without any practical capacity in the members of either House to reject what had been done."[50] Garrett Davis, a Democratic senator from Kentucky, built on Casserly's argument and objected to the rider on the grounds that the treaty-making relationship between Indian tribes and the U.S. federal government was "as fixed and immutable in the foundations of the Constitution as any other power," and that no committee or conference, not even the Senate or House, could change that.[51] Senator Casserly concluded the debate. "I know what the misfortune of the tribes is," he said; "they hold great bodies of rich lands, which have aroused the cupidity of powerful corporations and of powerful individuals. . . . I greatly fear the adoption of this provision . . . is the beginning of the end in respect to Indian lands. It is the first step in a great scheme of spoliation, in which the Indians will be plundered, corporations and individuals enriched, and the American name dishonored in history."[52] His words seem eerily prophetic to modern ears.

THE YEAR 1871 MARKED the end of the treaty-making system; it was the same year that Parker was ousted from the Office of Indian Affairs—the result of political pressure instigated by the Board of Indian Commissioners and William Welsh, an Episcopal layman and activist in Philadelphia who served as the board's first chairman. While it is unnecessary to review the events of his ouster in great detail, it is worth noting the intensity with which opposing reformers moved to combat Parker's efforts. Welsh and the board were also invested in the larger issues of the Reconstruction era, including the inclusion of Natives within the broader polity, but their vision of Indian affairs rested on the common postwar reasoning that the government had the power to coerce Native peoples to assimilate and should use it. As Elliott West has asserted, "Always the Greater Reconstruction was as much about control as liberation, as much about unity and power as about equality."[53] Although they initially saw Parker as a potential ally, they advanced a policy agenda that focused on confining Indians within increasingly smaller reservations and on cultural assimilation by any means necessary. Their driving philosophy, animated by Welsh's evangelism, was that the wealthy, educated Christian philanthropists of the United States understood the best interests of Native people better than Native people did themselves. Perhaps then it is no coincidence that Parker's ouster and the cessation of treaty making happened at the same time.

The intensity with which Welsh and the board attacked Parker, evidenced by the short tenure of his career on the federal level (1869–71), reveals how threatening the possibilities of his reform agenda appeared to those invested in the longer-term trajectory of federal Native policy premised on dispossession and assimilation. It also demonstrates the consequences of the shifting discourses in Reconstruction-era Indian policy debates, from a focus on tribal sovereignty to racial inclusion. Parker's efforts, reflecting the optimism of the late 1860s, focused on enforcing existing treaties, using the military to protect Native communities from settler violence when necessary, slowing the pace of assimilation, and providing opportunities for Indigenous nations in the form of money, goods, and especially education, so that they might incorporate themselves when and how they chose. Finally, more so than most of his contemporaries, Parker was fully convinced of the capabilities of Native people. While all the reformers working in Indian affairs in the mid-nineteenth century focused on inclusion in one way or another, Parker's program posed alternate and perhaps less disruptive methods that acknowledged or sought to maintain sovereignty in a variety of ways, also seeking to provide Native communities with multiple paths to peaceful coexistence with non-Native ones as their relationships with an expanding settler-colonial United States developed.

Ely Parker articulated a vision of the relationship between Native communities and the federal government at a temporal and discursive pivot point—a moment when policymakers and the broader public shifted the discussion of the "Indian Problem" from an early-nineteenth-century iteration based on Native sovereignty into a late-century discourse on race that was shaped by Reconstruction politics aimed at incorporating freedpeople into American society more completely. Recognition of tribal sovereignty seemed increasingly impossible amid the growing impulse to bring into the nation people of all races and the continuing expansion of white settlement in the West. Immersing ourselves in this transitory moment and making sense of several events in Parker's career forces us to bridge a historiographical disjuncture; that is, it requires that we layer three concurrent narratives (often artificially untangled) atop one another: the development of nineteenth-century Indian policy; the mid-century story of the coming of the Civil War and its aftermath; and the evolution of American settler colonialism. It is the latter narrative that ties the others together, reminding us that the history of U.S. conquest in the West, slavery, the Civil War, and the struggle for freedom were intimately connected.[54]

NOTES

The author owes a special debt of gratitude to James J. Buss and Boyd Cothran for their insights, comments, and thoughtful suggestions through several drafts of this chapter.

1. Arthur C. Parker, *The Life of General Ely S. Parker: Last Grand Sachem of the Iroquois and General Grant's Military Secretary* (Buffalo: Buffalo Historical Society, 1919), 99–104; William Armstrong, *Warrior in Two Camps: Ely S. Parker, Union General and Seneca Chief* (Syracuse, N.Y.: Syracuse University Press, 1978), 77.

2. *Investigation into Indian Affairs, before the Committee on Appropriations of the House of Representatives, Argument of N.P. Chipman, on Behalf of Hon. E.S. Parker, Commissioner of Indian Affairs* (Washington, D.C.: Powell, Glinck, 1871), vi–vii.

3. *Congressional Globe*, 41st Cong., 2nd sess., 1870, 4087–88.

4. Parker, perhaps as much as anyone working in federal policymaking in the immediate postwar period, echoed the broader optimism of the moment. Hannah Rosen recently characterized it as "a brief era in the United States of an imperfect but nonetheless far more inclusive political community and nation." Hannah Rosen, *Terror in the Heart of Freedom: Citizenship, Sexual Violence, and the Meaning of Race in Postemancipation South* (Chapel Hill: University of North Carolina Press, 2009), 4. Indeed, the historian Mark Summers's work reiterates this point in his assertion that, for reform-minded individuals, "it *was* a new world . . . the Civil War left them with a sense of purpose renewed . . . a new commitment to make America better, if only to requite the lives lost." Mark Summers, *The Era of Good Stealings* (New York: Oxford University Press, 1993), 21. Parker's vision of the federal government as caretaker also illustrates Drew Gilpin Faust's findings about the relationship of death and dying during the Civil War to the heightened expectations citizens had for federal responsibility. "Sacrifice and the state became inextricably intertwined," she argues. Those sacrifices "required that the government attend to the needs of those who had died in its service . . . [which] would prove an important vehicle for the expansion of

federal power that characterized the transformed postwar nation," she concluded. See Drew Gilpin Faust, *This Republic of Suffering: Death and the American Civil War* (New York: Random House, 2008), xiii–xiv.

5. The concept of American settler colonialism helps link events in Indian affairs with broader midcentury history. Scholars including Patrick Wolfe, who work at the intersections of anthropology, literary criticism, and cultural theory, have encouraged us to think in nuanced and specific ways about the forms colonization has taken throughout global history. Most important, as the Osage anthropologist Jean Dennison has asserted, "in the United States and other settler colonies, the process of conquest has been neither completed nor abandoned." It has always been caught in repetition and in a constant state of rearticulation. See Jean Dennison, *Colonial Entanglement: Constituting a Twenty-First-Century Osage Nation* (Chapel Hill: University of North Carolina Press, 2012), 6. Other recent works in Indigenous studies that have influenced my thinking on settler colonialism and its relationship to other historical developments include Kevin Bruyneel, *The Third Space of Sovereignty: The Postcolonial Politics of U.S.-Indigenous Relations* (Minneapolis: University of Minnesota Press, 2007); Malinda Maynor Lowery, *Lumbee Indians in the Jim Crow South: Race, Identity, and the Making of a Nation* (Chapel Hill: University of North Carolina Press, 2010); and Scott Richard Lyons, *X-Marks: Native Signatures of Assent* (Minneapolis: University of Minnesota Press, 2010).

6. For a lengthier discussion of these ideas, and especially the resistance Parker faced by assimilationist reformers, see C. Joseph Genetin-Pilawa, "Ely Parker and the Contentious Peace Policy," *Western Historical Quarterly* 41 (Summer 2010): 196–217.

7. Laurence Hauptman, *The Iroquois in the Civil War: From Battlefield to Reservation* (Syracuse, N.Y.: Syracuse University Press, 1993), 47–58. Hauptman devoted one brief chapter to a discussion of Parker entitled "'Grant's Indian': Ely S. Parker at the Battle of Chattanooga." Armstrong, *Warrior in Two Camps*, 87.

For more on Parker's life, especially before the war, see Parker, *The Life of General Ely S. Parker*; Armstrong, *Warrior in Two Camps*; Philip J. Deloria, *Playing Indian* (New Haven: Yale University Press, 1998), 71–94; William Fenton, "Tonawanda Longhouse Ceremonies: Ninety Years after Lewis Henry Morgan," in *Smithsonian Institution, Bureau of American Ethnology Bulletin* 128 (1941): 139–48. See also Elisabeth Tooker, "Ely S. Parker," in *American Indian Intellectuals*, ed. Margot Liberty (St. Paul, Minn.: West, 1978), 15–30; "Ely Samuel Parker: From Sachem to Brigadier General," *New York State and the Civil War* 1 (1961): 1–5; D. A. Brown, "'One Real American,'" *American History Illustrated* 4 (1969): 12–21; and Arthur C. Parker, "Ely S. Parker—Man and Mason," *Transactions—American Lodge of Research* 8 (1961): 229–47. I draw heavily on Parker's and Armstrong's biographies, but assert that both of them are fundamentally flawed. For more on this issue, see C. Joseph Genetin-Pilawa, "Confining Indians: Power, Authority, and the Colonialist Ideologies of Nineteenth-Century Reformers," (Ph.D. dissertation, Michigan State University, 2008), especially 77–117.

8. *Annual Report of the Commissioner of Indian Affairs*, 39th Cong., 1st sess., 1865, H. Ex. doc. 1, pt. 2, 522; and Armstrong, *Warrior in Two Camps*, 118–19. I addressed this council and Parker's role in greater detail in *Crooked Paths to Allotment: The Fight*

over Federal Indian Policy after the Civil War (Chapel Hill: University of North Carolina Press, 2012), especially 59–61.

9. Minutes of Meetings of the Special Commission, March 4–June 12, 1867, Records concerning an investigation of the Fort Phil Kearney (or Fetterman) massacre, 1867, Records of the Civilization Division, 28–30, Record Group 75, National Archives and Records Administration, Washington, D.C.

10. *Letter from the Secretary of War, Addressed to Mr. Schenck, chairman of the Committee on Military Affairs, transmitting a report by Colonel Parker on Indian Affairs,* 39th Cong., 2nd sess., 1867, House Misc. Doc. 37, 1.

11. Ibid.

12. For example, Andrew Denson refers to the report of the 1867–1868 Peace Commission as "a blueprint for the peace policy." See Denson, *Demanding the Cherokee Nation: Indian Autonomy and American Culture* (Lincoln: University of Nebraska Press, 2004), 92. In Karl Jacoby's brief discussion of the development of the Peace Policy, the author only mentions the 1867–1868 commission, ignoring the earlier and significant one. See Jacoby, *Shadows at Dawn: A Borderlands Massacre and the Violence of History* (New York: Penguin, 2008). I examined the Fort Phil Kearney investigation in much greater detail in *Crooked Paths to Allotment*, 61–62.

13. Jacoby, *Shadows at Dawn*, 227. Jacoby's work is otherwise incredibly insightful.

14. *Letter from the Secretary of War*, 1–2.

15. Ibid., 2.

16. For more, see David Blight, *Race And Reunion: The Civil War in American Memory* (Cambridge: Harvard University Press, 2001); Theda Skocpol, *Protecting Soldiers and Mothers: The Political Origins of Social Policy in the United States* (Cambridge: Belknap Press of Harvard University Press, 1992); Stuart McConnell, *Glorious Contentment: The Grand Army of the Republic, 1865–1900* (Chapel Hill: University of North Carolina Press, 1992); Patrick Kelly, *Creating a National Home: Building the Veterans' Welfare State, 1860–1900* (Cambridge: Harvard University Press, 1997); and Scott Ainsworth, "Electoral Strength and the Emergence of Group Influence in the Late-1800s: The Grand Army of the Republic," *American Politics Quarterly* 23 (1995): 319–38.

17. Armstrong, *Warrior in Two Camps*, 123.

18. Ibid.; emphasis added.

19. Skocpol, *Protecting Soldiers and Mothers*, 103. See also Eugene Murdock, *One Million Men: The Civil War Draft in the North* (Madison: State Historical Society of Wisconsin, 1971); and James Geary, *We Need Men: The Union Draft and the Civil War* (Dekalb: Northern Illinois University Press, 1991). For more on the expansion of the military bureaucracy, see Robert Angevine, *The Railroad and the State: War, Politics, and Technology in Nineteenth-Century America* (Stanford: Stanford University Press, 2004). For more on the significance of the development of the War Department during the Civil War, see Richard Bensel, *Yankee Leviathan: The Origins of Central State Authority in American, 1859–1877* (New York: Cambridge University Press, 1990), especially chap.3, entitled "War Mobilization and State Formation in the Northern Union and Southern Confederacy."

20. Michael Fitzgerald, "Emancipation and Military Pacification: The Freedmen's

Bureau and Social Control in Alabama," in *The Freedmen's Bureau and Reconstruction: Reconsiderations*, ed. Paul Cimbala and Randall Miller (New York: Fordham University Press, 1999), 53.

21. For the classic study of the Freedmen's Bureau, see George Bentley, *A History of the Freedmen's Bureau* (Philadelphia: University of Pennsylvania Press, 1955).

22. Bruyneel, *The Third Space of Sovereignty*, 57.

23. Henry Wilson to Ely S. Parker, 28 Jan. 1867, Ayer MS 1009, Edward E. Ayer Collection, Newberry Library, Chicago.

24. Letter from Christopher Columbus Andrews, Minister to Sweden, to E. B. Washburne, Minister of the United States in Paris, May 25, 1870, forwarded to Parker, Miscellaneous Letters, Ayer MS 22, Ayer Collection, Newberry Library, Chicago.

25. *Report of the Peace Commissioners*, 40th Cong., 2nd sess., 1868, H. Doc. 97, 21.

26. Ibid.

27. William T. Sherman to Senator E. G. Ross, Jan. 7, 1869, quoted in Henry G. Waltmann, "The Interior Department, War Department, and Indian Policy, 1865–1887" (M.A. thesis, University of Nebraska, 1962), 149.

28. The lone civilian holdout, the commissioner of Indian affairs Nathaniel Taylor, made an impassioned and strongly worded argument against the recommendation. He argued that Congress should support only a small army on a "peace footing." Citizens, he contended, would not abide the expense of tax dollars to fund a large and ongoing army that seemed to have no set endpoint or system for measuring success. Arguing that moving Indian affairs to the War Department would be "offensive" to Indian people, and an indication of "perpetual war," he concluded that the transfer would result in "demoralization and disease," as past military management already had failed, and would "always prove a failure." Finally, Taylor asserted that he could find no new evidence to change the decision the peace commissioners made only a few months earlier not to recommend the transfer. See Vine Deloria and Raymond DeMallie, *Proceedings of the Great Peace Commission 1867–1868* (Washington, D.C.: Institute for the Development of Indian Law, 1975), 165–70.

29. *Report of the Peace Commissioners*, 7.

30. Deloria and DeMallie, *Proceedings of the Great Peace Commission*, 169.

31. *Annual Report of the Commissioner of Indian Affairs*, 41st Cong., 2d sess., 1869, H. Ex. Doc. 1, pt. 2, 447.

32. Ibid. 448.

33. *Memorial of Yearly Meetings of the Society of Friends Relative to the Treatment of the Indians*, 40th Cong., 3d sess., House Misc. Doc. 29, 1869, 2.

34. See, for example, Scott Beck, "Freedmen, Friends, Common Schools, and Reconstruction," *Southern Friend* 17 (Spring 1995): 5–31; and Damon Hickey, "Pioneers of the New South: The Baltimore Association and North Carolina Friends in Reconstruction," *Quaker History* 72 (Spring 1985), 1–17.

35. Paul Hutton, *Phil Sheridan and His Army* (Lincoln: University of Nebraska Press, 1985), 189–91.

36. *Message of the President of the United States Communicating the Second Annual Report of the Board of Indian Commissioners*, 41st Cong., 3d sess., Senate Ex. Doc. 39,

1871, 90. See also Hutton, "Phil Sheridan's Pyrrhic Victory: The Piegan Massacre, Army Politics, and the Transfer Debate," *Montana: The Magazine of Western History* 32 (Spring 1982): 32–43.

37. Ely S. Parker to Sec. of the Interior Jacob D. Cox, 26 Apr. 1870, Report Books of the Bureau of Indian Affairs, 1838–1881, vol. 19, 327–28, Record Group 75, National Archives and Records Administration, Washington, D.C.

38. As Elliott West has argued, territorial expansion and the Civil War combined to pressure the federal government to decide how diverse peoples might be incorporated into the republic. According to West, Native Americans and freedpeople in the South "would be ushered in, assimilated, via strikingly similar programs of Christian mission, common school education, and integration into the economy of agriculture and the manual arts." He continued, "If the approach was the same, however, responses were not. Freedpeople embraced these programs and the vision behind them. So did some Indians." But those who did not faced the full force of a federal government that emerged from the Civil War exponentially more powerful and with a new willingness to deploy that power, as evidenced by the expanded jurisdiction of Congress outlined in the Reconstruction amendments and the Military Reconstruction Act. Elliott West, *The Last Indian War: The Nez Perce Story* (New York: Oxford University Press, 2011), xxi.

39. Patricia Limerick defined "shiftiness of language" as the "verbal behavior" within the process of colonization that allowed American settlers to "justify, promote, sell . . . congratulate, persuade, and reassure" themselves about their roles. Patricia Limerick, "Making the Most of Words," in *Under an Open Sky: Rethinking America's Western Past*, ed. William Cronon, George Miles, and Jay Gitlin (New York: W. W. Norton, 1993), 168–69. In his recent book, the historian James Buss has masterfully expanded Limerick's notion into a full treatment of "the role of language and the cultural expressions of language . . . as linguistic forms of domination" focused, in his case study, on the Lower Great Lakes region. See James Buss, *Winning the West with Words: Language and Conquest in the Lower Great Lakes* (Norman: University of Oklahoma Press, 2011), 4. For the second quote in the sentence, see Jodi Byrd, *The Transit of Empire: Indigenous Critiques of Colonialism* (Minneapolis: University of Minnesota Press, 2011), 54.

40. Bruyneel, *The Third Space of Sovereignty*, 69.

41. *Commissioner of Indian Affairs*, 1869, 448.

42. Ely S. Parker to William Welsh, 19 June 1869, Records of the Office of Indian Affairs, Letters Sent, vol. 90, 30 Apr. 1869–7 August 1869, 406, Record Group 75, National Archives and Records Administration, Washington, D.C.

43. Ely S. Parker to Henry Rowe Schoolcraft, 25 Mar. 1853, Folder 4, 1853–1858, Ely S. Parker Papers, American Philosophical Society, Philadelphia.

44. Ely S. Parker to Nicholson Parker, 21 June, 1846, Box 2, 1846–1848, Ely S. Parker Papers, American Philosophical Society, Philadelphia.

45. *ARCIA*, 1869, 448; emphasis added.

46. Ely S. Parker, "Draft for lecture containing autobiographical notes, notes on

the history of Indian-White relations and on religion," ca. 1878, MS 674, Folder 2, Parker Papers, Ayer Collection, Newberry Library, Chicago.

47. Deloria and DeMallie, *Documents of American Indian Diplomacy*, 233.

48. *Congressional Globe*, 41st Cong., 2d sess., 1870, 4080.

49. *Congressional Globe*, 41st Cong., 3d sess., part 3, 1871, 1811.

50. Ibid., 1824.

51. Ibid., 1822.

52. Ibid., 1824.

53. Elliott West, "Reconstructing Race," *Western Historical Quarterly* 34 (Spring 2003): 24.

54. See Byrd, *The Transit of Empire*, 10.

8 WASHINGTON NOVELS AND THE MACHINERY OF GOVERNMENT

Amanda Claybaugh

At loose ends after the death of her husband and increasingly bored with life in New York, Madeleine Lee, the protagonist of an anonymously published novel named *Democracy* (1880), decides to spend a season in Washington. In Washington, she would learn how national union was reconstituting itself in the aftermath of the Civil War, but she is more interested in learning what has happened to the nation's government. Indeed, her intention in visiting the city is to learn how "the machinery of government worked."[1] Madeleine Lee was not alone in her curiosity. The 1870s saw the beginning of a vogue for writings about Washington, for travel guides, etiquette books, and, most significantly, for novels like *Democracy*. These writings offered to readers what Madeleine Lee hoped a visit to Washington would afford: an encounter with the entity for which Americans had as yet no stable name, an entity they variously called the national government, the general government, and the government at Washington, D.C.

Historians have long debated whether the Civil War transformed the federal government. Some have argued that the war created, as Eric Foner put it, a "national state possessing vastly expanded authority and a new set of purposes."[2] Others have argued that the transformation was only temporary, or that it actually occurred significantly after the war, or that analogous kinds of governments had existed even before the war.[3] But as we debate whether the federal government actually changed, we should also ask how it was perceived at the time by ordinary citizens. This is a question that Heather Cox Richardson has explored, surveying postbellum newspapers and magazines and finding in them ample evidence that the federal government "continued to grow in Northerners' imaginations even more quickly than it did in real life."[4] And it is a question that I will take up in this essay, as I survey nineteenth-century literary works about Washington, novels most significantly. In these novels, I find further evidence that postbellum citizens believed that the war had changed the federal government. Only a handful of antebellum novels had been set in Washington, and these, I will show, remained largely indifferent to the government, focusing almost exclusively on questions of national feeling. In the postbellum period, by contrast, scores of such novels were written, and they all focused their attention, as *Democracy* did, on the federal government and its machinery.

But if these Washington novels suggest that postbellum citizens perceived a change in the federal government, they more importantly grapple with the question of what perceiving and depicting the federal government actually entails. There is a long tradition of observing that the U.S. federal government is uniquely difficult to perceive, with some arguing that this difficulty shows that the government is weak and attenuated, while others argue that the government's seeming invisibility is precisely the source of its power.[5] But by focusing exclusively on the United States, these accounts fail to reckon with the fact that all governments are difficult to grasp.

This difficulty becomes apparent when we contrast governments with nations. The nation, constituted as it is by persons, seems easy enough to perceive in one's fellow citizens and easy enough to depict in novelistic characters and plots. For this reason, theorists from Benedict Anderson to Homi K. Bhabha have argued that the novel played a key role in consolidating feelings of nationhood, and we will see this work done in the antebellum novels set in Washington.[6] Government, by contrast, comprises a vast array of institutions and activities, some of which are easy to see and depict, some of which are not. In part, the perceptual difficulties are ideological. As H. G. Wells argues, modern people suffer from "state-blindness." We have blinded ourselves to the state because we prefer to think of our "business activities" and "private employments" as purely individual acts, rather than acts that occur within—and are made possible by—a "large collective process."[7] And in part, the perceptual difficulties are phenomenological. As Michael Walzer argues, the state is "invisible" and so must be brought into visibility by representation. "It must be personified before it can be seen," he claims, and "symbolized before it can be loved."[8] Walzer's state is not quite coextensive with what I discuss as government, of course, and many aspects of government can in fact be seen and depicted quite easily: congressional debates, presidential campaigns, oral arguments at the Supreme Court. These, too, can be found in the antebellum Washington novels. But the federal government of the postbellum era was specifically a government of bureaucratic apparatuses and anonymous functionaries, and these things postbellum novels struggled to depict.

In grappling with difficulties of perception and depiction, postbellum novels about Washington also gradually arrived at a set of conventions for capturing a federal government that had, in the view of many postbellum Americans, grown dramatically in size and function. These conventions were borrowed, I will show, from contemporaneous discourses attacking this dramatic growth, a phenomenon that these discourses named "corruption." But while these conventions resulted from a specific set of political debates, they proved so successful at depicting the federal government that they long outlasted their original moment, continuing to shape how we experience and think about the federal government today.

WASHINGTON IN LITERATURE
BEFORE AND DURING THE CIVIL WAR

Even before its founding, the city of Washington was understood as a representation. There were debates about where in the country the city should be placed, and debates, too, about its built environment. Would the capital be a governmental village organized as a grid, a form that Thomas Jefferson took to be republican? Or would it be what George Washington wanted, a metropolis organized on a radial plan, with avenues extending to connect the city to the entire nation and projecting beyond the nation's borders across the continent: a federal city and an imperial one?[9]

This early conviction that the city's built environment would do representational work was taken up eagerly by the earliest important genre of Washington writing, ekphrastic poetry. Ekphrastic poetry translates visual art into verbal form, and these poems treat the buildings and streets of Washington like works of art. Early in the nineteenth century, many of these streets were still being laid, and many of the buildings remained half undone. But the early poets found in this incompleteness figures of a national greatness yet to come. In his "Poem on the Future Glory of the United States of America" (1804), for instance, David Humphreys describes Washington as a "future city" and an "embryo capital," one that requires of its citizens a willingness to imagine "Squares in morasses, obe-lisks in trees."[10] Another poet, Lydia Sigourney, would do much the same thing in reverse. Her "Conflagration at Washington" (1815) uses the now-burned Capitol, whose dome once rose "aspiring to the skies," as a figure for a national greatness postponed by the British attack on Washington.[11] A few decades later, reform-minded poets used the city's buildings to em-body democratic values that the nation had not yet fulfilled. Hannah Flagg Gould's "The Cherokee at Washington" (1839) imagines a Cherokee chief, his treaties betrayed, come to Washington in search of a monument to the man whose treaties the Cherokee could trust.[12] But this reformist strategy was put to its fullest use by antislavery poets. James Russell Lowell's "On the Capture of Fugitive Slaves Near Washington" (1845) argues that slav-ery has rendered meaningless the city's monuments to liberty, while John Greenleaf Whittier would call Washington the "City of the Slaves" in his "At Washington" (1845).[13]

In addition to these poems, a handful of novels appeared. Entirely for-gotten today, they had little impact even in their own era. They were often published by small regional houses and rarely reviewed or even mentioned in the press.[14] These novels divide into two groups. Some were written as political satires, to lampoon the rival political party, such as C. R. Wil-liams's and Clifton Waller Barrett's *Aristocracy: A National Tale* (1832) or William Price's *Clement Falconer; or, The Memoirs of a Young Whig* (1838). But another trio of novels focuses not on politics, but on Washington society: George Watterston's *The L. . . . Family at Washington* (1822), Margaret Ba-yard Smith's *A Winter in Washington* (1824), and *Scenes at Washington*, by a Citizen of Baltimore (1848).

The L. . . . Family establishes the paradigm for the rest. The novel be-gins when the L. family arrives in Washington to spend the season. After settling into a boarding house, the family tours the city. They visit the most important buildings, which are described much as they would be in contemporary poetry. In *Scenes at Washington*, for instance, the char-acters admire the unfinished Capitol and what they call the President's House, both of which are surrounded by "large blocks of unhewn stone" that figure coming grandeur.[15] The characters also do what the poets do not, namely, enter the buildings and witness the work of governing. They go to Congress and see the representatives at work, judging that body to possess "peculiar dignity and wisdom"; they go to the White House and meet the president and his wife, by whom they are cordially received.[16] The L. family even pays a visit to the Supreme Court, where they find the judges at their desks, busily writing.

Once the scene is fully set, the plots begin to unfold, and it becomes clear that these novels are more interested in the nation than in its government. The L. family has come to Washington from Connecticut in search of what a knowing observer telegraphically glosses as "husbands, offices, &" (18). The city functions as the source of whatever young women and men need to take their places in the adult world. The city functions, that is to say, much as London does in the courtship novels of Anthony Trollope or as Paris does in the *Bildungsromane*, or novels of education, by Stendhal or Honoré de Balzac. The courtship plots unfold smoothly, and, in the process, they do nation-building work.[17] Washington is the place where all of the country's "fashion, beauty, and much of the wealth and intellect" convene (Citizen 25). But it is also the place that gathers citizens from among all the nation's regions, the place where "the south intermingl[es] with the north, and the east with the west" (Citizen 40). As the L. family travels to Washington, they encounter a comic array of regional types, but in the city, once the courtship plot begins, love unites Americans across regional lines. The L. daughter, born in New England, marries a Kentucky man.

It is in the search for offices that we would expect to find an account of the federal government. The father of the family, having already served as a magistrate at home, hopes to be appointed minister to London, an aspiration the novel dismisses as unrealistic. More troubling, for Watterston, is the son's conviction that a government office is "the only thing worth having, or worth looking for in these times" (19). The son must learn that Washington is a city to visit, not to settle in, a lesson that all three of the novels teach. In another of these novels, the young man and woman flee for the countryside as soon as they are married, while the family in the third maintains a house in the country through their entire winter in Washington. These temporary sojourns in Washington, like the delimited legislative season, circumscribe the workings of the federal government, limiting it to the electoral circuits that put the nation's center in touch with the nation's regions. The novels do not want to imagine any federal government beyond that. The one acknowledgment that the federal government comprises something more than congressmen, presidents, and justices comes when Watterston's novel acknowledges the existence of government clerks. Visiting Congress one day, the L. family comes across forgotten notes for a debate about what clerks should be paid. But the antebellum novels have no interest in depicting the lives of clerks, nor the kind of work they do. And for the same reason, they have no interest in seeing their male characters secure the offices they desire. These antebellum novels remain fundamentally indifferent to the federal government.

During the Civil War, Washington was transformed. The city grew in size and changed in character. It became a garrison city, filled with new recruits training before being sent south and wounded veterans cared for in army hospitals. It also became a freedmen's city, as the city's large population of free men and women of color and recently emancipated slaves was joined by contrabands flooding in from Union lines. Only a handful of novels or poems about the city were published during these years, few of them of note. But a novelist, Louisa May Alcott, and a poet, Walt Whitman, did write some sketches that capture the city and its transformation more vividly than anything else. Alcott and Whitman had both come to Washington to help care for wounded soldiers. While Alcott was in Washington, she wrote a handful of sketches, which she first published in newspapers. When she returned from the capital, an abolitionist publisher reissued them as a book, *Hospital Sketches* (1863). Whitman, for his part, came to Washington to nurse his brother, who had been wounded in battle, and then stayed to tend to other soldiers as well. He, too, wrote sketches about his experiences, and he sent them to Alcott's publisher, who rejected them. Whitman finally published his sketches in 1875, in a volume entitled *Memoranda during War*, and he later incorporated them into his great autobiographical prose work, *Specimen Days* (1882).

In their wartime writings, both Alcott and Whitman grapple with national questions. For Whitman, the problem is the obvious one, secession. Before arriving in Washington, he had thought of the city as infiltrated by secessionists. And when he tried to imagine the city that he had not yet seen, the thought of secessionists unsettled his depictions. Imagining a crowd of citizens on a Washington street, presuming that half of them are "secesh of the most venomous kind," he is unable to move with his customary skill through his depiction of the crowd.[18] Where the Whitmanian catalogue typically moves with ease from item to item, this one remains an unseemly jumble of incommensurate categories: the street is "crowded, jamm'd with citizens, darkies, clerks, everybody, lookers-on" (733). When Whitman actually arrived in Washington, however, he found in the hospital powerful resources for depicting the nation that had been sundered and now needed to be healed. As he moved from patient to patient, he found in the lines of hospital beds a kind of literal embodiment of a poetic catalogue, which he was then quick to record. Among the wounded soldiers he saw, "representatives from all New England, from New York, and New Jersey, and Pennsylvania—indeed from all the States and all the cities—largely from the west" (743). An expansive list, but still only half the nation; subsequent sketches would, however, include wounded Confederates as well. One, whom Whitman had been tending for days, finally identifies himself as "a rebel soldier," and Whitman responds in the flat idiom of assured equality that the fact "made no difference" (795).

For Alcott, the problem facing the nation was that of the former slaves. As soon as she arrives in Washington, she sees a city filled with fugitives. At first, she finds them strange, unlike the free persons of color she had known in Concord. But she soon embraces these fugitives, quite literally in the case of the children, and celebrates their emancipation from slavery by dancing and cheering in her room the night that the Emancipation Proclamation comes into effect. In these ways, Alcott tries to create and sustain the affective ties that would undergird the postemancipation nation. But Alcott also realized that something more than national feeling might be required. This is the import of her book's strangest scene, in which Alcott wanders at night through empty Washington streets. Already succumbing to the typhoid fever that would ultimately force her to return home, Alcott sees the city with feverish intensity. In this state she enters the Capitol. As she wanders from room to room, she finds the building empty yet blazing with light. Empty, until she enters the Senate Chamber, where she beholds a rather unexpected sight. "I found," she recalls, "the Speaker's Chair occupied by a colored gentleman."[19] It is an extraordinary sight, until her fevered vision clears and she realizes that the "colored gentleman" is actually a ten-year-old boy, hired to clean the chamber after the session, now resting in the Speaker's chair. But even after Alcott's vision clears, the scene lingers in the mind. For if it is a fever vision during the war, it is also a prophecy of what the end of the war would bring about, namely, black officeholders occupying, if not the Speaker's chair, certainly other seats in Congress. More generally, the scene also anticipates a new role for the federal government in securing and guaranteeing racial equality.

Whitman, too, wanders the city's streets at night and enters empty buildings, but for him these wanderings offer a chance to consider how the buildings might figure a changing federal government. The government had, indeed, changed. During the war, the federal government took on a range of new powers and responsibilities. It created a national currency, established a national bank, and imposed a national income tax. It established land-grant universities, supported a transcontinental railroad, and distributed western lands through the Homestead Act. The process made the executive branch preeminent, and Whitman became an early poet of the presidency. The president, for all his power, is nonetheless a person—and thus easy to perceive and depict. "I see very plainly ABRAHAM LINCOLN's dark brown face," Whitman writes; "We have got so we exchange bows, and very cordial ones" (757). But the governmental apparatus that Lincoln heads is far more remote and abstract, and Whitman seeks it in empty buildings, alone and at night.

Again and again, his wartime sketches present the same scene. Whitman stands contemplating a building that he has entered many times by day, a building such as the Patent Office, now transformed into a hospital, or the Capitol or the White House. But the building is now estranged for him, by the silence, by the loneliness, by moonlight or by gaslight. And in this estrangement, Whitman pauses to reflect on what the building means. We can see this process at work most clearly in a passage entitled "The White House at Moonlight":

February 24th.—A spell of soft fine weather. I wander about a
good deal, sometimes at night under the moon. To-night took a
long look at the President's house. The white portico—the palace-
like, tall, round columns, spotless as snow,—the walls also—the
tender and soft moonlight, flooding the pale marble, and making
peculiar faint languishing shades, not shadows—everywhere a
soft transparent hazy, thin, blue moon-lace, hanging in the air—
the brilliant and extra-plentiful clusters of gas, on and around the
facade, columns, portico, &—everything so white, so marbly pure
and dazzling, yet soft—the White House of future poems, and of
dreams and dramas, there in the soft and copious moon—the gor-
geous front, in the trees, under the lustrous flooding moon, full of
reality, full of illusion—the forms of the trees, leafless, silent, in
trunk and myriad-angles of branches, under the stars and sky—
the White House of the land, and of beauty and night—sentries
at the gates, and by the portico, silent, pacing there in blue over-

coats—stopping you not at all, but eyeing you with sharp eyes, whichever way you move. (742)

Whitman's other sketches describing Washington buildings at night had been characteristically concise. This one, however, circles around, returning again and again to describe the moon, the facade, and the trees, extending the moment of contemplation, but crucially failing to advance it. Whitman's aspiration is clear, but it has not yet been fulfilled. The sketch is not so much a depiction of the federal government as an effort to capture both the necessity and the difficulty of such depictions. What this passage does, in its repetition and fragmentation, is hold open up a space in which the "White House of future poems" might one day be written.

Speciman Days is best known for Whitman's claim that "the real war will never get in the books" (802). But the wartime sketches should also be remembered for grappling with the difficulties of seeing and depicting the federal government. Finding a way to capture the government would prove the central task of Washington literature after the war.

WASHINGTON IN LITERATURE AFTER THE WAR

Not everything had changed by the end of the war. Poets continued to write about Washington, and they continued to do so in roughly the same ways as they had always done.[20] Yet after the war, the novel came into its own as the chief genre for depicting the city. Where the antebellum novels had been written by unknown authors and had gone largely unread, three prominent men began the postbellum vogue for Washington novels. Mark Twain was already well known as a frontier humorist when he jointly authored *The Gilded Age* (1873), the novel that would inaugurate his career as a novelist as well as giving the postbellum era its most enduring name.[21] John W. De Forest, the author of *Playing the Mischief* (1875), is now largely forgotten, but he was at the time even better known than Twain, routinely publishing essays and fiction in all the leading northeastern magazines. As for the anonymous author of *Democracy*, he was revealed to be Henry Adams, an important essayist and historian, as well as the grandson and great-grandson of presidents.

Diverging widely in style and tone, the three novels these men wrote nonetheless tell the same story. An experienced woman, having lost her husband, comes to Washington in search of something only Washington can provide. Adams's protagonist, Madeleine Lee, seeks experience; Twain's and De Forest's protagonists seek something more concrete. De Forest's protagonist has come to pursue a private claim, more specifically, she wants the government to compensate her for a barn destroyed during the War of 1812. Twain's protagonist, on the other hand, has come in hopes of selling the government some worthless land.

Set at the 1870s moment of their writing, these novels unsurprisingly take up the national questions raised by the recent civil war. In the antebellum novels, the city had brought together citizens from various states; now it brings together former enemies, and some tact, the protagonists discover, is required. In Twain, hostesses must learn that they should no longer refer to their southern guests as "rebels," while in De Forest congressmen must learn that the southern members, all born in the north, bridle at having their "yankeeism and carpet-baggism" referred to.[22] And Madeleine Lee catches herself in a faux pas when she asks whether a Virginian of her acquaintance will be paying a call on the president, only to be told that he is "not sufficiently reconstructed" (47) to do so. Twain and De Forest also grapple with the other national question posed by the war, the place of the former slaves. (Adams, writing a few years later, ignores race almost entirely, and after him the only authors to pay significant attention to the city's black population were themselves African American.) Twain acknowledges that the new "colored citizens" are now free to petition the government (172), while De Forest says that they are also now free to hold office. This fact enrages his protagonist so much that when she finds herself pressed up against an African American representative in a crowded levee, she stabs him with her umbrella. De Forest seems to share her rage, making his own attack on black office holding through a virulently racist short story, "The Colored Member" (1872).[23]

But these novels, unlike their antebellum predecessors, devote much less attention to the nation than to its government. In depicting the government, the authors would grapple with the same difficulties that Whitman had faced. And the solutions they arrived at would be shaped by two conflicting imperatives, one literary, one political. Adams and De Forest belonged to a northeastern elite that Twain ambivalently wanted to join, and this elite championed literary realism. The most influential postbellum critic had singled out one of De Forest's earlier novels, *Miss Ravenel's Conversion from Secession to Loyalty* (1867), as the first to "treat the war really and artistically," and the postbellum publishing world eagerly sought other phases of American life captured with similar fidelity.²⁴ At the same time, this northeastern elite was increasingly convinced that government had somehow gone wrong since the war, a view that would cause some elites to lose faith in the Republican Party and nearly all to lose faith in Reconstruction. All three novelists agreed that government had gone wrong. De Forest had lamented, in *Miss Ravenel*, the fall of an army officer tempted by increased governmental expenditures, and he would go on to attack corruption in an allegorical novel, *Honest John Vane* (1875), and in an allegorical short story, "An Inspired Lobbyist" (1872), before turning his attention to his more realist novel of Washington. Adams, for his part, wrote influential essays criticizing the spoils system and advocating a civil service that laid the groundwork for the reform efforts of the Liberal Republicans in the early 1870s. Twain alone stayed out of these 1870s political debates, remaining personally loyal to Ulysses Grant, but he, also, would finally turn, bolting from the Republican Party with other mugwumps in the mid-1880s. Taken together, the literary and political imperatives created novels that judged the government even while still seeking to understand it—and prompted the novelists to create depictions that neutrally describe, even as they also condemn.

Arriving in Washington to learn how government works, these protagonists must first realize that nothing is as they had thought it would be. Madeleine Lee prides herself on knowing more than the average woman does, on knowing, for instance, that the government is divided into three branches and that "the President, the Speaker, and the Chief Justice" are "important personages" (7). She is a bit contemptuous when her sister is bored by listening to congressional debates, a bit chagrined when she herself is bored by reading the *Congressional Register*, all because she believes that congressmen's speeches actually matter. "This is a very common conception of Congress," the narrator intervenes to observe, "many Congressmen share it" (11). Madeleine Lee will soon learn that the Speaker is not an important personage at all. Power resides, she discovers, in the senator who is courting her, or rather with his "secret senatorial ring" (41), with the secret service at its command. The other protagonists make similar discoveries about Congress. De Forest's quickly learns of Congress's corruption, avowedly so with an official "Committee on Spoilation" (161), and it takes her only a little longer to recognize that power does not lie in congressmen's hands. This account of Congress reflects a general postbellum sense that the executive branch had come into power at the expense of the legislative branch, but the president proves not to be an important personage either. Twain makes this claim dismissively, when a character notes in passing that a certain place is so unfashionable that it is frequented only by "persons of no position in society... and the President" (233). De Forest makes this point more elegiacally. When his protagonist visits a presidential levee, she is filled with sympathy for the president, a former war hero now charged with doing nothing more than shaking, by the thousands, the peoples' hands. Adams, too, uses a presidential levee as a way to capture the impotence of the presidency. When Madeleine Lee encounters the spectacle of a handshaking president and his wife, she succumbs to something like an "opium-eater's vision" (45) of an otherwise hidden truth, a recognition that the president and his wife have become nothing more than "mechanical figures," "toy dolls," "automata" (44).

Evacuating power from Congress and the presidency, these novels relocate it to the penumbra of institutions that surround them. Twain refers to this penumbra as "the lobbies and Newspaper Row" (276), and De Forest and Adams also settle on the term "lobby," along with the related concept of "influence." The terms perform two functions at once. They refer to behind-the-scenes advocacy in the service of a particular interest, but they also help name and organize the novels' depictions of a government that has grown in size, expanding to include new executive departments and new government employees. When one of Twain's characters informs another that all jobs in Washington are secured through political influence, from the "highest bureau chief" to "the maid who scrubs the Department halls, the night watchmen of the public buildings, and the darkey boy who purifies the Department spittoons" (178), he registers both the government's corruption and its new expansiveness.

The same holds true of the schemes that the lobbyists pursue. In pursuit of their own profit, lobbyists show a keen eye for the new functions that the government has come to perform, and in this way the figure of the lobbyist enables the depiction of those functions. Arriving in Washington in the hopes of being compensated for a barn destroyed long ago, De Forest's protagonist at first fears that a private claim might be beneath her, but then she falls in with a lobbyist and a more experienced claimant who encourage her to demand ever more. Soon she is demanding "twenty thousand—forty thousand—eighty thousand, for it... any sum that one was pleased to mention" (151). But through her time among the lobbyists, she learns that the real money lies not in private claims, but in public works, in "public building contracts, grading and paving contracts, banking commissions and interests" (437). Twain's protagonists are aware of public works from the beginning, seeking money for ill-conceived railroad, canal and steamship subsidies. But even better than public works, Twain emphasizes, is public aid. If De Forest's Congress has a Committee on Spoilation, Twain's offers an even more lucrative Committee on Benevolent Appropriations (258), and the existence of such a committee guides his protagonist's schemes. Arrived in Washington with some worthless land to sell, she soon realizes that she must present herself as wanting to sell it not for her own benefit but for those in greater need. Other lobbyists, she soon learns, have already monopolized the Indians, so she turns her attention to the freedpeople. She presents herself as devoted solely to "the uplifting of the down-trodden negro" (229), and she begins advocating for the government to build a university for freedpeople, so long as they build it, at great expense, on her lands.

In Adams's novel, the lobby is paired with another institution, Washington society, and it is here that the distance from the antebellum novels becomes most clear. The antebellum novels had certainly depicted society—that is where the courtships took place. But what they portrayed was not Washington society, but rather a national society gathered temporarily in Washington.

In the postbellum novel, however, Washington society has become both permanent and cut off from the rest of the nation. Twain had been the first to observe changes in Washington society. His narrator divides Washingtonians into three groups. First, the "antiques," which is to say, the "cultivated, high-bred old families" (230). Then, the "parvenues," newly arrived and eager to take their permanent place (230). And finally, the group that the antebellum Washington novels had described, the "Middle Ground," the uncorrupted legislators who make the annual circuit between the capital and the district they have been sent to the capital to represent (241). This last group is, for Twain, both admirable and tedious. "Beyond reproach" (241), they reside outside the scope of his novel, as do the admirable antiques; what interests him are the machinations of the parvenues.

It would fall to Adams to recognize that Washington society, whether parvenu or antique, offers an alternative to the lobby for depicting the penumbra of institutions and acts that he sees as constituting the federal government. In the antebellum novels, society and government had been kept carefully distinct. The ladies are mocked when they attend Congress to show off their new dresses, while the gentlemen are chided when they fall into political debates in a drawing room. But it is precisely in Madeleine Lee's drawing room that Adams will locate his account of government. Adams sketches a standard story of political corruption, with the Republican senator at its center. We learn, but we do not see, that the senator exercises his subtle power to dominate the newly elected president, much as he had dominated the previous one; that he influences the president to appoint him to the most powerful position in all the government, namely, secretary of the Treasury; that "office seekers" throng to his private rooms in the evening (74); and that he dispenses "public money" in exchange for votes (95). Instead of narrating these events, the novel tells of Madeleine Lee's progress in Washington society. In search of nothing but experience, she establishes a salon and soon finds herself hosting leading politicians, the Republican senator among them, as well as an array of cultivated European diplomats. Her drawing room becomes the site of a distinctly undemocratic politics, in which the offices that most matter (secretaryships and ministries) are appointed, not elected, and the appointments can be influenced by women and foreigners. In the midst of all these machinations, Madeleine Lee begins to influence the senator. First, she persuades him to dress and act like a more respectable man; then she begins to imagine that she might shape his political commitments and guide his political acts. The novel reaches a crisis with a pair of revelations. Madeleine Lee has accepted the senator's proposal of marriage when she learns that he is involved in a corrupt scheme, the "Inter-Oceanic Mail Steamship Company" (163). Learning this, she realizes that she been involved in similar scheming. Exercising her influence, she was acting as a subtler—and thus more powerful—version of the lady lobbyists she had disdained, and her dreams of influencing the senator were no different from his efforts to influence the president. She had been corrupted, precisely as he had been drawn in by "ambition, thirst for power, restless eagerness to meddle in what did not concern her" (166). She breaks the engagement and flees the city.

Whether these novels focus on the lobby or on society, they tell the same story about postbellum government. It is a story about democratization, about the extension of power to new persons, to ordinary people rather than patricians, to recently freed slaves, even, implicitly, to women. But it is also a story about governmental expansion, about a government that had grown in size and taken on new functions, and, in the process, cut itself off from electoral accountability. "Democracy," Adams's narrator tells us, "rightly understood, is the government of the people, by the people, for the benefit of Senators" (17). But that is not nearly cynical enough. The federal government is, these novels imply, government for the benefit of lobbyists and speculators and private claimants, for the benefit of the foreign ministers who crowd Madeleine Lee's salon, and for the freedpeople and Indians Twain's lady lobbyist claims to speak on behalf of. This is, of course, a very familiar account of government: it is the account that James S. Pike would give of the South Carolina state legislature, that Thomas Nast's cartoons would give of Tammany Hall, that seemingly every northern newspaper was giving of the Grant administration. It is difficult to gauge the accuracy of these accounts, difficult to ascertain whether corruption was as widespread as reformers claimed, whether it was uniquely bad in the postbellum era. (Certainly, Pike wrote the articles that were the core of *The Prostrate State* (1874) before he had even visited South Carolina, and he did very little research once he finally got there.)[25] What is easier to gauge is the effect these accounts had. Corruption, as Mark Summers has argued, did not play an important role in postbellum politics, but the controversy over corruption certainly did. It associated bad government with expansion and innovation, good government with a return to the more limited powers of the past.[26]

Very much the product of their times, this trio of novels would outlive them. Unlike the novels about Washington written during the antebellum period, which were forgotten almost as soon as they were published, the novels written by Twain, De Forest, and Adams were widely read and warmly received, inspiring other novelists to also write about Washington. In doing so, they drew heavily on the conventions already established for depicting the federal government: the city tour, the visit to Congress, the presidential levee; the ring and the scam, the lobby and the drawing room. But since most of the latter postbellum novelists did not share Twain's, De Forest's, and Adams's partisan agenda, they used these conventions in a new way. For later postbellum novelists, the conventions did not reveal the truth of a government in need of reform, but rather fulfilled purely literary functions. They served, as they had served for Twain, De Forest, and Adams, to depict aspects of government that would otherwise evade perception and depiction. But they also did something new, namely, please a readership that had become accustomed to these conventions.

One of the 1880s novelists, Frances Hodgson Burnett, appears unusually canny about readerly expectations. The narrator of her novel, *Through One Administration* (1881), is half amused and half appalled by what visitors now come to Washington to see. They still go to Congress, but no longer to hear the congressmen debate. They now come in hopes of seeing "the member connected with the last investigation" and learning of new "'jobs'" and "'schemes.'"[27] And yet, even as the narrator mocks the cheap popularity of stories about corruption, Burnett ends up offering one herself. Her novel will describe a wife forced, by her base husband, to become a kind of lobbyist on his behalf, and the plot enables Burnett to capture what interests her, the workings of the executive departments. Without a corruption plot, the departments remain as inaccessible as the buildings that contain them, concealing within themselves "tremendous communities, regulated by a tremendous system" (66).

If Burnett relies, almost despite herself, on the lobby to figure a changing government, most of her contemporaries would follow Adams in using society to figure that government instead. The canniest account of this strategy can be found in the writings of Madeline Vinton Dahlgren, the author of an etiquette guide, *Etiquette of Social Life in Washington* (1873), as well as a novel, *A Washington Winter* (1883). Both of these books respond to the same perceptual problem. The novel attempts to capture the workings of a government that can only be described, in the words of its knowing protagonist, as "wheels within wheels."[28] The etiquette guide attempts to answer the question of precedence, the question of whose wives should pay calls on whose. The two questions, it turns out, are the same. To ask whether the wife of the secretary of the Treasury should pay a call on the wife of the Speaker of the House is to ask whether the ramifying executive departments with their unelected officials have finally taken precedence over the legislature. To create, as Dahlgren advocates, a clear hierarchy of all officials would be to offer a transparent account of how the new federal government works. But this, ultimately, is not what the Washington novelists wanted to do. All the novels that focus on Washington society recognize, as Dahlgren did, the homology between the domains of society and government, but each provides a different account of how these domains work. Madeline Lee may learn that the real power lies with the secretary of the Treasury, but another protagonist will learn that the president is a mere puppet in the hands of party bosses or of the Speaker of the House. In one novel, the protagonist discovers that the receptions held by the secretary of state are more prestigious than those held by the Speaker of the House; in another, the protagonist discovers that the State Department has lost its power and prestige. The particular account a given novel or etiquette guide offers proves less significant, however, than the mere fact that the government is vast and complicated enough for these accounts to disagree.

Drawing when needed on the conventions established by Twain, De Forest, and Adams, the later postbellum novelists preserve and transmit the partisan arguments those conventions had once expressed. And they do so all the more effectively for being unpartisan. Reviews of Twain, De Forest, and Adams acknowledged that these men were writing with a political agenda, but reviews of the later postbellum novels about Washington often classify them as seemingly apolitical genres. Some of the novels were seen as society novels or novels of manners, while others were identified as realist, set alongside works by Henry James, and still others were discussed as romances. As for the novels written by Pauline E. Hopkins and W. E. B. Du Bois, these were destined, irrespective of genre, to be classified as race writing. Dispersed across so many different genres, severed from their partisan origins, the conventions that Twain, De Forest, and Adams had consolidated now seemed less like literary convention and more like unmediated truth.

This matters because the conventions they established continue to shape depictions of Washington into the present day. The lobbyists are familiar, of course, and the bribes and the scams, but more fundamentally, political observers continue to describe Washington as a place of sophisticated insiders and social relations that are as important as the political ones. In this way, the postbellum Washington novels predict everything from novels like Allen Drury's *Advise and Consent* (1959) to Sally Quinn's notorious complaint that Bill Clinton had violated the rules of a town to which he had never belonged.[29] And it is a way of thinking about our modern government that we learned at the very moment that government first emerged, during the Civil War and Reconstruction.

THE MACHINERY OF GOVERNMENT
AND THE STOCKADE STATE

Whatever the reality of the federal government may have been, postbellum Americans clearly believed that it was changing. Writing during the Civil War, Walt Whitman was one of the first to recognize what twentieth-century political theorists would later conclude, that seeing and depicting this changing federal government would prove both necessary and difficult. Writing in the immediate aftermath of the war, Mark Twain, John W. De Forest, and Henry Adams took the government to be expanding rapidly in both size and function, and they sought ways to represent this. They found that lobbies and Washington society could perform their representational work.

In lobbyists and hostesses, in the more and less obviously corrupted forms of influence, they found a way of capturing a government constituted by an interconnected network of institutions, some elected, some appointed, some official, some unofficial, some acknowledged, some denied. Hence the "machinery of government" that Madeline Lee had come to see.

How to reconcile this "machinery" with the "Stockade State" that other authors in this volume describe? The two depend on one another. The machinery of government names a fear; the Stockade State describes the reality that this fear creates. If federal power was limited, confined to a string of outposts on an ungovernable frontier, this situation occurred at least in part because of a fear that federal power was actually vast, rapidly expanding beyond visible institutions, with influence ramifying everywhere. And if federal power was described as so vast in Washington, it became possible to miss how attenuated it was everywhere.

NOTES

1. [Henry Adams], *Democracy* (1880; New York: Library of America, 1983) 12. All further references will be marked in the text.

2. Eric Foner, *Reconstruction: America's Unfinished Revolution: 1863-1877* (1988; New York: History Book Club, 2005), xxvi. Another study that shares this view is Drew Gilpin Faust, *This Republic of Suffering: Death and the American Civil War* (New York: Knopf, 2008).

3. For the view that the change was only temporary, see Richard Franklin Bensel, *Yankee Leviathan: The Origins of Central State Authority, 1859-1877* (New York: Cambridge University Press, 1990); and Theda Skocpol, *Protecting Soldiers and Mothers: The Political Origins of Social Policy in the United States* (Cambridge: Belknap Press of Harvard University Press, 1992). For the view that the change occurred significantly after the war, see Stephen Skowronek, *Building a New American State: The Expansion of National Administrative Capacities, 1877-1920* (New York: Cambridge University Press, 1982), 3. For the view that a regulatory state existed even before the war, see William J.

Novak, *The People's Welfare: Law and Regulation in Nineteenth-Century America* (Chapel Hill: University of North Carolina Press, 1996).

4. Heather Cox Richardson, *The Death of Reconstruction: Race, Labor, and Politics in the Post–Civil War North, 1865–1901* (2001; Cambridge: Harvard University Press, 2004), xv.

5. For the view that the state did not yet exist, see G. W. F. Hegel (quoted in Novak, *The People's Welfare*, 3); and Skowronek, *Building a New American State*, 3. For the view that its power lay in its invisibility, see Brian Balogh, *A Government Out of Sight: The Mystery of National Authority in Nineteenth-Century America* (New York: Cambridge University Press, 2009), 4.

6. Benedict Anderson, *Imagined Communities: Reflections on the Origins and Spread of Nationalism* (London: Verso, 1983); Homi K. Bhabha, "Introduction: Narrating the Nation," in *Nation and Narration*, ed. Homi K. Bhabha (London: Routledge, 1990).

7. H. G. Wells, *The Future in America: A Search after Realities* (New York: Harper, 1906), 153.

8. Michael Walzer, "On the Role of Symbolism in Political Thought, *Political Science Quarterly* 82 (June 1967): 194. See also my essay on the necessity and difficulty of representing the state, "Government in Good," *Minnesota Review* 70 (Spring/ Summer 2008).

9. For a summary of these debates, see Fergus M. Bordewich, *Washington: The Making of the American Capital* (New York: Harper Collins, 2008). For a discussion of Washington's representations, see Carl Abbott, *Political Terrain: Washington, D.C., from Tidewater Town to Global Metropolis* (Chapel Hill: University of North Carolina Press, 1999).

10. David Humphreys, "A Poem on the Future Glory of the United States of America," *The Miscellaneous Works of David Humphreys: Late Minister Plenipotentiary . . .* (New York: T. and J. Swords, 1804), 62.

11. [Lydia Sigourney], "The Conflagration at Washington," *Moral Pieces: Prose and Verse* (Hartford, Conn.: Sheldon and Goodwin, 1815), 32.

12. Hannah Flagg Gould, "The Cherokee at Washington," *Poems: Second Edition with Additions* (Boston:: Hilliard, Gray, and Co., 1839).

13. James Russell Lowell, "On the Capture of Fugitive Slaves Near Washington," in *The Poetical Works of James Russell Lowell in Five Volumes*, vol. 1: *Earlier Poems* (1845; Boston: Houghton, Mifflin, and Co., 1890), 227; John Greenleaf Whittier, "At Washington," in *Anti-Slavery Poems, Songs of Labor and Reform*, vol. 3 of *The Poetical Works* (1845; New York: 1892), 109.

14. The best guide to these novels is James A. Kaser's bibliography, entitled *The Washington, D.C., of Fiction: A Research Guide* (Lanham, Md.: Scarecrow Press, 2006). He counts thirteen novels published about Washington before the Civil War, and I have not been able to find any more. Exact figures are difficult to determine, but Kaser's bibliographical research has found fifteen Washington novels published before 1865, and another six published during Reconstruction. Between 1876 and the century's end, however, he found fifty-nine more, with no sign of the genre abating as the twentieth century began. (I have located two more.)

15. Citizen of Baltimore, *Scenes at Washington* (New York: Harper, 1848), 37–38. All further references are to this edition.

16. George Watterston, *The L. . . . Family at Washington; or, A Winter in the Metropolis* (Washington, D.C.: Davis and Force, 1822), 77. All further references are to this edition.

17. For an account of the nation-building work done by the courtship plot, see Doris Sommer, *Foundational Fictions: The National Romances of Latin America* (Berkeley: University of California Press, 1991).

18. Walt Whitman, *Specimen Days*, in *Walt Whitman: Poetry and Prose* (1882; New York: Library of America, 1996), 733. All further references are to this edition.

19. Louisa May Alcott, *Hospital Sketches and Camp and Fireside Stories* (1869; Boston: Roberts Brothers, 1892), 68.

20. Indeed, so persistent are the conventions of these poems that postbellum poems are just as likely to use the city's buildings to make arguments against a slavery that no longer exists. John James Piatt, for instance, devotes "Transfiguration" (1872) to describing the statue on the top of the Capitol dome and noting that the statue, an allegory of freedom, was crafted by the sculptor's slaves. John James Piatt, "Transfiguration," in *Landmarks: The Lost Farm and Other Poems* (1872; Boston: James R. Osgood, and Co., 1879).

21. Twain's coauthor was Charles Dudley Warner, but I refer to the novel as Twain's because the two divided the writing between them and the Washington chapters were written by Twain.

22. Mark Twain and Charles Dudley Warner, *The Gilded Age: A Tale of Today* (1873; New York: Modern Library, 2006), 268. John W. De Forest, *Playing the Mischief* (1875; State College, Pa.: Bald Eagle Press, 1961), 239. All further references will be to these editions.

23. John W. De Forest, "The Colored Member," *Galaxy* 13, no. 3 (March 1872): 293–302.

24. [William Dean Howells], review of *Miss Ravenel's Conversion from Secession to Loyalty*, *Atlantic Monthly*, July 1867, 121.

25. Robert F. Durden, "The Prostrate State Revisited: James S. Pike and South Carolina Reconstruction," *Journal of Negro History* 39, no. 2 (April 1954): 87–111.

26. Mark Wahlgren Summers, *The Era of Good Stealings* (New York: Oxford University Press, 1993), xi.

27. Frances Hodgson Burnett, *Through One Administration* (1881; Ridgewood, N.J.: Greenwood Press, 1967), 381–83.

28. Madeline Vinton Dahlgren, *A Washington Winter* (Boston: James R. Osgood, 1883), 8.

29. Sally Quinn, "In Washington, That Letdown Feeling," *Washington Post*, November 2, 1998.

A Long History of Emancipation

Barbara Krauthamer

In the summer of 1937, well over half a century after her emancipation from slavery, Kiziah Love welcomed a field worker from the Oklahoma office of the Federal Writers' Project into her home. Love was one of more than seven thousand black people owned and emancipated by a Native American master in Indian Territory, the region we now know as Oklahoma.[1] Ninety-three years old, blind, and bedridden, Love kept a sharp memory of her days in bondage. After speaking about her work, religion, health, and family life in slavery, the interview concluded with Love's recollection about emancipation. Yes, Love, stated, "I was glad to be free." She continued, "What did I do and say? Well, I jest clapped my hands together and said, 'Thank God Almighty, I'se free at last!'" Almost as an afterthought, Love added, "I live on the forty acres that the government give me."[2]

This brief excerpt from Love's narrative evokes a history of slavery and emancipation at once familiar and unexpected. From the late eighteenth century through the end of the Civil War, Native American slaveholders held thousands of people of African descent in bondage, exploiting their labor and reproduction for power, prestige, and wealth. During the 1830s era of Indian Removal, the federal government forced Indian nations to leave Mississippi, Alabama, and Georgia, and resettled people in the region known as Indian Territory, where the nations retained limited sovereignty over their people and land. Slaveholding Indian men and women brought their human chattel to their new territory in the West, where enslaved people labored on small farms and large plantations, producing both subsistence and commodity crops for their masters' benefit. Native slaveholders vigorously defended their nations' sovereignty but also recognized how their economic and social investments in slavery and its bedrock ideology of black inferiority linked them to white slaveholders in the southern states. In 1861, consequently, Native political leaders entered treaty relations with the newly created Confederate government, believing that this alliance offered the best means of safeguarding both sovereignty and slavery in Indian Territory.

Kiziah Love's recollection of her emancipation from slavery in Indian Territory as a moment of jubilee and deliverance echoes the universal sentiment of black people throughout the United States. Her passing mention of receiving "forty acres" from the federal government, however, highlights the unusual consequences and conditions of black people's emancipation in Indian Territory. Despite a brief, wartime flirtation with the notion of granting land to former slaves in coastal Georgia, the U.S. government did not authorize land redistribution to freed slaves in the southern states. At the end of the nineteenth century, however, federal efforts to terminate Indian nations' sovereignty and land title in Indian Territory entailed allotting land to citizens of the Indian nations, including former slaves and their descendants. The history of black people's emancipation from slavery in Indian Territory is thus both familiar and distinctive, reflecting the shared experience of black people in the United States and the particular conditions in Indian Territory.

Emancipation came late to Kiziah Love and the other seven to ten thousand enslaved people in Indian Territory. The Emancipation Proclamation (January 1, 1863) did not extend to Indian Territory, though in 1863 the loyalist faction of the Creek nation acknowledged the proclamation's authority.[3] The U.S. victory in 1865 did not ensure the abolition of slavery in the quasi-sovereign Indian nations. Though the Choctaw, Chickasaw, Cherokee, Creek, and Seminole nations had allied with the Confederacy, they were not recognized as states in the Confederacy, leaving their governments and laws effectively untouched by General Lee's surrender. Enslaved people in the Indian nations did not fall under the provisions of the Thirteenth Amendment, which Congress approved in January 1865 and the states ratified by December 1865.[4] Months after the war's end, many Indian lawmakers remained wary of ending chattel slavery and refused to contemplate the possibility of legally and socially redefining people of African descent as something other than slaves. In the Indian nations the central point of contention in the months after the war ended was not, *How would black people's freedom be defined?* Rather, the question was, *Would the nations abolish slavery and establish black people's freedom at all?*

In 1866, a full year after the Civil War had ended, leaders of the Cherokee, Creek, Seminole, Choctaw, and Chickasaw nations entered new treaties with the United States that cemented the abolition of racial chattel slavery in each nation. When Cherokee, Creek, Choctaw, and Chickasaw leaders had entered treaties with the Confederacy in 1861, they severed their nations' treaty relations with the United States. Of the five slaveholding nations in Indian Territory, only the Seminoles had remained loyal to the U.S. The end of the war did not automatically restore the previous treaties or diplomacy between the United States and the Confederacy's Indian allies. From the autumn of 1865 through the spring of 1866, leaders of the nations in Indian Territory, as well as those from Kansas and the southern Plains, conferred with each other and met with envoys from the federal government to negotiate new treaties. Finally, by the summer of 1866, the Cherokee, Creek, Seminole, Choctaw, and Chickasaw nations entered new treaties with the U.S. government. Each nation's treaty provided for the abolition of slavery and the rights of freedpeople and their descendants to citizenship. The 1866 treaties also included an array of provisions that had little to do with emancipation. The treaties insisted on the right of way for railroads through Indian Territory, for example. And treaty language clearly indicated that the days of Indian sovereignty and land title would come to a close by the end of the century.[5]

Slavery's delayed and protracted demise in Indian Territory, especially in the Choctaw and Chickasaw nations, requires that we rethink the familiar timeline and geographic scope of slavery and emancipation. The Choctaw/Chickasaw treaty is noteworthy because of the twisted path it laid out for establishing black people's freedom and citizenship in the Indian nations. Though in 1866 the Choctaw and Chickasaw nations stood as separate entities, their treaty required them to act in concert regarding black people's freedom and citizenship rights. In the Choctaw/Chickasaw treaty of 1866, much more so than in the Cherokee, Creek, and Seminole treaties, the issues of abolishing slavery and establishing black people's status and rights as citizens were firmly linked to provisions that curbed Indian sovereignty and eroded the nations' hold on its land. The long history of slavery and emancipation in Indian Territory reveals some of the ways in which post–Civil War debates over race and citizenship necessarily encompassed Native peoples in the West as much as black and white people in the South.

In the summer of 1865, President Johnson appointed Dennis N. Cooley, the commissioner of Indian affairs, to head up the U.S. treaty commission and negotiate new treaties with the Choctaw, Chickasaw, Cherokee, Creek, and Seminole nations. The other members of the U.S. treaty commission were Elijah Sells, the superintendent of Indian affairs for the southern superintendency; Thomas Wistar, a prominent Quaker; Brigadier General William S. Harney; and Colonel Ely S. Parker, a member of the Seneca nation and part of General Ulysses S. Grant's staff. Choctaw and Chickasaw delegates to the Fort Smith council reportedly responded favorably to Parker's presence on the council.[6]

Shortly before Cooley set out for Fort Smith, Arkansas, where the treaty council was to convene, he received his instructions from the secretary of the interior, James Harlan. Not long before his appointment as head of the Interior Department, Harlan, a Republican from Iowa, had served in the Senate, where he had introduced a bill proposing the extension of federal authority over Indian Territory, the first step toward statehood. The bill authorized the organization of Indian Territory as a formal territory of the United States and gave the president the power to name the secretary of Indian affairs as its governor. Harlan's bill made it through the Senate by an almost two-to-one margin, but the House adjourned before voting on it. Once Harlan was named secretary of the Interior Department, he pushed ahead with his plans for territorialization.

As Harlan's bill and subsequent instructions to Cooley indicate, western territorial expansion was very much on the minds of lawmakers in the years following the Civil War.[7] In his letter to Cooley, Harlan outlined a set of treaty provisions designed to diminish the Indian nations' land claims and sovereign governments. The treaty commission was to "insist upon a cession by [the Indian nations] of all lands not needed," a determination that would be made by federal officials, not Indians. To underscore the seriousness of this demand, Harlan directed the commission to "impress upon them, in the most forcible terms, that the advancing tide of immigration is rapidly spreading over the country, and that the government has not the power or inclination to check it." Harlan also required that the treaties ensure the abolition of slavery and the enactment of "adequate measures" for granting former slaves full equality as tribal members.[8]

The Fort Smith treaty council opened on September 8, 1865, in a cloud of confusion. Commissioner Cooley began the proceedings with a short statement, informing the Indian representatives that the president of the United States required each nation to enter into a new treaty with the United States. Chickasaw, Choctaw, Cherokee, Creek, Seminole, Wyandot, Osage, Seneca, and Shawnee delegates all responded that they had not been previously informed that the council's purpose was to renegotiate treaties with the United States. Moreover, the Choctaw and Chickasaw delegates, who had been selected by the U.S. Indian agent, indicated that they only represented a few hundred Choctaw and Chickasaw loyalists. Speaking through their black interpreter, Maharda Colbert, the Chickasaw delegates stated that they had no authority to speak or act on behalf of their nations. The leading men of the Choctaw and Chickasaw Confederate governments did not arrive at Fort Smith until almost a week later.[9]

Commissioner Cooley proceeded with the Fort Smith council, and on the second day he read through the United States' requirements for new treaties. Prominent among the federal demands were the creation of a single government for Indian Territory, the abolition of slavery, and the "incorporation [of freedpeople] into the tribes on an equal footing with the original members, or suitably provided for."[10] The U.S. Senate Judiciary Committee had debated using similar language of equality in the Thirteenth Amendment but had ultimately struck it from the final text. Its inclusion in the proposed treaty likely reflects Harlan's views on the subject of black people's rights as free people; Harlan was among the Iowa Republicans who endorsed black men's suffrage as early as 1866. Still, the treaty offered no further guidelines on the subject of freedpeople's status or rights in the Indian nations. The vague language regarding ex-slaves' freedom in the Indian nations mirrored the extent to which the definition of black people's freedom remained unclear and contested in the United States.[11]

Choctaw and Chickasaw representatives responded to the U.S. treaty provisions regarding abolition and black people's standing in the nations in equally ambiguous terms. The Chickasaw loyalists indicated that they were willing "to make suitable provisions for [ex-slaves'] future homes." The Chickasaw loyalist Lewis Johnson added, "I have heard much said about the black folks. They suffered as much as we did. I have always understood that the President esteemed the colored people, and we are willing to do just as our Father may wish, and take them in and assist them, and let them help us." It is not clear, however, how Johnson or other loyalists envisioned black people's future in the Chickasaw or Choctaw nations. Perhaps they imagined a return to the practices of kin-based adoption and reciprocity that characterized earlier generations' interactions with outsiders and captives, or perhaps they had something else in mind.

Robert M. Jones, a wealthy Choctaw planter who owned more than two hundred slaves, headed the Choctaw and Chickasaw Confederate delegation. He delivered an opening statement to Cooley that the historian Clara Sue Kidwell describes as breathtakingly defiant. Jones maintained that Choctaw and Chickasaw slaveholders believed the Southern cause was "just" and that the two Indian nations had sided with the Confederacy to safeguard "our independence and national identity." The Choctaw and Chickasaw delegation acknowledged U.S. authority over slavery in the nations but took the position that the subject was "open to further negotiation."[12] In the end, the Fort Smith council restored diplomatic relations between the Choctaw and Chickasaw nations and the United States but did not produce a formal treaty, leaving open myriad questions about the status of some five thousand enslaved people in the two nations.[13]

After the Fort Smith council adjourned, Choctaw and Chickasaw lawmakers considered measures that would abolish slavery but preserve slavery's social and economic subordination of black people. Though Choctaw slaveholders had "abandon[ned]" their property rights in slaves, Peter Pitchlynn, then the nation's principal chief, explained, they expected that black people's freedom would nonetheless "be consistent with the rights of their late owners."[14] What emerged was a set of regulations that functioned like the Black Codes adopted in the southern states. On October 14, 1865, the Choctaw General Council decreed that "such persons as have to the present time, been considered as slaves" could either remain with their former masters or select a new employer and then enter into a written labor contract. Wages were set by a standardized schedule divided by ability into eight ranks, including children, but undistinguished by gender. The law not only coerced freedpeople into farmwork but also positioned them as sharecroppers by specifying that their wages would be the first lien on the crop. Vagrants, those former slaves without such contracts, were liable to arrest by the Choctaw Lighthorsemen who would auction them to the highest bidder.[15]

The Chickasaw governor Winchester Colbert addressed his nation's legislature in the first week of October. "Emancipation is inevitable," he told lawmakers as he urged them to "bring about the manumission of slaves at the earliest practicable period." Colbert also informed the legislature that the good of the nation required them to "lay down a uniform rule of action for all in reference to slaves, so that there may be no confusion growing out of this subject among the people or among the slaves themselves."[16] Chickasaw lawmakers, however, only went so far as to approve a future discussion of a constitutional amendment to abolish slavery. Citing a constitutional provision prohibiting the legislature from emancipating slaves without first compensating the slaveholder, lawmakers refused to abolish slavery outright.[17]

The legislature did authorize Colbert to instruct slaveholders to enter into labor contracts with their slaves. The following week, on October 11, 1865, Colbert issued a proclamation on the subject of slavery and labor. In it he suggested that slaveholders implement a system of compulsory apprenticeship for minors and wage labor for adults while providing subsistence for the elderly and infirmed. Colbert informed federal officials at Fort Smith of his proclamation, noting that it should meet with their approval as it not only fulfilled the Fort Smith council requirements but also was much like the gradual emancipation laws implemented decades earlier by the northern states. Any declaration of universal emancipation, Colbert added, would have to come from the president or other U.S. authorities.[18]

Black people in the Choctaw and Chickasaw nations waited longer than most before gaining their freedom and a clear picture of their future. Still, they had plans and ideas about what their lives as free people in the nations should look like. While Choctaw and Chickasaw leaders spent the autumn of 1865 debating among themselves and negotiating with U.S. policymakers over the abolition of slavery and the place of freed slaves in Indian Territory, black people pursued their own visions of freedom, which centered on social and economic independence from their former owners. In their efforts to make their freedom meaningful, former slaves helped shape the debates over race, citizenship, property, and sovereignty that engulfed the Indian nations and informed U.S.-Indian relations through the latter half of the nineteenth century.

From the months leading up to the war through the winter of 1865, enslaved people of all ages envisioned and pursued their liberation in ways that demonstrated their acute understanding of the local and national politics shaping the meanings of race, slavery, property, and freedom in both Indian Territory and the United States. As in so many places across the slaveholding south, enslaved people in the Choctaw and Chickasaw nations neither needed nor waited for official declarations of slavery's demise to begin organizing their lives in accordance with their own visions of freedom. During the war, some slaves freed themselves from bondage by running away and establishing refugee camps near U.S. Army posts, while others joined the U.S. military as soldiers and laborers. Many black refugees from the Choctaw and Chickasaw nations settled near Fort Smith, Arkansas, just east of Indian Territory. Some fled the nations on their own, and a few left with the small contingent of Chickasaw and Choctaw loyalists.

Just before the end of November 1865, an enslaved man named Robert Looman and other fugitive slaves camped near Fort Smith drafted a written petition that reached the assistant commissioner of the Freedmen's Bureau for Arkansas. Though Indian Territory did not initially fall under the bureau's jurisdiction, black refugees from the Indian nations successfully gained the attention and assistance of the Arkansas bureau officers and other military personnel at Fort Smith. Looman and the other petitioners complained that slavery remained intact in the Choctaw and Chickasaw nations, where their families were still held as slaves. The head of the bureau's Arkansas division initially entertained the notion of sending soldiers into the nations "to liberate" the slaves. A month later, hoping to stave off an exodus of self-liberated slaves from Indian Territory, army officers at Fort Smith decided they would "furnish an escort to a number of colored men" and accompany them into the Choctaw and Chickasaw nations to visit their families.[19] If this Christmastime reunion cheered the refugees and their enslaved families, surely it also confirmed the efficacy of their enlisting a powerful and sympathetic ally in their efforts to undercut their master's control.

Through the autumn of 1865, enslaved people, men and women, routinely attempted to liberate themselves from bondage in Indian Territory. Like Looman, some of these self-liberated people brought their complaints to U.S. military personnel in Arkansas. Slavery continued unabated, they said. Not only did thousands of black people remain in bondage but those who had freed themselves during the war risked capture and re-enslavement. In September the Choctaw slaveholder Michael Leflore crossed into Arkansas and kidnapped four men who had run away from his plantation during the war. Having returned them to the plantation, Leflore tied them up and beat them before informing them that no slaves in the Choctaw nation had been freed. One of the kidnapped men escaped again from Leflore's custody and brought the matter to the Freedmen's Bureau. Black people protested to bureau officers that those who "claim their freedom" were threatened and abused.[20] They informed the authorities that the Choctaws and Chickasaws equivocated as to the freedpeople's status and that black people were subjected to violent and often fatal assaults.

Writing from Fort Smith, Major General Henry Hunt alerted the commissioner of Indian affairs to the unsettled state of affairs: "I have had representations made to me by negroes from the territory that their lives are threatened, that some murders have been committed upon them, that they are informed by some that they are free, by others that they are still slaves and [they desire] to know which is their actual condition and what they should do." Hunt then elaborated on the subject of these alleged murders, stating that the accounts were unsubstantiated and that there were no witnesses or evidence of any murders. Not wanting to discredit or dismiss the freedpeople's concerns, however, Hunt concluded, "it is evident that an uneasy feeling prevails that may lead to mischief." He assured the commissioner that when he saw the Choctaw and Chickasaw delegates, who were soon expected to pass through Fort Smith on their journey to Washington, D.C., for the final treaty negotiations, he would apprise them of the government's unwillingness to tolerate any violence against former slaves.[21]

Across Indian Territory, as in the southern states, former slaves testified to the violence that punctuated their daily lives in the months and years after emancipation. They brought their complaints about recalcitrant masters, abusive employers, and volatile white neighbors to U.S. military officers, agents of the Freedmen's Bureau, and other federal officials. Freedpeople's accounts of violence reveal the ways in which Indians sought to maintain their grip on black people's bodies, labor, and mobility after slavery's demise. Black people's testimonies about murder and terror were narrated along with accounts of withheld wages, seized property, and stolen goods. As Kidada E. Williams argues, black people reported episodes of violence and exploitation in an effort to "activate their citizenship." Freedpeople's collective accounts of violence revealed not only the horrors they had endured but also their determination to make their freedom meaningful by insisting on their rights to control their bodies, labor, and families.[22]

Not long after the Fort Smith council, military personnel in the region deemed black people's condition "one of great hardship." In October 1865, Choctaws and Chickasaws had reportedly "commenced a most deadly persecution upon" their former slaves, beating and shooting them.[23] In an effort to facilitate a smoother transition from slavery to freedom, the commissioner of Indian affairs appointed Major General John Sanborn as a special commissioner of the Freedmen's Bureau to Indian Territory. Sanborn made his first report in November 1865, before he traveled to the Choctaw and Chickasaw nations. He based his evaluation of those nations on his communication with loyal Chickasaws. According to Sanborn, despite the fact that both the Choctaw and Chickasaw national councils had acknowledged "a change in the relations of the former masters and slaves," the majority of Choctaws continued to treat the freedpeople as slaves. "The public sentiment" in the Choctaw nation, Sanborn concluded, was "radically wrong."

The Chickasaws' conduct was reportedly even more egregious. In that nation, Sanborn explained, the black people were still held as slaves and the Chickasaws "entertain[ed] a bitter prejudice against them all." Sanborn's Chickasaw contact, the loyalist chief Lewis Johnson, claimed that Governor Colbert had stated publicly that Chickasaws "should hold the slaves until [the delegates] could determine at Washington whether or not they could get pay for them, and if they could not then they would strip them naked and drive them either south to Texas, or north to Fort Gibson."[24]

In his second report, filed at the end of January 1866, Sanborn's assessment had changed only slightly. He found that "there is still much that is wrong and cruel" in the way the Chickasaws and Choctaws treated their former slaves.[25] Even as slaveholders conceded that slavery was over and grudgingly hired black men and women as paid laborers and sharecroppers, the reports of antiblack violence did not subside. In one especially gruesome account, Sanborn reported, "The fresh skull of a negro is now hanging on a tree . . . with a bullet hole through it."[26] Rumors circulated that up to six hundred freedpeople had been murdered in the Indian Territory's Red River Valley.[27] Military personnel in the region blamed Indians for isolated incidents and concerted campaigns of antiblack violence. Their pronouncements regarding Indians' brutality against black people frequently played on common images of Indians as "savage," and they also cited Indians' alliance with the Confederacy as evidence of their "backwardness."[28]

In Indian Territory, the postwar violence directed toward black people represented not only efforts to maintain slavery's social and economic hierarchies but also new concerns arising from federal efforts to curb Indian sovereignty. Indian leaders' opposition to federal efforts to curb their governments and land title often found expression in racist rhetoric and violence directed toward black people. Choctaw and Chickasaw leaders, for example, contended that black communities in Indian Territory beckoned black migrants from the states who entered the Indian nations without authorization. Claiming that freedpeople's migration from the states into the Red River area contributed to cattle and horse rustling, Choctaws and Chickasaws formed vigilante groups. Like vigilantes elsewhere, Indian patrols traveled on horseback, monitoring black people's labor, mobility, and acquisition of property. Any black person found with a slaughtered cow or hog, or with a horse, was presumed a thief and risked summary execution by hanging.[29] The freedwoman Polly Colbert remembered both slave patrols and postwar vigilantes, whom she called "Ku Kluxers."[30] Choctaw Loring Folsom, in a letter to Peter Pitchlynn, who was serving as a Choctaw delegate to Washington at the time, recounted an incident in which a freedman and a Choctaw woman were found in bed together. Folsom surmised that news of this scandal would mean that "the Klu Klax will be thick in this nation at a short notice [and] lots of such men in Texas would come in a hurry for that business."[31]

Many of the military personnel and Freedmen's Bureau agents took the reports of brutality against freed slaves seriously, but their dramatic accounts of the violence and lawlessness in Indian Territory can also be read as a sign of their waning regard for Indian territorial sovereignty. After receiving Robert Looman's complaints about his family's continued enslavement, one Freedmen's Bureau officer looked forward to impressing on "the Indians that the U.S. is committed to protecting negroes' rights." He also hoped to find an Indian who had committed an "outrage" against a black person, so that he could punish and make an example of the offender. Sanborn, likewise, maintained that the federal government could not successfully protect former slaves in the Choctaw and Chickasaw nations "until there is a proper military force stationed" at various posts in their territory. General Grant, who was inclined to think that Sanborn had overstated the extent of antiblack violence in the region, nonetheless endorsed the idea of placing Indian Territory under military control "for the purpose of protecting the Freedmen."[32]

Sanborn elaborated on the connections between black people's freedom and U.S. authority in Indian Territory, urging Interior Secretary Harlan to appropriate land in Indian Territory for former slaves. With a vision that vastly exceeded Major General William Sherman's proposed forty-acre land allowance to freedpeople on the Georgia coastal islands, Sanborn suggested extending the 1862 Homestead Act to freedpeople in Indian Territory. Were black people to receive 320-acre allotments, he reasoned, Indians would quickly submit to U.S. authority without "any open resistance, perhaps without a murmur, and the Freedmen will rejoice.[33]

The desire to see Indian Territory opened to U.S. settlers and under the control of U.S. law was not confined to military personnel, however. In the early weeks of 1866, dramatic reports of "murders of whites and blacks" appeared in *The New Era*, a Fort Smith newspaper supportive of Republican interests. The paper claimed, "The slave code is yet in full blast in the Choctaw and Chickasaw country, and the supreme law of the land, proclaiming the freedom of every human being, is ignored and derided." Not surprisingly, such accounts also included a call for a heightened military presence in the region. Some military officers, however, suspected the paper's editor of exaggerating wildly with the aim of undermining the Indian delegates' bargaining position in their final treaty negotiations with the United States.[34]

In the spring and summer of 1866, the Choctaw, Chickasaw, Cherokee, Creek, and Seminole nations agreed to the final terms of their treaties with the United States. The treaties confirmed the abolition of slavery and laid out the terms of black people's citizenship in each nation Yet each treaty was different. The Seminoles' treaty granted "persons of African descent and blood" and their descendants "all the rights of native citizens." The Cherokee treaty conferred "all the rights of native Cherokees" on ex-slaves and their descendants, but also required that refugee freedpeople return to the nation within six months to secure their citizenship. Creek leaders signed a treaty that allowed former slaves up to one year to return to that nation, and it extended "all the rights and privileges of native citizens, including an equal interest in the soil and national funds," to former slaves and their descendants.

The Choctaw/Chickasaw treaty also addressed the matter of freedpeople's citizenship and right of return, but it set forth a convoluted set of provisions that in retrospect could only have resulted in confusion and turmoil. On April 28, 1866, commissioners representing the Choctaw and Chickasaw nations approved a joint treaty of "permanent peace and friendship" with the United States. This treaty, like the Cherokee, Creek, and Seminole treaties, expanded on the laws and ideals governing Reconstruction in the southern states. But the Choctaw/Chickasaw treaty most firmly linked the issue of black people's citizenship to federal policies designed to undercut Indian landholdings and tribal sovereignty.[35]

The treaty language extended Congress' reach past the geopolitical boundaries of the United States. In language that echoed the recently approved Thirteenth Amendment, the second article of the Choctaw/Chickasaw treaty required the nations to abolish slavery and involuntary servitude. Choctaw delegates did not obtain the financial compensation for abolition they had desired.[36] The third article laid out a lengthy and circuitous plan for establishing freed slaves' equal citizenship in the Indian nations. The sixth article granted right-of-way for two railroads through the nations, one running north-south and the other running east-west. Other sections proposed the creation of a unified government of Indian Territory, composed of delegates from each nation or tribe, and called on the Choctaws and Chickasaws to "agree to such legislation as Congress and the President of the United States may deem necessary for the better administration of justice and the protection of the rights of person and property within the Indian Territory."[37]

The treaty sections that dealt with black people's freedom and the Choctaw and Chickasaw nations' land did not address these issues as discrete matters but wove them together, effectively linking freedom and land as fungibles. Under the terms of their 1866 treaty, the Choctaw and Chickasaw nations ceded around 4.6 million acres of land, known as the Leased District, to the United States in exchange for $300,000. The treaty allowed the federal government to retain control of the money until Choctaw and Chickasaw lawmakers enacted the "laws, rules and regulations" needed to grant "all persons of African descent" and their descendants "all the rights, privileges, and immunities, including the right of suffrage, of citizens, except in the annuities, moneys, and public domain claimed by, or belonging to, said nations respectively."

Eligibility for citizenship was limited to those black people who were "resident" in the nations in September 1865, when the Fort Smith council had convened. Unlike the Cherokee and Creek treaties, the Choctaw/Chickasaw treaty did not allow a window of time for black war refugees to return to the nations.

The treaty's fourth article elaborated on the subject of freedpeople's rights and reiterated the call for Indian and black equality under the law. Black people were to be recognized as "competent witnesses in all civil and criminal suits and proceedings in the Choctaw and Chickasaw courts." In keeping with U.S. ideals of free labor, Indian employers were expected to enter "reasonable and equitable contracts" with freedpeople, providing "fair remuneration" for their labor. Lastly, black people, like Indians, were to have unrestricted access to the nations' land commons to build their own homes and farms.[38]

According to the treaty, the United States would pay out the $300,000 only if the Choctaw and Chickasaw nations legally recognized black people's citizenship within two years—by June 1868. Three-quarters of the money would be paid to the Choctaw nation and one-quarter to the Chickasaw nation, the proportions reflecting the relative size of their populations. The final amount disbursed, however, was to be reduced by $100 for every former slave who voluntarily emigrated from the Choctaw and Chickasaw nations within ninety days of the citizenship legislation's enactment. If the nations failed to grant full citizenship to former slaves within the allotted time, the federal government would no longer hold the $300,000 in trust for the Choctaw and Chickasaw nations. Instead, the government would remove from those nations "all such persons of African descent as may be willing to remove" within ninety days and would retain the funds for those people's "use and benefit." Black people who opted to remain in the Choctaw and Chickasaw nations forfeited their claims to a share of the $300,000 and would be subject to the same laws "as other citizens of the United States in the said nations."[39]

The treaty further compounded the issues of black people's citizenship and Indian nations' land claims in sections that proposed the survey and allotment of the Choctaw and Chickasaw lands. In these nations, as in the Cherokee, Creek, and Seminole nations, custom and law had long recognized people's collective ownership of the land. By the mid-nineteenth century, Indians' communal town fields had given way to individual family farms, pastures, and plantations bounded by rough-hewn worm fences. Yet even with the rise of individually controlled farms and plantations, Indian men and women still owned only their improvements, livestock, and slaves, not the land.[40]

The treaty of 1866 signaled Americans' growing impatience with Indian nations' collective land title and shoved them in the direction of private landownership. Warming up for the mandatory allotment policies of the late 1880s, the treaty of 1866 temporarily placed land policy in the hands of Choctaw and Chickasaw legislators, leaving them to accept or reject the survey and allotment of their land in 160-acre parcels. If the Choctaw and Chickasaw governments agreed to this allotment scheme, land distribution would follow a racial grid designed by federal bureaucrats to distinguish between "negroes" and "Indians" and would limit black people to allotments of just forty acres.[41]

After the 1866 treaty was ratified, the Choctaw principal chief Peter Pitchlynn and the Chickasaw governor Winchester Colbert credited their delegates with securing this unequal distribution of land.[42] Determined to protect their financial interests established in earlier treaties, leading Choctaws had hired John H. B. Latrobe, a Baltimore attorney, as their advocate in the 1866 treaty negotiations. Latrobe claimed the credit for authoring the treaty, though he also acknowledged the input of the Indian delegates. There is little in Latrobe's writing that explains the reasoning behind the complicated provisions regarding black people's citizenship. Clara Sue Kidwell explains that the Choctaw and Chickasaw treaty delegates enlisted Latrobe's assistance because they wanted the federal government to resume payment of prewar annuities and other financial settlements, and to prevent the United States from gaining control of the Leased District.[43]

As the work of Stephen Kantrowitz and Joe Genetin-Pilawa in this volume shows, Indian nations and their land claims were often central in the minds of federal policymakers during the post–Civil War period. Their reasons for expanding federal authority and U.S. settlement westward into Indian Territory onto land taken from Indian peoples were as varied as the individuals who voiced them. Still, it is clear, as the 1866 treaties reveal, that the issues of slavery, emancipation, and black people's freedom went hand in hand with a significant assertion of federal power over the people and land in Indian Territory. Federal authorities' insistence that they could define the terms of black people's citizenship in the Indian nations constituted a direct attack on Indian sovereignty. On the surface, the measure appeared necessary to protect former slaves by ensuring their freedom and thus their free labor and property rights. At the same time, the steps to safeguard black people's freedom were not simply a sleight of hand to divert attention away from the concomitant federal assault on tribal governments and land claims. In the same manner that the "civilization programs" of the early nineteenth century had fused ideas about Indians' capacity for assimilation into the American mainstream with theories of racial hierarchy, many post-Civil War policymakers believed that terminating Native sovereignty and allotting Indian lands in severalty would uplift, not oppress, Indians.[44]

The demands that the Choctaw, Chickasaw, Cherokee, Creek, and Seminole nations emancipate their slaves, abolish slavery, and recognize former slaves and their descendants as citizens marked a dramatic intrusion into the nations' domestic affairs that did not go unnoticed or unchallenged by Indian leaders and their constituents. Individual planters and employers lashed out against freedpeople, unwilling to acknowledge black humanity and autonomy. Indian leaders, likewise, presented their opposition to federal authority in racist language that blamed black people for Indians' loss of land and sovereignty. At the same time, however, many Indian leaders recognized that they could not hold off the federal assault on their sovereignty and land claims.[45]

After the treaty was ratified, Principal Chief Pitchlynn and Governor Colbert delivered a joint statement to the Choctaw and Chickasaw nations in which they explicated the treaty's provisions regarding black people's citizenship and the Indian nations' land. In their account of the treaty negotiations, Pitchlynn and Colbert indicated that the issue of land, namely, control over the Leased District, became "complicated with . . . the negro question" because of U.S. insistence on protecting and providing for "our late slaves." "Hence," they stated, "the connection of the two questions." As Pitchlynn and Colbert framed the situation, if the nations' legislatures recognized former slaves as citizens—"adopted" was the term generally used by Choctaws, Chickasaws, and black people—then the nations would gain favor with the United States. This was no small matter.

The Choctaw and Chickasaw nations had been embroiled in financial disputes with the United States that dated back to the the 1830s, when the U. S. government called for the survey and sale of the Choctaws' Mississippi land. Fulfilling their treaty obligations by adopting black people as citizens, Pitchlynn and Colbert explained, might "materially aid" the nations, "as it will undoubtedly produce a strong influence in favor of our yet unsettled claims and demands upon the United States." On the other hand, Pitchlynn and Colbert warned, refusing to comply with the treaty by excluding former slaves from citizenship could prompt the United States to create a colony of former slaves "in our immediate vicinity." They predicted the dire consequences of such a colonization plan, arguing that as the first all-black colony of former slaves in the United States, it would "be sustained and fostered by the government, and the friends of the negro, now so numerous and powerful." The colony would then attract "thousands of other negroes," and this rapidly growing black community would be "anything but desirable neighbors." By contrast, adopting their former slaves as citizens would allow Choctaws and Chickasaws to outnumber and dominate black people within the nations.[46]

Pitchlynn's and Colbert's attentiveness to the subject of black colonization was hardly unwarranted. During the war, President Lincoln, members of his cabinet, and some senators had entertained various schemes for encouraging black emigration and colonization in Florida and the western United States, as well as in Haiti, Liberia, and Central America. Indian leaders' concerns about U.S. plans for colonizing freed slaves in the West had already surfaced in the Fort Smith negotiations. In fact, when the loyal Chickasaws were preparing to attend the council, they drafted a statement in which they opposed slavery but noted that "we will not allow any other coloured persons to live amongst us." During the Fort Smith council, a Seminole delegate similarly stated that his people were willing "to provide for the colored people of our own nation, but do not desire our lands to become colonization grounds for the negroes of other States and Territories." Even the spokesman for the Osage, who had not been slaveholders, decried the possibility that the federal government would settle black people from the United States in Indian Territory.[47]

The Choctaw/Chickasaw 1866 treaty conjoined the federal government's defense of black freedom with its assault on Indian land and governments. Indian leaders responded in kind by framing their opposition to federal authority in antiblack rhetoric and violence. The treaty conflated the issues of freedom and sovereignty, but historians need not follow this trajectory and frame black citizenship simply as a weapon for advancing the U.S. colonial mission. Instead, we can consider the 1866 treaty and the issues it raised as illustrative of Reconstruction's complex, contradictory, and continental scope. Certainly, one goal was to erase the boundaries between Indian nations and the United States by extinguishing tribal governments and territories. The issues of slavery, racial classification, and land distribution central to the Choctaw, Chickasaw, Cherokee, Creek, and Seminole 1866 treaties remained key points in U.S. policies toward these nations through the close of the nineteenth century. To be sure, demanding the abolition of slavery and the recognition of black people as citizens represented a major intrusion into the Indian nations' sovereign affairs. But to cast this moment only as strategic assault, as earlier generations of scholars have done, minimizes emancipation's profound meanings and consequences in black people's lives. In many respects, the story of emancipation and the early years of black people's freedom in Indian Territory falls in line with the broader, more familiar narrative of the transition from slavery to freedom in the southern states. Across the slaveholding South, including Indian Territory, freedpeople's expectations of and responses to freedom varied widely, reflecting the broad array of regional and local social, political, and economic conditions in the southern states. Black people in Indian Territory, like Robert Looman, shared with black people in the states an understanding of emancipation as deliverance from a litany of physical and psychic abuses. Yet former slaves, like Kiziah Love, and their descendants were also keenly aware of the ways the 1866 treaties fused black freedom with Indian subjugation. Indeed, the legacies of the 1866 treaties remain salient today for the descendants of those black people who were enslaved and emancipated in the Indian nations.

NOTES

1. The population statistics for enslaved people in the Indian nations are notoriously troublesome. The demographer Michael Doran used the 1860 U.S. census (census takers in Arkansas crossed into Indian Territory) and enumerated an enslaved population of 7,376 in the Choctaw, Chickasaw, Cherokee, and Creek nations. Censuses compiled later in the nineteenth century enumerate many more black people in the nations, raising the possibility that the 1860 census takers significantly undercounted the black population or that later censuses wildly overstated the number of black people in the nations. Michael F. Doran, "Population Statistics of Nineteenth Century Indian Territory," Chronicles of Oklahoma 53 (Winter 1975–76): 501.

2. T. Lindsay Baker and Julie P. Baker, eds., The WPA Oklahoma Slave Narratives (Norman: University of Oklahoma Press, 1996), 6–9.

3. Celia Naylor, African Cherokees in Indian Territory: From Chattel to Citizens (Chapel Hill: University of North Carolina Press, 2008), 151. In the Creek nation, the loyalist faction entered a treaty with the United States that abolished slavery and established black people's equal standing under Creek law. See Claudio Saunt, Black, White and Indian: Race and the Unmaking of an American Family (New York: Oxford University Press, 2005), 104. For an extended discussion of slavery and emancipation in the Seminole nation, see Kevin Mulroy, The Seminole Freedmen: A History (Norman: University of Oklahoma Press, 2007), especially chaps. 3, 6 and 7.

4. Eric Foner, *Reconstruction: America's Unfinished Revolution, 1863–1877* (New York: Harper and Row, 1988). Michael Vorenberg, *Final Freedom: The Civil War, the Abolition of Slavery, and the Thirteenth Amendment* (New York: Cambridge University Press, 2001).

5. Charles Kappler, comp., *Indian Affairs: Laws and Treaties*, vol. 2 (Washington, D.C.: Government Printing Office, 1904).

6. Joseph Genetin-Pilawa, *Crooked Paths to Allotment: The Fight over Federal Indian Policy after the Civil War* (Chapel Hill: University of North Carolina Press, 2014). William H. Armstrong, *Warrior in Two Camps: Ely S. Parker, Union General and Seneca Chief* (Syracuse, N.Y.: Syracuse University Press, 1978), 114–17. In 1871, in his capacity as commissioner of Indian affairs, Parker advocated putting an end to U.S. treaty making with Indian peoples, calling on the government to "cease the cruel farce of thus dealing with its helpless and ignorant wards." Quoted in Clara Sue Kidwell, *The Choctaws in Oklahoma: From Tribe to Nation, 1855–1970* (Norman: University of Oklahoma Press, 2009), 92.

7. Heather Cox Richardson, *West from Appomattox: The Reconstruction of America after the Civil War* (New Haven: Yale University Press, 2007).

8. James Harlan to D. H. Cooley et al., Aug. 16, 1865, reprinted in Annie Heloise Abel, *The American Indian and the End of the Confederacy, 1863–1866* (Lincoln: University of Nebraska Press, 1993), 219–26. Reprinted from the original edition titled *The American Indian under Reconstruction* and published in 1925 by the Arthur H. Clark Company, Cleveland, Ohio.

9. *Report of the Secretary of the Interior*, 39th Cong., 1st sess., 1865, House Ex. Doc. 1, pt. 2, 497–98, 500–502. Cyrus Bussey to Peter Pitchlynn, Aug. 2, 1865, Box 4, folder 33; Peter Pitchlynn to Winchester Colbert, Aug. 9, 1865, Box 4, folder 36; Winchester Colbert to Peter Pitchlynn, Aug. 24, 1865, Box 4, folder 38, Peter Perkins Pitchlynn Papers, Western History Collection, University of Oklahoma. For longer descriptions of the Fort Smith council, see Abel, *The American Indian and the End of the Confederacy*, chap. 6; Kidwell, *The Choctaws in Oklahoma*, chap. 6.

10. *Report of the Secretary of the Interior*, 1865, 502.

11. Eric Foner, *Reconstruction*, 66–68. Vorenberg, *Final Freedom*, chap. 2. Robert R. Dykstra and Harlan Hahn, "Northern Voters and Negro Suffrage: The Case of Iowa, 1868," *Public Opinion Quarterly* 32 (Summer 1968): 208–9.

12. *Report of the Secretary of the Interior*, 1865, 504, 518, 529. For a discussion of Indians' thinking about the meaning of freedom in their respective nations, see Claudio Saunt, "The Paradox of Freedom: Tribal Sovereignty and Emancipation during the Reconstruction of Indian Territory," *Journal of Southern History* 60 (January 2004): 63–94. Kidwell, *The Choctaws in Oklahoma*, chap. 6.

13. Agreement with the Cherokee and Other Tribes in the Indian Territory, 1865, in Kappler, *Indian Affairs: Laws and Treaties*, 2:1050–52. *Report of the Secretary of the Interior*, 1865, 440, has population estimates of three thousand slaves in the Choctaw nation and two thousand in the Chickasaw nation.

14. Peter Pitchlynn to Denis Cooley, Sept. 21, 1865, reprinted in Abel, *The American Indian and the End of the Confederacy*, 285.

15. "An act temporarily providing for such persons as have been to the present time

considered as slaves," Records of the Choctaw General Council, microfilm roll CTN-9, Oklahoma Historical Society, Oklahoma City, Oklahoma. Angie Debo, *The Rise and Fall of the Choctaw Republic* (Norman: University of Oklahoma Press, 1961), 99–101.

16. Colbert's address to the legislature is reprinted in Abel, *The American Indian and the End of the Confederacy*, 286–87.

17. Ibid., 289. Daniel F. Littlefield Jr., *The Chickasaw Freedmen: A People without a Country* (Westport, Conn.: Greenwood Press, 1980), 23–25.

18. Colbert's proclamation is reprinted in Abel, *The American Indian and the End of the Confederacy*, 288–89. Governor Winchester Colbert to Major General Henry J. Hunt, Oct. 11, 1865, Document 110, *Report of the Commissioner of Indian Affairs*, 1869 (Washington, D.C.: Government Printing Office, 1869), 357–58.

19. General John W. Sprague to Major General Reynolds, Nov. 20, 1865; General John W. Sprague to O. O. Howard, December 18, 1865; *Records of the Arkansas Bureau of Refugees, Freedmen and Abandoned Lands* (National Archives Microfilm Publication 979, roll 1); Francis Springer to General Sprague, December 4, 1865, *Registers and Letters Received by the Commissioner of the Bureau of Refugees, Freedmen, and Abandoned Lands, 1865–1872* (National Archives Microfilm Publication 752, roll 22).

20. J. W. Ballard, Nov. 30, 1865; Francis Springer to General Sprague, Nov. 28, 1865, *Registers and Letters Received by the Commissioner of the Bureau of Refugees, Freedmen, and Abandoned Lands, 1865–1872* (National Archives Microfilm Publication M752, roll 22).

21. Brevet Major General Henry Hunt to the Honorable D. H. Cooley, Commissioner of Indian Affairs, Nov. 28, 1865, *Records of the Office of Indian Affairs, Letters Received, Southern Superintendency, 1851–1871* (National Archives Microfilm Publication 234, roll 836).

22. Kidada E. Williams, *They Left Great Marks on Me: African American Testimonies of Racial Violence* (New York: New York University Press, 2012), 25. Dylan Penningroth makes a similar point in his analysis of former slaves' efforts to file claims with federal officials for property that was lost or destroyed during the war. Dylan C. Penningroth, *The Claims of Kinfolk: African American Property and Community in the Nineteenth-Century South* (Chapel Hill: University of North Carolina Press, 2003).

23. Assistant Commissioner Leard to O. O. Howard, Oct. 24, 1865, *Registers and Letters Received by the Commissioner of the Bureau of Refugees, Freedmen, and Abandoned Lands, 1865–1872* (National Archives Microfilm Publication M752, roll 21).

24. *Report of the Commissioner of Indian Affairs*, 1866 (Washington, D.C.: Government Printing Office, 1866), 283–84; Bvt. Maj. Genl. John Sanborn to James Harlan, Jan. 5, 1866, *Records of the Office of Indian Affairs, Letters Received, Southern Superintendency, 1851–1871* (National Archives Microfilm Publication M234, roll 837).

25. *Report of the Commissioner of Indian Affairs*, 1866, 286. Littlefield, *The Chickasaw Freedmen*, 30–38; Debo, *The Rise and Fall of the Choctaw Republic*, 100; Abel, *The American Indian and the End of the Confederacy*, 296–98.

26. General Sanborn's report, Jan. 8, 1866, *Records of the Office of Indian Affairs, Letters Received, Southern Superintendency, 1851–1871* (National Archives Microfilm Publication M234, roll 837).

27. Capt. W. Wood, to Lt. Col. J. Craig, Jan. 29, 1866; John Sanborn to Maj. Genl.

Hunt, Jan. 9, 1866; John Levering to Maj. Genl. Reynolds, Feb. 7, 1866, *Records of the Office of Indian Affairs, Letters Received, Southern Superintendency, 1851–1871* (National Archives Microfilm Publication M234, roll 837).

28. Col. William A. Phillips to Secretary of the Interior, Jan. 17, 1865, Document 91–A, *Report of the Commissioner of Indian Affairs*, 1865 (Washington, D.C.: Government Printing Office, 1865). Elijah Sells to D. H. Cooley, Aug. 5, 1865, in House Exec. Doc. 1, 39th Cong., 1st sess., 449.

29. In his multivolume history of Oklahoma, Joseph Thoburn wrote that he interviewed Choctaw and Chickasaw men who told him of their participation in the Vigilante Committee. Annie Abel quotes part of a letter from an officer at Fort Gibson who wrote about receiving freedmen's accounts of murder and assault and concluded that "the blacks are suffering a reign of terror" at the hands of Confederate Choctaws and Chickasaws. Joseph B. Thoburn and Muriel H. Wright, *Oklahoma: A History of the State and Its People* (New York: Lewis Publishing, 1928), 375–76. Debo, *The Rise and Fall of the Choctaw Republic*, 99–100. Abel, *The American Indian and the End of the Confederacy* 273n518.

30. Baker and Baker, *The WPA Oklahoma Slave Narratives*, 89. Colbert also said that she suspected her master, Mr. Holmes, "was one of de leaders" of this Klan activity.

31. Loring Folsom to Peter Pitchlynn, Aug. 29, 1870, Box 4, folder 48, Pitchlynn Papers.

32. Francis Springer to General Sprague, Dec. 4, 1864, *Registers and Letters Received by the Commissioner of the Bureau of Refugees, Freedmen, and Abandoned Lands, 1865–1872* (National Archives Microfilm Publication M752, roll 22); Ulysses S. Grant, endorsement on letter from James Harlan to Edwin M. Stanton, April 18, 1866, in *The Papers of Ulysses S. Grant*, ed. John Y. Simon, vol. 16, 1866 (Carbondale: Southern Illinois University Press, 1988), 496.

33. Major General John Sanborn to James Harlan, Jan. 5, 1866, *Records of the Office of Indian Affairs, Letters Received, Southern Superintendency, 1851–1871* (National Archives Microfilm Publication M234, roll 837).

34. "Letter from the Indian Nations and Texas," *The New Era*, January 31, 1866; Captain W. Wood to Lt. Col. J. Craig, Jan. 29, 1866; John Levering to Maj. Genl. Reynolds, Feb. 7, 1866, *Records of the Office of Indian Affairs, Letters Received, Southern Superintendency, 1851–1871* (National Archives Microfilm Publication M234, roll 837).

35. Kappler, *Indian Affairs: Laws and Treaties*. Circe Sturm, *Blood Politics: Race, Culture, and Identity in the Cherokee Nation of Oklahoma* (Berkeley: University of California Press, 2002), 74–75; 171–74; Tiya Miles, *Ties That Bind: The Story of an Afro-Cherokee Family in Slavery and Freedom* (Berkeley: University of California Press, 2005); Claudio Saunt, *Black, White, and Indian*; David A. Chang, *The Color of the Land: Race, Nation, and the Politics of Landownership in Oklahoma, 1832–1929* (Chapel Hill: University of North Carolina Press, 2010).

36. After the Fort Smith Council, on October 9, 1865, the delegates reported to the Choctaw General Council. They advised that the council instruct the men selected to go to Washington for the final treaty negotiations, "to insist upon the payment for the negroes to be emancipation in this nation. Though if the U.S. will not remunerate

it shall not be an obsticle [*sic*] to the completion of a Treaty." They also urged that the treaty delegates "request that no negro troops be stationed at any post in the Choctaw or Chickasaw nations." Statement to the General Council of the Choctaw Nation, Oct. 9, 1865, Records of the Choctaw General Council, microfilm roll CTN-9, Oklahoma Historical Society.

37. Kappler, *Indian Affairs: Laws and Treaties*. vol. 2, 918–31

38. Treaty with the Choctaw and Chickasaw, 1866, in ibid., 2:918–20. On federal efforts to promote free labor ideology and labor contracts during Reconstruction see, Amy Dru Stanley, *From Bondage to Contract: Wage Labor, Marriage, and the Market in the Age of Slave Emancipation* (New York: Cambridge University Press, 1998). For a history of the commons and land use in Indian Territory, see Chang, *The Color of the Land*; Alexandra Harmon, *Rich Indians: Native People and the Problem of Wealth in American History* (Chapel Hill: University of North Carolina Press, 2010), chap. 4.

39. Treaty with the Choctaw and Chickasaw, 1866, in Kappler, *Indian Affairs: Laws and Treaties*, vol. 2, 918–31. The Leased District had been the subject of negotiations between the Choctaws, Chickasaws, and the United States since the 1850s. See Kidwell, *The Choctaws in Oklahoma*, chap. 2.

40. Israel Folsom to Peter Pitchlynn, Feb. 24, 1870, Box 4, folder 47, Pitchlynn Papers.

41. Some thirty years after the Civil War ended, congressional strivings to put a territorial government in place in Indian Territory were realized with the passage of the General Allotment Act of 1887, more commonly known as the Dawes Act. It authorized the president to compel reservation Indians to relinquish their common land title and accept land allotments in severalty. During the following fifteen years, the Dawes Commission worked to allot Indian land and recreate Indian Territory as an organized territory of the United States. Although the Cherokee, Choctaw, Chickasaw, Creek, and Seminole nations were initially exempt from the Dawes Act, they remained under direct pressure to abandon tribal land title in exchange for individual allotments.

The question of land allotment in Indian Territory was put to rest finally on June 29, 1898, when Congress passed an *Act for the Protection of the People of the Indian Territory, and Other Purposes*. Dubbed the Curtis Act, this law transferred questions of citizenship, allotment, and property rights to the federal courts and effected the termination of the Indian nations' land title. By 1903, the Dawes Commission, having already compiled the rolls of Choctaw and Chickasaw citizens and freedpeople, commenced with issuing land patents. In the late nineteenth century, 23,405 people of African descent stood to gain ownership of land under federal law. This is the number of people included on the final tribal rolls for receiving land allotments, but it does not include the blacks rejected from the final rolls, making them ineligible for allotments. Angie Debo, *And Still the Waters Run* (Princeton: Princeton University Press, 1940), 47.

42. Address of Peter P. Pitchlynn and Winchester Colbert, July 12, 1865, Box 5, folder 8, Pitchlynn Papers.

43. John H. B. Latrobe, "An Address to the Choctaw and Chickasaw Nations, in

Regard to Matters Connected with the Treaty of 1866," Ayer Collection, Newberry Library, Chicago; John Edward Semmes, *John H. B. Latrobe and His Times, 1803-1891* (Baltimore: Norman, Remington, 1917): 544–45; Kidwell, *Choctaws in Oklahoma*, 79–80.

44. Harmon, *Rich Indians*, 136, 157.

45. Barbara Krauthamer, *Black Slaves, Indian Masters: Slavery, Emancipation, and Citizenship in the Native American South* (Chapel Hill: University of North Carolina Press, 2013); Chang, *The Color of the Land*; Saunt, "The Paradox of Freedom."

46. Address of Peter P. Pitchlynn and Winchester Colbert, July 12, 1865, Box 5, folder 8, Pitchlynn Papers.

47. Statement of Loyal Chickasaws, Sept. 17, 1865, *Records of the Office of Indian Affairs, Letters Received, Southern Superintendency, 1851–1871* (National Archives Microfilm Publication M234, roll 837); *Report of the Secretary of the Interior, 1865*, 508–9; Eric Foner, *The Fiery Trial: Abraham Lincoln and American Slavery* (New York: W. W. Norton, 2010), 199–259; Abel, *The American Indian and the End of the Confederacy*, 270, and see 514.

Black Women's Campaigns for Sexual Justice and Citizenship
Crystal N. Feimster

In a public lecture given in 1830, Maria W. Stewart, a pioneer black abolitionist and women's rights advocate, invoked black women's demands for sexual justice by asking, "What if I am a woman?"[1] Her query asserted the essential humanity of black womanhood and challenged long-held notions that denied women the political and civil rights of consenting citizenship. It was a question with profound implications if answered in the affirmative. What would it mean to acknowledge women, especially black women, as full citizens with legal capacity and political consent? If black women were granted not just the rights of life, liberty, and happiness, but also self-sovereignty, then they would also be entitled to the legal protection of those rights. Indeed, by asking the question, Stewart joined antebellum Americans in debates about the meanings of freedom and citizenship and called for the inclusion of women as fully human and autonomous beings, the "owners" of their own bodies with the ability to withhold consent. Placing black women at the center of discussions about slavery and women's rights, Stewart, like many black women, insisted on sexual justice as a natural right.

This essay traces black women's resistance to sexual violence during the transition from slavery to freedom and how their campaigns against rape shaped national debates about the emerging meanings of freedom and black citizenship. Highlighting slave women's sexual vulnerability and efforts to defend themselves, I argue that black women and their allies influenced the Republican Party's vision of racial equality from the 1850s until the end of Reconstruction. Taken together, black women's radical campaigns for sexual justice and Republican ideas about legal equality make visible the emergence of a new sexual citizenship that culminated during the Civil War, when newly freed black women gained the right to withhold consent and to legally testify as victims of sexual assault in military courts.[2] During Reconstruction, as Republican governments lost political power in the South and night riders and Klansmen raped and sexually brutalized black women for political gain, black women's campaigns for sexual justice took on new urgency.[3] Drawing on their wartime experience and the Fourteenth Amendment's guarantee of equal protection under the law, black women renewed their efforts to redefine citizenship to include all women and their right to determine when and with whom they had sexual relations.[4] The editors argue that the postwar era itself "tested the reach and authority of the national government." One source of that testing was black women, who called on the army and the Freedmen's Bureau to protect them from sexual violence. Emboldened by their wartime experiences and eager to test the limits of their newly won constitutional rights, black women articulated a radical vision of sexual citizenship during Reconstruction and the postwar years.

MASTER/SLAVE RAPE

Maria Stewart called for women's rights and joined the abolitionist fray in 1831 with the publication of "Religion and the Pure Principles of Morality, the Sure Foundation on Which We Must Build" in William Lloyd Garrison's antislavery newspaper, *The Liberator*.[5] Acknowledging black women's sexual vulnerability, Stewart opened the essay with a prayer, "O that my head were waters, and mine eyes a fountain of tears, that I might weep day and night [Jeremiah 9:1], for the transgressions of the daughters of my people."[6] Stewart knew that in most states black women, free and enslaved, were excluded from rape laws.[7] Regardless of status or region, black women were "usually de facto (if not de jure) prevented from even bringing criminal charges against almost any defendant."[8] In fact, no southern states made it legally possible for slave women to file rape charges against a white man before 1861. Even in the rare cases that involved a sex crime against a slave woman, it was her master who filed for damages. For example, in 1855 a white slave owner brought charges against James Keyton, a white man he claimed had raped one of his female slaves. Charged with committing a crime against property, Keyton was indicted but eventually acquitted. In 1859, Mississippi was one of the first states to pass legislation that made rape or attempted rape of a female slave under twelve illegal if her assailant was black. Georgia in 1861 included slave women in its legal definition of rape, but punishments were not nearly as harsh as those meted out to men who raped white women.[9] Thus existing outside the legal definition of rape and in the cultural imagination as a prostitute at best and a sexual beast incapable of morality and virtue at worst, a slave woman had few options.

In the decades before the Civil War, Stewart was not alone in raising the question of black women's rights. These were years in which black women (free and enslaved) and their allies waged war against slavery and began to imagine a new kind of American citizenship—one that included women and recognized a woman's right to withhold consent and gain legal protection. In claiming black female humanity, they managed to draw national attention to master/slave rape and articulated a new discourse of sexual citizenship. Their campaigns for sexual justice took many forms, from written protest to violent resistance.[10] They challenged the panoply of laws, traditions, and ideas that reinforced white men's sexual power and placed black women outside the legal and moral definitions of rape.

In the same year that Stewart published her antislavery pamphlet calling for the protection of black womanhood, Mary Prince introduced the antebellum slave narrative script on master/slave rape with the publication of *The History of Mary Prince, A West Indian Slave*. The first female slave narrative, Prince's autobiography exposed master/slave sexual violence and made visible black women's resistance. Born a slave in Brackish Pond, Bermuda, in 1788, Prince experienced all the horrors of slavery, from the breakup of her family to brutal beatings and sexual assaults. She recounted in graphic detail the physical and psychological violence that slaves suffered at the hands of their masters and mistresses. It was under Captain Ingham's ownership that Prince was first whipped. She recalled how her new mistress taught her not only "to do all sorts of household work" but also "to know the exact difference between the smart of the rope, the cart-whip, and the cow-skin" when applied to her naked body.[11] Prince described how two of her masters, Captain Ingham and Mr. D, beat her unmercifully. She remembered, "Mr. D—has often stripped me naked, hung me up by the wrists, and beat me with the cow-skin, with his own hand, till my body was raw with gashes."[12] The sexualized beatings that Prince withstood at the hands of both mistress and master functioned as brutal reminders that her body was not her own.

Master/slave rape proved a difficult subject for Prince to write about openly. Part of the challenge had to do with putting into words unspeakable violence while also adhering to Victorian ideals of womanhood that censored what a "respectable" woman could say publicly about rape.[13] Limiting her discussion of explicit sexual violence to a single paragraph, Prince described Mr. D as an "indecent master" who forced her to bathe him. "This," she confessed, "was worse to me than all the licks." Unable to state overtly the sexual violence implicit in Mr. D's demands, Prince instead spoke of her "shame" and her efforts to resist. She explained that when she ignored Mr. D's calls, he did not hesitate to beat her into submission. On one occasion, she recalled, "He struck me so severely for this, that at last I defended myself, for I thought it was high time to do so. I then told him I would not live longer with him, for he was a very indecent man—very spiteful, and too indecent; with no shame for his servants, no shame for his own flesh." After seeking refuge in a neighboring house, she returned the next morning, "not knowing what else to do."[14] By highlighting her resistance without transgressing Victorian norms of delicacy and propriety, Prince challenged the notion that slave women lacked virtue and welcomed white men's sexual advances.

By the 1850s master/slave rape was a standard part of the American abolitionist bill of indictment against slavery, and there were few slave narratives that did not mention the sexual exploitation of female slaves.[15] Sojourner Truth, most remembered for her alleged "Ar'n't I a Woman?" speech, also exposed the sexual violence that slave women suffered at the hands of their masters. Born a slave in New York in 1797, Truth joined the abolitionist movement in the 1840s after gaining her freedom and published The Narrative of Sojourner Truth in 1850. Truth, like so many black women, only spoke "obliquely" and in "scattered pages about sexual abuse."[16] Interestingly, Truth revealed sexual exploitation by her mistress. Nonetheless, it was a tough balancing act for black women who wanted to expose the "evils of slavery" while also maintaining a sense of privacy and respectable dignity.

In her narrative, Incidents in the Life of a Slave Girl, the best-known slave account on the impact of sexual violence on black women, Harriet Jacobs left little doubt about slave women's sexual vulnerability and the challenges of recounting rape for a public audience.[17] Like Prince, she highlighted her master's sexual power over her in ways that revealed her resistance. Jacobs recalled, "He told me that I was made for his use and made to obey his command in every thing; that I was nothing but a slave, whose will must and should surrender to his."[18] She explained, "There is no shadow of law to protect [slave women] from insult, from violence, or even from death; all these are inflicted by fiends who bear the shape of men."[19] Jacobs, who published her narrative using the pseudonym Linda Brent, claimed she resisted sexual assault by willingly giving herself to another white man. Both the pseudonym and her insistence that her consensual sexual relationship was a strategy of resisting her master reflect the moral constraints of the antebellum slave narrative. Moreover, such efforts revealed Jacobs's Herculean efforts to expose master/slave rape while maintaining an image of respectable womanhood.[20]

White female abolitionists had less difficulty writing and speaking publicly about master/slave rape than black women, but they too had to keep their criticisms within the bounds of Victorian respectability. Writing antislavery fiction proved the best platform for white women to express their views on slavery and rape. The abolitionist and women's rights activist Lydia Maria Child published a host of antislavery short stories—including "Slavery's Pleasant Home. A Fateful Sketch," and "The Quadroons"—that grappled with the problem of master/slave rape. The white abolitionist Harriet Beecher Stowe was the most successful fiction writer to bring national attention to the sexual exploitation of slave women. With the 1852 publication of her novel *Uncle Tom's Cabin*, Stowe became the most read abolitionist in the country. In *A Key to Uncle Tom's Cabin*, Stowe credits her black cook, Eliza Buck, a former slave, with giving her insight into the master/slave rape narrative. Stowe explained that Eliza's "last master" was the father of all her children and revealed how Victorian ideals of respectability informed Eliza's narrative. "On this point she always maintained a delicacy and reserve that seemed to me remarkable," recounted Stowe. "She always called him her husband, and it was not till after she had lived with me some years that I discovered the real nature of the connection."[21] Like Jacobs, Eliza had recounted her sexual vulnerability in the terms that would not undermine her respectability.

The rape of slave women and their resistance figured prominently not only in slave narratives and abolitionists' literary imaginings but also in some of the most momentous legal and political battles over slavery in the decade leading up to the Civil War. The 1855 case of Celia, an eighteen-year-old slave woman in Missouri who was tried and executed for killing her master after years of rape, raised the question of a slave woman's right to defend herself against sexual violence. Despite popular belief that black women were sexually lascivious and could not be raped, Celia insisted on her right to withhold consent and defend herself.[22] Her actions enabled a variety of responses by those who took up her case. Following Celia's lead, her lawyers argued that she had a right to use force to resist her master's sexual assault. Self-defense was the sole legal argument extended by southern courts to slaves accused of capital crimes, and Celia's lawyers did not hesitate to mobilize it on her behalf. Celia, however, could not speak on her own behalf, because Missouri law prevented blacks from testifying against white people. Nonetheless, Celia's defense argued that Missouri rape laws, which made it a crime "to take any woman unlawfully against her will and by force, menace or duress, compel her to be defiled," applied to Celia, a slave woman. If the court ruled that the law's declaration of "any woman" not only included enslaved women but also gave Celia the right to resist rape by her master with deadly force, then more was at stake than Celia's innocence. In fact, Celia's case proved a challenge to both master/slave rape and the institution of slavery. To recognize Celia as a rape victim would require acknowledging her as a person deserving of humane treatment and legal protection; indeed, such recognition would call into question the entire legal system of slavery. While Celia's lawyers failed to save her life or to overturn legal precedent that defined slave women outside the criminal definition of rape, Celia had succeeded in making visible black women's campaigns for human dignity and sexual justice.

More than grist for the antislavery mill, Celia's case was a powerful signifier of pending war. The battle lines were drawn. And the struggle would be waged not only between North and South, abolitionists and slaveholders, Republicans and Democrats, but also between slaves and masters. The war would be fought in humble slave cabins, like Celia's, and in courtrooms across America. Indeed, only a month after Celia's execution, Margaret Garner would join her in the ranks of legendary slave women who violently fought to free themselves from the sexual bondages of slavery. Garner's case, one of the most tragic challenges to the 1850 Fugitive Slave Law, captured the traumatic consequence of master/slave rape.[23]

In an effort to break the cycle of sexual violence that had forced her to give birth to three of her master's children, Garner attempted to escape with her slave husband and children from Kentucky to the free state of Ohio. Pursued by federal marshals and her master, Margaret and the seven members of her family sought refuge in the cabin of her uncle Joseph Kite, a free man of color in Cincinnati. Shortly after their arrival, the fugitives found themselves surrounded by slave catchers. In the ensuing battle, Margaret decided she would rather die than return to slavery. Thus in a desperate attempt to protect her children, especially her little girls, from having to suffer the brutalities of slavery, she killed her two-year-old daughter Mary before being subdued by federal marshals.

A rallying point for abolitionists, Margaret's daring escape over the frozen Ohio River and the tragic murder of her daughter provoked the longest and most visible fugitive slave trial of the pre–Civil War decade.[24] While abolitionists had long defended the right of slaves to escape and urged armed resistance to slave catchers and federal marshals, Garner's actions suggested another form of resistance: death. Abolitionists magnified the political significance of the case by aligning Margaret's actions with the heroes of the American Revolution, who, like her, had linked resistance with freedom. For example, on the last day of Garner's trial, the white abolitionist and women's rights advocate Lucy Stone interrupted the proceedings and spoke at length. Pointing to master/slave rape and comparing Margaret's escape and murder of her daughter to Patrick Henry and the American soldiers at Bunker Hill, Stone declared: "The faded faces of the negro children tell too plainly to what degradation female slaves must submit. Rather than give her little daughter to that life, she killed it. If in her deep maternal love she felt the impulse to send her child back to God, to save it from coming woe, who shall say she had no right to do so? That desire had its root in the deepest and holiest feelings of our nature—implanted alike in black and white by our common Father."[25] Stone framed the case as a powerful challenge to proslavery arguments that portrayed slaves as content with their status. She argued that it was Margaret's wish to free herself and her daughter from sexual violence that lay at the heart of the case. Integrating Margaret's claims for sexual justice into her antislavery arguments, she held that Margaret was justified in her actions and deserving of all the rights of freedom and citizenship. According to Stone, Margaret's choice of death over slavery not only revealed her wish for freedom but also reinforced the idea that a woman of honor and virtue preferred death to sexual violation.

The 1857 *Dred Scott* decision fueled political debates about a range of issues including the sexual exploitation of slave women. Indeed, the case reveals that by the late 1850s Republicans had begun to integrate black women's campaigns for sexual justice into their political ideas about equality and citizenship. Abraham Lincoln best articulated the Republican

Party's response to the Court's decision. He reminded his audience that not just Dred Scott's freedom was at stake in the case, but also the freedom of Scott's wife, Harriet Robinson, and their two young daughters, Eliza and Lizzie. Making clear his opinion, Lincoln explained, "We desired the courts to have held that they were citizens . . . that they were in fact and in law really free. Could we have had our way, the chances of these black girls, ever mixing their blood with that of white people, would have been diminished at least to the extent that it could not have been without their consent."[26] He insisted that Democrats and their pro-slavery allies "delighted" in the Court's decision that the girls were slaves and "not human enough to have a hearing, even if they were free." Moreover, he concluded, the ruling meant the girls would be "left subject to the forced concubinage of their masters, and liable to become the mothers of mulattoes in spite of themselves."[27] Drawing attention to master/slave rape, Lincoln flipped the sexual script to argue for Eliza's and Lizzie's rights as citizens to withhold consent and to testify.

Lincoln's counterargument reflected Republican ideas that recognized the essential humanity of black people and the party's commitment to certain basic rights for free blacks (and in this case fugitive slaves).[28] Republicans were not immune to racial prejudices, but as Lincoln made clear, the party believed free blacks were entitled to the natural rights of mankind articulated in the Declaration of Independence. Moreover, some Republicans, including Lincoln, felt basic civil rights, such as the protections of individual liberty, the security of person and property, and the right to testify, ought to be enjoyed by black women. Equal protection under the law, however, did not include political or social rights as far as Lincoln was concerned, or the majority of the Republican Party, for that matter, though it did include a vision of sexual justice articulated by black women.

CIVIL WAR AND MILITARY LAW

The arrival of Union troops in the south intensified master/slave violence and exposed black women to a new kind of sexual violence at the hands of soldiers. At the same time that the war made black women even more vulnerable to rape, the passage of new military laws under Lincoln's Lieber Code of 1863 brought all southern black women under the umbrella of legal protection. Defining rape as a war crime without regard to race, the code reflected the Republican Party's commitment to legal equality.[29]

Moreover, black women's use of the new military law made visible their continued resistance to sexual violence and claims for sexual justice.

The code established strict laws regarding the crime of rape. Three articles under Section II declared that soldiers would "acknowledge and protect, in hostile countries occupied by them, religion and morality; strictly private property; the persons of the inhabitants, especially those of women" (Article 37); that "all robbery, all pillage or sacking, even after taking a place by main force, all rape, wounding, maiming, or killing of such inhabitants, are prohibited under the penalty of death" (Article 44); and that "crimes punishable by all penal codes, such as . . . rape, if committed by an American soldier in a hostile country against its inhabitants, are not only punishable as at home, but in all cases in which death is not inflicted the severer punishment shall be preferred" (Article 47).[30] Together, the articles conceived and defined rape in women-specific terms as a crime against property, as a crime of troop discipline, and as a crime against family honor. Most significantly, the articles defined rape as a war crime without regard to race or former status and set the stage for black women's wartime citizenship claims. Such explicit prohibition against rape without regard to race reflected Republican ideals about the natural rights of black citizenship and equal protection under the law.

Because Republican ideas about consent and legal equality included free blacks, federal officials certainly did not condone the rape of slave women. Yet sexual violence was common to the wartime experience of all southern women, black and white.[31] Whether they lived on large plantations or small farms, in towns, cities, or in contraband camps, white and black women throughout the American South experienced the sexual trauma of war. Black women, however, were in even more danger not only because soldiers raped indiscriminately but also because northern white men were not immune to perceptions of black women as sexually lascivious.[32] Undergirding the exploitation of black women by white U.S. soldiers was a basic misconception about the degrading influence of slavery.[33] Testifying before the American Freedmen's Inquiry Commission in 1863, Major General Benjamin Butler declared, "The women are all brought up to think that no honor can come to them equal to that of connection with a white man." As an afterthought, Butler added that he was "sorry to say that white men are not all above taking advantage of this feeling."[34] Butler was not alone in his thinking. Captain John H. Grabill confided to his wife that some of the officers in his regiment believed that "no colored woman will deny gratification to a white man especially if he is an officer."[35] While such sexual attitudes enabled the officers to rationalize their exploitation of black women, their ideas and actions did not go unchallenged by black women and their Republican allies.

A recent historical study found that U.S. military courts prosecuted at least 450 cases involving sexual crimes during the war, many of them brought by black women.[36] A close examination of cases involving the rape of black women reveals that, while they may have been particularly vulnerable to wartime rape, they did not hesitate to make use of the Lieber Code. For example, in July 1863, Harriet Elizabeth McKinley, "a mulatto woman," appeared in Murfreesboro, Tennessee, before a Military Commission to testify against Private Perry Pierson of the 33rd Indiana Volunteer Infantry, who had allegedly raped her.[37] After McKinley was sworn in, her white assailant, Pierson, objected "to the reception of [her] testimony on the grounds that 'she was not a qualified witness, being a colored woman.'" The commission cleared the room for deliberation, and after "mature consideration" the objection was dismissed and McKinley was allowed to testify against the white man she claimed had brutally raped her.

McKinley's testimony shows not only how black women took advantage of military courts, but also their efforts to resist sexual assault. McKinley recounted how Pierson and two other men had come up on mules late in the afternoon: "He asked me whether I was a slave and I told him I was and he asked me to get up behind him on the mule, and I would be a slave no longer."[38] When McKinley told the soldier she was not interested in his offer, he tried to pull her up onto the mule. Before an all-white and all-male commission as well as her assailant, McKinley recounted in vivid detail her efforts to fend off the sexual assault: "He dragged me past a post, and I caught hold of it, and he told me if I did not let loose, he would slap the hell out of me. Then he dragged me around the smokehouse, and tried to make me lay down, and I wouldn't. He then caught hold of my shoulders, flung his knee in my back and threw me to the ground . . . he got on top of me and held me down; he pulled up my clothes . . . he run his hand over my mouth, to keep me from hallowing as much as he could." When asked bluntly, "Did the prisoner actually accomplish sexual intercourse with you: that is, did he or did he not insert his private part into you?" she answered solemnly, "Yes Sir, he did."[39]

In McKinley's case as in others, military courts called black women as witnesses for the prosecution. Matilda McKinley, who also took the witness stand, collaborated Harriet's account:[40]

Q: Did you see him on that day doing anything improper with Harriet Elizabeth McKinley?

A: Yes, Sir, I saw him ravish her.

Q: What do you mean when you say you saw him "ravish her?"

A: I saw him throw her down and get on her and do what he wanted to—that's what I call "ravishing her."[41]

Based on Harriet's and Matilda's testimonies, the commission found that Pierson "did by force and violence have carnal knowledge of the body of Harriet Elizabeth McKinley, a colored woman, without her consent or will." Found guilty of rape, Pierson was "put to hard labor for one year" and deprived of pay for four months.

Even General Butler, who in New Orleans had become notorious for the disrespect he showed Confederate women, held that black women had a right to sexual justice. In the summer of 1864, a Lieutenant Andrew J. Smith, 11th Pennsylvania Calvary, was sentenced to ten years of hard labor for "committing a rape on the person of a colored woman" in Richmond, Virginia. His victim testified, "He threw me on the floor, pulled up my dress. He held my hands with one hand, held part of himself with the other hand and went into me. It hurt. He did what married people do. I am but a child."[42] In reviewing the sentence of the court-martial, General Butler supported the guilty verdict. Summarizing the case, he explained, "A female negro child quits Slavery, and comes into the protection of the federal government, and upon first reaching the limits of the federal lines, receives the brutal treatment from an officer, himself a husband and a father, of violation of her person." Unwilling to entertain pleas for mercy on Smith's behalf, Butler defended the sentence and declared the officer lucky to walk away with his life. "A day or two since a negro man was hung, in the presence of the army, for the attempted violation of the person of a white woman," he argued. "Equal and exact justice would have taken this officer's life; but imprisonment in the Penitentiary for a long term of years, his loss of rank and position—if that imprisonment be without hope of pardon, as it should be—would be almost an equal example."[43]

During the Civil War black women armed themselves with new legal tools to negotiate a deeply abusive sexual terrain, but one that, for the first time, admitted that they could be raped in the eyes of the law. The black women, many of them former slaves, who testified before military courts mobilized military law in defense of themselves and their new rights as wartime citizens.

RECONSTRUCTION AND THE RISE OF JIM CROW

During Reconstruction and the rise of Jim Crow, black women remained vulnerable to sexual violence and continued their campaigns for sexual justice. Refusing to accept the racial and sexual politics of the antebellum hierarchy that had allowed white men to rape and brutalize them with impunity and that defined protection as a right guaranteed only to white women, black women sought to build on their wartime experiences to broaden their claims that female protection was a basic right of citizenship.

Their efforts were particularly clear in Memphis, where in summer of 1866 white rioters killed forty-six blacks, raped at least five black women, and injured hundreds more. The riot drew national attention, and a congressional committee traveled to Memphis to investigate.[44] Black women bravely testified before the committee and asserted their legal claim to personal and sexual autonomy.[45] Sixteen-year-old Lucy Smith testified that seven white men, two of them police officers, broke into her home during the riot and brutally raped her. "One of them," she explained, "choked me by the neck. . . . After the first man had connexion with me, another got hold of me and tried to violate me, but I was so bad he did not. He gave me a lick with his fist and said I was so damned near dead he would not have anything to do with me. . . . I bled from what the first man had done to me. I was injured right smart."[46] Denied legal protection against rape under slavery, Smith and the four other rape victims challenged long-held beliefs that black women welcomed white men's sexual advances.

In response to their testimonies, the committee's final report reflected the Republican Party's commitment to black women's claim to sexual justice. The committee concluded, "The crowning acts of atrocity and diabolism committed during these terrible nights were the ravishing of five different colored women by these fiends in human shape."[47] For black women, such a declaration confirmed their new rights as citizens and marked the Republican Party's commitment to those rights.[48] Black women had long insisted on their right to sexual justice. First expressed in slave women's resistance to sexual violence and then articulated in slave narratives and captured in abolitionist literature, black women's claims gained political currency with the rise of the Republican Party and took root during the Civil War, when black women testified about sexual assaults at court-martials. In the postwar context, such testimony gave new voice to black women's suffering and their demands for legal protection. The congressional committee's declaration acknowledged black women's right to federal protection against racial and sexual violence.

Yet the white and black Americans who wanted to ensure equal protection under the law faced profound opposition in the white South. As southern white anxiety about the political, economic, and social meanings of emancipation intensified, different constituencies assembled a convergent set of racial and sexual fantasies that would soon strip black women of the rights they had acquired under military law. Whereas prior to the war, abolitionists had espoused a political narrative that centered on the rape of black women by white men, in the postwar years southern white men developed a political discourse that defined rape as a crime committed by black men against white women. In constructing the image of the "black rapist," southern white men sought to challenge black men's and women's rights as citizens, while expanding their own sexual power over African Americans. The portrayal of black men as beastly and unable to control their sexual desires served to justify lynching, segregation, and disfranchisement. At the same time as the justification of lynching as the protection for white womanhood allowed for unprecedented violence against African Americans, it also served to terrorize women and place limitations on their sexual freedom and political rights.[49]

When federal troops withdrew from the South, black women's hopes of protection vanished with them. By the late 1870s, a pattern of political oppression and intimidation of black voters and their white Republican allies was well established. The possibility of black female citizenship dwindled as white Democrats regained complete power in the former Confederacy. Sexual justice for black women disappeared as the Jim Crow South denied their claim for equal protection under the law.

By the 1890s southern white men had found in the image of the black rapist a powerful political tool for maintaining white male supremacy.[50] While the rape justification of mob violence never cohered with reality, it shaped southern politics into a cautionary tale for southern women. Lynching and the threat of rape served as warnings that the New South was a dangerous place for women who transgressed the narrow boundaries of race and gender.[51] In fact, the stories that southern white men told and used in their white supremacy campaigns both increased and masked violence against women, black and white.

Indeed, a conjunction of shifting sexual practices, black protest, and female political mobilizations provided the conditions for the elaboration of the rape/lynch narrative. Out of this maelstrom emerged a powerful anti-rape movement led Ida B. Wells. The publication of Wells's 1892 pamphlet, *Southern Horrors*, marked a renewed campaign on the part of black women for sexual justice. Wells understood what black women had gained in the Civil War and its aftermath, and had lost in winning the peace. Yet like the black women who had fought for freedom before her, Wells insisted on black women's rights as citizens to equal protection under the law. Like Stewart and Prince, Wells turned to the press to make her case. In doing so, she provoked the emergence of the black club women's movement that would carry the campaign for sexual justice well into the twentieth century.

NOTES

1. Marilyn Richardson, *Maria W. Stewart: America's First Black Woman Political Writer* (Bloomington: Indiana University Press, 1988), and "'What If I Am a Woman?' Maria W. Stewart's Defense of Black Women's Political Activism," in *Courage and Conscience: Black and White Abolitionists in Boston*, ed. Donald M. Jacobs (Bloomington: Indiana University Press, 1993); and Valerie C. Cooper, *Word, Like Fire: Maria Stewart, the Bible, and the Rights of African Americans* (Charlottesville: University of Virginia Press, 2011).

2. For studies that discuss the sexual exploitation of slave women, see Deborah Gray White, *Ar'n't I a Woman* (New York: W. W. Norton & Company, 1999); Thelma Jennings, "'Us Colored Women Had to Go through a Plenty': Sexual Exploitation of African-American Slave Women," *Journal of Women's History* 1, no. 3 (1990): 45–74; Brenda Stevenson, *Life in Black and White: Family and Community in the Slave South* (New York: Oxford University Press, 1996); Jacqueline A. Jones, *Labor of Love, Labor of Sorrow: Black Women, Work, and the Family, from Slavery to the Present* (New York: Basic Books, 2009); Elizabeth Fox-Genovese, *Within the Plantation Household: Black and White Women of the Old South* (Chapel Hill: University of North Carolina Press, 1988); Stephanie M. H. Camp, *Closer to Freedom: Enslaved Women and Everyday Resistance to the Plantation South* (Chapel Hill: University of North Carolina Press, 2004); and "The Pleasures of Resistance: Enslaved Women and Body Politics in the Plantation South, 1830–1861," *Journal of Southern History* 68, no. 3 (2002): 533–72; Peter Bardaglio, *Reconstructing the Household: Family, Sex, and the Law in the Nineteenth Century South* (Chapel Hill: University of North Carolina Press, 1995); and "Rape and the Law in the Old South: 'Calculated to Excite Indignation in Every Heart,'" *Journal of Southern His-*

tory 60, no. 4 (1994): 749–82; Adrienne Davis, "Don't Let Nobody Bother Yo' Principle: The Sexual Economy of American Slavery," in *Sister Circle: Black Women and Work*, ed. Sharon Harley (New Brunswick: Rutgers University Press, 2002): 108–127; and "Slavery and the Roots of Sexual Harassment," in *Directions in Sexual Harassment Law*, ed. Catharine MacKinnon and Reva Siegel (New Haven: Yale University Press, 2003): 457–79; Thavolia Glymph, *Out of the House of Bondage: The Transformation of the Plantation Household* (New York: Cambridge University Press, 2008); Jennifer Morgan, *Laboring Women: Reproduction and gender in New World Slavery* (Philadelphia: University of Pennsylvania Press, 2004); Sharon Block, *Rape and Sexual Power in Early America* (Chapel Hill: University of North Carolina Press, 2006); Kristin Fischer, *Suspect Relations: Sex, Race, and Resistance in Colonial North Carolina* (Ithaca: Cornell University Press, 2001); Diane Miller Somerville, *Rape and Race in the Nineteenth-Century South* (Chapel Hill: University of North Carolina Press, 2004); and Kathleen Brown, *Good Wives, Nasty Wenches, and Anxious Patriarchs: Gender, Race, and Power in Colonial Virginia* (Chapel Hill: University of North Carolina Press, 1996).

3. For studies that discuss black women and sexual violence during Reconstruction, see Elsa Barkley Brown, "'To Catch the Vision of Freedom: Reconstructing Southern Black Women's Political History, 1865–1880," in *African American Women and the Vote, 1837–1965*, ed. Ann Gordon, Bettye Collier-Thomas, John H. Bracey, Arlene Voski Avakian, and Joyce Avrech Berkman (Amherst: University of Massachusetts Press, 1997), 66–99; Leslie Schwalm, *A Hard Fight for We: Women's Transition from Slavery to Freedom in South* (Urbana-Champaign: University of Illinois Press, 1997) and "'Sweet Dreams of Freedom': Freedwomen's Reconstruction of Life and Labor in Low Country South Carolina," *Journal of Women's History* 9, no. 1 (1997): 9–38; Catherine Clinton, "Bloody Terrain: Freedwomen, Sexuality, and Violence during Reconstruction," *Georgia Historical Quarterly* 76, no. 2 (1992): 313–32; Laura F. Edwards, "Sexual Violence, Gender, Reconstruction, and the Extension of Patriarchy in Granville County, North Carolina," *North Carolina Historical Review* 68, no. 3 (1991): 237–60 and *Gendered Strife and Confusion: The Political Culture of Reconstruction* (Urbana Champaign: University of Illinois Press, 1997); Hannah Rosen, *Terror in the Heart of Freedom: Citizenship, Sexual Violence, and the Meaning of Race in the Postemancipation South* (Chapel Hill: University of North Carolina Press, 2008), and "'Not That Sort of Women': Race, Gender, and Sexual Violence during the Memphis Riot of 1866," in *Sex, Love, Race: Crossing Boundaries in North American History*, ed. Martha Hodes (New York: New York University Press, 1999), 267–93; Glymph, *Out of the House of Bondage*; Tera Hunter, *To 'Joy My Freedom: Southern Black Women's Lives and Labor after the Civil War* (Cambridge: Harvard University Press, 1998); Jacquelyn Dowd Hall, "'The Mind That Burns in Each Body': Women, Rape, and Racial Violence," in *Powers of Desire: The Politics of Sexuality*, ed. Amy Snitow, Christine Stansell, and Sharon Thompson (New York: Monthly Review Press, 1983): 328–49, and *Revolt against Chivalry: Jessie Daniel Ames and the Women's Campaign Against Lynching (Ithaca: Cornell University Press, 1993)*; Jones, *Labor of Love, Labor of Sorrow*; Martha Hodes, *White Women, Black Men: Illicit Sex in Nineteenth-Century South* (New Haven: Yale University Press, 1998), 144, and "The Sexualization of Reconstruction Politics: White Women and Black Men in the

South after the Civil War," *Journal of the History of Sexuality* 3, no. 3 (1993): 402–17; Karen L. Zipf, "Reconstructing 'Free Woman': African-American Women, Apprenticeship, and Custody Rights during Reconstruction," *Journal of Women's History* 12, no. 1 (2000): 8–31; Lisa Cardyn, "Sexual Terror in the Reconstruction South," in *Battle Scars: Gender and Sexuality in the American Civil War*, ed. Catherine Clinton and Nina Silber (New York: Oxford University Press, 2006), 140–67; Kidada E. Williams, *They Left Great Marks on Me: African American Testimonies of Racial Violence from Emancipation to World War I* (New York: New York University Press, 2012); and Crystal N. Feimster, *Southern Horrors: Women and the Politics of Rape and Lynching* (Cambridge: Harvard University Press, 2009).

4. For discussions regarding links between rape and rights, see Hall, *Revolt against Chivalry*; Rosen, *Terror in the Heart of Freedom*; Feimster, *Southern Horrors*; Danielle L. McGuire, *The Dark End of the Street: Black Women, Rape, and Resistance* (New York: Knopf, 2010). Estelle B. Freedman, *Redefining Rape: Sexual Violence in the Era of Suffrage and Segregation* (Cambridge: Harvard University Press, 2013); Saidiya V. Hartman, *Scenes of Subjection: Terror, Slavery, and Self-Making in Nineteenth- Century America* (New York: Oxford University Press, 1997); Block, *Rape and Sexual Power in Early America*; Nell Irvin Painter, *Southern History across the Color Line* (Chapel Hill: University of North Carolina Press, 2002); and Glymph, *Out of the House of Bondage*.

5. Maria W. Stewart, "Religion and the Pure Principles of Morality, the Sure Foundation on Which We Build," 1831, in *America's First Black Woman Political Writer*, 28–42.

6. Ibid.

7. Block, *Rape and Sexual Power*, 64–74; Freedman, *Defining Rape*, 27–31; Bardiglio, "Rape and the Law," 759–60; and Melton A. McLaurin, *Celia, A Slave* (New York: Avon, 1999), 88–93.

8. Block, *Rape and Sexual Power in Early America*, 164–79. Block's study shows that legal cases involving African American women victims of rape were "exceptionally uncommon" in antebellum America. In the few cases in which black women were able to bring charges in the North, many of them involved assaults by African American men.

9. Bardiglio, "Rape and the Law," 759–60; and Diane Miller Sommerville, "'I Was Very Much Wounded': Rape Law, Children, and the Antebellum South," in *Sex without Consent: Rape and Sexual Coercion in America*, ed. Merril Smith (New York: New York University Press, 2002), 160–62.

10. Sabine Sielke, *Reading Rape: The Rhetoric of Sexual Violence in American Literature and Culture, 1790–1990* (Princeton: Princeton University Press, 2002); Kristen Hoganson, "Garrisonian Abolitionists and the Rhetoric of Gender, 1850–1860," *American Quarterly* 45, no 4 (1993): 558–595; Nell Painter, *Sojourner Truth: A Life, a Symbol* (New York: W. W. Norton, 1996), 16; Camp, *Closer to Freedom*; and Freedman, *Redefining Rape*, 30.

11. Mary Prince, *The History of Mary Prince, a West Indian Slave: Related by Herself* (London: F. Westley and A. H. Davis, 1831), 6.

12. Ibid., 10

13. Darlene Clark Hine, "Rape and the Inner Lives of Black Women in the Middle

West: Preliminary Thoughts on the Culture of Dissemblance," *Signs* 14, no. 4 (1989): 912–20. Few female slaves openly admitted in their slave narratives to being raped, yet most acknowledged it was common to slave women's experiences. Elizabeth Keckely, *Behind the Scenes; or, Thirty Years a Slave and Four Years in the White House* (New York: G. W. Carleton,1868).

14. Prince, *The History of Mary Prince*, 13.

15. For slave narratives that acknowledge sexual violence, see Frederick Douglass, *My Bondage and My Freedom* (1855); Solomon Northrup, *Twelve Years a Slave: Narrative of Solomon Northup* (1853); Moses Roper, *Narrative of the Adventures of Henry Bibb, an American Slave* (1849); and William J. Anderson, *Life and Narrative of William J. Anderson, Twenty-Four Years a Slave* (1857).

16. Painter, *Sojourner Truth*, 16–18.

17. In 1842, Harriet Jacobs, a slave in Edenton, North Carolina, escaped to New York and joined the antislavery feminist movement. Harriet A. Jacobs, *Incidents in the Life of a Slave Girl* (Cambridge: Harvard University Press, 1987). Also see Sharon Davie, "'Reader, My Story Ends with Freedom': Harriet Jacobs's *Incidents in the Life of a Slave Girl*," in *Famous Last Words: Changes in Gender and Narrative Closure*, ed. Alison Booth (Charlottesville: University of Virginia Press, 1993), 86–109; Winifred Morgan, "Gender-Related Differences in the Slave Narratives of Harriet Jacobs and Frederick Douglass," *American Studies* 35, no. 2 (1994): 73–94; Jean Yellin, "Through Her Brother's Eyes: *Incidents* and 'A True Tale,'" in *Harriet Jacobs and "Incidents in the Life of a Slave Girl*," ed. Deborah M. Garfield and Rafia Zafar (New York: Cambridge University Press, 1996), 44–56; and Nell Irvin Painter, "Of *Lily*, Linda Brent, and Freud: A Non-Exceptionalist Approach to Race, Class, and Gender in the Slave South," *Georgia Historical Quarterly* 76, no. 2 (1992): 241–59; Maggie Sale, "Critiques from Within: Antebellum Projects of Resistance," *American Literature* 64, no. 4 (1992): 695–718; Harryette R. Mullen, *Freeing the Soul: Race, Subjectivity, and Difference in Slave Narratives* (London: Cambridge University Press, 2000); Hartman, *Scenes of Subjection*, 103–12; and Claudia Tate, "Allegories of Black Female Desire; or, Rereading Nineteenth-Century Sentimental Narratives of Black Female Authority," in *Changing Our Own Words: Essays on Criticism, Theory, and Writing by Black Women*, ed. Cheryl A. Wall (New Brunswick: Rutgers University Press, 1989), 98–126.

18. Jacobs, *Incidents in the Life of a Slave Girl*, 18.

19. Ibid., 27–28.

20. In fact, it was only after the war that most former slave women were able to talk about white men's sexual power over them, and even then it proved difficult. See Keckley, *Behind the Scenes*, first published in 1868: "The savage efforts to subdue my pride were not the only things that brought me suffering and deep mortification during my residence at Hillsboro. I was regarded as fair-looking for one of my race, and for four years a white man—I spare the world his name—had base designs upon me. I do not care to dwell upon this subject, for it is one that is fraught with pain. Suffice it to say, that he persecuted me for four years, and I—I—became a mother. The child of which he was the father was the only child that I ever brought into the

world. If my poor boy ever suffered any humiliating pangs on account of birth, he could not blame his mother, for God knows that she did not wish to give him life; he must blame the edicts of that society which deemed it no crime to undermine the virtue of girls in my then position" (38–39).

21. Harriet Beecher Stowe, *A Key to Uncle Tom's Cabin* (Boston: John P. Jewett and Company, 1852).

22. For a discussion of slave women's resistance, see Glymph, *Out of the House of Bondage*, 55–57; Winthrop Jordan, *Tumult and Silence at Second Creek,: An Inquiry Into a Civil War Slave Conspiracy* (Baton Rouge: Louisiana State Press, 1996), 164–65, 201–2, 279; White, *Ar'n't I a Woman*, 74–76; and Camp, *Enslaved Women and Everyday Resistance*, 36–40.

23. Steven Weisenburg, *Modern Medea: A Family Story of Slavery and Child-Murder from the Old South* (New York: Hill and Wang, 1999).

24. Ibid.

25. Lucy Stone, "Speech of Lucy Stone Blackwell," in *Who Speaks for Margaret Garner?*, by Mark Reinhardt (Minneapolis: University of Minnesota Press, 2010), 219–21. Also see, Andrea Moore Kerr, *Lucy Stone: Speaking Out for Equality* (New Brunswick: Rutgers University Press, 1992); and Joelle Million, *Woman's Voice, Woman's Place: Lucy Stone and the Birth of Woman's Rights Movement* (New York: Praeger, 2003).

26. Abraham Lincoln, "Speech on the *Dred Scott* Decision Delivered in Springfield, Illinois, June 26, 1857," in *Lincoln: Speeches and Writings: 1832–1858*, ed. Don E. Fehrenbacher (New York: The Library of America, 1989), 398.

27. Ibid.

28. For a discussion of Republican ideas about black citizenship and rights see, Kate Masur, "Civil, Political, and Social Equality after Lincoln: A Paradigm and a Problematic," *Marquette Law Review* vol. 93, no. 4 (2010): 1399–1406, and *An Example for All the Land: Emancipation and the Struggle over Equality in Washington, D.C.* (Chapel Hill: University of North Carolina Press, 2010); and Eric Foner, *Free Soil, Free Labor, Free Men: The Ideology of the Republican Party Before the Civil War* (New York: Oxford University Press, 1995).

29. General Orders, No. 100: The Lieber Code, April 24, 1863, in *The War of the Rebellion: A Compilation of the Official Records of the Union and Confederate Armies* (Washington, D.C.: Government Printing Office, 1899), series III, vol. 3, 148–64.

30. Ibid.

31. E. Susan Barber and Charles R. Ritter, "'Physical Abuse... and Rough Handling': Race, Gender, and Sexual Justice in the Occupied South," in *Occupied Women: Gender, Military Occupation, and the American Civil War*, ed. LeeAnn Whites and Alecia P. Long (Baton Rouge: Louisiana State University Press, 2009), 49–64.

32. On female contraband, see Schwalm, *A Hard Fight for We*; Thavolia Glymph, "'This Species of Property': Female Slave Contrabands in the Civil War," in *A Woman's War: Southern Women, Civil War, and the Confederate Legacy*, ed. Edward D. D. Campbell Jr. and Kym S. Rice (Richmond: Museum of the Confederacy, 1997), 55–71; and "Noncombatant Military Laborers in the Civil War," *Magazine of History* 16, no. 2 (2012): 25–29; and Stephanie McCurry, "War, Gender, and Emancipation in the Civil War

South," in *Lincoln's Proclamation: Emancipation Reconsidered*, ed. William A. Blair and Karen Fisher Younger (Chapel Hill: University of North Carolina Press, 2009), 120–50.

33. Schwalm, *A Hard Fight for We*, 141.

34. Testimony of Maj. Gen. B. F. Butler before the American Freedmen Inquiry Commission file no. 5, see also testimony of J. Redpath, file no. 9, Capt. E. W. Hooper file no. 3A, O-328, 1863, Letters Received, ser. 12, RG 94, National Archives and Records Administration, Washington, D.C.. For a discussion of abolitionist views on sexual depravity in the South and the immorality of female slaves, see Reid Mitchell, *The Vacant Chair: The Northern Soldier Leaves Home* (London: Oxford University Press, 1993), 108–9; Ronald G. Walters, *The Antislavery Appeal: American Abolitionism after 1830* (New York: W. W. Norton & Company, 1984), 70–110. For comments on the role of women as the guardians of domestic virtue, see James McPherson, *Battle Cry of Freedom: The Civil War Era* (London: Oxford University Press, 2003), 34–35; Mitchell, *The Vacant Chair*, 74–75. For a description of antebellum stereotypes of black female slaves, see Fox-Genovese, *Within the Plantation Household*, 291–93; White, *Ar'n't I a Woman?*, 29–34, 46–50; Feimster, *Southern Horrors*; and Jennifer Morgan, *Laboring Women*.

35. Capt. E. Gabrill to wife, June 20, 1865, Elliot F. Grabill Papers, Oberlin College Archives; Herbert G. Gutman, *The Black Family in Slavery and Freedom, 1750–1925* (New York: Vintage, 1977), 385–402, 613–14.

36. Barber and Ritter, "Physical Abuse . . . and Rough Handling."

37. Trial of Perry Peirson, Records of the Office of the Judge Advocate General, Record Group 153, National Archives and Records Administration, Washington, D.C.

38. Testimony of Harriet McKinley in Trial of Perry Peirson, Records of the Office of the Judge Advocate General, Record Group 153, National Archives and Records Administration, Washington, D.C.

39. Ibid.

40. Ibid.

41. Testimony of Matilda McKinley in Peirson Trail.

42. Quoted in Thomas P. Lowry, *Sexual Misbehavior in the Civil War* (Xlibris Corp. 2006), 122.

43. Ibid.

44. Rosen, "'Not That Sort of Women'"; and *Terror in the Heart of Freedom*; Kenneth W. Goings, *"Unhidden" Transcripts: Memphis and African American Agency, 1862–1920* (Thousand Oaks, Calif.: Sage, 1995); Kevin R. Hardwick "'Your Old Father Abe Lincoln Is Dead and Damned': Black Soldiers and the Memphis Race Riot of 1866," *Journal of Social History* 27, no. 1 (1993): 109–28; Altina L. Waller, "Community, Class, and Race in the Memphis Riot of 1866," *Journal of Social History* 18, no. 2 (1984): 223–46; and James Gilbert Ryan, "The Memphis Riots of 1866: Terror in a Black Community During Reconstruction," *Journal of Negro History* 62, no. 3 (1977): 243–57.

45. Rosen, "'Not That Sort of Women.'"

46. Testimony of Lucy Smith, in *Memphis Riots and Massacres*, 39th Cong., 1st sess., 1866, House Rept. 101, 197.

47. *Memphis Riots and Massacres* quoted in Rosen, "'Not That Sort of Women,'" 282–83.

48. Rosen, *Terror in the Heart of Freedom*, 61–83.

49. Nell Irvin Painter, *Standing at Armageddon: The United States, 1877–1919* (New York: W. W. Norton, 1987); Glenda Elizabeth Gilmore, *Gender and Jim Crow: Women and the Politics of White Supremacy in North Carolina, 1896–1920* (Chapel Hill: University of North Carolina Press, 1996); Jane Dailey, *Before Jim Crow: The Politics of Race in Postemancipation Virginia* (Chapel Hill: University of North Carolina Press, 2000).

50. Edwards, *Gendered Strife and Confusion*; Hodes, *White Women, Black Men*; and Rosen, *Terror in the Heart of Freedom*.

51. Feimster, *Southern Horrors*; Hall, "'The Mind That Burns in the Body,'" and *Revolt against Chivalry*; Joel Williamson, *A Rage for Order: Black-White Relations in the American South since Emancipation* (New York: Oxford University Press, 1986); W. Fitzhugh W. Brundage, *Lynching in the New South: Georgia and Virginia, 1880–1930* (Urbana: University of Illinois Press, 1993); and Fitzhugh Brundage, ed., *Under Sentence of Death: Lynching in the South* (Chapel Hill: University of North Carolina Press, 1997); Nancy MacLean, *Behind the Mask of Chivalry: The Making of the Second Ku Klux Klan* (New York: Oxford University Press, 1994); E. M. Beck and Stewart E. Tolnay, *Festival of Violence: An Analysis of Southern Lynchings, 1882–1930* (Chicago: University of Illinois Press, 1995); Ashraf H. A. Rushdy, *American Lynching* (New Haven: Yale University Press, 2014); Leon Litwack, *Trouble in Mind: Black Southerners in the Age of Jim Crow* (New York: Vintage, 1999); and Amy Louise Wood, *Lynching and Spectacle: Witnessing Racial Violence in America, 1890–1940* (Chapel Hill: University of North Carolina Press, 2011).

SLAVE EMANCIPATION AND THE REVOLUTIONIZING OF HUMAN RIGHTS

11

Amy Dru Stanley

Did the abolition of slavery create a right to go to the theater? The question arose in the long debate over the Civil Rights Act of 1875, a measure enacted by Congress to sweep away the vestiges of chattel bondage. It arose again in the courts, within a month after the act was signed into law, brought first in a case about a Memphis playhouse. At issue was the liberty of a black theatergoer, as well as the sovereignty of the national state established by the antislavery amendments to the Constitution. "I would have selected some more precious and beneficent privilege for protection," wrote Judge Halmer Hull Emmons of the United States Circuit Court. "We turn from this almost grotesque exercise of national authority, and express our regret only that it cannot be exerted to protect from pillage and murder the humble homes of those peaceful toilers, who quietly and inoffensively labor . . . and who do not officiously and distastefully thrust themselves . . . among theatrical audiences."[1] In other words, the guarantees of slave emancipation should protect a laboring freedman from violence but not an amusement seeker at a theater.

By no means was the Civil Rights Act of 1875 an ascetic article of freedom. It was intended as a culminating decree of slave emancipation, and newly defined pleasurable liberties as affirmative rights. The act stated: "All persons within the jurisdiction of the United States shall be entitled to the full and equal enjoyment of the accommodations, advantages, facilities, and privileges of inns, public conveyances on land or water, theaters, and other places of public amusement."[2] Emancipation would bring a fundamental right to be an amusement seeker, in particular to be a theatergoer. This conception of freedom was both sensuous and steeped in the ways of the marketplace—and nowhere found in prior declarations of the rights of man.

The 1875 act was grounded in the Thirteenth and Fourteenth Amendments. It was called the *Supplementary Civil Rights Act,* because it was meant to supplement the 1866 Civil Rights Act, which entitled all citizens of the United States to rights of contract, property, security of the person, and equality before the law. It figured in the rights aspirations not only of freedpeople in the South but of freeborn blacks across the country. Notably, the supplement was enacted by a Congress in which sat both ex-slaves and ex-Confederates.[3]

Famously, the United States Supreme Court struck down the supplement as an encroachment on state sovereignty, the ruling in the *Civil Rights Cases of 1883.* It was not until a century after the Civil War, in the Civil Rights Act of 1964, that Congress resurrected the pleasurable entitlements of public amusement seeking—but under the Commerce Clause, which regulates the traffic in commodities, rather than under the Thirteenth Amendment, which safeguards the freedom of human beings.[4]

The supplement bears reconsidering as a human rights decree. My argument is that slave emancipation transformed the human rights tradition inherited from the Age of Revolution. It did so by vindicating amusement seeking as a right belonging to all persons by virtue of their humanity. And therefore it altered the very conception of being human—enshrining the idea that intrinsic to a person was a right to seek amusement, to pursue pleasure, to experience rapture in public, and that this right must be written into the positive law of the nation-state. This was a revolutionary transformation of Enlightenment understandings of human rights and humanity that were rooted in proprietorship and wealth accumulation.[5]

Evidence lies in the theater of politics—the debates of Congress. The argument also concerns the world of the stage—the theater itself. Connecting the realms of the Capitol and the playhouse, lawmaking and social experience, was the outcry of ex-slaves and free black persons against the violation of their human dignity.

My purpose is not to join scholarly disputes about the value of searching the past for precursors of contemporary human rights doctrine. Nor is it to deny the paradox of human rights that are rooted in the sovereignty of a nation—the paradox revealed in Hannah Arendt's classic study of the Rights of Man that hinge on citizenship.[6]

Nonetheless, my argument about slave emancipation does challenge scholarship on the human rights tradition. A prevailing interpretation holds that the language of human rights did not emerge until the era of the Holocaust, and that abolitionists spoke of common humanity but rarely of human rights.[7] The history of the 1875 supplement contradicts these findings. Explicit invocations of human rights justified the legislation as the final act of abolition. But the issue is not just one of semantics.

My point is that the supplement—though aborted—represents a turning point in both the death of slavery and the emergence of human rights. Abolitionism had long held that slavery violated natural law. But in the supplement lay the unprecedented conception that being human included the inherent right to pursue amusement in public, and, particularly, to behold an imaginary world created on stage. The legislation spoke in universalist terms of "all persons," not only citizens. And the freedoms enumerated did not simply echo the natural rights declarations of revolutionary America, France, and Haiti, nor simply transcend the color line.[8]

Rather, the supplement of 1875 transformed human rights doctrine. Newly, the status of not being a slave, a thing, a brutish creature, but a human being endowed with free will entailed the right to experience amusement in a public sphere mediated by market exchange. Newly, guarantees of volition extended beyond the liberties of work, contract, and property accumulation as exercised by self-disciplined citizens. A century earlier, in the era of the American Revolution, the Continental Congress had banned the theater as a pleasure adverse to the industry and economy of a self-governing people. Yet for a moment, until it was nullified, the 1875 act vindicated amusement seeking as a condition of free personhood. The rights bearer was not a mere *homo economicus* or a possessive individual. From the revolution of slave emancipation emerged the idea of a sensuous, affective, and sociable entitlement, protected by the national state, for the purchase price of a ticket. Here was something new in the history of human rights: a public right to play, born of the transition from property to person—a right to nonacquisitive happiness as the negation of chattel slavery.[9]

In the next century, the Universal Declaration of Human Rights would guarantee the freedom to partake of cultural life, including the arts. That cosmopolitan guarantee—the conversion of the vexed pleasure of theatergoing into a human right—arose as an antislavery invention, from the overthrow of America's peculiar institution.[10]

For the most part, the supplement is remembered as a landmark defeat in the battle against Jim Crow. Its career has been seen as evidence of the unfinished promise of Reconstruction and as a lesson in the limits of the

Thirteenth Amendment and in the constraints of the state action requirement of the Fourteenth Amendment, a distinctly American problem. Its lasting legacy has been understood in terms of race and space and public rights: the claim of citizens to use public space as civic equals.[11]

At stake, I argue, was a project no less revolutionary, of widening the expanse of freedom and redefining the nature of the rights that constitute being human, the slave's opposite—a project of significance beyond American borders. Historically, writes the theorist Jürgen Habermas, the appeal to human rights has insisted on an inviolable "domain of free will," originating in the protest of the humiliated against affronts to their dignity and premised on the moral principle that all of humanity is an end in itself.[12]

Such a human rights perspective casts new light on the meaning of the supplementary Civil Rights Act of 1875 in counting amusement seeking and theatergoing as an essential part of freedom's domain, an act of national sovereignty as unprecedented as the uncompensated slave emancipation that it was meant to complete. A former slave named John Roy Lynch, who became a Mississippi congressman, put it simply. "This bill," he told the United States House of Representatives, "has for its object the protection of human rights."[13]

IN THE ERA OF slave emancipation, Congress became a theater of debate over human rights. Before the Civil War, the language of human rights had sometimes emerged in congressional conflict over slavery extension, the slave trade, and the Fugitive Slave Law. With emancipation, it became more pronounced, especially in the adoption of the antislavery amendments. And in the debate on the supplement—which dragged on for more than three years—the usage intensified, transcending divisions of region and race.[14] In the making of a world without slavery, the language of human rights expressly infused political and constitutional arguments, long before its emergence amid world war and genocide in the twentieth century.

At the same time, Congress became a forum for the outcry of black people, whether born into freedom or slavery, against insults to their personhood. In December 1871, a recitation of the grievances of black petitioners opened the long debate on the supplement. A remonstrance from Brooklyn began: "We, the undersigned citizens . . . feeling ourselves aggrieved . . . and degraded . . . for the want of a law . . . supplementary to the civil rights bill, do respectfully pray for the passage of the same."[15]

To antislavery advocates, inside and outside of Congress, the supplement represented a guarantee of human rights. A freeborn black congressman from South Carolina, Alonzo Ransier, quoted resolutions sent by his state legislature, where black men held sway—men who called for the measure's enactment to end "the violation of their rights as human beings." Ransier quoted also from *Macbeth*, as he rebuked former slave owners for their opposition, prophesying that one day they would falsely mourn: "Thou canst not say I did it: never shake thy gory locks at me."[16]

From the galleries of Congress spectators of both races viewed the drama below. The author of the supplement, Senator Charles Sumner of Massachusetts, spoke of human rights in justifying congressional power to protect the freedom of amusement seekers and sojourners. "I invoke the sentiments of mankind and posterity," Sumner said. "The national Constitution is the charter of a great Republic dedicated to Human Rights, dedicated at its very birth by the Declaration of Independence . . . whoever fails to enlarge and ennoble it by that interpretation, through which human rights are most advanced, will fail in his oath to support the Constitution." But the author of the 1866 Civil Rights Act, Senator Lyman Trumbull of Illinois, objected that the supplement was an unnecessary, and unconstitutional, intrusion on state authority over private institutions. "We believe in human rights"—property, contract, and equality at law, the "rights of men" already recognized by the 1866 act—Trumbull said, averring that only amnesty remained, "the peace of the country restored."[17]

The supplement's guarantees reached to all persons, unlike those of the 1866 act, which applied only to citizens. Sumner's original draft of 1870 would have afforded entitlements in a broad expanse of places: incorporated churches, cemeteries, and benevolent associations; common schools and other public institutions of learning; all juries; as well as inns, railroads and steamboats, licensed theaters, and other places of public amusement. The bill languished, adversely reported by the Senate judiciary committee and failing as an amendment attached to an 1872 amnesty law that restored the right of most Confederate leaders to hold public office. "Sufficient unto the day is the evil thereof," warned a Georgia senator, Joshua Hill, a former slave owner, quoting from the Sermon on the Mount. "When it pleased the Creator of heaven and earth to make different races of men it was His purpose to keep them distinct and separate." As the vituperation continued, the measure shed some of its provisions. When finally adopted in 1875, the supplement applied to inns, public conveyances, theaters and other public amusements, and all juries, with no specification about incorporation or licensing. It withstood objections that guaranteeing the rights of persons—as if Congress legislated for "all the world and the rest of mankind" in a universalist spirit—would protect "foreigners" such as the Chinese on American soil. It gave exclusive jurisdiction to the federal courts and defined violations as misdemeanors, punishable by imprisonment for as long as a year and a fine no greater than $1,000. It also created a private right of action, enabling the aggrieved to sue offenders and claim a sum of $500 in damages. All would be entitled to be theatergoers: noncitizens, citizens, and the stateless alike.[18]

Paeans to human rights flowed forth in Congress even as the framers of Reconstruction argued over the supplement's legitimacy. "We cannot agree upon the best way of maintaining human rights," acknowledged a Connecticut senator, Orris Ferry, who had been a Civil War general. A contest was occurring on the "great subject of human rights," said a South Carolina senator, Frederick Sawyer, who opposed the effort to "bring in a speech upon human rights on every bill." It was "in the name of human rights" that Senator John Sherman of Ohio insisted on the "unenumerated powers" of Congress to recognize entitlements as "innumerable as the sands of the sea." Stating the claims of black Republicans, the South Carolina congressman Richard Harvey Cain, a pastor in the African Methodist Episcopal Church, declared that "revolutions never go backward" and explained that the supplement embodied the "understanding of human rights . . . all rights to all men."[19]

The crux of the constitutional argument on behalf of the supplement was that the power granted to Congress by the antislavery amendments must be interpreted in accordance with the higher law tenets of the Declaration of Independence. "These amendments to the Constitution do not define all the rights of American citizens," said Senator Sherman, calling on Congress to look "to the Declaration of Independence, to every scrap of American history." In Sumner's words: "The Constitution is full of power; it is overrunning with power. . . . I say a new rule of interpretation for the Constitution, according to which, in every clause and every line and every word, it is to be interpreted uniformly for human rights. . . . [I]t must be interpreted by the Declaration of Independence to advance human rights."

Fulfilling the freedom won at Appomattox—"victories of many bloody fields"—the legislation expressed the newfound power of the nation-state to overturn rules "alien to human rights."[20]

By contrast, in the eyes of former slaveholders, the supplement brought the nightmare of Black Reconstruction ever closer, compelling social equality and race mixing. States' rights men condemned the legislation as an unconstitutional trespass of Congress into the private sphere, a violation of the private liberties of contract, property, and association. As a Maryland senator protested: "You boast of having struck the manacles from the hands of the slaves, while you place them upon the volition of the whites. Suffer not . . . to weigh down the mighty balances of human rights."[21]

At issue were momentous questions: the relationship of rights and sovereignty, moral norms and positive law, freedom and coercion. To defenders of the old order, the supplement made a "hotch-potch" of the Constitution, debasing American government, with Congress overreaching its authority by "descending" to interfere with "institutions of pleasure," as well as with inns and conveyances, enterprises of "private means" that involved neither involuntary servitude nor state action. It threatened to protect what was "not the right of any colored man on earth," to associate everywhere as equals, even to "intermarry with any caste," eroding the boundary between domestic affairs governed by local law and national civil rights. "I think that such matters are subject to municipal regulation by the States for their own people," said the Georgian Joshua Hill. "I confess to having a little *penchant* for the white race." But to visionaries of a new order, the supplement expressed the antislavery ascent of the nation by extending the reach of fundamental rights. "No question of human rights is small," affirmed Sumner, condemning "indignity to the colored man." Rather, the supplement was "transcendent," amplifying the slave's transformation from property to person.[22]

Meanwhile, appeals for rights flooded into the Capitol from both ex-slave and freeborn black petitioners, and as they were read into the record, the congressional debate was punctuated by the testimony of the wronged about insults to their dignity and aspirations for freedom that encompassed pleasure in public. For example, there were resolutions adopted by four thousand colored persons in Macon, Georgia; correspondence from public meetings in Rhode Island; a petition from Virginia freedpeople; a memorial from a mass meeting of three thousand colored people in

Philadelphia, whom one of their leaders called "the downtrodden and the despised." Southern lawmakers were horrified by the image of black men traversing the country, arousing ex-slaves to agitate for supplementary rights.[23]

The agitation had begun before the debate opened in Congress. Early in 1871, petitions came to Sumner: "A memorial was sent to you . . . asking the Senate to pass your bill supplementary to the Civil Rights bill. This should have been accompanied by a note, politely asking you to present it." Letters told of mustering the "support of the colored people . . . in securing them in their civil rights."[24]

Soon the protests of freedpeople rang out in Congress, read aloud by antislavery statesmen. A speech of a Georgia ex-slave, John Quarles, delivered at the Convention of Colored People in South Carolina in 1871, became a text for Sumner. "We are weary of being treated as outcasts and strangers," said Quarles, describing being a pariah as an inheritance of slavery: "In whatever direction we go . . . in public places of amusement . . . upon the railroad . . . in the wayside inn, we encounter . . . this inhuman outrage upon our manhood. . . . We are weary of being hunted down by the ghost of the defunct system of slavery. . . . Let the abominable crimes against humanity be buried in the grave of oblivion." The freedman gloried in "a grand and a moral power in the spectacle of a whole people arising to assert their rights."[25]

In turn, the petitioners derived inspiration from the speeches in Congress. As a freedman named Edwin Belcher, the president of the Georgia Civil Rights Association, wrote to Sumner in January 1872, "I thank you for the copy of the speech which you kindly sent me. . . . No more bitter disappointment will ever be felt by the colored race than the defeat of your bill . . . the Magna Charta of our liberties."[26]

In greater detail, a Virginia ex-slave named London Kurdle explained his understanding of fundamental rights in a letter prompted by reading Sumner's words. Kurdle wrote that he had been enslaved most of his life — "never to shool . . . but work hard a nights my self to be able to Read and was being (32) year of my life in Bondage the best of my day was spent that time" — as he offered thanks to Sumner for seeking to safeguard freedom:

Having read your Speech, that you delivered to the Senate of these United States on the 15th of January, I feel it my duty for the noble manner in wich you appeals to the members of the Senate to do Jus-

tice to a people that have just bin made Citizens of this Nation. . . .
I have attempted to write to you hoping that the might God may
bless you to live to accomplish that greate work you have began.

But the purpose of Kurdle's letter was to interpret the doctrine expressed
in the supplement. "Let me come to the Point," he wrote. Invoking moral
and legal and economic principles, he reasoned that the right to seek public amusement should depend simply on the ability to buy a ticket and
good conduct, not on the discretion of property owners and color:

> For one Class of people, to use proscription upon another . . . on
> account of Color is a sin a gainst God and a Crime a gainst man. . . .
> Look at the white man and the black man; they bouth have one
> bone; one blood. . . . you Calls the Senates attention to . . . how
> Colored men have bin treated . . . and all living under one Common
> Law; and that too Where the Constitution makes no distinction on
> account of Color, if I pay my money at place of public entertain-
> ment; it is as good as if a white man had paid his, at the same place.
> What dose it matter so each man behaves himself as he should. . . .
> All that are sacred will be found at one heaven.[27]

As the ex-slave imbued the supplement with the authority of divine law
and the Constitution, he affirmed both the equity of the marketplace and
the unity of humanity. Having been property for the best of his days, he
envisioned amusement seeking as a natural right guaranteed by the abolition of slavery.

An interchange thus developed between the outcry of the aggrieved
and expansive congressional constructions of newfound national sovereignty under the antislavery amendments. The pleas of unfreedom served
as a moral justification for the supplement; at the same time, ex-slaves
circulated transcripts of the proceedings in Congress as they drew up their
appeals. From that charged interchange the logic of the supplement took
shape as an antislavery vindication of human rights.

IT WAS THE ORATORY OF Sumner so praised by the freedmen that set
forth the revolutionary meaning of the supplement as a human rights
decree. In a Senate speech of January 15, 1872, Sumner announced the
new proposition that seeking amusement at a theater was a human right
grounded in the pursuit of happiness and owed to ex-slaves as an outcome

of abolition. "Here are institutions whose peculiar object is the 'pursuit of happiness,' which has been placed among the equal rights of all," Sumner said. His argument justified the sovereignty of the national state—asserting the power of Congress to tap the Declaration of Independence in enforcing the Thirteenth and Fourteenth Amendments—while proclaiming the supplement as "truly efficacious for human rights."[28]

The supplement renovated the Rights of Man. Recognizing the human dignity of ex-slaves, it amplified the fundamental rights long conceived as natural. At the heart of its logic lay the transformation of the slave from property to person—and therefore a conception of the rights inherent in all human beings. The supplement was intended as a legal consummation of that transformation. It extended the guarantees of emancipation and the sphere of individual volition—beyond property and contract, speech and association, marriage and family, citizenship and political enfranchisement. "The slave is free. No longer a chattel, he is a man justly entitled to all that is accorded by law to any other man," Sumner said. Self-owning, the freedman was entitled to his labor and its fruits, inalienable rights of the liberal tradition. There was no auction block, no violation of the household, no sanctions against knowledge, no exclusion from the courtroom or the ballot box. "But this is not enough," claimed Sumner. "The new-made citizen is called to travel for business, for health, or for pleasure. . . . He longs, perhaps, for respite and relaxation, at some place of amusement. . . . The denial of any right is wrong."[29]

The supplement therefore enshrined the seeking of amusement, of respite, of pleasure in public as a human right of freed slaves. It did not only efface the color line, including black persons within the community of citizens; nor did it afford simply the dignity of social exchange that money could buy. An antislavery amendment to the rights declarations of the Age of Revolution, it codified new freedoms defined by the destruction of chattel bondage. It would protect the volition of freed persons, whether acting out of desire or necessity, whether pursuing happiness or fulfilling duties. As the freedman Kurdle wrote, "I pay my money at place of public entertainment; it is as good as if a white man had paid his."[30] The ex-slave would be entitled to cross the threshold from a pain economy to a pleasure economy, from a cotton field to a city theater, a passage marking a new conception of innate rights.

The ideal of happiness itself was amplified by the supplement—as an end sought by rights bearers. The experience available at a place of public amusement was affective, sensuous, and sociable, such as a theatergoer might desire at a playhouse. It did not involve individual property accumulation and wealth creation, or a rational calculus of pain and pleasure, or works of benevolence, or the felicities of a well-constituted state, forms of happiness elucidated by Enlightenment thinkers. Sumner expressly cited "insulting at the theater" as an act of subjugation. He said nothing of the debate that had occurred among French philosophes on the theater's vices and virtues. Rather, he relied on the Declaration of Independence—"by which the 'pursuit of happiness' is placed with life and liberty, under the safeguard of axiomatic self-evident truth"—to count public amusement seeking as an inviolable right of freedom.[31]

Newly, therefore, the supplement defined the right to seek nonacquisitive forms of happiness—sensual amusements once considered sinful—as the antithesis of slavery. It broadened not only the domain of free will protected by law but the very idea of a human being: the slave's opposite. In Sumner's words, the freed person came "within the pale of humanity" under the supplement: "As a man he is entitled to all the rights of man."[32] To be a theatergoer was a right belonging to ex-slaves by virtue of their status as human beings.

At least one point was not contested—that the supplement had no precedent in transforming the amusement seeker into a bearer of fundamental rights. It was as unfounded in constitutional doctrine on the privileges and immunities of national citizenship as it was in common law principles. Sumner strived to argue that the theater was a place "kindred" to a railroad, steamboat, and inn, in that all were "public institutions": creatures of law, subject to municipal licensing, with a duty to admit all paying persons. Southerners held that no national legislation could require "sitting together." But Sumner claimed that the touch of the law, establishing, maintaining, or regulating private ventures operating in public, empowered Congress to protect human rights in those places: "From essential reason, the rule should be the same," he said. "Whoever seeks the benefit of the law, as the owners and lessees of theaters do, as the common carriers do, as hotel keepers do. . . . Everything that they do and all their regulations shall be in conformity with the supreme law of the land which is the Declaration of Independence." Yet even Sumner admitted that the analogy was inexact, remarking that "places of public amusement, licensed by law, are . . . less noticed by jurisprudence." The treatises he cited, Chancellor Kent's *Commentaries*, Joseph Story on *Bailments*, offered no authority for the theater clause. Nor did the landmark case of *Corfield v. Coryell* (1823), which spoke of the right to "obtain happiness" but not to pursue public amusement, defining entitlements "in their nature, fundamental," as freedom to own property, petition for habeas corpus, bring law suits, vote, and produce wealth by traveling or residing in any state "for purposes of trade, agriculture, professional pursuits, or otherwise." Never had amusement seeking at the theater been a pursuit of happiness or a form of social intercourse protected by government. To slave owners, the legislation seemed both a "monstrous absurdity" and a congressional act of "revolution and violence."[33]

Accordingly, the defense of the supplement joined the pleas of black petitioners with the Declaration of Independence as sources of moral authority. "One once a slave knows whereof he speaks," argued Sumner, as he justified the supplement's constitutionality as an antislavery human rights decree that abolished practices enduring from "those unhappy days before the war."[34]

OF THE PLACES governed by the supplement, only the theater had once been an illicit place, a place of blaspheme.[35] That it came to represent an aspirational realm of freedom was eloquently expressed in an appeal for the supplement appearing in 1874 in a religious journal, the *Independent*—an appeal that told of the emotive and political experience of a black theatergoer. It was written by a freeborn black antislavery leader named George Downing, who had been an operator of the Underground Railroad, and then a brigade quarter master of Colored Troops during the war. He described viewing *The Merchant of Venice* as a young man. He recalled how his emotions had overflowed as he felt Shylock's wrongs. He wrote of his "rights and feelings," attesting to a sentience that distinguished him from a brute.[36]

"I feel keenly. I have listened to . . . the words which Shakespeare put in the mouth of Shylock to let it be known that even a despised Jew had feelings. Shylock's words depict the feelings that animate with great intensity the outraged colored man."[37] Responding to a profound artistic work, Downing conveyed his own humanity. The protagonist's condition had been as if his own.

And then Downing wrote of the supplement and rights to be won. "I am not demanding a pound of human flesh; but I am demanding exact and even-handed justice, as denominated in the bond between me and my

Government."[38] For Downing, the artifice of the stage truly held a mirror up to nature.

A century earlier, the Continental Congress had outlawed all theaters and stage plays as subversive of revolutionary republicanism. The sensations produced by spectacles such as *The Merchant of Venice* appeared contrary to liberty, virtue, and economy. The Articles of Association of 1774 forbade the "extravagance and dissipation" of diversions such as "shews" and "plays" in requiring habits of "frugality, economy, and industry." Resolves of 1778, adopted to protect the independence of the American people, renewed the ban, declaring the theater inimical to "public liberty and happiness" and to "true religion and morals." Perversely, in suppressing theatrical pleasures, the rebellious nation echoed British measures, the ordinances adopted by the Long Parliament during the English Civil War that prohibited "Spectacles of pleasure . . . expressing laciuious Mirth and Levitie." But it also drew on colonial edicts that condemned the "great mischiefs which arise from publick stage-plays" and the production of "a taste for intriguing, amusement and pleasure."[39]

Nor was there a common law right to go to a playhouse. The common law had long recognized an entitlement to travel in public conveyances and to stop at inns. This was a right rooted in necessity, which traced back to medieval understandings of natural law principles of self-preservation, and which obliged innkeepers and common carriers to take in all paying travelers as space allowed.[40]

But the theater lay beyond the realm of necessity, as a place that animated emotion and imagination through the arts of illusion. Since the early modern era, theaters had come under municipal licensing laws, which allowed property owners to admit paying spectators to view stage plays involving the "excitement of emotion" and the "representation of action." The licenses also protected actors from vagabond laws that imposed punishments — public whipping, hard labor in a house of correction, burning through the gristle of the ear — on wanderers who mounted amusements that drew crowds of idle people. But the licenses afforded no rights to theatergoers. Nor was there a customary right to seek public amusement.[41]

In the era of revolution, then, the inalienable right to pursue happiness hardly entailed seeking pleasure at a theater. Rather, an ethos of asceticism sustained American ideals of independence, obliging work and self-denial, as opposed to the "idleness" and "dissipation" deplored by the

Continental Congress. In revolutionary France, theaters released from royal authority were required by the National Convention to stage dramas promoting republican virtues, a rule recalling Rousseau's theories about the effect of theatrical amusements on the passions. But the Declaration of the Rights of Man and Citizen guaranteed no rights to theatergoers or amusement seekers. Neither did the slave emancipation decrees of the French republic; nor the antislavery constitutions of Saint Domingue and Haiti. The British Abolition Act of 1833 detailed the labor owed by ex-slaves and the compensation due to ex-masters in the West Indies but accorded no pleasurable rights to freedpeople. And American moralists continued to warn against theaters as sinful places. An *Essay on the Stage* by the minister Timothy Dwight decried the sensuous experience inspired by pretense. The theater offered "visionary delusions" that "excite too strongly the passions" in an "empty waste of feeling," wrote Dwight. "If the Stage, immoral and polluted, impious and usurping . . . afford amusement to a moral being, his conscience must be seared with a hot iron."[42]

By the era of the Civil War, the theater was no longer an illicit place. Both the many and the few, black and white, were unrepentant spectators in playhouses that reflected the contradictions of American democracy. If nothing else, the presence of the martyred Lincoln at Ford's Theatre indicated that moral beings were theatergoers. Indeed, the value of the playhouse had interested none other than Adam Smith, who had endorsed the pleasures of the masses almost a century earlier, dissenting against austere religiosity and denying a necessary conflict between amusement seeking and profit making, in *The Wealth of Nations*. "To amuse and divert the people," reasoned Smith, liberal states should encourage "gaiety of public diversions": "all sorts of dramatic representations and exhibitions, would easily dissipate . . . melancholy and gloomy humour."[43]

Yet across America, on both sides of the Mason-Dixon line, the races were kept separate at the theater. Black people sat apart in the upper galleries, or were excluded entirely, by custom, and, in some southern cities, by law. As hybrid places—private associations open to the public—theaters were subject to municipal authority, but property owners possessed the liberty to exclude or restrict at will. On the eve of the war, even the Massachusetts Supreme Judicial Court had upheld the color line at theaters, adhering to the common law tradition that recognized no right of amusement seeking.[44] After emancipation, statehouses controlled by Radical Republicans banned distinctions of race and color in public conveyances and resorts. But the legislation was evaded simply by tickets stating that proprietors had discretion to exclude anyone. Nor did it carry a positive grant of rights; it regulated places rather than entitling persons.[45]

In appealing for the supplement, former slaves told of their unfreedom at the theater. "We cannot go into a decent place at the theater," wrote a member of the Virginia House of Delegates, Richard G. L. Paige, who was born into slavery in Norfolk, and had lived free in Boston before returning to the South after the war. Sometimes, he explained, there was not even a "separate place in the hall for 'niggers.'" An Alabama freedman spoke about wrongs of sex, protesting that, cordoned off in the upper galleries, "colored women, no matter . . . of how much dignity and refinement . . . sit among the harlots." Emancipation yielded no parity in pleasurable market exchange as a token of common humanity.[46]

The relation of freedom to amusement seeking had not always been a premise of antislavery doctrine. Ascetic injunctions had figured in abolitionism since its emergence. In 1796, a convention of American Abolition Societies had issued an address "To the Free Africans and other free People of color" warning against vicious dissipation: "Avoid frolicking, and amusements which lead to expense and idleness." That doctrine persisted, particularly shaping indictments of the theater as inimical to productive labor and generative of evil passions. According to a lesson imparted by an 1836 report of the Massachusetts Anti-Slavery Society, the playhouse was a place of "sin and misery." Abstain from "sensuous indulgences," taught *An Address to the Free Colored People of the United States* presented by the Anti-Slavery Convention of American Women: "We entreat you not to expend your earnings at theatres and other places of idle amusement." The virtuous were said to abhor both slavery and the temptations available to a theatergoer.[47]

But the deepening of sectional crisis gave new meaning to the theater as a public place. Abolitionists appreciatively noted its political influence. "The theater, bowing to its audience, has preached immediate emancipation," declared Wendell Phillips at an 1853 meeting of the Massachusetts Anti-Slavery Society, held in Boston's Melodeon, a hall used for entertainments, lectures, and concerts. By then *Uncle Tom's Cabin* had become a sensation in theaters across the North, generating abolitionism, as Phillips said, with "all the radical doctrines and all the startling scenes. . . . Slaves shoot their hunters to loud applause." In a column entitled "Satan Transformed," the *Liberator* affirmed that the "harlotry" of the playhouse had been "exorcized by the spirit of Anti-Slavery." But the exorcism had started earlier, in 1821, when a drama company of free black men created the African Grove Theatre in New York City and staged plays for two years, beginning with Shakespeare's *Richard III*, in which an ex-slave played the tormented king. The repertoire included scenes of southern bondage—*Life in a Slave-Market in Charleston* and *Low Life of Slaves in a Cotton Field*—and a drama about a Caribbean slave rebellion, written by the troupe's leader, the West Indian black ship steward William Alexander Brown, which was titled *King Shotaway: Founded on Facts Taken from the Insurrection of the Caravs in the Island of St. Vincent, Written from Experience.*[48]

And asceticism formed only one strain of the antislavery moral ethos. Scarcely all abolitionists associated emancipation with the renunciation of amusement and sensuous pleasures. Consider the longing expressed by Frederick Douglass to be a spectator at a public amusement as a right of free personhood. Writing from England in 1846, he contrasted his own unhappy pursuit of pleasure as an ex-slave in America with the expanse of his liberty abroad. Out on the Boston Common, he recalled, he had been turned away from a place of public amusement—not a theater but a menagerie: "I had long desired to see such a collection. . . . Never having had an opportunity while a slave, I resolved to seize this, my first, since my escape. . . . I was met and told by the door-keeper, in a harsh and contemptuous tone, 'We don't allow niggers in here.'" Yet everywhere in England, wrote Douglass, his "equal humanity" was unquestioned, and he was admitted into "any place of worship, instruction, or amusement, on equal terms." Douglass reveled, "Lo! The chattel becomes a man."[49]

A decade earlier, the Unitarian preacher William Ellery Channing had offered a meditation on antislavery principles of happiness. His 1835 treatise, *Slavery*, explained the meaning of happiness as a human right—a right of all persons as moral beings and a negation of a system of bondage that denied slaves a will of their own, as nothing but instruments of the pleasure of masters. "Airs from heaven . . . fan such a flame in the mind of Channing," Sumner later observed, "and the appeal is felt by the world."[50]

Slavery, wrote Channing, "calls us to inquire into the foundation, nature, and extent of human rights, into the distinction between a person and a thing, into the true relations of man and man . . . and above all into the true dignity and indestructible claims of a moral being." As an article of chattel property—a brute always working as an "instrument of another's will and pleasure," a thing "forced and broken into a tool to another's physical enjoyment"—the slave was a creature stripped of the "fundamental right to . . . seek his own happiness." Therefore slavery struck at man's "divine faculties" as a moral agent and the "foundation of human rights in human nature." Every human being, Channing stated, "was plainly made for an End in Himself. He is a Person, not a Thing. He is an End, not a mere Instrument or Means. He was made for his own virtue and happiness." His thoughts on the human right to happiness echoed the terms of Kant's idea of a categorical imperative.[51]

But what was happiness? Surely it lay in rights of proprietorship, family life, and free labor, as well as in dignity and social belonging based on "moral worth," Channing taught. Yet the deepest root was perfectibility, the right of a free person to self-culture—"the most sacred right of human nature."[52]

In his 1839 treatise, *Self-Culture*, Channing explained why theatergoing and amusement seeking were antislavery sources of happiness, emancipatory pursuits creating "pleasures worthy of men." He explicitly disowned asceticism, declaring that "public amusements" and "dramatic performances" and "pleasures" elevated human beings above brutes and that only a slave was raised to be a "mere drudge" and "do nothing but work."[53]

Notably, Channing's argument anticipated the moral critique of acquisitive self-denial, the image of the free laborer as an *"ascetic* but *productive* slave,"* which Marx would offer in his *Economic and Philosophic Manuscripts of 1844*: "The less you go to the theatre, the dance hall, the public house; the less you think, love, theorize, sing, paint . . . the more you save, the greater becomes your treasure."[54]

That was Channing's point as he condemned the "chains of bodily necessity." He argued that self-culture, "the expansion of the free illimitable soul," required much more than the right of human beings to work and save in pursuing happiness, "to toil for their animal subsistence, and to minister to the luxury and elevation of the few." He did not deny that impurities degraded the stage. But he defended the essential virtue of the theater in liberating the spirit, diffusing happiness to the "mass of the people," conveying "grand, beautiful, touching conceptions," and producing "a pleasure at once exquisite and refined" as the audience was "electrified by a sublime thought."[55]

It was precisely the sublimity of the theater that George Downing had felt as a spectator touched by *The Merchant of Venice*: the exquisite pleasure in the poet's conception and the exquisite anguish of Shylock's condition—the memory of such emotions infused his appeal for the supplement.

The antislavery ethos of human rights that Channing expressed thus resonated in vindications of the supplement. It emerged in the remonstrance of black petitioners that their unfreedom as amusement seekers violated their human dignity. So, too, it echoed in the argument of Sumner that pursuing happiness at the theater—once an act of doubtful virtue—constituted a right of man.[56] And it horrified former slave owners, who claimed in Congress that it was "disgusting to us, in our social relationships," to envision releasing freedpeople from labor to become, of their own volition, "partakers of common joys."[57]

At stake was nothing less than the emancipation that Douglass had sought by viewing a menagerie on Boston Common: "Lo! The chattel becomes a man." Or as an Alabama ex-slave, a Baptist preacher, wrote in appealing for the supplement as a guarantee of his human status: "We are men . . . having the same faculties . . . the same aspirations, passions, and weaknesses as other men."[58] The supplementary legislation codified a profound change in moral perception.

IN THE EYES OF statesmen opposed to the supplement, the theater clause appeared as both tragedy and farce: tragedy in violating the constitutional limits set on the sovereignty of the nation-state, but farce in equating theatergoing with the rights of life, liberty, and property. Ire and irony filled the speeches delivered by lawmakers on both sides of the sectional divide who argued that nothing in the Constitution could be construed to guarantee amusement seeking at a theater as a birthright of free men.

A diatribe by Senator Garrett Davis of Kentucky summed up the views of former slaveholders. "It is preposterous to claim authority for the passage of such a measure," he claimed, "an enactment as offensive, as oppressive, and annoying . . . in all the old slave States." Abolition of property in man did not involve "theatrical companies," whose members retained a "right to make the association exclusive." The supplement was "violative of the universal rights and powers of private associations" belonging to property owners. "How stale the Constitution has become, how low it has sunk," Davis fulminated. "Why do they not burn it by the public hangman?"[59]

Especially abhorrent to legislators from the old slave states was the prospect of persons who had been chattel property liberated from labor to become theatergoers. Freed slaves should not be "associates in pleasure," said a Georgia senator. It was unimaginable to a Kentucky congressman that a "well-dressed negro with money in his pocket shall call and demand entertainment." As a former Confederate leader, Congressman Hiram P. Bell of Georgia, objected, entitling former slaves to pursue amusement at a playhouse would "divert the negro from the pursuit of remunerative labor and honest industry."[60] The condemnation of masterless men as theater-goers echoed the censure of idle rogues centuries before.

Opposition came also from antislavery men, who argued that the the-ater guarantee lacked constitutional foundation and made a travesty of both abolition and natural rights principles. Speaking for Republicans who denied that the authority of Congress reached to public amusements staged on private property throughout the states, Senator Lot Morrill of Maine asked incredulously: "What is a theater? A place of amusement. May a man be said to be denied a natural right who is denied admission there? . . . Is it an incident, a badge of slavery . . . if you cannot show that you have got a free ticket under the authority of the United States to a the-ater?" Scathingly, he continued, "How many shameless shams in the way of amusements and questionable shows . . . are here to be made reputable by the presence of the authority of the United States?" The antislavery amendments granted Congress no power "to make freedmen freemen" as amusement seekers: "to open the doors of the theater, owned by a corpo-ration . . . in order to perfect the freedom of the former slaves!"[61]

As the debate continued, the enactment of state civil rights acts ban-ning discrimination in public places based on race and color deepened opposition to supplementary congressional legislation, as did rulings by the Supreme Court limiting the scope of the antislavery amendments. While black officials in the South reported that the state protections went unenforced in local courts — "a dead letter on . . . statute books" — states' rights men in Congress maintained that guarantees of national citizen-ship were irrelevant to theaters. As an Ohio Democrat scoffed, "a man's life does not depend on whether he can go into a theater or not; his liberty does not depend on whether he can go into a theater or not; his property does not depend on whether he can go into a theater or not." The protest against the theater clause also drew on the *Slaughterhouse Cases* of 1873, in which the Supreme Court circumscribed the prohibition on slavery under the Thirteenth Amendment and the entitlements of national citizenship under the Fourteenth Amendment. Presciently, Senator Matthew Hale

Carpenter of Wisconsin, who had prevailed as counsel in *Slaughterhouse*, conjectured that the Commerce Clause might be tried instead, "perhaps, upon the theory that a cheerful mind is favorable to enterprise" and that every person transacting business "should be admitted to theaters and other places of public amusements in the States wherein he might be temporarily sojourning." Sardonically, however, he added, "Such provision in regard to theaters would be somewhat fantastic as a regulation of commerce." Another unserious proposal was to replace the theater guarantee with a church provision in keeping with divine law.[62]

The very expansiveness of the protected rights and places evoked ridicule. Was the purpose to safeguard the pursuit of happiness as a human right at all forms of theater and all places of public amusement, no matter how base? Was the intent to reach the circus and menagerie and cockfight and wax-work exhibition and variety show? Such a project of emancipation was again and again said to demean Congress. Sarcasm dripped from the lips of Senator William Thomas Hamilton of Maryland as he asked where an amusement seeker could not be excluded:

> What is it that this clause does embrace? Come let us know. . . . What does the language mean? What can it mean — 'other places of public amusement?' A Fourth of July celebration, a barbecue, a harangue, an exhibition of large men, of small men, or of fat men? A large woman, a small woman, a fat woman? Or it may be a collection of monkeys, or a cage of snakes?. . . The exhibition of the Punch and Judy show? . . . . What is a 'public amusement?' . . . Does it mean a menagerie? Does it mean a circus?

Lingering on the question of the menagerie, he inquired if an animal owner would be punished for "taking around his lions or tigers or zebras or monkeys" while choosing to "exclude a negro." He decried the "sweeping intention," wondering at the outcome if public amusements lawful in some places were forbidden as licentious in others.[63]

The theater itself seemed a category full of ambiguity—but insignificant. "This is trifling with great subjects. Theaters!. . . This is a very strange subject, and we must see the folly . . . in its thorough absurdity," said Senator Hamilton, pointing out that there were all sorts of theaters, "as various as there are tastes and fancies . . . high and low, pure and vulgar." Irately, he asked, "What do you call a theater? What kind of a theater is it to be?" — "variety theaters" or "theaters comique" or "the kind in which Booth is now performing . . . ?" But none was a realm of inalienable rights. "A theater is not . . . a substantial of life. . . . The theater is for amusement."[64]

The argument was that the supplement would enact "terror" in transforming even a theatergoer into a bearer of human rights. "There is nothing . . . to be left untouched," as Hamilton lamented, warning against the "fanatics" in the North who claimed to speak on behalf of freedpeople: "If there were Africans upon this floor now I would appeal to them and tell them to depend rather upon their old masters at home."[65] Surely the words were meant not only for legislators in Congress but for former slaves seeking greater freedom.

IN THE HOUSE OF Representatives, abstract claims about the supplement became personal and palpable, for there black statesmen and former slaveholders argued as equals about the nature of human rights. The Fifteenth Amendment brought freedmen to the Capitol, while the amnesty law allowed officers of the Confederacy to return to the reconstructed Congress. The encounter of men with such opposing experiences on the floor of the House deepened the conflict over the supremacy of the national government and the ambit of slavery abolition.

"Liberty, Equality, and Fraternity . . . the watchword of people seeking a higher plane of manhood and a broader comprehension of the earthly destiny of the human family": that was the language of rights spoken by the slaveborn Florida congressman Josiah Walls in justifying the supplement. The Georgia congressman Alexander Stephens, the former vice president of the Confederate States, spoke differently. Emancipation required "no leveling of the population . . . no equality and fraternity," said Stephens, who had once called slavery the "corner-stone" of the South, but now explained that he was "properly weighing every word that may be uttered by me" and that justice had been done concerning "the status of the African race" — "This thorn in the flesh, so long the cause of irritation between the States, is now out for all time to come."[66]

The outcry of the freeborn black congressman from South Carolina, Alonzo Ransier, condemned the violation of inalienable rights. "We are circumscribed within the narrowest possible limits on every hand, disowned, spit upon, and outraged in a thousand ways." Just as slaves had been "made less than human," so freed persons were not yet endowed with "ordinary privileges attaching to them as human beings."[67]

Ransier knew well the limits of freedom and the outrage against human dignity. Less than a year after the Civil War's end he had been set apart as a spectator, on account of color, in the gallery of Congress—just as in a theater. Alongside Ransier sat George Downing, and both joined in a letter of protest, which explained that the grievants wrote on behalf of delegations of black men from across the country who had come to Washington to witness the debates on the Fourteenth Amendment and seek "impartial liberty." But at the Senate a doorkeeper had stopped them, with "orders not to admit colored persons but to direct them to a particular spot." The letter objected: "The delegation cannot in self respect consent to be colonized."[68]

So Ransier argued anew, less than a decade later, as a member of Congress speaking on behalf of the supplement, quoting from *Macbeth* in warning against the apparitions that would haunt lawmakers who withheld rights of "practical freedom." Whether born slave or free, Ransier protested, colored people were not entitled to "engage in the 'pursuit of happiness' as rational beings." He spoke directly after Alexander Stephens, explaining that he felt "called upon to say a word." He said that Congress must protect the rights belonging to all persons simply by reason of being human: "Nature's blackest blot—American slavery—no longer curses our land; yet, sir, a relic of it remains."[69]

Such arguments—from the lips of a black man—were anathema to redeemers of the South. Consider the bitter colloquy in January 1874 between Ransier and a Virginian, John Harris, who was dilating about white supremacy, states' rights, and the wrongs of entitling ex-slaves to be amusement seekers.

> MR. HARRIS: . . . What would the elder patriots of our country think
> if they could come on earth and find the American Congress
> legislating as to how persons . . . should sit in the theaters. . . .
> I say there is not one gentleman upon this floor who can honestly
> say he really believes that the colored man is created his equal.
> MR. RANSIER: I can.
> MR. HARRIS: . . . Of course you can; but I am speaking to the white
> men of the House . . . . It was born in the children of the South;
> born in our ancestors . . . that the colored man was inferior to
> the white.
> MR. RANSIER: I deny that.
> MR. HARRIS: . . . I do not allow you to interrupt me. Sit down. I am
> talking to white men. I am talking to gentlemen.[70]

Thus the debate on the supplement became a form of revolutionary drama as the conflict of words—and the antagonism of wills—expressed the upheaval of emancipation. Yet the statesmen once enslaved did not dwell on the past; they offered no accounts of the experiences revealed in slave narratives, no memories of the debauchery at the will of the master, the inhuman theater of the auction block, or the moments of stolen happiness, of slaves secretly dancing in the starlight. Rather, they spoke of their rights aspirations. "Yes, the time is at hand when you must cease to take us for cringing slaves. . . . You talk about humanity. . . . Gracious Heaven!" said the South Carolina freedman, Congressman Joseph Rainey. "The negro will never rest until he gets his rights."[71]

That the debate over the outcome of abolition occurred in a Congress where ex-slaves and ex-masters orated as equals about the emancipatory decrees of the nation-state marked a turning point in the development of the human rights tradition. A freeborn black congressman from Alabama, James Rapier, explained the threshold that had been crossed, using an allusion to the theater. "Most of us have seen the play of Rip Van Winkle, who was said to have slept twenty years in the Katskill Mountains." That was the Southerner's situation—his "life and actions . . . illustrate this character," said Rapier, who had grown wealthy as a cotton planter after the war, capitalizing on the revolution that had destroyed the slaveholder's world. "He, Bourbon-like, comes back saying the very same things he used to say, and swearing by the same gods. . . . He seems not to know that the ideas which he so ably advanced for so many years were by the war swept away, along with the system of slavery. . . . And worse to him than all, he finds the negro here, not only a listener but a participant in debate." Denying the authority of apostles of slavery to oppose the supplement—condemning the second coming of Alexander Stephens—the freeborn black congressman from South Carolina, Robert Elliott, a typesetter who had become a lawyer, cried out: "it is not from him that the American House of Representatives should take lessons in matters touching human rights."[72]

As the debate drew to a close in the House, in February of 1875, its meaning was stated anew. "The mills of the gods grind slowly, but surely and exceeding fine," affirmed the South Carolinian, Richard Harvey Cain, a freeborn black man. "There are periods in the history of nations and of peoples when it is necessary that men belonging to a race or races whose rights and interests are at stake . . . vindicate their rights. . . . My understanding of human rights . . . is all rights to all men. . . . All rights, all liberty, all law, all government, all progress, all science, all arts, all literature."[73] From an emancipatory creed of human rights derived the rebuke to the living relics of the slave South.

A decade after the end of the Civil War, Congress at last enacted the supplement. Some of the final words on its logic belonged to the theatergoer, Congressman Rapier, who simply said, "This question resolves itself into this: either I am a man or I am not a man."[74]

AFTER THE YEAS and nays had been cast, George Downing wrote matter-of-factly of the fateful event to his sons: "The civil rights bill has passed, I will send you a paper tomorrow." Downing had begun petitioning for the supplement in 1871, writing on behalf of people with "dark skins" to Sumner, who did not live long enough to see antislavery Republican radicalism prevail for the last time in Congress. Not a single Democrat supported the enactment in either house.[75]

The final act of the supplement is well known. In 1883, in the *Civil Rights Cases*, the Supreme Court struck it down as unconstitutional, without foundation in either the Thirteenth Amendment or the Fourteenth Amendment. Two of the cases before the Court concerned the violation of the right to be a theatergoer. "Where does any slavery or servitude, or badge of either, arise from such an act of denial?" asked the Court. "What has it to do with the question of slavery?"[76]

In fact, the kinds of theater in question in the *Civil Rights Cases* had everything to do with slavery. In one case, a black porter named George M. Tyler was turned away from a program of "slave songs"—performed by the Jubilee Singers, a troupe of freedpeople from Fisk University—at the door of the dress circle of Maguire's theater in San Francisco. A letter of grievance from "A Colored Man" described why the spirituals would give happiness to amusement seekers who had been slaves: "It is but natural that their own race should desire to hear them . . . particularly as many colored residents of this city have heard and joined in singing the same melodies on the plantation." In another case, a freedman named William R. Davis was cast out of the Grand Opera House in New York City. The play was *Ruy Blas*, a drama by Victor Hugo about a slave disguised as a nobleman who wins the love of a queen. Edwin Booth, the brother of Lincoln's assassin, played the slave.[77]

But to uphold the supplement, the Court famously ruled, "would be running the slavery argument into the ground." It did not consider whether the plenary power of Congress over interstate commerce authorized the statute, explaining that this source of constitutional power had not been invoked. Instead, adhering to the interpretation first offered in the Memphis case of 1875, the Court found that nothing of bondage endured in the denial of a theatergoer's freedom: "Such an act of refusal has nothing to do with slavery or involuntary servitude."[78]

Less well known is the eulogy that Frederick Douglass delivered on the supplement. Douglass spoke bitterly of human rights and slavery and the rule of law. "O for a Supreme Court which shall be as true, as vigilant, as active and exacting in maintaining law enacted for the protection of human rights as in other days was that Court for the destruction of human rights!" But he grew lyrical in foreseeing the supplement's emancipatory legacy, quoting from Shakespeare's *As You Like It*: "There are tongues in trees, books, in the running brooks, — sermons in stones. This law, though dead, did speak."[79]

A century after the downfall of slavery, the ethos of the supplement was resurrected. Under Title II of the Civil Rights Act of 1964, Congress entitled all persons, irrespective of race, color, religion, or national origin, to the full and equal enjoyment of the theater as well as other places of public amusement — motion picture houses, concert halls, stadiums, and arenas. Notably, the 1964 act was grounded not in the antislavery Thirteenth Amendment but in the Commerce Clause, and, should state action be involved, in the Fourteenth Amendment.[80] The theatergoer's freedom would owe to commodity exchange among the states. Paradoxically, as America celebrated the centennial of slave emancipation, human rights newly came to amusement seekers by virtue of the untrammeled flow of commerce.

NOTES

I thank Craig Becker, Dan Edelstein, Walter Johnson, Dirk Hartog, Melissa Lane, Timothy Murphy, Emily Remus, Daniel Rodgers, Emma Rothschild, Leslie Rowland, John Stauffer, and Kristin Warbasse; and participants at seminars at the Charles Warren Center, the Princeton University Center for Human Values, the Princeton University Modern America Workshop, the University of Virginia Law School, and the Richards Civil War Era Center at Penn State University.

1. *Charge to Grand Jury — Civil Rights Act*, 30 F. Cas. 1005 (Circuit Court, Western District Tennessee, 1875). See "Current Topics," *Albany Law Journal: A Weekly Record of the Law and the Lawyers*, March 27, 1875, 197.

2. "An Act to Protect All Citizens in Their Civil and Legal Rights," *U.S. Statutes*

at Large 18, part 3, chap. 114 (Washington, D.C.: Government Printing Office, 1875), 335–37. The 1875 act also entitled all citizens to serve on juries in all courts. It differed from early postbellum state legislation that banned discrimination but created no positive right to seek amusement in public.

3. The formal title was "A bill supplementary to an act entitled 'An act to protect all citizen of the United States in their civil rights, and to furnish means for their vindication,' passed April 9, 1866," *Congressional Globe*, 41st Cong., 2nd sess., 1870, 3434; 42nd Cong., 1st sess., 1871, 21. On black petitioners' appeals, see, for example, *Congressional Globe*, 42nd Cong., 2nd sess., 1872, 429–33. Scholarship on the Civil Rights Act of 1875 is extensive; for example, see L. E. Murphy, "The Civil Rights Law of 1875," *Journal of Negro History* 12, no. 2 (1927): 110–27; James M. McPherson, "Abolitionists and the Civil Rights Act of 1875," *Journal of American History* 52, no. 3 (1965): 493–510; John Hope Franklin, "The Enforcement of the Civil Rights Act of 1875," *Prologue* 6 (1974): 225–35; Eric Foner, *Reconstruction: America's Unfinished Revolution, 1863–1877* (New York: Harper and Row, 1988), 504–5, 532–34, 552–56); Joseph William Singer, "No Right to Exclude: Public Accommodations and Private Property," *Northwestern University Law Review* 90, no. 4 (1996): 1283–1497; Kate Masur, *An Example for All the Land: Emancipation and the Struggle over Equality in Washington, D.C.* (Chapel Hill: University of North Carolina Press, 2010), 224–32; Stephen Kantrowitz, *More Than Freedom: Fighting for Black Citizenship in a White Republic, 1829–1889* (New York: Penguin, 2012), 389–91, 412. See Bruce A. Ragsdale and Joel D. Treese, *Black Americans in Congress, 1870–1989* (Washington, D.C.: Office of History and Preservation, 1990).

4. *Civil Rights Cases*, 109 U.S. 3 (1883). The 1875 Memphis case anticipated the Supreme Court's ruling in the *Civil Rights Cases*. Public accommodations provisions of the 1964 act, which include theaters, are codified at 42 U.S.C. Sec. 2000a. See George Rutherglen, "The Thirteenth Amendment, the Power of Congress, and the Shifting Sources of Civil Rights Law," *Columbia Law Review* 112, no. 7 (2012): 1551–84; Robert John Kaczorowski, *The Politics of Judicial Interpretation: The Federal Courts, Department of Justice, and Civil Rights* (New York: Fordham University Press, 2005). In enacting the 1964 Civil Rights Act, Congress relied principally on the Commerce Clause, while also drawing ancillary support from the Fourteenth Amendment, but the U.S. Supreme Court upheld the legislation only under the commerce power. See *Heart of Atlanta Motel, Inc. v. United States*, 379 U.S. 241 (1964).

5. On the development of rights doctrine, see Brian Tierney, *The Idea of Natural Rights: Studies in Natural Rights, Natural Law, and Church Law, 1150–1625* (Atlanta: Scholars Press, 1997); C. B. MacPherson, *The Political Theory of Possessive Individualism: Hobbes to Locke* (1962; New York: Oxford University Press, 2011); David Brion Davis, *The Problem of Slavery in the Age of Revolution, 1770–1820* (New York: Oxford University Press, 1975); Amy Dru Stanley, *From Bondage to Contract: Wage Labor, Marriage, and the Market in the Age of Slave Emancipation* (New York: Cambridge University Press, 1998).

6. Hannah Arendt, *The Origins of Totalitarianism* (1951; New York: Harcourt, 2004), 290–302. On the scholarly controversy over the historical origins of modern human rights doctrine, see Jeffrey Wasserstrom, Lynn Hunt, and Marilyn B. Young, eds.,

Human Rights and Revolutions (Lanham, Md.: Rowman and Littlefield, 2000); Lynn Hunt, *Inventing Human Rights: A History* (New York: W. W. Norton, 2007); Charles R. Beitz, *The Idea of Human Rights* (New York: Oxford University Press, 2009); Samuel Moyn, *The Last Utopia: Human Rights in History* (Cambridge: Harvard University Press, 2010); Robin Blackburn, *The American Crucible: Slavery, Emancipation, and Human Rights* (New York: Verso, 2011); Jenny S. Martinez, *The Slave Trade and the Origins of International Human Rights Law* (New York: Oxford University Press, 2012); Eric D. Weitz, "Self-Determination: How a German Enlightenment Idea Became the Slogan of National Liberation and a Human Right," *American Historical Review* 120, no. 2 (April 2015); Akira Iriye, Petra Goedde, and William I. Hitchcock, eds., *The Human Rights Revolution: An International History* (New York: Oxford University Press, 2012).

7. Moyn finds that "'human rights' entered the English language in the 1940s ... unceremoniously, even accidentally." Moyn, *Last Utopia*, 44. Blackburn finds that the "modern term 'human rights' was rarely used but anti-slavery advocates often denounced the institution in the name of 'common humanity' or some similar locution." Blackburn, *American Crucible*, 480. But Martinez finds that opponents of the slave trade "conceptualized the issue in terms of human rights." Martinez, *Slave Trade*, 17.

8. "An Act to Protect All Citizens in Their Civil and Legal Rights," (hereafter "Supplement"), 336. See Laurent Dubois, *Avengers of the New World: The Story of the Haitian Revolution* (Cambridge: Belknap Press, 2004); Davis, *Problem of Slavery*; Blackburn, *American Crucible*; Lynn Hunt, ed., *The French Revolution and Human Rights: A Brief Documentary History* (Boston: Bedford Press, 1996), 1–32. On emancipation, commerce, and public life, see Rebecca J. Scott, "Public Rights and Private Commerce: A Nineteenth-Century Atlantic Creole Itinerary," *Current Anthropology* 48, no. 2 (2007): 237–56; and on theatrical life in Saint-Domingue, see Bernard Camier and Laurent Dubois, "Voltaire, Zaïre, Dessalines: Le Théâtre des Lumières dans l'Atlantique français," *Revue d'histoire moderne et contemporaine* 54, no.4 (2007): 36–69. On the public sphere, equality and the commodity form, see William H. Sewell Jr., "Connecting Capitalism to the French Revolution: The Parisian Promenade and the Origins of Civic Equality in Eighteenth-Century France, *Critical Historical Studies* 1, no. 1 (2014): 5–46.

9. *Journals of the Continental Congress: The Articles of Association*: October 20, 1774, http://avalon.law.yale.edu/18th_century/contcong_10-20-74.asp; Worthington Chauncey Ford, ed., *Journals of the Continental Congress: 1774–1789* (Washington, D.C.: Government Printing Office , 1904–37), 12 (1778): 1001–2; Heather S. Nathans, *Early American Theatre from the Revolution to Thomas Jefferson: Into the Hands of the People* (New York: Cambridge University Press, 2003), 36–38, 44. On slaves as bestial things, see David Brion Davis, *Inhuman Bondage: The Rise and Fall of Slavery in the New World* (New York: Oxford University Press, 2006), 1–35, 178–79, 198. The entitlement to security of person and property stretches back to the medieval era; see Tierney, *Idea of Natural Rights*, 79–89, 187–88, 230–40, 296–97. On aspirations of slaves and freedpeople to assert autonomy through pleasure and amusement, see Saidiya Hartman, *Scenes of Subjection: Terror, Slavery, and Self-Making in Nineteenth-Century America* (New

York: Oxford University Press, 1997), 17–78; Stephanie M. H. Camp, "The Pleasure of Resistance: Enslaved Women and Body Politics in the Plantation South, 1830–1861," *Journal of Southern History* 68, no. 3 (2002): 533–72; Tera W. Hunter, *To 'Joy My Freedom: Southern Black Women's Lives and Labors after the Civil War* (Cambridge: Harvard University Press, 1997); Daphne A. Brooks, *Bodies in Dissent: Spectacular Performances of Race and Freedom, 1850–1910* (Durham: Duke University Press, 2006); Camier and Dubois, "Voltaire, Zaïre, Dessalines."

10. The Universal Declaration of Human Rights states, in Article 27, "Everyone has the right freely to participate in the cultural life of the community, to enjoy the arts," http://www.un.org/en/documents/udhr/.

11. On the supplement and the limits of Reconstruction, see C. Vann Woodward, *The Burden of Southern History* (Baton Rouge: Louisiana State University Press, 1993), 78–87; William Gillette, *Retreat from Reconstruction, 1869–1879* (Baton Rouge: Louisiana State University Press, 1982), 259–79; Foner, *Reconstruction*, 553–56; Franklin, "Enforcement of the Civil Rights Act." According to Woodward, "equality was a far more revolutionary aim than freedom," since it surpassed abolition; see Woodward, *Burden*, 79. My point is that expanding freedom's scope to include amusement as a human right constituted a revolutionary redefinition of rights. On equal citizenship and public space, see Rebecca J. Scott, "Public Rights, Social Equality, and the Conceptual Roots of the *Plessy* Challenge," *Michigan Law Review* 106, no. 6 (2008): 777–804; Rebecca J. Scott, *Degrees of Freedom: Louisiana and Cuba after Slavery* (Cambridge: Harvard University Press, 2005), 43–45; Masur, *An Example*.

12. Jürgen Habermas, "The Concept of Human Dignity and the Realistic Utopia of Human Rights," in *The Crisis of the European Union: A Response* (Cambridge, UK: Polity, 2012), 90. See Rebecca J. Scott, "Dignité/ Dignidade: Organizing against Threats to Dignity in Societies after Slavery," in *Understanding Human Dignity*, ed. Christopher McCrudden (New York: Oxford University Press, 2013), 61–77; David Kretzmer and Eckart Klein, eds., *The Concept of Human Dignity in Human Rights Discourse* (New York: Klumer International Law, 2002); George Kateb, *Human Dignity* (Cambridge: Harvard University Press, 2011); Patrick O. Gudridge, "Privileges and Permissions: The Civil Rights Act of 1875," *Law and Philosophy* 8, no. 1 (1989): 83–130; Immanuel Kant, *Grounding for the Metaphysics of Morals*, trans. James W. Ellington (Indianapolis: Hackett, 1981), 34–40.

13. *Congressional Record*, 43rd Cong., 2nd sess., 1875, 947.

14. On prior antislavery usages of human rights language, see, for example, "The American Slave Trade"(1843), in *Speeches in Congress by Joshua R. Giddings* (Boston: John P. Jewett, 1853), 38; *Speech of Hon. Horace Mann, on the Right of Congress to Legislate for the Territories of the United States, and Its Duty to Exclude Slavery Therefrom* (Boston: J. Howe, 1848); *No Compromise on Human Rights: Speech of Hon. Charles Sumner*, March 7, 1866 (Washington, D.C.: Congressional Globe Office, 1866); "Speeches of Thaddeus Stevens on Reconstruction," *Globe*, 39th Cong., 1st sess., 1866, 535–38, 4304–5.; W. E. B. Du Bois, *The Suppression of the African Slave-Trade to the United States of America, 1638–1870* (New York: Russell and Russell, 1896), 94; Martinez, *Slave Trade*.

15. *Globe*, 42nd Cong., 2nd sess., 1871, 2.

16. *Record*, 43rd Cong., 1st sess., 1874, 1311–12; William Shakespeare, *Macbeth*, III, iv; *Journal of the House of Representatives of the State of South-Carolina, for the Regular Session of 1873–1874* (Columbia: State Printers, 1874), 19–20, 42, 168–69, 182–83, 191. See Thomas C. Holt, *Black over White: Negro Political Leadership in South Carolina during Reconstruction* (Urbana: University of Illinois Press, 1977), 96–97, 166–67; Steven Hahn, *A Nation under Our Feet: Black Political Struggles in the Rural South from Slavery to the Great Migration* (Cambridge: Harvard University Press, 2003), 260–61.

17. *Globe*, 42nd Cong., 2nd sess., 1872, 828, 901. On the galleries, see Masur, *An Example*, 91–97. On congressional power and the 1866 act, see Robert J. Kaczorowski, "To Begin the Nation Anew: Congress, Citizenship, and Civil Rights after the Civil War," *American Historical Review* 92, no. 1 (1987): 45–68.

18. *Globe*, 42nd Cong., 2nd sess., 1871–1872, 241, 242, 896, 901; "Supplement," 336. On early texts of the bill, see *Globe*, 41st Cong., 2nd sess., 1870, 3434; 42nd Cong., 1st sess., 1871, 21; 42nd Cong., 2nd sess., 1871, 244. On revisions, see *Globe*, 42nd Cong., 2nd sess., 1872, 453, 847, 899, 842. On an "emasculated" version passed in the Senate and rejected in the House in 1872, see ibid., 3705, 3727–43, 3762. The act's final text restated the limited version of 1872; see *Globe*, 42nd Cong., 2nd sess., 1872, 3730. On the supplement's legislative history, see Alfred Avins, "The Civil Rights Act of 1875: Some Reflected Light on the Fourteenth Amendment and Public Accommodations," *Columbia Law Review* 66, no. 5 (1966): 873–915; Foner, *Reconstruction*, 504–5, 532–34, 553–56. On its adoption as a compromise to avert voting rights legislation granting further executive authority to suspend habeus corpus, see Gillette, *Retreat from Reconstruction*, 280–99. On the overthrow of Republican rule in the South as the bill moved through Congress, see Hahn, *Nation under Our Feet*, chap. 6.

19. *Globe*, 42nd Cong., 2nd sess., 1872, 871, 874, 875, 844, 843; *Record*, 43rd Cong., 2nd sess., 1875, 956.

20. *Globe*, 42nd Cong., 2nd sess., 1872, 843, 844, 727, 729, 727. On antislavery and the Declaration of Independence, see Eric Foner, *The Fiery Trial: Abraham Lincoln and American Slavery* (New York: W. W. Norton, 2010), 65–72.

21. *Globe*, 42nd Cong., 2nd sess., 1872, 391. See Hartman, *Scenes of Subjection*, 163–68.

22. *Record*, 43rd Cong., 2nd sess., 1875, appendix, 113; *Globe*, 42nd Cong., 2nd sess., 1871, 242, 243.

23. Letter of Richard Greener to Sumner, Jan. 15, 1872, *The Papers of Charles Sumner* (Chadwyck-Healey, 1988), series I, reel 56; *Globe*, 42nd Cong., 2nd sess., 1872, 429–34, 448, 491, 517, 722. See "Civil Rights Meeting of Colored Citizens to Take Action Favoring Sumner's Supplementary Civil Rights," *Cleveland Morning Daily Herald*, January 24, 1872.

24. Letter of George T. Downing to Charles Sumner, Jan. 20, 1871, *Papers of Charles Sumner*, series I, reel 52; Letter of George T. Downing to Charles Sumner, Dec. 12, 1871, *Papers of Charles Sumner*, series I, reel 55.

25. *Globe*, 42nd Cong., 2nd sess., 1872, 429. On Quarles, see Nathan R. Johnston, *Looking Back from the Sunset Land: Or People Worth Knowing* (Oakland, Calif., 1898).

26. *Globe*, 42nd Cong., 2nd sess., 1872, 727. See also letter of Richard Greener to Sumner. On Belcher, see Eric Foner, ed., *Freedom's Lawmakers: A Dictionary of Black Officeholders during Reconstruction* (New York: Oxford University Press, 1993), 15–16.

27. Letter of London Kurdle to Sumner, Feb. 3, 1872, *Papers of Charles Sumner*, series I, reel 56.

28. *Globe*, 42nd Cong., 2nd sess., 1872, 383; Charles Sumner, *The Works of Charles Sumner*, vol. 14 (Boston: Lee and Shepard, 1870–83), 385.

29. *Globe*, 42nd Cong., 2nd sess., 1872, 381.

30. Letter of London Kurdle to Sumner, Feb. 3, 1872, *Papers of Charles Sumner*.

31. *Globe*, 42nd Cong., 2nd sess., 1872, 384, 382. On happiness and rational calculations, see Garry Wills, *Inventing America: Jefferson's Declaration of Independence* (New York: Doubleday, 1978), 229–58; Wai Chee Dimock, *Residues of Justice: Literature, Law, Philosophy* (Berkeley: University of California Press, 1997), 140–81. On the philosophes' debate, see Jean-Jacques Rousseau, *Politics and the Arts: Letter to M. D'Alembert on the Theatre*, trans. Allan Bloom (1758; Ithaca: Cornell University Press, 1960)

32. *Globe*, 42nd Cong., 2nd sess., 1872, 385.

33. Ibid., 383; *Record*, 43rd Cong., 2nd sess., 1875, 939; *Globe*, 42nd Cong., 2nd sess., 1871, 280; *Globe*, 42nd Cong., 2nd sess., 1872, 383, 764, 765; *Corfield v. Coryell*, 6 Fed. Cas. 546 (1823); Joseph Story, *Commentaries on the Law of Bailments: With Illustrations from the Civil and Foreign Law*, 4th ed. (Boston: Little, Brown, 1846); James Kent, *Commentaries on American Law*, ed. Oliver Wendell Holmes, 4 vols., 12th ed. (Boston: Little Brown, 1873). On licensing and state regulatory power, see William J. Novak, *The People's Welfare: Law and Regulation in Nineteenth-Century America* (Chapel Hill: University of North Carolina Press, 1996), 90–95.

34. *Globe*, 42nd Cong., 2nd sess., 1872, 727.

35. William Nevill Montgomerie Geary, *The Law of Theaters and Music-Halls: Including Contracts and Precedents of Contracts* (London: Stevens, 1885). On the theater, see Jean Christophe Agnew, *Worlds Apart: The Market and the Theater in Anglo-American Thought, 1550–1750* (New York: Cambridge University Press, 1986); Ann Fairfax Withington, *Toward a More Perfect Union: Virtue and the Formation of American Republics* (New York: Oxford University Press, 1991).

36. George T. Downing, "Christianity, Law, and Civil Rights," *Independent*, February 26, 1874. On Downing, see Letter of Frederick Douglass to Edwin M. Stanton, July 13, 1863, Tracy Collection, Connecticut Historical Society; S. A. M Washington, *George Thomas Downing: Sketch of His Life and Times* (Newport, R.I.: Milne Printery, 1910); Sumner, *Works of Charles Sumner*, vol. 14, 357; Kantrowitz, *More Than Freedom*, 35, 129, 134, 206–10, 248, 276–77, 335–58, 384–94. On the theater, see Lawrence Levine, *Highbrow/Lowbrow: The Emergence of Cultural Hierarchy in America* (Cambridge: Harvard University Press, 1988).

37. Downing, "Christianity, Law, and Civil Rights."

38. Ibid.

39. *Journals of the Continental Congress*, 1 (1774), 76, 78; *Journals of the Continental Congress*, 12 (1778), 1001; Geary, *Law of Theatres and Music Halls*, 7; Arthur Hornblow, *A History of Theatre in America from its Beginnings to the Present Time*, vol. 1 (Philadelphia:

J. B. Lippincott, 1919), 23–24. See Withington, *Toward a More Perfect Union*, xiv–xv, 12–54; David Scott Kasten, *Shakespeare after Theory* (New York: Routledge, 1999), 202–20.

40. Story, *Commentaries on the Law of Bailments*, 311, 487, 589; Joseph Chitty, *A Practical Treatise on the Law of Contracts, Not under Seal, and upon the Usual Defenses to Actions Thereon* (London: S. Sweet, 1834), 377–86. See Tierney, *Idea of Natural Rights*, 79–89, 187–88; Andrew Sandoval-Strausz, "Travelers, Strangers, and Jim Crow: Law, Public Accommodations, and Civil Rights in America," *Law and History Review* 23, no. 1 (2005): 53–94; Gregory S. Alexander and Eduardo M. Peñalver, *An Introduction to Property Theory* (New York: Cambridge University Press, 2012), 140.

41. Geary, *Law of Theatres and Music-Halls*, 1–34, quote at 18; "Vagabond Act of 1714," http://www.londonlives.org/browse.jsp?div=LMSMPS50136PS501360026. See Hornblow, *History of Theatre*, 343–44.

42. *Journals of the Continental Congress*, 12 (1778), 1001; Timothy Dwight, *An Essay on the Stage: In Which the Arguments in Its Behalf, and Those Against It Are Considered and Its Morality, Character, and Effects Illustrated* (London: Sharp, Jones, 1824), 54, 122, 129, 130; William Warland Clapp, *A Record of the Boston Stage* (Boston: James Munroe, 1853); 1801 Saint-Domingue Constitution, http://thelouvertureproject.org/index .php?title=Haitian_Constitution_of_1801_%28English%29; "An Act for the Abolition of Slavery throughout the British Colonies; for promoting the Industry of the Manumitted Slaves; and for Compensating the Persons hitherto Entitled to the Services of Such Slaves" (3&4 Will. IV, cap. 73), http://www.pdavis.nl/Legis_07.htm; Rousseau, *Politics and the Arts*. See Wendy Bellion, *Citizen Spectator: Art, Illusion, and Visual Perception in Early National America* (Chapel Hill: University of North Carolina Press, 2011); Frederick W. J. Hemmings, *Theater and State in France, 1760-1905* (New York: Cambridge University Press, 1994); Marvin A. Carlson, *Voltaire and the Theatre of the Eighteenth Century* (Westport: Greenwood Press, 1998), 97–120; Jeffrey Ravel, *The Contested Parterre: Public Theater and French Political Culture, 1680-1791* (Ithaca: Cornell University Press, 1999); Susan Maslan, *Revolutionary Acts: Theater, Democracy, and the French Revolution* (Baltimore: Johns Hopkins University Press, 2005); Laurent Dubois and John D. Garrigus, *Slave Revolution in the Caribbean, 1789-1804: A Brief History with Documents* (New York: Palgrave Macmillan, 2006), 120–25, 191–96; Dubois, *Avengers of the New World*; Thomas C. Holt, *The Problem of Freedom: Race, Labor, and Politics in Jamaica and Britain, 1832-1938* (Baltimore: Johns Hopkins University Press, 1991).

43. Adam Smith, *An Inquiry into the Nature and Causes of the Wealth of Nations* (1789; Chicago: University of Chicago Press, 1976), 5:i, 318. See Levine, *Highbrow/Lowbrow*, 6, 20–36, 56–57; Timothy Gilfoyle, *City of Eros: New York City, Prostitution, and the Commercialization of Sex, 1790-1920* (New York: W. W. Norton, 1992), 110–14; Gordon Wood, *Empire of Liberty: A History of the Early Republic, 1789-1815* (New York: Oxford University Press, 2009), 562–63; Nathans, *Early American Theatre*, 70; Michael Knox Beran, "Lincoln, *Macbeth*, and the Moral Imagination," *Humanitas* 11, no. 2 (1998): 4–21.

44. See Henry J. Leovy, *The Laws and General Ordinances of the City of New Orleans* (New Orleans: E. C. Wharton, 1857), 17; Hornblow, *History of Theater*, 343–44; *McCrea v. Marsh*, 78 Mass. 211 (1858); *Burton v. Scherpf*, 83 Mass. 133 (1861); "Places of Amusement—Rights of Ticket-Holders," *Albany Law Journal*, April 12, 1873, 225–26; Rose-

marie K. Bank, *Theater Culture in America, 1825–1860* (New York: Cambridge University Press, 1997), 50, 96–98; Leonard Curry, *The Free Black in Urban America: The Shadow of the Dream, 1800–1850* (Chicago: University of Chicago Press, 1981); Shane White, *Stories of Freedom in Black New York* (Cambridge: Harvard University Press, 2002), chap. 2; Ira Berlin, *Slaves without Masters: The Free Negro in the Antebellum South* (New York: Pantheon, 1974); August Meier and Elliot Rudwick, *From Plantation to Ghetto: An Interpretive History of American Negroes* (New York: Hill and Wang, 1966), 95; Max W. Turner and Frank R. Kennedy, "Exclusion and Segregation of Theater Patrons," *Iowa Law Review* 32, no. 4, (1947): 625–58.

45. In declaring an affirmative entitlement, the supplement differed from state legislation that barred discrimination; see, for example, "An Act Forbidding Unjust Discrimination on Account of Color or Race," *Acts and Resolves Passed by the General Court of Massachusetts, in the Year 1865* (Boston: Wright and Potter, 1865), chap., 277, 650; "An Act in Relation to Public Places of Amusement," *Acts and Resolves Passed by the General Court of Massachusetts, in the Year 1866* (Boston: Wright and Potter, 1866), chap., 252, 242; "Civil Rights," *The Revised Statute Laws of the State of Louisiana* (New Orleans: Republican Office, 1870), sec. 458, 93; "An Act to Enforce the Provisions of the Civil Rights Bill of the United States Congress, and to Secure to the People the Benefits of a Republican Government in this State," *Acts and Joint Resolutions of the General Assembly of the State of South Carolina, Part I* (Columbia: John W. Denny, 1870), no. 279, 387; "An Act to Provide for the Protection of Citizens in Their Civil and Political Rights," *New York Statutes at Large*, chapter 186, vol. 9 (1875), 583–84 (passed Apr. 9, 1873). See also Scott, "Public Rights, Social Equality"; Singer, "No Right to Exclude"; Masur, *An Example.*

46. *Globe*, 42nd Cong., 2nd sess., 1872, 726, 432. See Scott, "Dignité/Dignidade"; Camier and Dubois, "Voltaire, Zaïre, Dessalines"; Sewell, "Connecting Capitalism to the French Revolution"; Jürgen Habermas, *The Structural Transformation of the Public Sphere: An Inquiry into a Category of Bourgeois Society* (Cambridge: MIT Press, 1989), 36–37. On Paige, see *African American Legislators in Virginia*, Virginia General Assembly, Dr. Martin Luther King Jr., Memorial Commission, http://mlkcommission.dls .virginia.gov/lincoln/african_americans.html.

47. The American Convention for Promoting the Abolition of Slavery, *Minutes of the Proceedings of the Third Convention of Delegates from the Abolition Societies Established in Different Parts of the United States Assembled at Philadelphia, January 1, 1796* (Philadelphia: Zachariah Poulson, Jr., 1796), 14; *Fourth Annual Report of the Board of Managers of the Massachusetts Anti-Slavery Society* (Boston: Isaac Knapp, 1836), 31; *Proceedings of the Fourth New-England Anti-Slavery Convention, Held in Boston, May 30, 31, and June 1 and 2, 1837* (Boston: Isaac Knapp, 1837), 46–48; *Address to the Free Colored People of the United States* (Philadelphia: Matthew and Gunn, 1838), 8.

48. *Speech of Wendell Phillips, at the Melodeon, Thursday Evening, Jan. 27, 1853* (Boston: Printed for the American Anti-Slavery, 1853), 8, 17; "Satan Transformed," *Liberator*, November 4, 1853; "'Uncle Tom' on the Stage," *Liberator*, September 9, 1853; Parker Pillsbury, "Uncle Tom's Cabin at a Boston Theatre," *Liberator*, December 14, 1852. See

James Ford Rhodes, *History of the United States*, vol. 5 (New York: Macmillan, 1904), 116, 211–12, 425–27; Justin Winsor and Clarence Jewett, eds., *The Memorial History of Boston: Including Suffolk County, Massachusetts 1630–1880*, 4 vols. (Boston: Ticknor, 1881), 4:371; David S. Reynolds, *Mightier Than the Sword: Uncle Tom's Cabin and the Battle for America* (New York: W. W. Norton, 2011), 145–48; Jeffrey D. Mason, *Melodrama and the Myth of America* (Bloomington: University of Indiana Press, 1993). See Eric Lott, *Love and Theft: Black Minstrelsy and the American Working Class* (New York: Oxford University Press, 1993), 45–47; Marvin McAllister, *White People Do Not Know How to Behave at Entertainments Designed for Ladies and Gentlemen of Colour: William Brown's African and American Theater* (Chapel Hill: University of North Carolina Press, 2003); George Thompson, *A Documentary History of the African Theatre* (Evanston, Ill.: Northwestern University Press, 1998), 129–36; Anthony D. Hill and Douglas Q. Barnett, *Historical Dictionary of African American Theater* (Lanham, Md.: Scarecrow Press, 2009), 6–7; Brooks, *Bodies in Dissent*; Camier and Dubois, "Voltaire, Zaïre, Dessalines."

49. Letter reprinted in Frederick Douglass, *My Bondage and My Freedom* (New York, 1855), 371. See John Stauffer, "Frederick Douglass and the Aesthetics of Freedom," *Raritan Review* 25, no.1 (Summer 2005): 114–36.

50. Letter of Sumner to Lord Morpeth (1842) in Edward Lillie Pierce, *Memoir and Letters of Charles Sumner*, 4 vols. (Boston: Robert Brothers, 1877–93), 2:225; letter of Sumner to his brother (1842), ibid., 223.

51. William Ellery Channing, *Slavery* (Boston: James Munroe, 1835), 8, 13, 15, 16, 18, 20, 25, 26, 32, 33, 49. On Channing and Kant, see William Henry Channing, *Memoir of William Ellery Channing: With Extracts from His Correspondence and Manuscripts*, 3 vols. (Boston: Crosby and Nichols, 1851), 2:95; Andrew Delbanco, *William Ellery Channing: An Essay on the Liberal Spirit in America* (Cambridge: Harvard University Press, 1981); Herbert W. Schneider, *A History of American Philosophy* (New York: Columbia University Press, 1946); Richard O. Curry and Lawrence B. Goodheart, eds., *American Chameleon: Individualism in Trans-National Context* (Kent, Ohio: Kent State University Press, 1991), 1–19.

52. Channing, *Slavery*, 35, 36, 50.

53. William Ellery Channing, *Self-Culture: An Address Introductory to the Franklin Lectures, Delivered at Boston, September, 1838* (Boston: Dutton and Wentworth, 1839), 53, 54, 49.

54. Robert C. Tucker, ed., *The Marx Engels Reader*, 2nd ed. (New York: W. W. Norton, 1978), 95–96.

55. Channing, *Self-Culture*, 55, 54.

56. On Channing's influence on Sumner, see Charles Sumner, *The Scholar, the Jurist, the Artist, the Philanthropist: An Address before the Phi Beta Kappa Society of Harvard University, at Their Anniversary, August 27, 1846* (Boston: W. D. Ticknor, 1846).

57. *Record*, 43rd Cong., 1st sess., 1874, appendix, 237.

58. Douglass, *My Bondage and My Freedom*, 371; *Globe*, 42nd Cong., 2nd sess., 1872, 432.

59. *Globe*, 42nd Cong., 2nd sess., 1872, 764, 765.

60. *Record*, 43rd Cong., 1st sess., 1874, appendix, 237; *Globe*, 42nd Cong., 2nd sess., 1872, appendix, 217; *Record*, 43rd Cong., 1st sess., 1874, appendix, 3. See Hartman, *Scenes of Subjection*, 163–68.

61. *Globe*, 42nd Cong., 2nd sess., 1872, appendix, 4.

62. *Globe*, 42nd Cong., 2nd sess., 1872, 430, 496; *Record*, 43rd Cong., 2nd sess., 1875, 1861, 1868–69. See *Slaughter-House Cases*, 83 U.S. 36 (1873); Heather Cox Richardson, *The Death of Reconstruction: Race, Labor, and Politics in the Post–Civil War North, 1865–1901* (Cambridge: Harvard University Press, 2001).

63. *Record*, 43rd Cong., 1st sess., 1874, appendix, 362–66.

64. Ibid., 364–65.

65. Ibid., 365, 369.

66. *Record*, 43rd Cong., 1st sess., 1874, 416, 379, 378, 381. For Stephens's 1861 "Corner-Stone Speech," see Henry Cleveland, *Alexander Stephens in Public and Private* (Philadelphia: National Publishing Company, 1866), 717–29.

67. *Record*, 43rd Cong., 1st sess., 1874, 383, 382.

68. Letter of George T. Downing and Alonzo Ransier et al. to Charles Sumner, Feb. 1, 1866, *Papers of Charles Sumner*, series I, reel 35. Other signers included the ex-slave minister, John Francis Cook, from Washington, D.C., and the prosperous Baltimore freeborn lawyer, William E. Matthews. See Linda C. Tillman, ed., *The Sage Handbook of African American Education* (Thousand Oaks, Calif.: Sage Publications, 2008), 37; Loren Schweninger, *Black Property Owners in the South, 1790–1915* (Urbana: University of Illinois Press, 1990), 221.

69. *Record*, 43rd Cong.,1st sess., 1874, 383, 382, 1311.

70. Ibid., 376–77.

71. *Record*, 43rd Cong., 2nd sess., 1875, 959; *Record*, 43rd Cong., 1st sess., 1873, 344. On slavery, pleasure, and subjection, see Douglass, *My Bondage and My Freedom*, 254–55; Solomon Northup, *Twelve Years a Slave* (Buffalo: Derby, Orton and Mulligan,1853), 218; Robert Collins, *Essay on the Treatment and Management of Slaves* (Macon: Benjamin F. Griffin, 1852); Hartman, *Scenes of Subjection*, 1–78; Camp, "Pleasures of Resistance"; Robert Conrad, *Children of God's Fire: A Documentary History of Black Slavery in Brazil* (University Park: Pennsylvania State University Press, 1994). On the theater of the slave auction, see Walter Johnson, *Soul by Soul: Life inside the Antebellum Slave Market* (Cambridge: Harvard University Press, 1999).

72. *Record*, 43rd Cong., 1st sess., 1874, 4783–84, 409.

73. *Record*, 43rd Cong., 2nd sess., 1875, 956.

74. Ibid., 1001.

75. Letter of George T. Downing to Philip B. Downing and Peter John Downing, Feb. 5, 1875, De-Grasse-Howard Papers, Massachusetts Historical Society, box 1, folder 19; Letter of George T. Downing to Charles Sumner, Jan. 20, 1871, *Papers of Charles Sumner*, series I, reel 52; *Record*, 43rd Cong., 2nd sess., 1875, 1011, 1870. On the supplement's passage on the eve of the loss of Republican control in Congress, see Foner, *Reconstruction*, 553–56.

76. *Civil Rights Cases*, 21.

77. The theater cases were *U.S. v. Ryan* (in error to the Circuit Court for the District of California) and *U.S v. Singleton* (from the Circuit Court for the Southern District of New York); *U.S. v. Ryan*, Transcript of Record, Oct. 14, 1876, 3. "Civil Rights and the Jubilee Singers," *San Francisco Chronicle*, January 7, 1876; "Amusements," *San Francisco Chronicle*, January 4, 1876, 3; "A Question of Color: Involving the Hue of a Ticket and a Man," *San Francisco Chronicle*, January 19, 1876, 3; William Winter, "Ruy Blas" in *The Miscellaneous Plays of Edwin Booth*, ed. William Winter, 3 vols. (Philadelphia: Penn Publishing Company, 1899). On George M. Tyler, see "United States Census 1880," Geo. M. Tyler, Oakland, Alameda, California, United States, citing 84C, family 0, NARA microfilm publication T9-0061; https://familysearch.org/pal:/MM9.1.1/M6G2-ZTS,. See Alan F. Westin, "The Case of the Prejudiced Doorkeeper," in *Quarrels That Have Shaped the Constitution*, ed. John A. Garraty (New York: Harper and Row, 1987), 128–44; Franklin, "The Enforcement of the Civil Rights Act of 1875"; Elizabeth Dale, "Social Equality Does Not Exist among Themselves, nor among Us: *Baylies v. Curry* and Civil Rights in Chicago, 1888," *American Historical Review* 102, no. 2 (1997): 331–39; Brooks, *Bodies in Dissent*.

78. *Civil Rights Cases*, 24, 18, 19, 24.

79. *Proceedings of the Civil Rights Mass Meeting, Lincoln Hall, Oct. 22, 1883* (Washington, D.C.: C. P. Farrell, 1883), 2, 5, 12; William Shakespeare, *As You Like It*, II, i.

80. *Civil Rights Act of 1964*, Pub. L. No. 88-352, 78 Stat. 241, Title II, Sec. 201(a)(3). The U.S. Supreme Court upheld the 1964 act only under the Commerce Clause, without addressing the Fourteenth Amendment grounds. See *Heart of Atlanta Motel*.

12 FROM THE SECOND AMERICAN REVOLUTION TO THE FIRST INTERNATIONAL AND BACK AGAIN

Marxism, the Popular Front, and the American Civil War

Andrew Zimmerman

Historians commonly describe the Civil War and Reconstruction as a revolution so profound as to merit comparison with the one that won the United States independence from Great Britain. Yet the revolution of 1861–1877 differed so greatly from the revolution of 1776 that it makes more sense to speak of the Civil War as a redefinition than as a repetition of revolution. When the North American colonies sought independence from Great Britain in 1776, this had amounted to a revolution. The Civil War is thought to have been a revolution because, with the defeat of slavery, it transformed the economy and society of the United States, in large part because Confederate attempts to win political independence failed. The Civil War changed the meaning of revolution profoundly, from the overthrow of a political sovereign to the transformation of society. It thus helped create the very concepts by which we still understand revolutions. The development of the Union war from a relatively conservative effort to preserve the territorial integrity of the United States into a revolutionary war that overthrew slavery gave rise to strategic and analytic concepts of revolution as change in society rather than change in government. Perhaps the most important observers to elaborate this new concept of revolution in relation to the American conflict, and certainly the most influential on twentieth- and twenty-first-century understandings of revolution, were Karl Marx and Friedrich Engels.

Marx and Engels did not apply ready-made concepts of revolution to the U.S. Civil War. Rather, the Civil War and Marxism developed in tandem, as components of a dynamic transnational set of revolutionary movements. Marx and Engels were members of an international community of revolutionary exiles, thousands of whom fought in the U.S. Civil

War, and tens of thousands of whom observed the conflict with keen attention. Through their observations and analyses of the war, Marx and Engels developed a recognizably Marxist understanding of revolutionary politics and the recognizable Marxism of the three volumes of *Capital*. Many liberal scholars with no overt commitment to Marxism also understand the U.S. Civil War as a social revolution. James McPherson, to cite just one prominent example, celebrated the Civil War as a social, as well as a political, revolution when he described the election of Abraham Lincoln as "the revolution of 1860" and secession as "the counterrevolution of 1861."[1] The entanglement of Marxism and the U.S. Civil War thus runs far deeper than the decision of particular writers to employ Marxist categories in their analyses of this conflict. It also extends far beyond the lifespans of Marx and Engels. Indeed, most of the history of Marxism has occurred since the deaths of its two founders.[2] One of the reasons to return to Marx and Engels's own writings on the Civil War is that they present a messier, more contentious, and potentially more revealing study of the Civil War as a revolution than the bourgeois revolution theory that has predominated much subsequent Marxist discussions of the conflict.[3]

Returning the history of revolution to the center of the American Civil War and the American Civil War to the center of the history of revolution appears especially important today, when revolution has come so out of favor that — apart from the U.S. Civil War — it can rarely even be discerned in the past. For whatever reason, the bicentennial of the French Revolution and the overthrow of the communist regimes of Eastern Europe in 1989 produced a political climate in the United States and in Europe in which radical social change was widely held to promise only 'totalitarianism,' and thus in which acceptable forms of democratic politics occurred strictly within the individualistic boundaries of a liberal civil society and the rule of law.[4] The focus on the law, the constitution, and individual civil rights in much recent Civil War historiography and popular culture reflects these recent more conservative understandings of revolution, much as earlier interpretations of the war reflected their own political contexts.[5] The ongoing centrality of the figure of Lincoln as "the Great Emancipator" in the face of, and in direct contradiction to, much work highlighting the importance of black self-emancipation is symptomatic of the conservative hegemony of our own period.[6] This is evident not only in Steven Spielberg's 2012 *Lincoln* but even in left-leaning and avowedly Marxist works.[7]

The struggle against slavery in the United States had been denounced and celebrated as a revolution decades before the American Civil War. Defenders of slavery turned to European antiradical terminology—contemporary equivalents of the twentieth-century pejorative use of the term "Bolshevik"—to denounce those who opposed slavery. Thus, just after the Denmark Vesey conspiracy in 1822, one South Carolinian described African Americans as "truely the Jacobins of the country."[8] Jacobin, the name of the radical party in the French Revolution, became a term to describe leftists for much of the nineteenth century. Later, supporters of slavery referred to the party of Lincoln as the "black republicans," pointing both to the supposed racial sympathies of party members and also to the bogeyman of European antirevolutionaries at that time, the "red republicans." The historian William Archibald Dunning, in his denunciation of African American political participation, similarly deemed the Civil War and Reconstruction "as reckless a species of statecraft" as the French Revolution for its "enthronement in political power" of freedmen.[9]

The Civil War had its revolutionary defenders as well. Black abolitionists like David Walker and Henry Highland Garnet, as well as John Brown and his followers, fought slavery with self-consciously revolutionary means. European immigrants, often veterans of the revolutions of 1848–49, brought their own revolutionary attitudes and experiences to the struggle against slavery.[10] There were multiple revolutionary currents at work during the Civil War, and these did not come to an end with Reconstruction, but continue to this day. Historians seeking to understand the American Civil War and Reconstruction as a revolution immerse themselves, more or less consciously, not only in evolving and conflicting understandings of nineteenth-century U.S. history but, equally, in evolving and conflicting interpretations of the nature of revolution, from 1789 to 1848 to 1861–77, to the October Revolution of 1917, to the Popular Front of 1934–39, and beyond.

The European revolutions of 1848–49, historians now agree, had a major impact on the U.S. Civil War. Civil War historiography dealing with the influence of these revolutions has tended, however, to portray them as liberal nationalist uprisings. In fact, there were many factions in these revolutions, and those veterans who fled to the United States tended to be, like Marx and Engels, socialist internationalists.[11] Only in the first year of the revolution in Germany did socialists, like Marx and Engels, cooperate with liberals, who were typically elite property owners. Marx and Engels had recommended such a working-class alliance with the bourgeoisie in the *Communist Manifesto*, published just before the revolutions broke out in 1848. In the first year of the revolution, Marx, much to the consternation of many communists, continued to advocate this interclass collaboration. The hopes of Marx and likeminded leftists for a socialist-democratic-liberal alliance in Germany were dashed when, after a year of debate, in 1849, the liberal Frankfurt Parliament proposed a constitutional monarchy for Germany. Even worse, when the proposed head of this monarchy, the king of Prussia, rejected this crown, liberals abandoned the revolution and cooperated with their erstwhile enemies to suppress those socialists and radical democrats who wished to continue the revolution. Marx, Engels, and many others responded to this liberal betrayal by abandoning their calls to participate in a democratic revolution that they had anticipated the bourgeoisie would lead.[12] By 1849 the moderate stage theory of the *Communist Manifesto*—in which the bourgeoisie vanquished feudalism, produced "its own gravediggers" in the proletariat, and then stepped aside for socialism—had been replaced by a more directly military and revolutionary model of history.

In 1849 German socialists and communists attempted a final revolution, this time also against some of their former liberal allies. The renewed revolution of 1849 broke out in several places in Germany, but the most important were in the Grand Duchy of Baden and in the Bavarian Palatinate in southwest Germany. This was also the most significant region of the revolution for American Civil War history, since its veterans provided the majority of the prominent German army officers, including Carl Schurz, Franz Sigel, Alexander Schimmelpfennig, August Willich, and Ludwig Blenker. Engels himself fought in this revolution as an adjutant to Willich, the future brigadier general of the Thirty-Second Indiana Infantry Regiment. Like the German revolution from which it emerged, the revolution in Baden also split into more liberal and more socialist factions, with liberals advocating collaboration with existing military and political elites, while socialists demanded revolutionary political and economic transformations in the former duchy. The Germans who would play such important roles in Civil War era America, including those, like Schurz, who would later become more conservative, mostly favored the revolutionary socialist position. Indeed, this is why they had to flee, first to Switzerland and later to the United States, when the Prussian army defeated the provisional government in Baden.

Revolutionary refugees from Baden and elsewhere did not bring a preformed socialist strategy to the United States. They had to flee to the United States, after all, because their revolution had failed, and they brought instead a set of self-criticisms and worries. While many texts record their doubts, one coauthored by Johann Phillip Becker and Christian Essellen proves especially significant, because the future army major general Franz Sigel consulted with them as they wrote, and also because Becker remained a close associate of Marx and Engels and later became a leader in the First International. Becker and Essellen proposed, first, that in an age of powerful state militaries, revolutionaries had to fight as armies in the field rather than as insurgents on barricades. They had to learn to combine more successfully "military calculation and revolutionary audacity." Second, they held that compromising with liberals who wished to preserve the constitution, private property, and much of the state structure garnered the revolution weak allies at best, and alienated more committed revolutionaries at home, as well as foreign fighters who might have rushed to their cause. "The proletariat," wrote Becker and Essellen, "had no desire to risk its life for an Imperial Constitution in which no word was written about the right to work, no word about relief of the poverty under which it suffered." Third, they thought that the revolution should spread itself as rapidly as possible to neighboring states, thus requiring its enemies to divide their forces.[13] Rather than attempting a final, decisive battle with the enemies of the revolution, Becker and Essellen counseled a wave of simultaneous revolutions that would force counterrevolutionaries to divide their forces. This is perhaps one of the origins of the strategy of "two, three, or many Vietnams" that Che Guevara proclaimed in Havana in 1967.[14]

The American Civil War had such important consequences for nineteenth-century revolutionary thought and politics at least in part because it appeared to be an extraordinarily successful instance of revolutionary political-economic change. After a string of political disappointments, the Civil War not only restored the morale of many revolutionaries but also offered as many positive lessons as the revolutions of 1848–49 had offered negative ones. The 1848–49 revolutions had, in Marx's view, merely defeated "prerevolutionary traditional appendages" to the revolution, that is, cleared the ground for some future revolution; the American Civil War, by contrast, sounded the "alarm bell" (*Sturmglocke*) for the European working class to take up the revolution that Marx had anticipated almost two decades earlier.[15]

Yet these U.S. lessons had little to do with the America that European émigrés found when they first crossed the Atlantic. Revolutionaries generally did not flee to the United States because they wished to pursue democratic politics there. The United States seemed to many already democratic enough and to others simply too far away from the European revolutions to hold their interest. Many revolutionaries had decided to move to the United States—temporarily, they hoped—after the coup d'état of Napoléon Bonaparte's nephew, Louis-Napoléon, in France. In the United States they could earn a better living than the meager existence they had eked out in London or in Swiss exile, while organizing and publishing freely and awaiting the first sign of renewed revolution in Europe.

These émigrés in the U.S. Army would pursue revolutionary strategies, often against a Union leadership that they feared was falling into the same national liberal trap that had defeated them in 1848–49. When these German radicals faced Lincoln's compromises with Missouri slaveholders, for example, their outrage stemmed in part from a sense that he was repeating errors that they had made in 1848–49. Then they had similarly tried to win property-holding allies to the revolution by minimizing socialist demands. They considered Lincoln's compromises not merely unethical but strategically suicidal. Marx and Engels absorbed and developed the concerns of their comrades across the Atlantic. One reason for returning to Marx and Engels on the Civil War is to offer present-day historians an escape from the same national liberal trap, which impairs understandings of the politics of the Civil War and Reconstruction.

Given the centrality of Louis-Napoléon Bonaparte's coup to the decision of many German revolutionaries to flee to the United States, it is not surprising that Marx first published "The Eighteenth Brumaire of Louis Napoléon" in a German-language journal in New York edited by his comrade Joseph Weydemeyer.[16] In that text, Marx revealed how class struggle could produce not a classless society but an antirevolutionary state that seemed, falsely, to stand above class conflicts. Bonaparte's apparently revolutionary legacy, inherited not only from his uncle but also from his own long-term involvement with the Italian Risorgimento and his Saint-Simonian socialism, caused much angst among those on the left, for it showed how their own struggles could be appropriated to aggrandize the power of their enemies. For Marx, the French coup called into question the future social revolution, which he now thought had to break sharply with the past and "draw its poetry . . . from the future." His poetic fancy and temporal musings in the famous first pages of the "Eighteenth Brumaire" come from a profound confusion about the nature of revolution, a confusion that the success of the war against slavery in America would help resolve.

While Marx may have written the "Eighteenth Brumaire" to help European exiles in the United States understand the challenges they would face when they returned for the next revolution, the text also drew him into conversations about democracy, society, and the state emerging in the United States. Some southern apologists for slavery who wished to present their institution as modern and progressive looked to this modern dictator as an example. Two years after Marx published his work on Bonaparte, the southern slavery apologist George Fitzhugh, wishing to convince readers that "slavery is a form, and the very best form, of socialism," lavished praise on Bonaparte. The French leader had, according to Fitzhugh, provided food and housing for workers and nurseries "for the children of the working women, just as we Southerners do for our negro women and children."[17] The year before, in 1853, the German-born Francis Lieber, an antislavery professor of law at South Carolina College, who would later serve as a legal advisor to the Union, had excoriated the French "elected despot" as a "political monstrosity" who exemplified false ideas of free government.[18] In 1861 Marx would compare the formation of the Confederacy to Napoléon's coup.[19] Though in the 1850s Marx and Weydemeyer thought the United States was simply a safe place in which to wait for the next European revolution, they were already, even if they did not know it, participating in American politics.

Marx began consciously participating in Civil War–era politics in 1851, with a regular column he wrote for the New York *Tribune*. While covering the European revolutions of 1848–49 for the *Tribune*, Charles A. Dana had sought out Marx in Cologne and later recruited him to write for the paper.[20] Marx contributed almost five hundred articles, mostly on European affairs, before the *Tribune* ended the relationship in 1861 and Dana left the paper for a prominent position in Lincoln's War Department. Dana informed Marx that he was "not only one of the most highly valued, but one of the best paid contributors attached to the journal."[21] Dana, easy to reach through the internationally known *Tribune*, also served as a go-between among German exiles in the United States and Europe.[22]

Writing for the *Tribune* not only drew Marx into political and economic debates around the emergence of the American Republican Party; it also brought him into the heart of socialist discussions in the United

States.[23] Before the Civil War, the most important variant of socialism in the country was that of the French thinker Charles Fourier, who inspired numerous utopian communities with his "associationist" economic and psychological ideas.[24] This model of socialism differed markedly from that of Marx and Engels and many German exiles, which focused on class conflict not only as a characteristic of society but also as a necessary strategy in pursuing socialism. Already in the *Communist Manifesto* Marx and Engels had spoken of a "more or less veiled civil war, raging within existing society."[25] Rejecting the associationist model of socialism without class conflict also entailed rejecting the gradualist antislavery common among U.S. Fouriersts and echoed by the economist Henry Carey. Carey, who would become one of the economists most severely criticized by Marx, had an important influence on *Tribune* editor Horace Greeley and many other Whigs who would become Republicans.[26] Carey argued that economic development, and especially the growth of industry, led to an ever increasing "harmony of interests" among workers and owners, industry and agriculture. He held that slavery would gradually disappear on its own with economic development, and that sudden abolition would only make things worse.[27] Far more than any classical political economist of the late eighteenth or early nineteenth centuries, Carey stood in stark contrast to Marx's view that class conflict was a necessary and foundational component of all history and politics.

It was Carey's view of slavery and its abolition that most drew Marx's ire. Marx was especially outraged when he found one of his *Tribune* articles cited by Carey to support his argument against immediate abolition in his 1853 *Slave Trade, Domestic and Foreign*.[28] In that article, "The Duchess of Sutherland and Slavery," Marx had chided British aristocrats for criticizing slavery in the United States while profiting from the expulsion of thousands of Scottish tenants to turn their fields into pasturage for sheep. While Carey similarly connected the misery of expelled Scottish tenants to the misery of American slavery, he did so to suggest that the failure to develop manufactures, rather than the exploitation of the poor by the rich or the institution of slavery, was responsible for this misery and that the "harmony of interests" would gradually free all.[29] Carey's book infuriated Marx, as did the *Tribune's* "puffing Carey's book for all it's worth." Carey and the *Tribune*, Marx concluded, supported the interests of the American industrial bourgeoisie "in the guise of Sismondian-philanthropic-socialist anti-industrialism." That, Marx concluded, explained "why the

Tribune, despite all its 'isms' and socialist flourishes, manages to be the 'leading journal' in the United States."[30] A common socialism may have drawn Greeley and Dana to Marx, but Marx also added a confrontational strategy of class conflict that diverged from the harmony of interests socialism of the *Tribune*.

In engaging with the American socialism of Greeley and Carey's harmony of interests doctrine, Marx not only added a German communist voice to debates in the United States, including about slavery, but also honed his own ideas about class conflict, which he would later publish just after the war in *Capital*. Already in his earliest economic notebooks, written in 1857 and published as part of the *Grundrisse* long after his death, Marx focused on Carey and, to a lesser extent, on the French economist Frédéric Bastiat. "Carey's entire bad joke," according to Marx, rested on his belief that increasing the productivity of labor would lead to greater wealth for the worker rather than for capital. "Carey's generality," Marx noted later, is "Yankee universality." Carey proceeded from the fact that American workers could "accumulate enough to become e.g. a farmer etc. (although that too is already coming to a halt now)."[31] The free soil doctrine, central to Carey's concept of the harmony of interests, as it was to much American Republicanism, Marx found anathema to the revolutionary strategy that he and others in his radical milieu continued to develop. (Later he would compare the free-soil practices of American "land-jobbers and pioneers" to "the worst horrors taking place, for instance, in Ireland."[32]) Marx would eventually respond to Carey with his theory of surplus value, which he would develop during the Civil War and explain, as we shall see, with analogies to slave labor.

Marx's dispute with Carey not only reveals how engaging with Civil War–era America helped Marx develop his own ideas. It also indicates how Marx's radical milieu contributed to the Civil War itself, when the "more or less veiled civil war, raging within existing society," which he and Engels had written of in the *Communist Manifesto*, broke out into a real civil war. Marx and Engels resolutely rejected every position that suggested that class conflict, including the conflict between slaves and slaveholders, might gradually disappear without a decisive confrontation. This set them at odds not only with proponents of slavery but also with a variety of gradualist positions within the antislavery camp.

Marx and Engels learned about the American Civil War through newspaper reports and through correspondence with members of their radical émigré community who had fled to the United States. Already in 1860, Marx wrote to Engels: "In my view the greatest thing happening in the world today is, on the one hand, the Americ[an] slave movement, opened by [John] Brown's death; on the other hand the slave [i.e. serf] movement in Russia."[33] By the time the war actually broke out more than a year later, the attention of the two would be more drawn to the United States than to Russia, not least because some of their old comrades and rivals in the Communist League played important roles in the fighting.[34] Marx saw the American Civil War as the first important conflict since the end of the 1848–49 revolutions, "distinguished, by the vastness of its dimensions and the grandeur of its ends, from the groundless, wanton, and diminutive wars Europe has passed through since 1849."[35] Soon after the war began, Marx even helped one German veteran of Garibaldi's Red Shirts to raise money to pay passage across the Atlantic to join the U.S. Army.[36]

At the outbreak of the American Civil War, many of the radicals along-side whom Engels had fought in Baden in 1849 found themselves concentrated in the western states, and especially in St. Louis, Missouri. While most had hoped to remain in New York, closer to the ships that could take them back to Europe at the outbreak of a revolution, economic circumstances had forced many to relocate to the West, where the demand for skilled labor in cities like St. Louis made them especially welcome. Germans created their own radical culture in the West, one enlivened by its proximity to the struggle over slavery in Kansas and made perhaps more earnest by the existence of slavery in their midst. At least since 1857, Marx's closest American associate, Weydemeyer, had lectured to Germans throughout the West on slavery, emphasizing that the attack on slavery was not simply a celebration of wage labor but also an attack on private property as a prerequisite to labor exploitation.[37] He also seriously considered joining the fight against slavery in Kansas, as a number of German émigrés already had.[38] He eventually settled in St. Louis. While Weydemeyer may have perceived himself as an agent of Marx, it seems just as likely that he served as a conduit for the experience of the struggle against slavery in the United States for his German comrade.[39]

Missourians were divided over the issues of slavery and secession even before Lincoln took office, and it was primarily German paramilitaries who defended the federal armory in St. Louis from secessionist forces under Governor Claiborne Fox Jackson and drove the governor from power. German revolutionaries regularly conducted military training in voluntary "gymnastics" associations, and in Missouri they were able to form themselves quickly into Home Guards units. They mustered into service under Nathaniel Lyon, an antislavery army officer who had been serving in Kansas. Franz Sigel, who had served as minister of war in the revolutionary government in Baden, became the top German general in the region, and he and other émigrés evidently applied in Missouri the lessons they had learned from their defeat by Prussia in 1849.[40]

German Home Guard units did not repeat the compromising liberal gradualism that many regarded as the mistake of 1848–49. They immediately began attacking slavery without regard to the rights of property or the provisions of the Constitution, not to mention the orders of their superior officers. Some not only welcomed fugitives from slavery into their lines but also into their ranks as fellow soldiers. One visitor to Boonville, Missouri, for example, complained that in a German Home Guard encampment "sundry runaway slaves . . . often appear in U.S. uniform and on one occasion at least had U.S. arms placed in their hands and acted the part of U.S. soldiers inside of the intrenchments here."[41] Understood in the context of this type of spontaneous antislavery action, the 1861 emancipation proclamation of John C. Frémont, commander at this time of the Western Department, does not simply anticipate the Second Confiscation Act of 1862 or the Emancipation Proclamation of 1863. It reflects, instead, German-American and African American revolutionary practices that liberal languages of property, constitution, and extraordinary war powers could only seek to approximate.

The extent of revolutionary collaboration between German socialists and African American enemies of slavery is hard to measure, since its success often depended on it going unreported. Conservative unionists, however, found it real enough. Henry W. Halleck, who took over the department after Lincoln removed Frémont from command, described a conspiracy by German soldiers and civilians to foment insurrection and with the help of "the German and Abolitionist Press" to restore Frémont's command.[42] When Frémont was reassigned to Virginia, many, both foreign and native born, rallied around his name as a sign of a radicalism they felt had been betrayed by the political machinations of men like McClellan and Lincoln.[43] A later conservative commander of Missouri sought to suppress the left-wing German press in St. Louis, which he described as "so radical that they cannot possibly be loyal to the Government."[44] Marx was as outraged as German radicals in Missouri about Frémont's dismissal as commander of the Western Department, but maintained—echoing, in a way, Halleck's fears—that Frémont could lead an eventual opposition to the Union's compromises with slaveholders and "smash the hitherto prevailing diplomatic system of waging war."[45]

It is conceivable that the collaboration between German and African American revolutionaries in the western theater of the Civil War was one of the earliest collaborations of socialists with a proletariat. The German socialist milieu had consisted primarily of artisans fearing proletarianization, rather than of the proletarians that thinkers like Marx and Engels thought might finally emancipate humanity from class altogether. The Mississippi Valley, where many German socialists fought, first in Missouri, then in Arkansas, then, under Grant, in Mississippi, was home to arguably the most proletarianized workforce in the world. Here enslaved workers produced cotton for the world market as part of a new rationalized plantation slavery that also emerged in sugar production in Cuba and coffee production in Brazil. Scholars have begun to describe the mode of production in these areas as a "second slavery" with especially industrialized, capitalist characteristics.[46]

The plantations of the Mississippi Valley emphasized the proletarian character that the slavery in the Americas had always possessed. The expansion of the cotton economy into the Mississippi Valley had led to a mass forced migration of slaves from the Upper South and the eastern seaboard in what Ira Berlin has called a "Second Middle Passage."[47] Slaves sent to the Mississippi Valley were separated from family networks of support. In this new frontier slavery, planters could often ignore customary limits on exploitation won over generations of resistance in other regions. Planters in the Mississippi Valley were more likely to prevent enslaved workers from provisioning themselves on their own gardens and, even where these workers were able to establish some independent production, the frontier afforded them little if any opportunity to market their produce. Mississippi Valley cotton workers also faced deskilling, for cotton production, in comparison with tobacco, rice, and other products of the East, required less skill in itself, and also brought in fewer other skilled workers, for example coopers, carpenters, or blacksmiths.[48] Organized in gangs on large cotton plantations, these enslaved workers constituted an early American proletariat, with nothing to lose but their chains. The Union would oversee some of the most conservative versions of free labor in the Mississippi Valley, as former slaves were often forced to work as nominally free laborers on plantations they had once worked as bondspeople.[49] But the region would also support some short-lived efforts at black economic autonomy, for example, purchasing cotton directly from freedpeople at Helena, Arkansas, or cooperative farming at Davis Bend, Mississippi.[50]

Some German émigrés in the Mississippi Valley came to understand slaves fleeing from such conditions as a revolutionary proletariat, but Marx and Engels did not. It would be for Marxists, rather than Marx and Engels themselves, to develop this understanding of an enslaved black proletariat in the Civil War. Marx and Engels attributed much black working-class agency to the white political leaders and workers with whom they collaborated. This was likely because they had trouble seeing modern slaves or African Americans as agents of history. Nonetheless, thanks to the efforts of enslaved black workers, Marx and Engels did recognize in the Civil War a proletarian revolution, even if they failed to identify the principal fraction of workers who made this revolution.

For Marx, the Civil War dispelled some of the mystery about the nature of the "social revolution of the nineteenth century" that had so troubled him only a decade earlier in the "Eighteenth Brumaire." From the beginning, both Marx and Engels understood the American Civil War as having two axes: a conventional war between the Union and the Confederacy and a social revolution against slavery with significant African American participation. Marx never doubted that slavery was the central issue of war, even while officials in the North still denied this.[51] Marx and Engels feared the South had a military advantage over the North, but Marx, at least, was confident that the North held social revolution as a kind of trump card that would ensure its final victory. Engels sometimes despaired at the North's lack of revolutionary energy.[52] Marx, meanwhile, thought that the dynamics of the war itself would force the "Yankees" to fight the war "in a revolutionary manner," particularly by arming slaves. "In the long run," Marx wrote, "the North will of course win, since in case of emergency it can play the final card of slave revolution."[53] In a private letter to Engels, Marx suggested, using the common racial epithet, that a single black regiment "would have a remarkable effect on southern nerves."[54] Marx also cautioned that the "constitutional manner of war," including the protection of slavery in border states, "violently suppressed the sympathies of Negroes for the North," made generals reluctant to employ black soldiers, and led slaves to continue working, thus enabling a larger number of whites to serve in the Confederate Army. He also ventured, echoing

Becker and Essellen's analysis of the Baden revolution, that northern men would volunteer more readily had Lincoln "carried out a revolutionary war and written 'abolition of slavery' as a battle cry on the Stars and Stripes."[55] Marx worried that the North would have difficulty taking such revolutionary steps because the United States was a "bourgeois republic where swindle has reigned supreme for so long."[56] For Marx and Engels the Civil War was not a bourgeois revolution but a workers' revolution carried out, sometimes in a "distasteful form," within a "'bourgeois' democracy."[57]

Perhaps Marx and Engels resorted to such a complex characterizations of the revolution in part because they had difficulty understanding enslaved black workers as workers and thus as authors of their own emancipation. Marx noted that "the indirect slavery of the white man in England" depended on "the direct slavery of the black man on the other side of the Atlantic," but he seems to have been less able to conceive the logical inversion of this relationship, and thus to have seen enslaved and free workers as interlinked class fractions.[58] Marx and Engels understood that the Union victory involved ending slave labor in the United States, but they did not recognize the enslaved themselves as the principal agents of this revolution. The first rule that Marx gave to the International Working Men's Association, which he helped found in London during the Civil War, stated that "the emancipation of the working classes must be conquered by the working classes themselves" and would consist of the "abolition of all class-rule."[59] Yet Marx seems to have conceived the antislavery revolution—from which he may have borrowed his language of the "emancipation" (*Befreiung*) of labor and the "abolition" (*Abschaffung*) of bourgeois property[60]—as anything but self-emancipation by blacks. Rather, for Marx and Engels, this revolution was initiated by white political and military leaders who called the slave uprising into existence out of military necessity and legislative decision. Even though, in their view, slave uprisings remained the final guarantee of Union victory, the conflict itself was between "the 20 million free men of the North" and "an oligarchy of 300,000 slaveholders." European workers, meanwhile, rallied to a war against slavery because they "consider the soil of the United States as the free soil of the landless millions of Europe, as their land of promise, now to be defended sword in hand, from the sordid grasp of the slaveholder."[61] All this shows a canny appreciation of the complex motives of some white opposition to slavery, but it also fails to recognize black workers as central participants in the class politics of the Civil War.

The repressed figure of the black proletariat perhaps returned in the writings of Marx and Engels in their fantasy-laden admiration for presidents Lincoln and Johnson as "two men of labour."[62] Marx and Engels's counterparts in the German revolutionary exile community in the United States remained furious throughout the war at what they perceived as Lincoln's timid attitude toward slaveholders from the moment he countermanded Frémont's August 1861 Missouri emancipation proclamation. While Marx and Engels shared the frustration of their overseas comrades concerning Lincoln, they nonetheless lavished praise on the president. Thus Marx hailed the Preliminary Emancipation Proclamation as "the most meaningful document of American history since the founding of the Union," and characterized it as revolutionary, "tearing up the old American Constitution." Lincoln, moreover, offered the world a new, democratic model by "doing the most significant things in the most insignificant manner, . . . without historical drapery." Lincoln was, for Marx, simply "a plebeian . . . without intellectual polish, without a particular greatness of character, without exceptional meaning—an average nature with good will" who became president through "the ordinary play of universal suffrage unconscious of the great destiny about which it had to decide." Marx regarded it as the greatest proof of the "political and social organization" of the United States that "average natures with good will can achieve what would have required a hero in the old world."[63] In a private letter, Marx contrasted Lincoln and Louis-Napoléon, comparing the lawyerly language in which Lincoln, in Marx's view, transformed the world with the "drapery in which the Frenchman wraps the most insignificant."[64]

After the assassination of Lincoln, Marx and Engels held similarly unrealistic hopes that Andrew Johnson, "as a former poor white," would have a "deadly hatred of the oligarchy" of the South and would "insist on confiscation of the great estates" to a greater degree than Lincoln would have.[65] In an open letter to Johnson, Marx encouraged him to continue "the arduous work of political reconstruction and social regeneration" and "initiate the new era of the emancipation of labour."[66] Marx and Engels quickly realized how wrong their assessment of Johnson had been, but their positive assessment of Lincoln remains less contested, even if few historians today would view Lincoln as having rejected a constitutional for a revolutionary path, as Marx did.

The Civil War demonstrated to Marx that revolution was possible. It provided him with a positive political vocabulary that contrasted with the bitter negativity that had characterized much of his writing in the 1850s, including his public and private comments about fellow socialists and communists with whom he disagreed. Many of these, after all, had been soldiers and officers in the revolutionary war he so admired. Even before the Union victory, the war seems to have persuaded Marx to resume his active role in revolutionary politics with the founding of the International Workingmen's Association, the First International, in London in 1864. This gave formal, institutional organization to the international network of exiled revolutionaries that had taken shape in the wake of the 1848–49 revolutions and played such an important role in the war.

In his famous inaugural address to the organization, Marx singled out the American members for special praise, noting that, after the 1848–49 revolutions, "the most advanced sons of labour fled in despair to the Transatlantic Republic." Marx also praised English workers who, through demonstrations and threatened political actions, had prevented "the West of Europe from plunging headlong into an infamous crusade for the perpetuation and propagation of slavery on the other side of the Atlantic," that is, supporting the Confederacy diplomatically or even militarily. The importance of the American struggle also reveals itself in Marx's praise for worker-controlled cooperatives. These cooperatives abolished wage labor from below, "by deed, instead of by argument," demonstrating that "like slave labour, like serf labour, hired labour is but a transitory and inferior form, destined to disappear before associated labour plying its toil with a willing hand, a ready mind and a joyous heart."[67] Workers' cooperatives, in short, suggested that the successful revolution against slavery in the United States might promise also an end of capitalism. Marx's famous 1864 letter to Lincoln on behalf of the International recapitulated much of his analysis of the war, presenting it as a preliminary to a struggle against wage labor and generalizing the "Slaveholder's Rebellion" as "a general holy Crusade of Property against Labour."[68]

Marx developed his theory of surplus value for the First International, basing it in part on his observations of the American struggle over slavery, as Raya Dunayevskaya was perhaps the first to suggest.[69] Marx's theory of surplus value was his final answer to the "harmony of interests" political economy of class compromise that Carey had proposed explicitly and that had been implicit in Louis-Napoléon's state socialism. Marx presented his first formulation of surplus value in two June 1865 lectures to the International Workingmen's Association to explain why strikes were a viable strategy for workers within capitalism. Apparently, in the face of "a real epidemy of strikes and a clamour for a rise of wages" in Europe, some members of the International had suggested that raising wages for workers would only raise prices (as some economists continue to do today with their concept of a wage-price spiral). Marx rejected the liberal understanding of wages as a free bargain between employer and employee and compared wage labor instead to another form of unfree labor, serfdom. Each week, Marx explained, the serf worked several days in his own fields for himself and several days on the lord's field for no remuneration. A similar separation of paid labor and unpaid labor existed in the wage system, Marx suggested, but it was invisible, not "separated in time and space" as these two types of labor were for serfs.

Marx then turned to slavery to describe the struggle over wages and the working day for free laborers. The amount paid to workers was based, Marx claimed, on a socially determined "traditional standard of life" and the amount capitalists took on their ability to both lower this "traditional standard" and on their ability to extend the working day (absolute surplus value) or make workers more productive (relative surplus value). Capitalists would, if they could, reduce workers to "all the miseries of the slave, without the security of the slave." Rather than accepting "the dictates of the capitalist as a paramount economical law" workers should fight, for the question of wages finally "resolves itself into a question of the respective powers of the combatants." While endorsing strikes, Marx also warned that this "guerilla war against the effects of the existing System" could not replace "the final emancipation of the working class, that is to say, the ultimate abolition of the wages system."[70] The language itself, not only of slavery, emancipation, and abolition, but also of warfare, suggests how important the recent Civil War was for Marx.

In the first volume of *Capital*, published in 1867, Marx built on similar analogies between slavery and wage labor. There he made his famous statement: "Labour in a white skin cannot emancipate itself where it is branded in a black skin," and noted with satisfaction that the movement for an eight-hour workday was "the first fruit of the American Civil War."[71] In drawing attention primarily to the struggles of wage laborers, Marx presented the fight against slavery as an auxiliary to the labor movement rather than as a labor movement in its own right. Nonetheless, the movement by slaves against slavery in the United States had shaped Marx's radical milieu. Indeed, some propaganda of the International concluded by quoting Marx's claim in the preface to *Capital* that the American Civil War had "sounded the alarm bell" for the European working class, much as the American War of Independence had for the "European middle class."[72]

From his vantage point as an officer who spent the entire war in Missouri, Weydemeyer gained a much better appreciation than his old friends Marx and Engels of the role of African Americans in the Civil War and Reconstruction. Just months after the war ended, Weydemeyer reminded readers of one of the St. Louis German-language newspapers that the interests of African Americans, the Union cause, and "Civilization and progress" all coincided and should not be separated. He denounced efforts to limit African American freedom, from "Banks's system of serfdom" in U.S.-occupied Louisiana to attempts by postwar southern elites to "bind former slaves to the soil." African American veterans with military training would not, Weydemeyer warned, tolerate these attempts to subordinate them anew, and the only alternative to future "race wars a la St. Domingo" was the "rapid reconstruction of Reconstruction, with political equality for the Negro as its basis." He suggested that the only way to end the military occupation of the South would be to enfranchise African American men and to develop Southern industry in alliance with southern workers, "regardless of what ancestry they have to thank for their skin color."[73]

Weydemeyer, perhaps Marx and Engels's most loyal ally in the United States, realized the potential in their common international revolutionary milieu to understand black workers as active agents of revolutionary transformations. It is also worth remembering that, while Marx and Engels were surely limited by their assumptions about black political subjectivity, by white standards of their own time, including those of many American radicals, they had a relatively good sense of black political agency. In the decades following the American Civil War they came to better understand the active role played by African American workers in U.S. history and, more broadly, in the struggles of oppressed peoples and nations globally. Still, their understanding was more than matched by those German exiles directly involved in the intersecting struggles of race and class in the United States.

The failure of the Civil War to yield radical social change for white workers and the continued racial oppression of blacks after the war disappointed the International, even while the memory and effects of the Civil War remained of paramount importance. In an 1865 address to the people of the United States, the International advised making all citizens "free and equal, without reserve," warning that if the country failed to do so, "there will yet remain a struggle for the future which may again stain your country with your people's blood."[74] The International also complained that American workers had suffered from the financial consequences of the war, "in glaring contrast to the new fangled luxury of financial aristocrats, shoddy aristocrats, and other vermin bred by war." Nonetheless, they continued to regard the Union victory as a valuable achievement: "Still the Civil War offered a compensation in the liberation of the slaves and the impulse which it thereby gave to your own class movement."[75] Marx continued to look to Reconstruction and the postwar American labor movement with hope, but the political vocabulary and the model of the Civil War played an even more important role in the development of Marxist politics and political economy.

In the years immediately following the Civil War, Marx began to focus on the efforts of the Fenians to achieve Irish independence. He noted that this paramilitary organization seeking independence of Ireland from Britain had emerged not in Ireland itself but in the United States. Indeed, Fenians employed tactics that they had learned as soldiers in the American Civil War, although Marx did not allude to this.[76] Their American origins, for Marx, meant that the Fenians, in contrast to earlier movements for Irish independence, were led by "the masses, the lower orders," rather than upper or middle classes and the clergy. This Irish movement thus fought not only against foreign rule but also against the poverty brought about by the local class structure that foreign rule supported. It was thus a "fight for life and death," which for Marx explained the particular violence of the Fenians.[77] When a number of Fenians in Manchester were sentenced to death for one of their actions, Marx compared their executions to "the fate of John Brown at Harper's Ferry" and claimed that they would "open a new period in the struggle between Ireland and England," as Brown's execution had in the American struggle.[78] By 1870 Marx had decided that if the English aristocracy could be overthrown in Ireland, this would topple the English bourgeoisie, and thus lead to international revolution. The main obstacle, he found, was English workers' "religious, social, and national prejudices against the Irish worker," which Marx compared to the attitude "of the 'poor whites' to the Negroes in the former slave states of the U.S.A." As the International had seen the emancipation of slaves in the United States as a prerequisite for the emancipation of wage workers, so the International would try to "awaken the English workers to a realization of the fact that for them the national emancipation of Ireland is no question of abstract justice or humanitarian sentiment but the first condition of their own emancipation."[79]

Marx's nearly contemporaneous account of the 1871 Paris Commune similarly revealed how much the American conflict shaped his later politics.[80] In a work titled the "Civil War in France," Marx contrasted national war and civil war, the latter of which now functioned as the form of warfare appropriate to the International. "The highest heroic effort of which old society is still capable is national war," Marx wrote, "and this is now proved to be a mere governmental humbug, intended to defer the struggle of classes, and to be thrown aside as soon as that class struggle bursts out into civil war. Class rule is no longer able to disguise itself in a national uniform; the national Governments are one as against the proletariate!" Marx described the decision by the leaders of the French Third Republic to make peace with the Prussians so they could make war on the Commune not merely as treason but as a "slaveholder's rebellion" — precisely the term he used to describe the Confederate secession.[81] Marx's use of a vocabulary borrowed from his account of the American Civil War suggests the deeper importance of the conflict for much postwar revolutionary socialism.

BUILDING ON BOTH Marx's and Engels's writings on the Civil War and on traditions of black radicalism, W. E. B. Du Bois presented in his 1935 *Black Reconstruction in America* what is still the greatest Marxist interpretation of the Civil War.[82] Developing concepts of revolution made newly relevant by the Bolsheviks in 1917, Du Bois also went beyond the limited perspective of Marx and Engels on African American workers. As Du Bois charitably put it in an article in the *Crisis* praising Marx and Engels's writings on the war, "Whatever he [Marx] said and did concerning the uplift of the working class must . . . be modified so far as Negroes are concerned by the fact that he had not studied at first hand their peculiar race problem here in America."[83] The Communist International (Comintern), which coordinated the activities of Communist Parties around the world, also called for direct struggles against racism and imperialism at this point, rejecting the earlier idea that these could be treated as epiphenomena of capitalism. As a number of historians have shown, this Communist antiracism played an important role also in the long development of the civil rights movement in the United States and anti-imperialism abroad.[84]

Du Bois identified a revolutionary "general strike" of enslaved black workers during the Civil War that, with Reconstruction, inaugurated what he termed "one of the most extraordinary experiments of Marxism that the world, before the Russian revolution, had seen." Many of the achievements won under what Du Bois, for the case of South Carolina, suggested approached a "dictatorship of the black proletariat," were undone by what he called the "counterrevolution of property."[85] Du Bois agreed with the 1913 Marxist account by the German American Hermann Schlüter that Lincoln could not be viewed as a revolutionary friend of labor, but where Schlüter emphasized the role that the white working class played in the fight against slavery, Du Bois pointed to the role of enslaved workers themselves.[86] Far from a bourgeois revolution, the Civil War and Reconstruction were, for Du Bois, a proletarian revolution partly undone by a bourgeois counterrevolution.

The thesis that the Civil War constituted a bourgeois revolution, when capitalism in the North defeated feudalism in the South, has become a staple of Marxist analysis, though neither Marx, Engels, nor Du Bois made this argument. Du Bois, in fact, rejected this idea as a "sweeping mechanistic interpretation," whose most prominent proponents at the time were the historians Charles and Mary Beard. The Beards applauded the Civil War and Reconstruction as a "Second American Revolution" that brought the victory of northern industry over southern agrarianism.[87] "Manufacturing and industry," as Du Bois characterized this view, "develop in the North; agrarian feudalism develops in the South. They clash . . . and the stronger forces develop the tremendous industrial machine that governs us so magnificently and selfishly today." Du Bois, like Marx and Engels after 1848, denied such mechanistic stage theories of history and focused instead on the historical contingencies of political and military conflicts between classes. "The real plot of the story," Du Bois explained, included "the abolition crusade," "the hurt and struggle of degraded black millions in their fight for freedom and their attempt to enter democracy," and, finally, "rebuilding a new slavery of the working class in the midst of a fateful experiment in democracy."[88] The idea that the slaveholding South was feudal or precapitalist still continued to have a strong career among non-Marxist modernization theorists, including Barrington Moore.[89]

Marxists turned to the interpretation of the Civil War as a bourgeois revolution during the period of the Popular Front of 1934–39, and as a component of the communist struggle against fascism. In 1934, shocked by the brutal success of the Nazi regime after its first year in power in Germany, the Comintern instructed Communist Parties around the world to make common cause with all antifascist parties, including various socialist and antifascist liberal parties.

The great hope of the Popular Front was the Spanish Civil War of 1936–39, during which a coalition of fascists and conservatives under General Francisco Franco sought to topple a popularly elected socialist government. Communists, Trotskyists, anarchists, and other antifascists from around the world volunteered to fight fascism in Spain, while Nazi Germany and Fascist Italy supported Franco. To make common cause with liberal regimes, the Comintern insisted that antifascists fight only against fascism and not against capitalism. This entailed opposing Trotskyists and anarchists, who did not think it worthwhile or strategically valid to defeat fascism without also defeating the capitalist system thought to be the root of fascism.[90] The liberal capitalist states, meanwhile, not only refused support to the Republican cause in Spain but also soon made peace with Hitler in the infamous Munich Agreement of 1938. The following year the Soviet Union followed suit, making its own short-lived peace with Nazi Germany. The Popular Front dissolved, discredited, in the brief accommodation of the world's great powers to fascism, although something like it continued in the U.S. and British cooperation with the USSR against the Axis in the Second World War.

For Communists in the United States, the Popular Front represented a time to celebrate progressive traditions they now supposed inhered in the United States. "Communism is twentieth-century Americanism," proclaimed Earl Browder, the general secretary of the Communist Party of the United States (CPUSA) through the period of the Popular Front and most of the Second World War. In this spirit, the CPUSA dubbed the contingent of soldiers it organized for the Spanish Civil War the Lincoln Brigade. The connections between the Lincoln Brigade and President Abraham Lincoln are more than nominal, but they are also far from linear. Marx and Engels's own identification with Lincoln (and, initially, with Johnson) stemmed from their perception that the Civil War constituted a proletarian revolution and from their inability to recognize enslaved black workers as the proletarian authors of this revolution. This identification with Lincoln was, nonetheless, hardly the central point of the writings of Marx and Engels on the Civil War. In the 1930s, however, identifying with Lincoln served to rally all antifascist forces, whether liberal, socialist, or communist, against fascism. The American Civil War was duly interpreted as a bourgeois revolution, just one stage behind a proletarian revolution, and Lincoln elevated to a red hero, including in the name of the U.S. brigade fighting Franco in Spain.

Herbert M. Morais, writing under the pseudonym Richard Enmale, offered perhaps the first Marxist reading of the Civil War as a bourgeois revolution in his introduction to a 1937 volume of writings by Marx and Engels on the American Civil War.[91] Morais endorsed the interpretation of Charles and Mary Beard that the Civil War was a bourgeois revolution in which modern northern free-labor capitalism defeated a supposedly feudal southern slavery. (Morais did, however, point out some shortcomings in the approach of these "liberal bourgeois" historians, particularly their failure to acknowledge the roles of white workers or any African Americans in the war.)[92] In this view, nations proceed through similar historical stages, for example, from feudalism to capitalism to socialism, varying primarily in the speed with which they complete their progress. While Morais's interpretation stood at odds with Marx and Engels's own interpretation of the war, crossing Marxism with American exceptionalism served an important political function in establishing the Popular Front. The belief that an ideal of freedom inheres in the United States suggested that the differences between the capitalist United States and the socialist Soviet Union came from temporary delays in an otherwise inevitable national U.S. progress rather than from fundamental political and economic differences. Yet this hybrid of Marxism and American exceptionalism continued to flourish in Civil War historiography long after the struggle against fascism ended.

In the atmosphere of political persecution that has long been the decidedly unexceptional reality in the United States, Morais elected to publish under a pseudonym to remain anonymous. He chose the name Enmale, combining the first two letters of the names Engels, Marx, and Lenin. The ruse failed, and Morais became one of the Brooklyn College faculty fired in 1941 after hearings on "subversive activities" in New York public education by the red-baiting Rapp-Coudert Committee. Apparently the committee was especially alarmed that, in the overheated words of a *New York Times* reporter, "Teachers Planned to Depict Franklin, Lincoln as Forerunners of Reds."[93] It is easy to see how those seeking to purge communists from public life might find in Morais's edition of Marx and Engels's writings on the Civil War a threatening echo of the CPUSA's Browderist slogan "Communism is twentieth-century Americanism."

Trotskyists, although they did not endorse the Popular Front, also took on a version of the CPUSA interpretation of the war as a bourgeois revolution. This was to criticize the limited extent of emancipation rather than to praise the United States as progressive. The Trotskyist intellectual and author of *Black Jacobins*, C. L. R. James, criticized Morais and other Communist Party historians, including James S. Allen and Herbert Aptheker, for treating both black and white workers as simply "manpower and shock troops" for white political elites. James characterized the work of these historians as an invasion by "American Stalinism" of Civil War history in service of the Popular Front policy. He also accused these historians of ignoring or dismissing Du Bois's *Black Reconstruction*, a charge that is plausible only with respect to Morais's edition of Marx and Engels. The claim is inaccurate about Allen's 1937 *Reconstruction*, including Morais's preface to that text, and about the work of Aptheker.[94] James also characterized the Civil War as a bourgeois revolution and thus criticized Du Bois, even while praising him for delivering a telling blow against "the whole Stalinist popular front conception." In depicting the Civil War as a revolution of black workers, James explained, Du Bois had revealed that "the Negroes in particular had tried to carry out ideas that went beyond the prevailing conceptions of bourgeois democracy."[95] George Novack, another Trotskyist, similarly criticized Morais as a Stalinist for presenting an overly rosy picture of the post–Civil War United States, while also characterizing the Civil War as a bourgeois revolution.[96]

The contested process of interpreting the American Civil War as a revolution is just one of the many avenues that connect present-day historians to the war itself, not as detached observers but as participants in what Eric Foner has aptly called "America's Unfinished Revolution." Most scholars of the Civil War influenced by Marx have continued to refine the Popular Front bourgeois revolution thesis. Noel Ignatiev has criticized Foner's *Reconstruction* for continuing the Popular Front interpretation of the Civil War as a bourgeois revolution. Where earlier ultraleftists had criticized CPUSA historians for ignoring Du Bois's interpretation of the Civil War as a revolution of black workers undermined by a counterrevolution of capital, Ignatiev criticized Foner for mischaracterizing Du Bois's interpretation as congenial to his own.[97] Eugene Genovese also maintained the bourgeois revolution thesis long beyond the Browderist period by identifying a precapitalist, feudal character of the southern slaveholding economy. Although this interpretation emerged from a Marxist perspective, it continued to flourish even after Genovese abandoned Marxism.[98] The stagist model presupposed by the bourgeois revolution thesis even had Genovese characterizing nineteenth-century slave uprisings as bourgeois revolutions.[99] Although Steven Hahn also characterizes the Civil War as a bourgeois revolution, he does not subsume African American politics into that category. Beginning with a section on African Americans as "the Jacobins of the country," Hahn both restores and develops Du Bois's understanding of the period.[100]

It is hard to dispute the basic point that, at least by the end of Reconstruction, capitalism based on nominally free labor was secure and dominant throughout the United States.[101] However, such an "outcome-based definition of bourgeois revolution," as Neil Davidson terms it, leaves unexamined the process of war and revolution, and, in doing so, obscures not only the history it is supposed to explain but also the theoretical concepts it is meant to elaborate.[102]

The interpretation of the Civil War as a bourgeois revolution is just one position in a contentious debate about the nature of liberalism, private property, war, and revolution that began well before the first shots were fired on Fort Sumter and that continues to this day. This reflexivity does not reveal some fallacious circular logic in Marxism, but rather highlights how dialectical categories of historical analysis emerge from the history they explain, rather than being applied from some outside, more or less correctly, to history. Marx and Engels did not regard the Civil War as a bourgeois revolution, although the understandings of class and revolution that they developed while observing the conflict have been especially influential on interpretations of the Civil War, including as a bourgeois revolution. For them, the Civil War offered a hopeful model of working-class revolution that contrasted favorably with the failed European revolutions of 1848. Comrades like Joseph Weydemeyer who participated in the war already began to overcome Marx and Engels's limited ability to appreciate the agency of black workers. By highlighting the agency of enslaved black workers, Du Bois's *Black Reconstruction* offered a new interpretation of the Civil War and Reconstruction that historians are still grappling with. One might agree with C. L. R. James and Noel Ignatiev that Popular Front interpretations of the Civil War as a bourgeois revolution continue to limit our ability to appreciate Du Bois's thesis. But it would also be incorrect to exaggerate the enmity among Marxists, even that between Trotskyists and Communists. Before the late 1960s, almost every Marxist interpreter of the Civil War—including Du Bois, Morais, Allen, and Aptheker—was suppressed not by each other but by an academy whose avowed hostility to racial equality and to all forms of Marxism was supported by U.S. government harassment and worse. In the face of this, and with support from Communist Parties, these individuals laid the groundwork for historians to drive the Dunning thesis from the field of Reconstruction history. The purpose of reviving the conflicts among these Marxists is not to watch them cancel each other out, but to revive their debates and unstick interpretations of the Civil War and Reconstruction from the single moment of the Popular Front and from the bourgeois revolution thesis.

NOTES

1. James M McPherson, *Battle Cry of Freedom: The Civil War Era*, vol. 6 of *The Oxford History of the United States* (New York: Oxford University Press, 1988). See also James M. McPherson, *Abraham Lincoln and the Second American Revolution* (New York: Oxford University Press, 1990).

2. To recover a more robust set of interpretations of the American Civil War as a revolution, this essay thus builds on three normally separate discussions about Karl Marx and the American Civil War, each of which is as old as the war itself. The first is the study of the contribution of varieties of German socialist radicalisms to the fight against slavery in the Civil War–era United States, what Robin Blackburn has recently termed the "German corrective" to American abolitionism. See Robin Blackburn, *An Unfinished Revolution: Karl Marx and Abraham Lincoln* (London: Verso, 2011). Blackburn relies especially on the excellent Bruce Levine, *The Spirit of 1848: German Immigrants, Labor Conflict, and the Coming of the Civil War* (Urbana: University of Illinois Press, 1992). See also Alison Clark Efford, *German Immigrants, Race, and Citizenship in the Civil War Era* (New York: Cambridge University Press, 2013); and Mischa Honeck, *We Are the Revolutionists: German-Speaking Immigrants and American Abolitionists after 1848* (Athens: University of Georgia Press, 2011). The second is the study of Karl Marx's and Friedrich Engels's own interpretations of the American Civil War. The classic text is the compilation edited by Richard Enmale, Karl Marx, and Friedrich Engels, *The Civil War in the United States* (New York: International Publishers, 1937). More recently, see Kevin B. Anderson, *Marx at the Margins: On Nationalism, Ethnicity, and Non-Western Societies* (Chicago: University of Chicago Press, 2010); Blackburn, *An Unfinished Revolution*; August H. Nimtz, *Marx, Tocqueville, and Race in America: The "Absolute Democracy" or "Defiled Republic"* (Lanham, Md.: Lexington Books, 2003); and Andrew Zimmerman, ed., *Marx, Engels, and the Civil War in the United States* (New York: International Publishers, forthcoming). The third is a long tradition of employing Marxist concepts of class conflict, politics, and revolution to interpret the American Civil War. The earliest version are Marx and Engels's own writings on the Civil War. The most recent is John Ashworth, *Slavery, Capitalism*,

and Politics in the Antebellum Republic, 2 vols. (Cambridge, UK: Cambridge University Press, 1995, 2007). See also the essays in the "Symposium on the American Civil War and Slavery," *Historical Materialism* 19 (December 2011).

3. Especially important in developing this history have been Noel Ignatiev, "'The American Blindspot': Reconstruction According to Eric Foner and W. E. B. Du Bois," *Labour / Le Travail* 31 (April 1993): 243–51; Neil Davidson, "The American Civil War Considered as a Bourgeois Revolution," *Historical Materialism* 19 (December 2011): 45–91; and Brian Kelly, "Introduction to the Illinois Edition," in *Labor, Free and Slave: Workingmen and the Anti-slavery Movement in the United States*, by Bernard Mandel (Urbana: University of Illinois, 2007), ix–lx.

4. For a critique, see Slavoj Žižek, *Did Somebody Say Totalitarianism?* (London: Verso, 2001).

5. For a recent, excellent example, see James Oakes, *Freedom National: The Destruction of Slavery in the United States, 1861–1865* (New York: W. W. Norton, 2013). This would seem to stand in contrast to Oakes's earlier "The Political Significance of Slave Resistance," *History Workshop* 22 (Autumn 1986): 89–107.

6. On popular emancipation from below by Union soldiers, see Chandra Manning, *What This Cruel War Was Over: Soldiers, Slavery, and the Civil War* (New York: Alfred A. Knopf, 2007); and Glenn David Brasher, *The Peninsula Campaign and the Necessity of Emancipation: African Americans and the Fight for Freedom* (Chapel Hill: University of North Carolina Press, 2012). On self-emancipation, see, among others, W. E. B Du Bois, *Black Reconstruction: An Essay Toward a History of the Part Which Black Folk Played in the Attempt to Reconstruct Democracy in America, 1860–1880* (1935; New York: Free Press, 1998); and Steven Hahn, *A Nation under Our Feet: Black Political Struggles in the Rural South from Slavery to the Great Migration* (Cambridge: Harvard University Press, 2003).

7. For an important critique of Spielberg's *Lincoln*, see Kate Masur, "In Spielberg's 'Lincoln,' Passive Black Characters," *New York Times*, November 12, 2012. For a recent left celebration of President Lincoln, see Blackburn, *An Unfinished Revolution*. Eric Foner offers a more sophisticated study of Lincoln that nonetheless leaves relatively intact the figure of the Great Emancipator in *The Fiery Trial: Abraham Lincoln and American Slavery* (New York: W. W. Norton, 2010).

8. Edwin C. Holland, *A Refutation of the Calumnies Circulated against the Southern and Western States, Respecting the Institution and Existence of Slavery among Them* (Charleston, S.C.: A. E. Miller, 1822), 86.

9. William Archibald Dunning, *Essays on the Civil War and Reconstruction and Related Topics* (New York: Macmillan Company, 1898), 250–51.

10. On 1848 and the Civil War, see, in addition to literature cited in note 2, Andre M. Fleche, *The Revolution of 1861: The American Civil War in the Age of Nationalist Conflict* (Chapel Hill: University of North Carolina Press, 2012); Larry J. Reynolds, *European Revolutions and the American Literary Renaissance* (New Haven: Yale University Press, 1988); Timothy M. Roberts, *Distant Revolutions: 1848 and the Challenge to American Exceptionalism* (Charlottesville: University of Virginia Press, 2009).

11. Bruce Levine captures the socialist politics of these '48ers perhaps better than any other scholar. See his *Spirit of 1848*.

12. On these events, especially as Marx participated in them, see Jonathan Sperber, *Karl Marx: A Nineteenth-Century Life* (New York: Liveright, 2013), 214–42.

13. Johann Philipp Becker and Christian Essellen, *Geschichte der Süddeutschen Mai-Revolution* (Geneva: Gottfried Becker, 1849), 203–5, 130. On Sigel's assistance with this work, see Franz Sigel, *Denkwürdigkeiten des Generals Franz Sigel aus den Jahren 1848 und 1849*, ed. Wilhelm Blos, 2nd ed. (Mannheim: J. Bensheimer, 1902), 139.

14. Che Guevara, *Message to the Tricontinental* (Havana: The Executive Secretariat of the Organization of the Solidarity of the Peoples of Africa, Asia, and Latin America, 1967).

15. Karl Marx, preface to the first edition of *Capital*, vol. 1, translated by Ben Fowkes (1867; New York: Penguin Books, 1992), 91. I changed the translation of *Sturmglocke* from its usual "tocscin" to the simpler "alarm bell."

16. Karl Marx, "Der 18te Brumaire des Louis Napoleon" (1852), in *Gesamtausgabe*, by Karl Marx and Friedrich Engels (Berlin: Dietz/ Internationale Marx-Engels-Stiftung, 1972–) (hereafter MEGA2), I/11, 96–173.

17. George Fitzhugh, *Sociology for the South; or, The Failure of Free Society* (Richmond: A. Morris, 1854), 41–42.

18. Francis Lieber, *On Civil Liberty and Self-Government* (London: Richard Bentley, 1853), 16.

19. Marx wrote of "the 2nd-December character of the whole secession maneuver." Karl Marx to Friedrich Engels, 5 July 1861, MEGA2 III/11, 529–32.

20. See Adam Tuchinsky, *Horace Greeley's New-York Tribune: Civil War–Era Socialism and the Crisis of Free Labor* (Ithaca: Cornell University Press, 2009).

21. Charles A. Dana to Karl Marx, Mar. 8, 1860, MEGA2 III/10, 362.

22. See the transfer of payments discussed in Sigismund Ludwig Borkheim to Friedrich Kapp, Dec. 27, 1860, Kleine Korrespondenz (Sozialdemokratische Partei Deutschlands), International Institute of Social History, Amsterdam, Netherlands (hereafter IISG).

23. Tuchinsky, *Horace Greeley's New-York Tribune*.

24. Carl Guarneri, *The Utopian Alternative: Fourierism in Nineteenth-Century America* (Ithaca: Cornell University Press, 1991).

25. See Étienne Balibar and Cory Browning, "On the Aporias of Marxian Politics: From Civil War to Class Struggle," *Diacritics* 39 (Summer 2009): 59–73.

26. Eric Foner, *Free Soil, Free Labor, Free Men: The Ideology of the Republican Party Before the Civil War* (New York: Oxford University Press, 1970), 18–23.

27. Henry Charles Carey, *Principles of Political Economy*, 4 vols. (Philadelphia: Carey, Lea and Blanchard, 1837), 2:206–7.

28. Henry Charles Carey, *The Slave Trade, Domestic and Foreign: Why It Exists, and How It May Be Extinguished* (Philadelphia: A. Hart, late Carey and Hart, 1853).

29. Ibid., 203–4.

30. Karl Marx to Friedrich Engels, 14 June 1853, MEGA2 III/6, 196–200.

31. Karl Marx, *Grundrisse* (1939; New York: Penguin Books, 1973), 883–84, 580, 579.

32. Karl Marx to Friedrich Engels, 26 Nov. 1869, MEGA1 III/4: 247–51.

33. Karl Marx to Friedrich Engels, 11 Jan. 1860, MEGA2 III/10, 152–53.

34. See, for example, Karl Marx to Friedrich Engels, 1 July 1861, MEGA2 III/11, 520–22, or Friedrich Engels to Joseph Weydemeyer, 24 Nov. 1864, Karl Marx and Friedrich Engels, *Der Bürgerkrieg in Den Vereinigten Staaten*, ed. Günter Wisotzki and Manfred Tetzel (Berlin: Dietz, 1976), 211–15.

35. Karl Marx, "The London *Times* on the Orleans Princes in America," *New York Daily Tribune*, November 7, 1861; Enmale, Marx, and Engels, *Civil War in the United States*, 20–25.

36. Karl Marx to Friedrich Engels, 28 Sept. 1861, MEGA2 III/11, 572–73. The individual soon set sail for the United States. See Ernst Oßwald, writing from Liverpool, to Karl Marx, 9 Oct. 1861, MEGA2 III/11, 524–25.

37. Joseph Weydemeyer, "Die ökonomischen Zustände des Südens (lecture manuscript)," 1857, Joseph Weydemeyer Papers, IISG, Nr. 334; Joseph Weydemeyer to Max Joseph Becker, 23 Feb. 1857, Joseph Weydemeyer Papers, IISG, Nr. 245.

38. Joseph Weydemeyer to Max Joseph Becker, 25 Jan. 1857, Joseph Weydemeyer Papers, IISG, Nr. 243. On Germans in the Kansas fight, see Frank Baron, "German Republicans and Radicals in the Struggle for a Slave-Free Kansas: Charles F. Kob and August Bondi," *Yearbook of German-American Studies* 40 (2005): 3–26.

39. August H. Nimtz argues that Weydemeyer was a conduit for Marx's ideas in the struggle against slavery in *Marx, Tocqueville, and Race in America*.

40. I develop this argument in "From the Rhine to the Mississippi: Property, Democracy, and Socialism in the American Civil War," *Journal of the Civil War Era* 5 (March 2015): 3–37.

41. The letter, from November 30, 1861, refers to a state that had been ongoing, and, while it is not clear when these troops began incorporating blacks into their ranks, it was well before any such thing was officially permitted. Isaac P. Jones to Henry W. Halleck, 30 Nov. 1861, *The War of the Rebellion: A Compilation of the Official Records of the Union and Confederate Armies*, 128 vols. (Washington, D.C.: Government Printing Office, 1880–1901), Ser. II, vol. 1, 779–81 (hereafter *OR*).

42. Henry W. Halleck to George B. McClellan, 2 Feb. 1862, *OR*, Ser. I, vol. 8, 828–29.

43. See Jörg Nagler, *Frémont contra Lincoln: Die deutsch-amerikanische Opposition in der Republikanischen Partei während des Amerikanischen Bürgerkrieges* (Frankfurt am Main: P. Lang, 1984).

44. John M. Schofield to Henry Wager Halleck, 20 Sept. 1863, *OR* Ser. I, vol. 22, pt. 2, 546.

45. Karl Marx, "The Dismissal of Frémont," *Die Presse*, November 26, 1861, in *Collected Works*, by Karl Marx and Friedrich Engels (New York: International Publishers, 1975) (hereafter MECW), 19: 86–88.

46. On slavery in the Mississippi Valley, see most recently Walter Johnson, *River of Dark Dreams: Slavery and Empire in the Cotton Kingdom* (Cambridge: Harvard University Press, 2013). On the second slavery in the United States, see especially Anthony E.

Kaye, "The Second Slavery: Modernity in the Nineteenth-Century South and the Atlantic World," *Journal of Southern History* 75 (August 2009): 627–50. The historian Dale Tomich has been most responsible for this important turn in the scholarship about slavery. For an overview, see Dale Tomich and Michael Zeuske, "The Second Slavery: Mass Slavery, World Economy, and Comparative Microhistories," *Review: A Journal of the Fernand Braudel Center* 31, no. 2 (2008): 91–100.

47. Ira Berlin, *Many Thousands Gone: The First Two Centuries of Slavery in North America* (Cambridge: Harvard University Press, 1998); Ira Berlin, *Generations of Captivity: A History of African-American Slaves* (Cambridge: Harvard University Press, 2004). On the expansion of slavery, see Adam Rothman, *Slave Country: American Expansion and the Origins of the Deep South* (Cambridge: Harvard University Press, 2007).

48. Berlin, *Generations of Captivity*, 177–81. See also Ira Berlin and Philip D. Morgan, eds., *Cultivation and Culture: Labor and the Shaping of Slave Life in the Americas* (Charlottesville: University of Virginia Press, 1993).

49. Lawrence N. Powell, *New Masters: Northern Planters during the Civil War and Reconstruction* (New Haven: Yale University Press, 1980).

50. On Helena, see Zimmerman, "Rhine to Mississippi." On Davis Bend, see especially Thavolia Glymph, "The Second Middle Passage: The Transition from Slavery to Freedom at Davis Bend, Mississippi" (Ph.D. dissertation, Purdue University, 1994).

51. Karl Marx, "The American Question in England," *New York Daily Tribune*, October 11, 1861, in *Civil War in the United States*, 3–15.

52. See, e.g., Friedrich Engels to Karl Marx, 12 May 1862, in *Karl Marx, Friedrich Engels historisch-kritische Gesamtausgabe*, ed. David Borisovich Rjazanov (Frankfurt am Main: Marx-Engels-Archiv, 1927) (hereafter, MEGA1) III/3, 68–69; Friedrich Engels to Karl Marx, 30 July 1862, MEGA1 III/3, 80–82; Friedrich Engels to Karl Marx, 5 Nov. 1862, MEGA1 III/3, 106–7.

53. Karl Marx to Lion Philips, 6 May 1861, MEGA2 III/11, 439–40.

54. Karl Marx to Friedrich Engels, 7 Aug. 1862, MEGA1 III/3, 91–92; *Bürgerkrieg*, 176–78.

55. Karl Marx, "Zur Kritik der Dinge in Amerika," *Die Presse*, 9 Aug. 1862, *Bürgerkrieg*, 171–76.

56. Karl Marx to Friedrich Engels, 10 Sept. 1862, MEGA1 III/3, 101–2; *Bürgerkrieg*, 179–80.

57. Karl Marx to Friedrich Engels, 29 Oct. 1862, MEGA1 III/3, 104–6.

58. Karl Marx, "The British Cotton Trade," *New York Daily Tribune*, October 14, 1861, in *Civil War in the United States*, 15–19

59. Karl Marx, "Provisional Rules of the International Working Men's Association" (London, 28 Sept. 1864), MEGA2 I/20, 13–14.

60. The use of the terminology of emancipation and abolition occurs regularly in the work of Marx and Engels. See, for example, *Manifest der Kommunistischen Partei* (1848), in *Werke*, by Karl Marx and Friedrich Engels, 37 vols. (Berlin: Dietz, 1956) (hereafter MEW) 4:459–93.

61. Karl Marx, "The London *Times* on the Orleans Princes in America," *New York Daily Tribune*, November 7, 1861, in *Civil War in the United States*, 20–25.

62. Karl Marx, "To Andrew Johnson, President of the United States," *The Bee-Hive*, May 20, 1865, MEGA2 I/20, 134–137.

63. Karl Marx, "Zu den Ereignisse in Nordamerika," *Die Presse*, 12 Oct. 1862, in MEW 15:339–47.

64. Karl Marx to Friedrich Engels, 29 Oct. 1862, MEGA1 III/3, 104–6. Eric Lott has suggested that Lincoln carried out his own "Eighteenth Brumaire" in wedding American traditions of revolution to his project of state building in "The Eighteenth Brumaire of Abraham Lincoln: Revolutionary Rhetoric and the Emergence of the Bourgeois State," *Clio* 22 (Winter 1993): 157–73.

65. Marx to Engels, May 1, 1865; Engels to Marx, May 3, 1865, MEGA2 III/3, 262–65.

66. Karl Marx, "To Andrew Johnson, President of the United States," *The Bee-Hive*, 20 May 1865, MEGA2 I/20, 134–37.

67. Karl Marx, "Address of the International Working Men's Association (Inaugural Address)" (London, Sept. 28, 1864), MEGA2 I/20, 3–12.

68. Karl Marx to Abraham Lincoln, 22 Nov. 1864, MEGA2 I/20.

69. Raya Dunayevskaya, "The Impact of the Civil War in the United States on the Structure of Capital," in *Marxism & Freedom: From 1776 until Today* (1958; Amherst, N.Y.: Humanity Books, 2000), 581–91.

70. Karl Marx, "Value, Price, and Profit," 20 and 27 June 1865, MEGA2 I/20, 141–86, 143, 171, 179–83.

71. Marx, *Capital*, vol. 1, 414.

72. See, e.g., Wilhelm Eichhoff, "Die Internationale Arbeiterassoziation: Ihre Gründung, Organisation, politisch-soziale Tätigkeit und Ausbreitung, 6. Juni bis 26./27. Juli 1868," 1868; Friedrich Lessner, "Aufruf an die deutschen Arbeiter Londons," *Hermann*, 15 Aug. 1868. MEGA2 I/21, 948–1003.

73. Joseph Weydemeyer, "Zur Neger-Stimmrechts-Frage," *Westliche Post*, September 8, 13, 14, 1865.

74. International Working Men's Association, "To the People of the United States of America," *The Workman's Advocate*, October 14, 1865, *Minutes of the General Council of the International Workingmen's Association, 1864–1886* (Moscow: Progress Publishers, 1964).

75. General Council of the International Workingmen's Association to International Labor Union, May 12, 1869, in Hermann Schlüter, *Lincoln, Labor, and Slavery: A Chapter from the Social History of America* (1913; New York: Russell and Russell, 1965), 229–33.

76. Niall Whelehan, "Skirmishing, the Irish World, and Empire, 1876–86," *Éire-Ireland* 42 (Spring/Summer 2007): 180–200.

77. Karl Marx, "Entwurf des Vortrages über den Fenianismus im Deutschen Arbeiterbildungsverein, London am 16. Dezember 1867," 16 Dec. 1867, MEGA2 I/21, 22–32.

78. Karl Marx, "Draft of a Speech on the 'Fenian Question' for the Meeting of the General Council of the International Working Men's Association," 26 Nov. 1867, MEGA2 I/21, 15–21. This lecture, apparently, was never delivered.

79. Karl Marx to Meyer and Vogt, 9 April 1870, Karl Marx and Friedrich Engels, *Letters to Americans, 1848–1895: A Selection*, ed. Alexander Trachtenberg and trans. Leonard E. Mins (New York: International Publishers, 1953), 77–80.

80. On this and much else, see Philip M. Katz, *From Appomattox to Montmartre: Americans and the Paris Commune* (Cambridge: Harvard University Press, 1998).

81. Karl Marx, *The Civil War in France* (London: Edward Truelove, 1871), MEGA2 I/22, 119–62, 158, 129–30, 138.

82. See Cedric J. Robinson, *Black Marxism: The Making of the Black Radical Tradition* (Chapel Hill: University of North Carolina Press, 2000), esp. 185–251.

83. W. E. B Du Bois, "Karl Marx and the Negro," *Crisis* 40 (March 1933): 55–56.

84. Glenda Elizabeth Gilmore, *Defying Dixie: The Radical Roots of Civil Rights, 1919–1950* (New York: W.W. Norton, 2008); Mark I. Solomon, *The Cry Was Unity: Communists and African Americans, 1917–36* (Jackson: University Press of Mississippi, 1998); Andrew Zimmerman, "Prussian Paths of Capitalist Development," in *Alabama in Africa: Booker T. Washington, the German Empire, and the Globalization of the New South* (Princeton: Princeton University Press, 2010), 237–50.

85. Du Bois, *Black Reconstruction*, chap. 4, 358, 381, chap. 14.

86. Schlüter, *Lincoln, Labor, and Slavery*. For two recent, compelling portraits of the of role that black and white workers played in the end of slavery and the Civil War, see Mandel, *Labor, Free and Slave*; and Bruce C. Levine, *Half Slave and Half Free: The Roots of Civil War* (New York: Hill and Wang, 1992).

87. Charles A. Beard and Mary R. Beard, *The Rise of American Civilization* (New York: Macmillan, 1927).

88. Du Bois, *Black Reconstruction*, 714–15.

89. Barrington Moore, "The American Civil War: The Last Capitalist Revolution," in *Social Origins of Dictatorship and Democracy: Lord and Peasant in the Making of the Modern World* (Boston: Beacon Press, 1966), 111–55.

90. George Orwell offers a compelling portrait of this process in *Homage to Catalonia* (1938; San Diego: Harcourt, Brace, 1980).

91. Karl Marx and Friedrich Engels, *The Civil War in the United States*, ed. Richard Enmale (New York: International Publishers, 1937).

92. Beard and Beard, *The Rise of American Civilization*.

93. "Communist Scheme to Rewrite History Bared at Hearing," *New York Times*, March 8, 1941.

94. James S. Allen, *Reconstruction: The Battle for Democracy (1865–1876)* (New York: International Publishers, 1937); Herbert Aptheker, *American Negro Slave Revolts* (1943; New York: International Publishers, 1983).

95. C. L. R. James writing as J. Meyer, "Stalinism and Negro History," *Fourth International* 10 (November 1949): 309–14.

96. George Novack, "Marx and Engels on the Civil War," review of *The Civil War in the United States* by Karl Marx and Friedrich Engels, edited by Richard Enmale, *New International* 4 (February 1938): 45–47.

97. Ignatiev, "The American Blindspot."

98. Eugene D. Genovese, *Roll, Jordan, Roll: The World the Slaves Made* (New York: Pantheon Books, 1974).

99. Eugene D. Genovese, *From Rebellion to Revolution: Afro-American Slave Revolts in the Making of the Modern World* (Baton Rouge: Louisiana State University Press, 1979).

100. Hahn, *A Nation under Our Feet*. For Hahn's conception of the Civil War as, nonetheless, a bourgeois revolution, see his "Class and State in Postemancipation Societies: Southern Planters in Comparative Perspective," *American Historical Review* 95 (February 1990): 75–98, and his afterword to this volume.

101. See Sven Beckert, *The Monied Metropolis: New York City and the Consolidation of the American Bourgeoisie, 1850–1896* (New York: Cambridge University Press, 2001).

102. Davidson, "The American Civil War," 62. Davidson endorses such an "outcome-based" approach.

AFTERWORD

What Sort of World Did the Civil War Make?
Steven Hahn

The theme of this volume, the world the Civil War made, is a large and capacious one, and it implicitly suggests that the Civil War made for a new and different world than the one that came before it. This would not seem to be a controversial idea. The Civil War is widely understood as one of the country's great turning points, if not *the* great turning point, and we often use rather powerful, dramatic, and occasionally extravagant language to describe what happened during and immediately after it. The quantity of blood spilled — epic even on an international stage[1] — is the most common measure of the war's impact, but to this may be added the abolition of slavery, the construction of new forms of centralized power, the decisive defeat of the Confederate rebellion, and the ability of the victorious Union to impose martial law and all manner of conditions attendant on securing a peace. If the war and what we generally call Reconstruction are regarded as inextricably connected, then historians often invoke the term "revolution" to characterize what went on, whether they were appalled by what the Republican Party did to a defeated South (the Dunningites),[2] sanguine or critical about the transformations effected (the progressives and revisionists),[3] or ultimately disappointed that the engine of change too quickly ran out of steam (the post-revisionists).[4]

Yet if we take a longer view, the picture — at least the picture constructed and argued over by scholars — is much less clear. And this volume raises further questions still. At the turn of the twentieth century, the United States appeared to be a far different place than it was forty years earlier. A sprawling, decentered, and overwhelmingly agricultural and small-town society had become an urban and industrial power, and a force in international relations. But how much of all this change owed

337

explicitly to the Civil War and Reconstruction? It is easy to forget the historiographical traditions that either emphasized fundamental continuities during the Civil War era, or failed to take direct stock of how what happened influenced the longer term. Economic historians have debated for years whether the Civil War advanced the course of industrialization, and a good many of them believe the data says no. A few claim that the war may in fact have retarded industrialization.[5]

The historian C. Vann Woodward, whose work has been of enormous influence inside and outside the academy, made a strong case for the Civil War's revolutionary consequences for the South, and in this he followed in the "progressive" path of Charles and Mary Beard and Howard Beale. But the centerpiece of Woodward's argument—the destruction of the old landed ruling class and the rise of a new one, urban and middle-class in character—has been challenged very forcefully by social historians who have demonstrated, with intensive quantitative studies, that in most places planter families held onto their land and reclaimed the reins of local power, not to mention control of the freed labor force.[6] Other historians who write about the postwar system of tenancy and sharecropping often puzzle over how different it was than slavery, marked as it quickly came to be by a raft of extraeconomic compulsions. Indeed, what I see as the general scholarly consensus (which I happen not to share) is that slavery constituted just another form of capitalism, and it makes one wonder what the destruction of slavery and the transition to different forms of labor exploitation mean in conceptual terms. Besides, scholars who regard slavery as a form of capitalism rarely confront the question of the transition themselves.[7] Those who also see the main theme of the period between 1865 and 1914 as the reconstruction and redeployment of white supremacy—as Ulrich B. Phillips did in his day—have good reason to ask if the South "lost the war" but ultimately "won the peace."[8]

Then, of course, there is the question of how wide an impact the Civil War might have had and how big a "world" it might have made. We have become well accustomed to viewing the Civil War and Reconstruction in international and comparative perspective, but mostly as it concerns a better understanding of what happened here.[9] We know next to nothing— other than conjecturally—about the international, the global, repercussions of the war, and the literature on world history does not proffer much help. C. A Bayly's recent world synthesis of the nineteenth century, *The Birth of the Modern World*, devotes only a few pages to the American Civil

War and makes relatively little of its international consequences outside the changing technology of warfare. Neither does Eric Hobsbawm's multi-volume history of the nineteenth century, including the one—*The Age of Capital, 1848-1875*—that directly covers the Civil War era. Nor does any other overview of the era that I know of.[10]

Although American historians have often claimed that the outcome of the Civil War effectively doomed slavery in Cuba and Brazil, the last places in the hemisphere where it still survived, neither the Cuban nor the Brazilian historical literatures makes such connections (or at least do not make very much of such connections). Even Rebecca Scott's highly regarded study of race and emancipation in Cuba and Louisiana devotes all of one paragraph to the meaning of the Civil War in Cuba. The war that concerns Cubanists is the Ten Years War in their own territory; the one that concerns Brazilianists is the Paraguayan War on their border.[11] Significantly, the American Civil War does not much register in the historiography of either Latin America more generally or Mexico in particular (consumed as it was during the period with the French invasion, the installation of Maximilian as emperor, and the construction of the regime of Porfirio Díaz, best known as the *Porfiriato*). Mexican eyes see more of a continuity of American imperial aggression throughout the nineteenth century, even though the distractions of the war likely played a role in France's decision to invade.[12]

The limited consideration of the Civil War's international influence is all the more surprising when we compare it to the literatures on the French Revolution, its Haitian component, the abolition of slavery in the British West Indies, or the revolutions of 1848. For in these the international ripple effects figure centrally in scholarly appraisals of their significance. If anything, scholars of the United States have taken much more account of these events in the coming of the Civil War than of the Civil War's impact on the international developments that followed. It is reasonable for us to ask why this is so.[13]

My intention is not to dismiss deeply laid understandings and argue that they make much ado about nothing. My intention, following the provocative and interesting essays here, is rather to suggest the wide-ranging and challenging conceptual and empirical work that we still have before us. And I am indebted to the authors in this volume who take on many of these challenges and move the interpretive discussion in very exciting ways. In a variety of respects, that is, they ask us to interrogate long-held perspectives on the Civil War era, to recast the geography and chronology, to embrace social groups and developments normally left to the margins, and to glimpse interconnections that have previously been overlooked or ignored. They also remind us of the limits of power, of the creative forms of resistance to it, of the bumpy and nonlinear course of change, and of the role of official and paramilitary violence in the making of the postwar era. Their picture of the world the Civil War made often defies, if not consciously rejects, familiar categories and assumptions; they can paint with unusual brush strokes. And they leave us with more than a few arresting questions: Gregory Downs and Kate Masur, in fact, introduce the volume by suggesting that we dispense with the idea of Reconstruction entirely.

Yet I would like to take us in a direction—one organized around issues of political economy—that few of the essays follow, and argue a bit more forcefully that the Civil War made, very directly, for a different, in some instances a far different, world, both domestically and internationally, and in the arenas that mattered most. The war and its specific outcome in my view dramatically reoriented the axes of power and the formation of social classes in the United States, redefined the nature and boundaries of governance, redirected the course of economic development, reconstituted the body politic, and extended the international revolutionary dynamic that appeared to have ended with the revolutions of 1848, reconfiguring the platform of international relations, especially as regards the Pacific (we make a mistake if we view the war and its impact chiefly as an Atlantic event).

Which is to say that what began as a slaveholders' rebellion in the context of an intense struggle for federal power, turned into a social and political revolution, bourgeois in nature, that simultaneously made for an imperial nation-state for the first time on the North American continent, as well as for a massive capitalist transformation "from above."[14] The main work of what we have customarily called Reconstruction, in other words, was reorganizing the political economy of the United States and setting the course for what became the next reconstruction—not in the 1950s and 1960s and associated with civil rights, as this is often made out to be—but in the 1890s and first decade and a half of the twentieth century, when what Martin Sklar calls the "corporate reconstruction of American capitalism" began to take place.[15]

Making this case in its fullness would require many more pages than I have here. Rest assured, I will not test the reader's patience. But I would like to make some claims and offer some ways of thinking about their viability. And this will require both a brief return to the world before the Civil War and a brief counterfactual excursion into a world in which the Civil War had not occurred or had turned out differently.

PART OF THE CHALLENGE in understanding the Civil War's impact more clearly is to get a firm handle on the nature of power and the trajectories of development in the antebellum United States. Historians often work off a number of ideas that, in my judgment, are dubious: that the Revolution and the Constitution produced a nation; that slavery quickly became organized along sectional lines; that the main axes of conflict were North versus South; and that the power of slaveholders was steadily declining; that the United States was well along the road of industrialization by the 1840s and that it moved down the industrial road with an enfranchised working class; and, of course, that capitalism was running rampant.

There are, it seems to me, good reasons to question all of this. We might like to think of our national-origins story commencing in the late eighteenth century with perhaps a highly embattled march to fruition being completed with Reconstruction. But the structure of governance created by the Articles of Confederation and then the Constitution scarcely made for a national state—for a nation-state—in its most basic of terms: as a political entity that could claim sovereign authority over the people and places within its presumed borders. After all, the majority of the voting public in the United States embraced some form of state rights, and the territory of the country was replete with competing forms of sovereignty, not only built around states and localities and spiritual movements but also around households, slavery being the most politically consequential, though hardly the most common of them. We might, in fact, think about a raft of "counter-sovereignties," some patriarchal, which not only limited the hold of the center but also threatened, at various points, to dismember the entire Union (not entirely unlike Mexico in this period). Secession in 1860–61 was only one of a number of rebellious challenges that erupted from the 1790s onward.[16]

For its part, slavery was anything but sectional in its geography. The states of the Northeast and Middle Atlantic abolished slavery very gradually (mostly freeing the children of slaves and not until they were adults), and the legal basis of emancipation in them was often so muddled that many of the states had to do it twice, New Hampshire as late as 1857. Slave hiring and transit could make a mockery of any dividing line between "free" and "slave" states—as did the persistence of servitude and lifetime indentures for the supposedly liberated—and the courts effectively privileged the demands of slaveholders to take their slaves wherever they saw fit and to recover slaves who tried to escape their captivity.[17]

Outside of New England and the Middle Atlantic, moreover, industrial activity and the spread of wage labor remained quite limited. The rural sector was still organized (North and South) around patriarchal landownership and personal domination (whether of household members or slaves), and manufacturing was chiefly the business of small shops and outworking of various sorts, including the garment trades. Wage labor was most densely in evidence in seaports and on infrastructure projects (most of it was foreign born), and in some places was used in close conjunction with slaves and other coerced workers. And, in truth, much of the antebellum working class was excluded from the franchise owing to race, gender, geographical mobility, and (during the 1850s in the heart of industrialism) place of birth.[18] Not incidentally, the workers in the leading economic sectors of the United States—the production and processing of the cotton staple—had few or no civil and political rights. What was happening during the era of the so-called market revolution, at least in my own judgment, was an intensification of existing exchange relations, of the circulation of goods and people, rather than a transformation in how goods were produced and people deployed. Merchants and large landowners remained the dominant economic actors, much as they had been since the time of European settlement.[19]

Without question, paths of capitalist development and nation-state formation were being carved in the Northeast and sections of the Midwest owing to networks of finance, capital accumulation, immigration, transportation, and state activism at several levels. Yet alternative paths were also being pursued—and alternative centers of power constructed—not only in the lower South but even more significantly in the Mississippi Valley. There, from at least the early nineteenth century onward, entrepreneurs, settlers, slaveholders, and policymakers who would find a political home in the Democratic Party imagined a massive agrocommercial empire stretching out from the riverine (and then rail) corridor linking Chicago and New Orleans, both to other parts of North America and into the Caribbean basin (mainly by way of Havana). Although the slaveholding imperialists of the Gulf Coast may have been the best known among them, midcontinent allies to the North, like Stephen Douglas (who thought Lincoln's "house divided" idea was ludicrous), were equally important.[20]

Indeed, I would like to suggest that the main developmental conflict in the first half of the nineteenth century did not set the North against the South; it set the Northeast against the Mississippi Valley. The disintegration of the valley political coalition in the face of slaveholding militants was crucial to the coming of the Civil War, and then to the impact the war would have on the American political economy. Significantly, one plank that the platforms of Northern and Southern Democrats held in common in 1860, even as they nominated separate candidates and differed over popular sovereignty, was the call for the annexation of Cuba.[21]

The war, then, would not award victory to the North over the South, or to the Union over the so-called Confederacy (I prefer the "so-called Confederacy," as Lincoln had it, recognizing its rogue character rather than dignifying it as a state), but rather to the Northeast developmental project over its various competitors. Yet this was hardly preordained. It came in the process of waging war, not in initiating war; and it was decisively influenced by the course of reconstructing the South and especially the West.

We are, of course, familiar with a constellation of federal measures, designed principally to fund the war and defeat the rebellion, that clearly tipped (or would tip) the balances of political economy in new directions (so long as the war was won): toward cities at the expense of the countryside, toward industry at the expense of agriculture, and toward the Northeast and national state at the expense of every place else. These included the Morrill tariff (and Anti-Bigamy Act), the National Banking Acts, the immediate and uncompensated emancipation of the slave labor force by the federal (as opposed to the state) government, military conscription and the enlistment of African Americans, and the imposition of martial law over much of the South once the rebels began to surrender (though the war and the rebellion would not be over for some time still).[22]

Yet especially important was the creation and dramatic empowerment of a new class of finance capitalists through the marketing of government bonds and securities, and their close alliance with the national state mediated chiefly by the railroads. This was the developmental wedge that transformed the trans-Mississippi West and, in the process, left a decisive mark on the nature and trajectory of American capitalism, domestically and internationally.

Now, there is some reason, as Richard White has recently shown, to question the economic wisdom of the transcontinental railroads that had their birth during the Civil War with the Pacific Railway Act. But the truth is that the transcontinentals were initially governed by a political rather than an economic logic (though the economic followed the political). Lincoln nearly lost the states of California and Oregon in the election of 1860; Democrats and southern sympathizers were the powers there; the New Mexico Territory had enacted a slave code; and rebel troops had quickly moved westward out of Texas with an eye on both Colorado and possibly California (and the precious metals to be found there—the so-called Confederate treasury was effectively bare). Transcontinental railroads had long been favorites of Lincoln's (he wanted to build three), and their authorization must be seen, alongside the creation of new military departments and territories in the West, as a means of extending federal authority over the American territory: as a means of turning a shaky Union into a nation-state. What nineteenth century nation-state did not seek to build some version of a transcontinental railroad as one of its first moves?[23]

The transcontinentals could have been left under public control as some in Congress had hoped, but in effect the government socialized most of the costs not only by means of land giveaways and generous financing but also by deploying the United States Army to facilitate construction through potentially hostile territory. Indeed, the army—with its top officers being veterans of the Civil War and southern Reconstruction—embodied the developmental alliance by destroying and marginalizing Native populations who, in their land use, social organization, subsistence strategies, and forms of surplus extraction, constituted the last significant pre- or non-capitalist societies west of the Mississippi. General William T. Sherman, who placed particularly high value on his career in the West, was not alone in seeing his goals as the promotion of railroad construction, white settlement, and regional economic expansion; in the early treaties that he supervised, Sherman carefully had Indian signatories surrender rights-of-way to the railroads. Then, of course, in one of the lesser-known acts of nation-state building during Reconstruction, the entire treaty system, and the status of Indians as "domestic dependent" nations, was abrogated.[24]

The alliance between new finance capital and the new nation-state proved of considerable developmental importance because it favored creditors over debtors, stabilized the formal political system in its general interests (those who opposed the money regime were left to cobble together their own coalitions and mostly fly-by-night political parties), and laid the groundwork for the next reconstruction in a variety of ways.[25] Equally important, the alliance helped establish the framework for the subsequent industrialization of the West, directly providing the capital and other resources for the many extractive industries—mining chief among them—that would be the hallmarks of the post–Civil War Western economy. Unquestionably, a slower process of railroad building that followed rather than preceded settlement would have made for less of a financial roller coaster during the last three decades of the nineteenth century and surely would have created more breathing room for Native Americans and small producers alike. But that would have been the result of a different Civil War than the one the country actually experienced.[26]

The abolition of slavery and soon thereafter debt peonage (at least in theory, as Stacey L. Smith shows here), as well as the consecration of birthright citizenship, did make new popular struggles possible, and may have advanced the political prospects of working people in parts of Europe (as Andrew Zimmerman suggests). If nothing else, they help us understand why the United States had the most vibrant and violent labor/political history in the world during the last third of the nineteenth century. And the most brutal showdowns clearly occurred in the South and West. We tend to think of radical Reconstruction in racial and political terms, but we must not forget that emancipation created a new working class chiefly in the rural districts of the South, and one that carried out the most impressive political mobilization of any section of the working class in the entire nineteenth century, if not in all of American history.[27] For a time, the federal government was an enabler in this regard, as it was in early agitation for the eight-hour day. Yet not by accident did the governing Republican Party almost simultaneously allow the last Reconstruction regimes, whose political base was overwhelmingly working class, to fall while sending its troops (for the first time) to suppress the Great Railroad Strikes of 1877. Jim Crow involved many different things, but it surely involved a counterrevolution by landed capital and its allies principally through the vehicle of state governments: new lien laws, fence laws, game laws, and vagrancy laws for the agricultural sector, together with the beginnings of a massive attack on the bases of black—read working-class—power.[28]

For the remainder of the century, the United States was convulsed by conflicts of various sorts between labor and capital, and many of the most intense and militarized occurred in the South (I do not think we can understand lynching aside from the reinvigoration of black labor mobility and activism during the 1880s and 1890s, especially in the cotton districts) and, especially, in the West. Here the Knights of Labor helped organize massive strikes against the Gould system in 1885 and 1886, as they did in the sugar districts of lower Louisiana; here the Colored Farmers' Alliance launched a widespread and bloody cotton pickers' strike; here the Populists mobilized thousands of small landowners and tenants in the rural areas while finding a working-class base mainly among silver miners in the Rocky Mountains; here the Western Federation of Miners engaged in some of the most militant actions in the country; and here the Industrial Workers of the World found support among a wide array of the new western working class, many highly mobile laborers who moved between the agricultural, lumbering, and mining sectors (as well as connections with radicals in northern Mexico).[29] Here, too, territorial governments, closely tied to the interests of the railroads and other finance capitalists, along with the courts, played crucial roles in tilting the balances of conflict in favor of capital, in fact in making it almost impossible for labor and its community-based allies to achieve *sustained* victories either through industrial organization or electoral politics.[30] In its forms of accumulation, the deployment of a multiethnic and multicultural labor force, the hyperexploitation of workers, and a close alliance between capital and the state, the trans-Mississippi West became something of a proving ground and crucible for the American form of capitalism.

So it did, too, for American nation-state building. In many respects, the postbellum West (at least the interior West), even more than the postbellum South, became a political and economic colony of both the Northeast and the federal government. This was true not only because northeastern capital was the great beneficiary of western economic development or because federal policy was so critical in promoting economic activity, but also because the federal government — during the Civil War — effectively territorialized most of the region and, with minor exception, blocked these territories from moving to statehood for a very long time. Territorialization, we must not forget, formed a central part of the discourse of "reconstructing" the South. The Dakotas, Idaho, Montana, and Wyoming remained territories for thirty-eight, twenty-seven, twenty-eight, and twenty-two years, respectively. Utah remained a territory for forty-six years, Arizona for forty-nine. And New Mexico was a territory for sixty-two years (territories east of the Mississippi, created before the Civil

War, made far more rapid moves to statehood). "There may be no difference between the form of government of a territory and that of a colony," a
member of Congress intoned who questioned whether the populations in
some of them, on ethnic and cultural grounds, were politically assimilable:
whether, that is, the Constitution would follow the flag there.[31]

Not surprisingly, these issues would soon resurface in the Philippines;
and not surprisingly, the experience of the territorial West would be regarded as foundational. Senator Henry Dawes, the sponsor of the Dawes
Severalty Act (which offered Native Americans citizenship in exchange
for their willingness to give up tribal affiliations), thought that efforts ex-
pended to manage Indians should guide dealings with "other alien races
whose future has been put in our keeping" owing to the Spanish-American
War, and those who arrived in the Philippines were well prepared to put
his idea into practice. From top to bottom—from the directors of the new
Bureau of Insular Affairs, to the appointed military governors, to the top
field officers, to the troops on the ground—most of the American personnel had military experience, and direct encounters with Indians, in the
West.[32]

THE INTERNATIONAL repercussions of the Civil War are not always easy
to measure and, in part owing to odd periodizations in the organization
and writing of American history, they have not adequately been measured.
But let me suggest a few areas where we might look. As the invocation
of the Philippines intimates, the Civil War and its outcome simultaneously secured American hegemony in the Caribbean basin and in much
of the Western Hemisphere—especially in the face of possible British interference—and had an enormously consequential effect on the advance
of American influence and power in the Pacific. From the purchase of
Alaska to the annexation of Hawaii to the proclamation of the Open Door
to the intervention in the Philippines, the reconstruction of the political
economy that the Civil War made possible proved decisive (southerners,
recall, formed the main part of the anti-imperialist bloc at the end of the
nineteenth century).[33]

At the same time, the new resources and bravado claimed by finance
capital fueled growing foreign investments, most immediately in Mexico,
where the Díaz regime, embarking on its own course of nation building,
allowed American companies a major hand in constructing railroads and
in other areas of the Mexican economy, most notably in the mines of

the northwest provinces. Indeed, American economic activity in Mexico began to develop during and immediately after the Civil War, partly at the behest of Mexican liberals looking to defeat the French and move toward the commodification of land and labor (or, as they might prefer, the "modernization" of the peasant sector). Which is to say that the Civil War not only dramatically advanced the development of capitalism in the United States; it also facilitated the expansion of capitalist relations of production and forms of resource exploitation well beyond American borders.[34]

Ironically, this happened too in the international spread of the cotton plant. We all know that cotton was truly king in the antebellum United States. It made the fortunes of a powerful slaveholding class, accounted for 60 percent of the value of all American exports at the time of the Civil War, and created developmental linkages between the South and the Northeast. It also limited what the victorious federal government was prepared to do to slaveholding rebels and do for liberated slaves, because the protection and reinvigoration of cotton production in the rebellious states became a central policy objective. But the U.S. blockade of southern ports encouraged the advance of cotton cultivation in places where it had been organized chiefly on a small scale, sometimes on the basis of peasant production, and both made for new competitors for the United States and a new labor process in the agricultural sectors of south Asia, parts of the Middle East, Africa, and Brazil. The Civil War, that is, may have contributed to the expansion of, and then the crisis of, new global capitalism during the last third of the nineteenth century.[35]

What often confounds a compelling assessment of the Civil War's impact is some sense of what the world might have looked like if the American Civil War had not taken place or if the Civil War had ended up differently: without the unconditional defeat of the Confederate rebellion. Most scholars who even approach the issue appear to think of a course of American development and American influence merely devoid of the military elements of the war, of the disruptions, the casualties, and the necessary reconfigurations of trade. But they also generally fail to consider the social, political, and institutional transformations that the war ushered in, and what these have meant.

It is, of course, difficult and dangerous to imagine a world, here or elsewhere, without the Civil War as we have come to know it. But there are some things that we can reasonably and safely say as a way of evaluating the difference that the war made.

Had the Civil War not taken place (because Buchanan decided to seek a second term, because the Republicans agreed to compromise a bit on the territorial issue during secession winter, because Lincoln abandoned Fort Sumter and bought more time) or had the war, far more likely, ended up with something short of a U.S. victory, say an armistice, there are a number of possible, and in some cases probable, scenarios. Most extreme would have been a steady disintegration of the country in which the so-called Confederate states may eventually have been joined in secession by other regions, led perhaps by a Pacific Coast republic, something in the manner of the Spanish-American colonies-turned-countries. Other separatist interests would undoubtedly have been encouraged, and the borders we have come to recognize both in the Southwest and Northwest could easily have shifted.[36]

More conceivable would have been a reunification in which power was effectively shared between big landed interests in the South and West and big industrial and financial interests in the Northeast and Midwest: an American version of the German marriage of "iron and rye" that linked Prussia and the Ruhr, though probably with a weaker center and with per-sisting limits to the federal government's ability to establish its sovereign authority.[37] At all events, slavery would have been abolished at some point, likely sooner rather than later, but this would have happened gradually under the authority of the states—not the federal government—though the federal government, if it survived, would have had to contribute at least some of its resources to stabilizing the transition—something like a slaveholders' bureau instead of a Freedmen's Bureau, or something like the stipendiary magistrates who supervised the transition in the British colonial possessions. Obviously there would have been no Thirteenth Amendment abolishing slavery without compensation to slaveholders; no Fourteenth Amendment or Civil Rights bills granting birthright citi-zenship and spelling out what some of those citizenship rights were; no Reconstruction Acts enfranchising black men in the South or the Fifteenth Amendment enfranchising black men in the North and West. Dred Scott would have remained the law of the land, and the conservative political impulses of the 1850s, which defeated black and women's suffrage and looked to disfranchise the immigrant working class, may well have con-tinued unabated, with serious consequences for popular politics in the second half of the nineteenth century.[38] For its part, the Republican Party would have faced a severe crisis, especially if the country became reunified, since it had little or no basis in the southern states and, without black enfranchisement, was unlikely to build any in the near term. A new, or multiparty, political system may well have taken shape, as Andrew Johnson and some Liberal Republicans had hoped.[39]

In all probability, the financiers of the Union war would not have come out in nearly as strong a position as they did, and some of the important wartime legislation that reshaped the political economy would have been revised, weakened, or repealed—tariffs, banking, and homestead legislation most conspicuously. The agrocommercial sectors would probably have remained on a stronger footing, and the industrial capitalist sectors on a shakier one. Landed interests would have been in a better position to weather the decline of commodity prices beginning in the 1870s, and could have expected more direct legislative help from the federal state. Which is to say that a Populist movement of the sort that raged in the South and Plains would not have gained much traction.

Internationally, Britain may well have been able to reassert itself as a major power in the Western Hemisphere (it was still an important economic power)—after all, the British were sure that the United States would fail to defeat the rebellion and hoped to mediate a peace—and France may have fared better in Mexico. At the very least, it is hard to imagine the United States, or any substantial part of it, being in a position, for a while at minimum, to throw its weight around quite as it did either in the hemisphere or in the Pacific basin. This would have been an advantage for many international political actors, large and small, not least perhaps for Japanese imperialists.

As for the trans-Mississippi West, the future patterns of development would have depended either on the reunification settlement that was reached as to the viability of slavery and other forms of coerced labor, or on which of the breakaway regions held the best position to exert its authority. Whatever the outcome, there likely would have been continuing conflict and political struggle with no clear end in sight. The countersovereignties there, Mormons and Indian peoples chief among them, may have consequently had more room for their ways of life (the Indians could hardly have fared worse than they did); and for the Canadian West and especially for Mexico, there may have been different social and political experiences, including a rather different dynamic to the revolution that erupted in Mexico in the 1910s.

These rather irreverent conjectures clearly raise many more questions than they provide satisfying answers, and they may raise the hackles of some readers as well. They surely do not reject the cautions that several of the essays here suggest about the limits of central power, the many ways it could be resisted or refashioned, and the very choppy and incomplete extension of federal authority over various parts of the new nation. And they are quite compatible with an extended period—and I think this to be the case—in which both the federal state and its allies among the capitalist classes struggled and largely failed to established their hegemony. But the results of the war did put them in a very strong position to do so by the end of the nineteenth century, fending off various challenges to their rule along the way, and enabling a more stable and enduring reconfiguration of their power and authority. All told, these conjectures suggest a very different world than the one that existed before the Civil War, and thus they demonstrate how very different a world the Civil War indeed came to make.

NOTES

1. Of all nineteenth-century wars and civil conflicts, only the Taiping Rebellion in China (1851–64) had greater casualties than the American Civil War. The most recent study estimates that the struggle of the Taiping Heavenly Kingdom against the Qing dynasty resulted in 20 million casualties owing to warfare and related disease and famine. See Stephen R. Platt, *Autumn in the Heavenly Kingdom: China, the West, and the Epic Story of the Taiping Civil War* (New York: Alfred A. Knopf, 2012).

2. See, for example, William A. Dunning, *Reconstruction, Political and Economic: 1865–1877* (New York: Harper & Row, 1907); Walter L. Fleming, *Civil War and Reconstruction in Alabama* (New York: Columbia University Press, 1905); Claude G. Bowers, *The Tragic Era* (Cambridge, Mass.: Houghton Mifflin, 1929); E. Merton Coulter, *The South during Reconstruction, 1865–1877* (Baton Rouge: Louisiana State University Press, 1947).

3. Charles A. Beard and Mary R. Beard, *The Rise of American Civilization* (New York: Macmillan, 1933); Kenneth M. Stampp, *The Era of Reconstruction, 1865–1877* (New York: Vintage, 1965); Willie Lee Rose, *Rehearsal for Reconstruction: The Port Royal Experiment* (Indianapolis: Bobbs-Merrill, 1964); James M. McPherson, *The Struggle for Equality: Abolitionists and the Negro in the Civil War and Reconstruction* (Princeton: Princeton University Press 1964).

4. Eric Foner, *Reconstruction: America's Unfinished Revolution, 1863–1877* (New York: Harper and Row, 1988); Leon F. Litwack, *Been in the Storm So Long: The Aftermath of Slavery* (New York: Alfred A. Knopf, 1979); Lawrence N. Powell, *New Masters: Northern Planters in the Civil War and Reconstruction* (New Haven: Yale University Press, 1980); Barbara J. Fields, *Slavery and Freedom on the Middle Ground: Maryland during the Nineteenth Century* (New Haven: Yale University Press, 1985); Ira Berlin et al., eds., *Freedom:*

A Documentary History of Emancipation, 1861-1867, 6 vols. (New York: Cambridge University Press, 1982-2013). The most powerful influence on all of these studies is W. E. B. Du Bois, *Black Reconstruction in America, 1860-1880* (New York: Harcourt, Brace, 1935).

5. See, for example, the essays collected in Ralph Andreano, ed., *The Economic Impact of the Civil War* (Cambridge, Mass.: Schenckman, 1962); and David T. Gilchrist and W. David Lewis, eds., *Economic Change in the Civil War Era* (Greenville, Del.: Eleutherian Mills-Hagley Foundation, 1965). Also see, Thomas C. Cochran, "Did the Civil War Retard Industrialization," *Mississippi Valley Historical Review* 48 (September 1961): 197-210.

6. C. Vann Woodward, *Origins of the New South, 1877-1913* (Baton Rouge: Louisiana State University Press, 1951). Woodward's critics on this account include Jonathan M. Wiener, *Social Origins of the New South: Alabama, 1860-1885* (Baton Rouge: Louisiana State University Press, 1978); Michael S. Wayne, *The Reshaping of Plantation Society: The Natchez District, 1860-1880* (Baton Rouge: Louisiana State University Press, 1983); Crandall A. Shiflett, *Patronage and Poverty in the Tobacco South: Louisa County, Virginia, 1860-1900* (Knoxville: University of Tennessee Press, 1982); Randolph B. Campbell, *A Southern Community in Crisis: Harrison County, Texas, 1850-1880* (Austin: University of Texas Press, 1983); Stephen V. Ash, *Middle Tennessee Society Transformed, 1860-1870: War and Peace in the Upper South* (Baton Rouge: Louisiana State University Press, 1982).

7. The literature portraying the slave South as capitalist and slavery as a form of capitalism include Walter Johnson, *Soul by Soul: Life Inside the Antebellum Slave Market* (Cambridge: Harvard University Press, 1999); James Oakes, *The Ruling Race: A History of American Slaveholders* (New York: Alfred A. Knopf, 1982); Robert Fogel and Stanley Engerman, *Time on the Cross: The Economics of American Negro Slavery* (Boston: Little Brown, 1974); Lacy K. Ford Jr., *The Origins of Southern Radicalism: The South Carolina Upcountry, 1800-1860* (New York: Oxford University Press, 1988). The major dissenter has been Eugene D. Genovese, especially in *The Political Economy of Slavery: Studies in the Society and Economy of the Slave South* (New York: Pantheon, 1965), but also see Fields, *Slavery and Freedom on the Middle Ground*; Julie Saville, *The Work of Reconstruction: From Slave to Wage Laborer in South Carolina, 1860-1870* (New York: Cambridge University Press, 1994); Steven Hahn, *The Roots of Southern Populism: Yeoman Farmers and the Transformation of the Georgia Upcountry, 1850-1890* (New York: Oxford University Press, 1983).

8. See, for example, Glenda Gilmore, *Gender and Jim Crow: Women and the Politics of White Supremacy in North Carolina, 1896-1920* (Chapel Hill: University of North Carolina Press, 1996); Stephen Kantrowitz, *Ben Tillman and the Reconstruction of White Supremacy* (Chapel Hill: University of North Carolina Press, 2000); David Blight, *Race and Reunion: The Civil War in American Memory* (Cambridge: Harvard University Press, 2001). For Phillips, see Ulrich B. Phillips, "The Central Theme of Southern History," *American Historical Review* 34 (October 1928): 30-43.

9. Think of Eric Foner, *Nothing But Freedom: Emancipation and Its Legacy* (Baton Rouge: Louisiana State University Press, 1982); Peter Kolchin, *A Sphinx on the Land: The Nineteenth Century South in Comparative Perspective* (Baton Rouge: Louisiana State University Press, 2003); Eugene D. Genovese, *The World the Slaveholders Made: Two*

Essays in Interpretation (New York: Pantheon, 1969), 3–113; C. Vann Woodward, "The Price of Freedom," in *What Was Freedom's Price?*, ed. David G. Sansing (Jackson: University Press of Mississippi, 1978), 93–113.

10. C. A. Bayly, *The Birth of the Modern World, 1780–1914* (Oxford, UK: Blackwell, 2004); Eric J. Hobsbawm, *The Age of Capital, 1848–1875* (New York: Pantheon, 1975).

11. Rebecca Scott, *Degrees of Freedom: Louisiana and Cuba after Slavery* (Cambridge: Harvard University Press, 2005), 29. On the Cuban literature, see Ada Ferrer, *Insurgent Cuba: Race, Nation, and Revolution, 1868–1898* (Chapel Hill: University of North Carolina Press, 1999); Rebecca Scott, *Slave Emancipation in Cuba: The Transition to Free Labor, 1860–1899* (Princeton: Princeton University Press, 1985); Ramiro Guerra y Sánchez, *La Guerra de los diaz Años, 1868–1878*, 2 vols. (Havana: Cultural, 1950–52); Arthur Corwin, *Spain and the Abolition of Slavery in Cuba, 1817–1886* (Austin: University of Texas Press, 1967). On the Brazilian literature, see Emilia Viotti da Costa, *Da senzala a colonia* (São Paulo: Difusão Européia do Livro, 1964); Robert Brent Toplin, *The Abolition of Slavery in Brazil* (New York: Atheneum, 1972); Rebecca Scott et al., *The Abolition of Slavery and the Aftermath of Emancipation in Brazil* (Durham: Duke University Press, 1988); Robert Conrad, *The Destruction of Slavery in Brazil, 1850–1888* (Berkeley: University of California Press, 1972). David Brion Davis's new volume, *The Problem of Slavery in the Age of Emancipation* (New York: Alfred A. Knopf, 2014), insists that the American Civil War and the war-era emancipations had a powerful effect on the fate of slavery in Cuba and Brazil, but he offers little direct evidence to sustain the point other than the temporal relation.

12. See, for example, Benjamin Keen and Keith Haynes, *A History of Latin America*, 9th ed. (New York: Houghton Mifflin, 2012); Marshall C. Eakin, *The History of Latin America: A Collision of Cultures* (New York: Palgrave, 2007); Edwin Williamson, *The Penguin History of Latin America* (New York: Penguin Books, 2010); Michael C. Meyer and William L. Sherman, *The Course of Mexican History* (New York: Oxford University Press, 1987).

13. Most recently, Edward Rugemer, *The Problem of Emancipation: The Caribbean Roots of the American Civil War* (Baton Rouge: Louisiana State University Press, 2009); Matthew J. Clavin, *Toussaint Louverture and the American Civil War: The Promise and Perils of a Second Haitian Revolution* (Philadelphia: University of Pennsylvania Press, 2011); Bruce Levine, *The Spirit of Forty-Eight: German Immigrants, Labor Conflict, and the Coming of the Civil War* (Urbana: University of Illinois Press, 1992).

14. Here I simultaneously embrace and part company with Barrington Moore Jr's. powerful interpretation of the American Civil War in *Social Origins of Dictatorship and Democracy: Lord and Peasant in the Making of the Modern World* (Boston: Beacon, 1965), 111–55.

15. Martin J. Sklar, *The Corporate Reconstruction of American Capitalism* (New York: Cambridge University Press, 1988). I share the interest of Gregory Downs and Kate Masur in interrogating the usefulness of "Reconstruction" as an era and analytical category, and in defining what its chronological boundaries might be.

16. Think, for example, of secessionist stirrings in New England and the Lower Mississippi Valley during the early years of the nineteenth century, of the nullifica-

tion crisis, various filibustering operations of the 1840s and 1850s, the Mormon "war" of the late 1850s, and disunion sentiment on the West Coast, in the Midwest, and in New York City during the winter of 1860-61.

17. See Don E. Fehrenbacher, *The Slaveholding Republic* (New York: Oxford University Press, 2001); Arthur Zilversmit, *The First Emancipation: The Abolition of Slavery in the North* (Chicago: University of Chicago Press, 1967); Joanne Pope Melish, *Disowning Slavery: Gradual Emancipation and "Race" in New England, 1780-1860* (Ithaca, N.Y.: Cornell University Press, 1998); James Oliver Horton and Lois E. Horton, *In Hope of Liberty: Culture, Community, and Protest among Northern Free Blacks, 1700-1860* (New York: Oxford University Press, 1997); Graham Russell Hodges, *Slavery and Freedom in the Rural North* (Madison: University of Wisconsin Press, 1997); Christopher M. Osborne, "Invisible Hands: Slaves, Bound Laborers, and the Development of Western Pennsylvania, 1780-1820," *Pennsylvania History* 72 (January 2005): 77-99.

18. See Christopher Clark, *The Roots of Rural Capitalism: Western Massachusetts, 1780-1860* (Ithaca, N.Y.: Cornell University Press, 1990); Alan Kullikoff, *Agrarian Origins of American Capitalism* (Charlottesville: University of Virginia Press, 1992), 34-59; Seth Rockman, *Scraping By: Wage Labor, Slavery, and Survival in Early Baltimore* (Baltimore: Johns Hopkins University Press, 2009); Peter Way, *Common Labor: Workers and the Digging of North American Canals, 1780-1860* (Baltimore: Johns Hopkins University Press, 1993); Alexander Keyssar, *The Right to Vote: The Contested History of Democracy in the United States* (New York: Basic Books, 2000), 26-116.

19. Sven Beckert, "Merchants and Manufacturers in the Antebellum North," and Adam Rothman, "The Slave Power in the United States, 1783-1865," both in *Ruling America: A History of Wealth and Power in a Democracy*, ed. Steve Fraser and Gary Gerstle (Cambridge: Harvard University Press, 2005), 64-122.

20. Robert May, *The Southern Dream of a Caribbean Empire, 1854-1861* (Baton Rouge: Louisiana State University Press, 1973); Thomas R. Hietala, *Manifest Design: Anxious Aggrandizement in Late Jacksonian America* (Ithaca, N.Y.: Cornell University Press, 1985); Robert Johannsen, *Stephen A. Douglas* (New York: Oxford University Press, 1973), 206-680; Walter Johnson, *River of Dark Dreams: Slavery and Empire in the Cotton Kingdom* (Cambridge: Harvard University Press, 2013). On slaveholder imperialism, see the outstanding doctoral dissertation of Matthew Karp, "The Foreign Policy of Slavery" (Ph.D. dissertation, University of Pennsylvania, 2011).

21. Joel H. Silbey, *A Respectable Minority: The Democratic Party in the Civil War Era, 1860-1868* (New York: W. W. Norton, 1977), 27.

22. Richard Franklin Bensel, *Yankee Leviathan: The Origins of Central State Authority in America, 1859-1877* (New York: Cambridge University Press, 1990); Heather Cox Richardson, *The Greatest Nation of the Earth: Republican Economic Policies during the Civil War* (Cambridge: Harvard University Press, 1997). On the war's complex ending, see Gregory P. Downs, *After Appomattox: Military Occupation and the Ends of War* (Cambridge: Harvard University Press, 2015).

23. Richard White, *Railroaded: The Transcontinentals and the Making of Modern America* (New York: W. W. Norton, 2011); Christian Womar, *Blood, Iron, and Gold: How the Railroads Transformed the World* (New York: Public Affairs, 2009), 45-190.

24. Robert G. Athearn, *William Tecumseh Sherman and the Settlement of the West* (Norman: Oklahoma University Press, 1956); Richard White, *The Roots of Dependency: Subsistence, Environment, and Social Change among Choctaws, Pawnees, and Navajos* (Lincoln: University of Nebraska Press, 1983); Pekka Hämäläinen, *Comanche Empire* (New Haven: Yale University Press, 2008); Francis Prucha, *The Great Father: The United States Government and the Indians*, 2 vols. (Lincoln: University of Nebraska Press, 1984), 527–33.

25. Richard Franklin Bensel, *The Political Economy of American Industrialization, 1877–1900* (New York: Cambridge University Press, 2000); Irwin Unger, *The Greenback Era: A Social and Political History of American Finance, 1865–1879* (Princeton: Princeton University Press, 1964); Robert Sharkey, *Money, Class, and Party: An Economic Study of the Civil War and Reconstruction* (Baltimore: Johns Hopkins University Press, 1959); Gretchen Ritter, *Goldbugs and Greenbacks: The Antimonopoly Tradition and the Politics of Finance in America, 1865–1896* (New York: Cambridge University Press, 1997).

26. Richard White concludes his important book with an interesting but I think misconceived counterfactual. See, *Railroaded*, 455–505.

27. See Steven Hahn, *A Nation under Our Feet: Black Political Struggles in the Rural South from Slavery to the Great Migration* (Cambridge: Harvard University Press, 2003), 163–313; Foner, *Reconstruction*, 228–343; David Montgomery, *Citizen Worker: The Experience of Workers in the United States with Democracy and the Free Market during the Nineteenth Century* (New York: Cambridge University Press, 1993), 115–62.

28. Hahn, *Nation under Our Feet*, 412–64; Harold D. Woodman, *New South — New Law: The Legal Foundations of Credit and Labor Relations in the Postbellum Agricultural South* (Baton Rouge: Louisiana State University Press, 1995)

29. Theresa A. Case, *The Great Southwest Railroad Strike and Free Labor* (College Station: Texas A&M University Press, 2010); Richard E. Lingenfelter, *The Hardrock Miners: A History of the Mining Labor Movement in the American West, 1863–1893* (Berkeley: University of California Press, 1974); John P. Enyeart, *The Quest for "Just and Pure Law": Rocky Mountain Workers and American Social Democracy, 1870–1924* (Stanford: Stanford University Press, 2009); James E. Wright, *The Politics of Populism: Dissent in Colorado* (New Haven: Yale University Press, 1974); Robert W. Larson, *Populism in the Rocky Mountain West* (Albuquerque: University of New Mexico Press, 1986); Frank Tobias Higbie, *Indispensable Outcasts: Hobo Workers and Community in the American Midwest, 1880–1930* (Urbana: University of Illinois Press, 2003), 98–204. On the political links with northern Mexico, see Benjamin Heber Johnson, *Revolution in Texas: How a Forgotten Rebellion and Its Bloody Suppression Turned Mexicans into Americans* (New Haven: Yale University Press, 2003); Claudio Lomnitz, *The Return of Comrade Ricardo Flores Magon* (New York: Zone Books, 2014).

30. See, especially, William E. Forbath, *Law and the Shaping of the American Labor Movement* (Cambridge: Harvard University Press, 1991); Karen Orren, *Belated Feudalism: Labor, the Law, and Liberal Development in the United States* (New York: Cambridge University Press, 1991).

31. Walter L. Williams, "U.S. Indian Policy and the Debate over Philippine Annexation: Implications for the Origins of American Imperialism," *Journal of American*

History 66 (March 1980): 810–31; Howard R. Lamar, *The Far Southwest, 1846–1912: A Territorial History* (New Haven: Yale University Press, 1970); Earl S. Pomeroy, *The Territories and the United States, 1861–1890: Studies in Colonial Administration* (Philadelphia: University of Pennsylvania Press, 1947). Arizona and New Mexico gained admission once the demographic balances assured Anglo political control; Utah was admitted once Mormon leaders there publicly renounced polygamy.

32. Williams, "U.S. Indian Policy and Debate over Philippine Annexation," 810–31.

33. See Walter LaFeber, *The New Empire: An Interpretation of American Expansion, 1860–1898* (Ithaca, N.Y.: Cornell University Press, 1963); Walter Nugent, *Habits of Empire: A History of American Expansion* (New York: Alfred A. Knopf, 2008), 237–317.

34. John Mason Hart, *Empire and Revolution: The Americans in Mexico since the Civil War* (Berkeley: University of California Press, 2002); Gilbert M. Joseph, *Revolution from Without: Yucatán, Mexico, and the United States, 1880–1924* (New York: Cambridge University Press, 1982); Samuel Truett, *Fugitive Landscapes: The Forgotten History of the U.S.-Mexico Borderlands* (New Haven: Yale University Press, 2006); Rachel St. John, *Line in the Sand: A History of the Western U.S.-Mexico Border* (Princeton: Princeton University Press, 2011); Julie Greene, *The Canal Builders: Making America's Empire at the Panama Canal* (New York: Penguin Press, 2009).

35. See Sven Beckert, *The Empire of Cotton: A Global History* (New York: Alfred A. Knopf, 2014).

36. Lincoln, in deciding to supply the troops at Fort Sumter, clearly worried about whether weakness on the part of the federal center would strengthen centripetal forces across the country. One cannot help but think, in this connection, of Iraq and Syria today.

37. See the discussion of unifications in Steven Hahn, "Class and State in Postemancipation Societies: Southern Planters in Comparative Perspective," *American Historical Review* 95 (February 1990): 75–98.

38. Keyssar, *The Right to Vote*, 81–116.

39. See Eric L. McKitrick, *Andrew Johnson and Reconstruction* (Chicago: University of Chicago Press, 1960), 364–420; John Sproat, *The Best Men: Liberal Reformers in the Gilded Age* (New York: Oxford University Press, 1971).

Contributors

AMANDA CLAYBAUGH is a professor of English at Harvard University, where she also chairs the program in History and Literature. She is the author of *The Novel of Purpose* (Cornell University Press, 2007) and is now at work on a project about the literary depiction of the federal government in the aftermath of the Civil War.

GREGORY P. DOWNS is an associate professor at City College and Graduate Center, CUNY, and is the author of *After Appomattox: Military Occupation and the Ends of War* (Harvard University Press, 2015) and *Declarations of Dependence: The Long Reconstruction of Popular Politics in the South, 1861–1908* (University of North Carolina Press, 2011). His short story collection, *Spit Baths* (University of Georgia Press, 2006), won the Flannery O'Connor award.

LAURA F. EDWARDS received her Ph.D. from the University of North Carolina at Chapel Hill and is now the Peabody Family Professor of History at Duke University. She recently completed *A Legal History of the Civil War and Reconstruction: A Nation of Rights* (Cambridge University Press, 2015) and is also the author of *The People and Their Peace: Legal Culture and the Transformation of Inequality in the Post-revolutionary South* (University of North Carolina Press, 2009).

CRYSTAL N. FEIMSTER is an associate professor in the Department of African American Studies and the American Studies Program at Yale University. Her publications include "'How Are the Daughters of Eve Punished?' Rape during the American Civil War," in *Writing Women's History*, ed. Elizabeth Anne Payne (University Press of Mississippi 2011), and *Southern Horrors: Women and the Politics of Rape and Lynching* (Harvard University Press, 2009).

C. JOSEPH GENETIN-PILAWA, an assistant professor of history at George Mason University, is the author of *Crooked Paths to Allotment: The Fight over Federal Indian Policy after the Civil War* (University of North Carolina Press, 2012), and the coeditor of *Beyond Two Worlds: Critical Conversations on Language and Power in Native North America* (SUNY Press, 2014). His new project is a study of urban Indigenous history in Washington, D.C.

STEVEN HAHN is the Roy F. and Jeannette P. Nichols Professor of History at the University of Pennsylvania. His book *A Nation Under Our Feet: Black Political Struggles in the Rural South from Slavery to the Great Migration* (Harvard University Press, 2003) won the Pulitzer, Bancroft, and Merle Curti prizes. His other books include *The Roots of Southern Populism: Yeoman Farmers and the Transformation of the Georgia Upcountry, 1850–1900* (Oxford University Press, 1993) and *The Political Worlds of Slavery and Freedom* (Harvard University Press, 2009).

LUKE E. HARLOW is assistant professor of history at the University of Tennessee, Knoxville. He is the author of *Religion, Race, and the Making of Confederate Kentucky, 1830–1880* (Cambridge University Press, 2014).

STEPHEN KANTROWITZ is Vilas Distinguished Achievement Professor of History at the University of Wisconsin-Madison. He is the author of *More Than Freedom: Fighting for Black Citizenship in a White Republic, 1829–1889* (Penguin, 2012), a finalist for the Douglass and Lincoln prizes, and *Ben Tillman and the Reconstruction of White Supremacy* (University of North Carolina Press, 2000).

BARBARA KRAUTHAMER is associate professor of history at the University of Massachusetts-Amherst. She is the coauthor of *Envisioning Emancipation: Black Americans and the End of Slavery* (Temple University Press, 2013), which received the 2013 NAACP Image Award for Outstanding Work in Non-Fiction, and she is also the author of *Black Slaves, Indian Masters: Slavery, Emancipation, and Citizenship in the Native American South* (University of North Carolina Press, 2013).

KATE MASUR is an associate professor of history and African American Studies at Northwestern University. She is the author of *An Example for All the Land: Emancipation and the Struggle over Equality in Washington, D.C.* (University of North Carolina Press, 2010), and a coeditor of the most recent volume in the series *Freedom: A Documentary History of Emancipation* (University of North Carolina Press, 2013).

K. STEPHEN PRINCE is an assistant professor of history at the University of South Florida. He is the author of *Stories of the South: Race and the Reconstruction of Southern Identity, 1865–1915* (University of North Carolina Press, 2014).

STACEY L. SMITH is associate professor of history at Oregon State University and the author of *Freedom's Frontier: California and the Struggle over Unfree Labor, Emancipation, and Reconstruction* (University of North Carolina Press, 2013). Her research focuses on race, labor, and civil rights in the nineteenth-century North American West.

AMY DRU STANLEY is a history professor at the University of Chicago. Her research focuses on the long nineteenth century—on slavery and abolition, capitalism, human rights, and the historical experience of moral problems. Her current book project, provisionally titled *From Slave Emancipation to the Commerce Power: An American History of Human Rights*, is forthcoming from Harvard University Press.

KIDADA E. WILLIAMS is the author of *They Left Great Marks on Me: African American Testimonies of Racial Violence from Emancipation to World War I* (NYU Press, 2012). She is an associate professor of history at Wayne State University, where she is researching a book on the impact of night riding on African American families.

ANDREW ZIMMERMAN is a professor of history at the George Washington University. He is the author of *Anthropology and Antihumanism in Imperial Germany* (University of Chicago Press, 2001) and *Alabama in Africa: Booker T. Washington, the German Empire, and the Globalization of the New South* (Princeton University Press, 2010). He is currently working on a global history of the American Civil War.

Index

civil rights legislation, 66, 141, 269, 275, 288, 292, 293; and Chinese immigration restriction, 67, 70; and recruitment of European laborers, 68; and Indian affairs, 194, 195, 238; in literature, 216–17, 221; committee investigating 1866 Memphis riot, 260–61; as theater, 272

Connecticut, 210, 274

Constitution, Confederate States of America, 137

Constitution, U.S., 23, 275, 276, 286, 318, 341; Civil War–era amendments to, 2, 23, 27, 34–35, 272, 287; and American Indians, 79, 84, 86, 90, 96, 198. *See also* Fifteenth Amendment; Fourteenth Amendment; Reconstruction, congressional; Thirteenth Amendment

Continental Congress, 271, 281–82

Contract labor, 60–61, 63, 67, 68. *See also* Chinese immigration; Coolie labor

Convention of Colored People (South Carolina), 276

Conyngham, David, 111, 118, 121

Coolie, definition of, 62–63

Coolie labor, 47, 48, 60–62, 64–65, 67, 69. *See also* Chinese immigration; Contract labor; Coolie, definition of; *Slaughterhouse Cases*

Cooley, Dennis N., 229, 230, 231

Corfield v. Coryell, 280

Cornish, Sandie, 122–23

Corruption, 220

Cox, Jacob, 194

Creek Indians, 227, 228, 230, 237, 238, 242

Crisis, The, 323

Crook, George, 188

Crow Creek, Dakota Territory, 80, 86

Cuba, 315, 339

Culture of Calamity, The (Rozario), 123

Curtis Act, 247 (n. 41)

Dabney, Robert L., 149

Dahlgren, Madeline Vinton, 221

Dakota Territory, 13, 80

Dakota War, 80

Dana, Charles A., 310, 312

Dandy (Roaring Thunder), 81–83, 98

Dandy's Band, 75, 76, 81, 83, 88, 91, 93, 104 (n. 92)

Daniel, Sir, 168

Darwin, Charles, 136

Das, Veena, 161

Davis Bend, Miss., 316

Davis, Garrett, 56, 198, 286

Davis, William R., 292

Dawes, Henry, 347

Dawes Severalty Act, 98, 240, 247 (n. 41), 347

Declaration of Independence, 273, 274, 277, 279, 280

Declaration of the Rights of Man and Citizen, 282

Decora family, 98

Deep South, U.S., 59

De Forest, John William, 214–17, 220, 222, 223

Delano, Columbus, 96, 97

Delgado, Felipe, 53

Democracy, 220, 282

Democracy (Adams), 206, 207, 214

Democratic Party, 2, 12, 342; postwar challenge to Republicans, 9, 66, 88, 159, 197–98; and Redemption in South, 46, 152; and Anti-Chinese movement, 48, 61, 63, 65, 67; blocking of civil rights legislation in California, 63–64; support for Ho-Chunk Indians, 88–89; and *Dred Scott* decision, 256; opposition to Civil Rights Act of 1875, 292; 1860 split, 343

Department of Dakota, 193

Department of Education, U.S., 7

Department of Justice, U.S., 7, 9, 59

Department of State, 222

Department of the Interior, U.S., 96; and Indian affairs, 185, 187, 188, 191–93, 229

Department of War, U.S., 7, 95, 310; and Indian affairs, 185–87, 191, 192; increased scope in Civil War and Reconstruction, 189–90

Dirty War (Argentina), 166

District of Columbia, 29, 139

Domestic captivity, 163

Doolittle, James, 83

Doty, James, 78

Douglass, Frederick, 127, 284, 286, 293

Downing, George, 280–81, 285–86, 290, 292

Downs, Gregory P., 96, 340

Dred Scott, 30, 75, 255, 349

Drury, Allen, 222

Du Bois, W. E. B., 222, 323, 327, 328, 329. See also *Black Reconstruction in America*

Dunayevskaya, Raya, 319

Dunning, William A., 22, 25, 306

Dunning School, 7, 22, 23, 25–27, 40 (n. 2), 329, 337

Dwight, Timothy, 282

Eager, Scipio, 169

Economic and Philosophic Manuscripts (Marx), 285

Education, 36–37, 199

Edwards, Laura F., 161

"Eighteenth Brumaire of Louis Napoléon, The" (Marx), 309–10, 316

Eight-hour-day movement, 2, 320, 345

Eight-Hour League, 69

Elkins, Stephen, 55

Elk v. Wilkins, 99

Elliott, Robert, 291

Emancipation. See African Americans; Civil War, American; Freedpeople; Slavery

Emancipation Proclamation, 212, 227, 318

Emmons, Halmer Hull, 269

Enforcement Acts, 91

Engels, Friedrich, 304. See also Marx, Karl

England, 284, 317

English Civil War, 281

Enlightenment, Age of, 270, 279

Episcopalians, 147, 198

Equality, 30, 31, 39, 90

Essays on the Civil War and Reconstruction and Related Topics (Dunning), 25

Essellen, Christian, 308, 317

Etiquette of Social Life in Washington (Dahlgren), 221

Federal government. See U.S. government

Federal Writers' Project, 226

Feimster, Crystal, 174

Fenians, 322

Ferry, Orris, 274

Fetterman Fight, 186

Fifteenth Amendment, 39, 64, 88, 134, 173–74, 289

Fisk University, 292

Fitzhugh, George, 310

Florida, 289

Folsom, Loring, 236

Foner, Eric, 5–6, 206, 327

Ford's Theatre, 282

Fort Gibson, 235

Fort Phil Kearney, 186

Fortress Monroe, Va., 139

Fort Selden, N.M., 53

Fort Smith, Ark., 2, 186, 229, 230, 233, 237

Fort Smith treaty council, 229–32, 234, 238, 242

Fort Sumter, S.C., 114, 124

Fourier, Charles, 311

Fourteenth Amendment, 30, 35, 39, 46, 58, 64, 134, 250, 290, 349; Ho-Chunk Indians and, 75, 90; and Indian citizenship, 83, 87, 89, 96, 102 (n. 20);

cation in, 37; labor movement in, 68, 69, 71; residents' interest in Southern ruins, 106–10, 112–13, 123–26, 128; antebellum era in, 114; residents and postwar southern recovery, 123–26; Civil War-era religion in, 137, 139–40; and fundamentalism, 151; residents and slavery as a cause of Civil War, 316–17. *See also* Northeast, U.S.; Old Northwest

North America, 48, 77, 81

North Carolina, 34, 37

Northeast, U.S., 49, 68, 215–16, 341, 342

Northern Cheyenne Indians, 186

Norwegian Americans, 98

Novack, George, 327

Novels: about national government, 206, 208; set in Washington, D.C., 206–8; and nationhood, 207; antebellum, 207, 209–11, 214, 215, 218–19, 220; Civil War-era, 211–12; set in postwar Washington, D.C., 214–25. *See also* Bureaucracy

Oberly, James, 79

Office of Indian Affairs, 2, 75, 76, 83, 84, 91, 193, 197; proposed transfer, 184, 186, 191. *See also* Indians, American; Parker, Ely S.

Oglala Indians, 186

Ohio, 88, 254, 274, 287

Ohio River, 255

Ojibwe Indians, 79

Oklahoma, 226

Old and New School Presbyterian Churches, 140

Old Northwest, 126

Old Testament, 132, 150

Open Door Policy, 347

Oregon, 344

Osage Indians, 230, 242

Pacific Railroad Act, 80, 344

Page, Horace, 66–67

Page Law, 67

Paige, Richard G. L., 283

Paine, Robert, 146

Painter, Nell Irvin, 160

Palmer, Benjamin M., 149

Palmyra, Mo., 142

Palmyra Manifesto, 142

Paris, France, 191, 210

Paris Commune, 323

Parker, Ely S., 2, 200; seeks army commission, 183; and Indian affairs reform, 184, 186–90, 192, 199, 200 (n. 4); Civil War service of, 185; and Indian sovereignty, 185; and Fort Kearney investigation, 186–87, 190–91; advocates transfer of Office of Indian Affairs to War Department, 187–90; as head of Office of Indian Affairs, 192; support for cessation of treaty making, 194–97; removed from Office of Indian Affairs, 198–99; and 1866 treaties, 229

Patent Office, U.S., 212

Patton, William W., 116

Pauline epistles, 135

Peace Commission of 1867–1868, 187, 191, 192

Peace Policy, 81, 84, 99, 186, 197

Peonage, 56–57, 60; in New Mexico, 1, 8, 9, 47–51, 53–55, 61, 70. *See also* Anti-Peonage Act; Indians, American; Involuntary labor; Sharecropping; *Slaughterhouse Cases*

Philadelphia, Pa., 116, 275–76

Philippines, 347

Phillips, Ulrich B., 338

Phillips, Wendell, 283

Philosophes, 279

Photographic Views of Sherman's Campaign (Barnard), 106

Piegan Indians, 193

Pierson, Perry, 258–59

Pike, James S., 220

Pitchlynn, Peter, 231, 236, 240–42